D1564696

PIOUS PURSUITS: GERMAN MORAVIANS IN THE ATLANTIC WORLD

EUROPEAN EXPANSION & GLOBAL INTERACTION

GENERAL EDITORS
Pieter C. Emmer, *Institute for the History of European Expansion, Leiden University*
Seymour Drescher, *University Professor, Department of History, University of Pittsburgh*

It may be said that the question of how the technology, languages, institutions, and even pastimes of Western Europe came to dominate global civilization—even came to create that civilization—is the greatest historical question of modern times. Yet scholars have paid relatively little attention to this veritable monumental phenomenon. This new series is designed to offer a forum for debate and bring new research to light.

PIOUS PURSUITS: GERMAN MORAVIANS IN THE ATLANTIC WORLD

Edited by
Michele Gillespie and Robert Beachy

Berghahn Books
New York • Oxford

First published in 2007 by

Berghahn Books
www.berghahnbooks.com

©2007 Michele Gillespie & Robert Beachy

Library of Congress Cataloging-in-Publication Data
Pious pursuits : German Moravians in the Atlantic World / edited by Michele
Gillespie and Robert Beachy.
    p. cm.
Includes bibliographical references and index.
ISBN-13: 978-1-84545-339-8 (hardback : alk. paper)
ISBN 10-84545-339-5 (hardback : alk. paper)
   1. Moravians—History. I. Gillespie, Michele. II. Beachy, Robert.
BX8565.P56 2007
284'.609—dc22   2007003687

British Library Cataloguing in Publication Data
A catalogue record for this book is available from the British Library
Printed in the United States on acid-free paper

ISBN 978-1-84545-339-8

CONTENTS

ABBREVIATIONS

The following abbreviations have been adopted for archives and texts frequently cited in the endnotes:

Katholiek documentatiecentrum (Nijmegen, Netherlands)—KDC

Moravian Archives (Bethlehem, PA)—MAB

Moravian Archives-Southern Province (Winston-Salem, NC)—MA-SP

Museum of Early Southern Decorative Arts (Winston-Salem, NC)—MESDA

New York Historical Society—NYHS

North Carolina Division of Archives and History (Raleigh, NC)—NCDAH

North Carolina Historical Review—NCHR

Records of the Moravians in North Carolina (7 vols., 1922–1943)—*RMNC*

Transactions of the Moravian Historical Society—TMHS

Unitäts Archiv (Herrnhut, Germany)—UA-Herrnhut

ACKNOWLEDGMENTS

THE IDEA FOR THIS VOLUME originated in a conference on "German Moravians in the Atlantic World" at Wake Forest University in Winston-Salem, North Carolina, in 2002. It has evolved substantially over the intervening years to explore new themes and highlight new outstanding scholarship by both young and established historians. The co-editors remain grateful to all the participants and supporters involved in the original conference, especially the History Department at Wake Forest, Daniel Crews and his staff at the Moravian Archives-Southern Province, the staff at Old Salem, Inc., and our own Wake Forest students. We herald our *Pious Pursuits* contributors for their patience in allowing the volume to expand and deepen in the years that have intervened. We are also most appreciative of our publisher, Marion Berghahn, our editor, Melissa Spinelli, and our series editors, P. C. Emmer and Seymour Drescher, for their counsel and support.

INTRODUCTION

☙❧

JOHANNETTE MARIA KIMBEL ETTWEIN (1725–1773), Westphalian-born, and her husband Johannes Ettwein (1721–1803), of Württemberg, spent their lifetimes making "hopeful journeys" on behalf of the Congregation of God—the Moravians. Both joined the Congregation at Marienborn (in the principality of Wetteravia) in their youth and traveled separately to Holland before being married in 1746. That same year they were ordained as deacons and helped found the Dutch Congregation of Zeist. Four years later the couple was sent to the House of Disciples in London, moving back and forth to Herrnhaag while caring for a growing family. The Ettwein family was then called to Bethlehem in Pennsylvania in 1754, to Wachovia in North Carolina in 1758, and back to Bethlehem in 1766. Johannes was subsequently ordained bishop, led the Bethlehem Congregation throughout the Revolutionary War, and is remembered as one of the leading organizers of two key North American Moravian communities.[1] One of their sons trained as a Moravian physician. The peripatetic lives of the Ettweins, as missionaries who proselytized in the most cosmopolitan of European cities as well as the newest of American backcountries, were not in the least exceptional among eighteenth-century Moravians.

Recent work on the history of migration in the Atlantic World has underscored the interdependence of the political economies and cultures of Europe, North America, Africa, Latin America, and the Caribbean in the eighteenth century. This scholarship has emphasized the impact of these exchanges on political relations, state building, economic structures, commerce, and wealth, and launched debates on the degree to which these exchanges did or did not shape a unique American society by 1750. At the same time, scholars have begun to delve into the cultural realities of this Atlantic World, including the multiple factors that played into the construction of identity, be it individual, community, state, or transnational, although this scholarship is in its relative infancy.

Much of this Atlantic World work, which has received strong encouragement from Bernard Bailyn and his school, has prioritized the Anglo-American context. Bailyn himself has recently argued that historians during the World War II era, in the process of watching a new Atlantic community take shape in the wake of monumental challenges to Anglo-American governments and liberalism, rediscovered the degree to which English-speaking people in the early modern period—whether they were in the Caribbean, the mid-Atlantic colonies of America, England, or the west coast of Africa—had understood themselves as part of a larger Atlantic culture.[2] Scholars since the 1960s, moreover, have been especially smitten by the idea of shared American and European mental worlds, as represented by the discovery of an Atlantic republican tradition that linked Machiavelli's fifteenth-century Italy with Jeffersonian democracy in the early nineteenth-century US.[3] Meanwhile, historians more interested in economic development in the Atlantic World have argued that the nature of plantation economies and their reliance on African slavery along with new consumer desires and commercial opportunities generated a new set of immigration patterns in the Americas that differed greatly from European migration movements and labor markets.[4]

These developing lines of scholarship have produced two interdependent Atlantic World models, the best-known being the Anglo-Atlantic (and implicitly Protestant), which deals with North America and the British Caribbean, and the other being the Iberian-Atlantic (and explicitly Catholic), which focuses on Latin America, the American Gulf South, and the Spanish Caribbean.[5] Although the Anglo-Atlantic model has allowed some room for the inclusion of Continental Europeans, be they French Huguenots or Dutch Calvinists, there is no question that its Anglocentrism has its limitations. This is especially true with respect to the limited place it holds for German Protestants in the Atlantic World. Although Germans were the second largest group of immigrants to the American colonies in the eighteenth century, they have received minimal consideration in this wider scholarship.[6]

It is also important to point out that while the powerful role of the Catholic Church in shaping the Iberian-Atlantic World networks of people, trade, and communication is well documented, we know much less about the role Protestant churches played in these processes. We may now understand that the Atlantic World was crisscrossed by networks of migrants, commerce, and cultures, but we are only beginning to grasp the centrality of Protestant religious networks to the construction of Euro-American, Native American, and African American identities. Limited scholarship makes clear that the Anglican Church, with its rigid hierarchies, was less effective at spreading the gospel than the Quakers, with their loose organization but effective itinerant ministry of men and women. Yet the British propagators in all their variety paled next to the German Pietists. Lutheran Pietists, under the leadership of August Hermann Francke, built a sophisticated system that webbed persecuted Salzburgers with London Methodists and Halle apothecaries with frontier midwives. What historians have yet to appreciate is the degree to which the German Moravians, more than any other Protestant sect, proved most adept not only at stretching themselves across the entirety of the Atlantic World, but in securing new adherents in the unlikeliest of communities and in the unlikeliest of places.

Moravians established missions in London, Greenland, Ireland, Stockholm, and Silesia, but also Tobago, Antigua, Barbados, the Danish West Indies, Surinam, and West and South Africa, as well as the British colonies from Georgia to Maine, and westward to Richard White's "middle ground" from their home base in Pennsylvania. Hence their converts were as likely to include displaced Delaware Indians and African-born slaves as German-born immigrants. Their success was all the more remarkable when one notes that the original members of the Moravian home community in Herrnhut, Saxony totaled under a thousand before 1750.[7]

The German-born Ettweins, therefore, along with thousands of other eighteenth-century Moravian immigrants, offer us a fresh vantage from which to examine the Atlantic World. First and foremost, Moravians were quick to traverse the conventional political boundaries that divided European states and American colonies. Moreover, their commitment to their faith and community was so strong that many quit their homelands to form new congregations in the most cosmopolitan of European cities, and then crossed the Atlantic Ocean to build fledgling settlements on the North American frontier or in the plantation Caribbean, all in a single lifetime. In addition, Moravians even modified traditional European constructs of difference. Because their doctrine held that women were spiritually equal to men, women garnered significant authority in the larger church community. Moravians also believed that it was their charge to teach all the peoples of the world—regardless of race or ethnicity—about Christ's martyrdom for their salvation, a mission they have pursued down to the present. Today, Moravians number about 700,000 worldwide; well over half of them are African.

The study of Moravian lives, beliefs, communities, and culture, especially over the course of the eighteenth century, provides a new framework for analysis of the Atlantic World, one that is not only comparative and transnational, but in many respects intercultural, moving us well beyond the more simplistic core-periphery model of colonization. Given their rather extraordinary life journeys, some of their values and beliefs, and the means by which they built this diasporic church community, Moravians were certainly citizens of the world, yet paradoxically, only loosely so. Even as the very tenets of their faith, rooted in a special kind of Protestant Pietism, helped the Moravians launch an impressive global network of missions, they also cultivated tightly knit, carefully controlled religious communities. The fifteen essays that make up this volume convey how these Moravians worked to spread their unique faith in an increasingly complicated Atlantic World undergoing the first throes of modernity. Because they found themselves in a revolutionary age, German Moravians deliberately harnessed many aspects of modernity—

from education, credit, and medical knowledge to modern travel and information networks—to build successful missions and settlements around the Atlantic. But modernity also brought with it a host of new challenges in the form of Enlightenment secularisms, democracies, and freedoms, each of which was fully capable of tearing apart the fragile fabric of this unique world church community.

Origins of the Moravian Church

Historians have traditionally identified two complementary sources for the establishment of the Renewed Unity of Brethren, or Moravian Church. The congregation began as a small gathering of exiles from Bohemia and Moravia (located in the modern Czech Republic), who settled in 1722 on the estate of the German aristocrat, Count Nicolaus Ludwig von Zinzendorf, at the southeastern border of the German territorial state of Electoral Saxony. These peasant and artisan immigrants claimed membership in a late medieval sect known as the Unitas Fratrum or Bohemian Brethren, which traced its history to the fifteenth century. The 1415 execution of the Czech religious reformer Jan Hus, whom Martin Luther viewed as his spiritual predecessor, inspired the organization of several Czech dissident religious groups. Among these, the Unitas Fratrum maintained a tenuous and underground organization into the eighteenth century, despite the persecution of the seventeenth-century Habsburg Counter-Reformation, which strove to eliminate all Protestant influence and religious observance.[8]

Count Zinzendorf—raised under the influence of the Halle Pietists—represents the second critical force behind the formation of the modern Moravian Church. Not only through his benevolent support as a German nobleman, but also with charismatic leadership, Zinzendorf indelibly shaped the Renewed Unitas Fratrum. Most of Zinzendorf's immediate family members belonged to a circle of Pietists with close ties to the Berlin- and Halle-based leaders Jakob Spener and August Hermann Francke, and this formed the Count's childhood environment. Spener even stood godfather at Zinzendorf's baptism in 1700. Within the framework of the confessional Lutheran Church, these early Pietists hoped to ignite a second Protestant reformation through their members' personal commitment to Christ. Disappointed with the rigidity of orthodox Lutheranism, the Pietists advocated a "new birth" in religious faith, and their evangelicalism drew new followers eager to rescind worldly ways and embrace a heartfelt piety. In 1710 the young Zinzendorf attended Francke's academy in Halle for his secondary schooling before studying at the University of Wittenberg.[9]

Both his schooling and family background represented the formative Pietist influences that inspired Zinzendorf as a young man to invite the Moravian and Bohemian exiles to his feudal estate in 1722. Under his visionary leadership the Renewed Unitas Fratrum was officially launched in 1727 in the newly founded congregation town of Herrnhut (which meant "Under the Lord's care"). With Zinzendorf at the helm, the Moravians adopted an ecumenical and expansionist outlook, while also developing a unique kind of spiritualism that shaped all aspects of their religious practice and society.

The social organization of the Moravians was much more restricted, however, especially as it evolved from the late 1720s. They adhered strictly to the New Testament, were expected to undergo a profound conversion experience, and obeyed a strict code of conduct. They made decisions by drawing lots, which they viewed as an expression of God's will. Thus covenanted as one, they believed themselves a chosen people living out God's word. Particularly in Herrnhut, the Moravians developed a communitarian ideal in which worshipers were divided into discrete "choirs" or cohorts by age, sex, and marital status, thereby attenuating traditional emotional ties of family. These choirs lived, worked, and worshipped in separate groups created for children, adolescents, single men, single women, married men, married women, and so on. Each choir had its own leader, kept its own records, and organized its own work and worship schedules. (It is important to note, however, that outside Moravian Church headquarters and a number of better known communities, not all Moravians maintained this rigorously compartmentalized living system.) This segregation also required an elaborate leadership structure that gave women authority over the worship and education of their half of the congregation. The Moravians, although they considered men and women spiritually equal and encouraged marriage, also believed that men and women had different religious experiences, and hence their inner lives needed nurturing by those of their own gender. During the period of the so-called General Economy, from the late 1720s through the early 1770s, the church also regulated all economic activity. Property was collectively owned and community members received no wages.

However, unlike those sects that withdrew from worldly temptation to foster insular agricultural communities, the Moravians managed to look simultaneously inward and outward. This unique ecumenicalism took many forms. Most prominently, the Moravians, many of whose leaders were noblemen, cared deeply about education and literacy, and demanded university education for all clergy members. They offered significant support to persecuted Pietists, and also worked hard to maintain cordial relations with the Lutheran state churches of the German territories, a difficult balancing act at the best of times. But the Moravians did not limit themselves to the particularities of religious and political life in Germany. Zinzendorf and the other leaders vigorously promoted evangelical work and sent missionaries far and wide, proselytizing and founding new congregation towns modeled on Herrnhut. Highly organized and increasingly talented financiers, the Brethren established colonies throughout Europe, North America, the Caribbean, Africa, South America, and

Greenland over the course of the eighteenth century, converting Native Americans, Africans, and African Americans as well as Europeans and European Americans. Despite this worldly approach to missions, a sophisticated understanding of commerce and industry, and the embrace of education, the religious communities they created were characterized by an intense piety embedded in a fervent spiritualism that led to the imposition of strict control among a small group of true believers.[10]

Like many Pietists and Protestant nonconformists of this period, Moravians held that individual believers with an intimate relationship to Christ formed a true and ecumenical church within the shell of the confessional churches. This position shaped Moravians' doctrine and colored their missionary work. Thus Church missionaries not only founded colonies and sought conversion to Moravianism: both ordained Moravian ministers and devout laypersons participated in evangelical work that promoted the Pietist Christian renewal of non-Moravian Protestants, but without appeals to conversion. These revivalist activities received sanction with a formal Church "diaspora" doctrine that promoted spiritual mentorship for all Protestant Christians, regardless of denomination. Moravians thus had significant early contacts in the London Fetter Lane Society with John and Charles Wesley and George Whitefield, all prominent leaders of the Anglo-American Great Awakening. Moravian "diaspora" revivalists also worked tirelessly in much of Northern Europe into the nineteenth century, contributing to the Pietist German evangelical movements that developed after the Napoleonic Wars.[11]

Despite, and perhaps directly because of their ecumenical intentions, however, Moravian Church leaders confronted a series of difficult tasks by the late 1730s. While fighting persecution at home, they needed to support missionary efforts and administer the General Economy. Political pressure from the Saxon court in Dresden compelled the Moravians to become masters of migration, adept not only at organization and planning, but at securing financial backing as well. When the Moravian headquarters were banished from Herrnhut by the Saxon government in 1738, they were then moved to Herrnhaag in Wetteravia, and Zinzendorf became increasingly hopeful that the Moravians could establish successful missions in North America, given its diverse religious milieu. He traveled across the Atlantic himself in 1741 to oversee the development of the Moravian town of Bethlehem, Pennsylvania. The Unity would found Wachovia, North Carolina, twelve years later to harbor European brethren seeking refuge and to generate income for the increasingly debt-heavy Church. Not surprisingly, given their ambition to unite all the German religious groups, the Moravians followed the settlement patterns of other German immigrants in North America, with the majority settling in backcountry Pennsylvania. Although their efforts were spurned by the Lutheran majority, the Moravians remained influential throughout the American colonies, in part because they comprised a fourth of all German-speaking congregations on the eve of the American Revolution. They were also especially successful at mastering one of the defining hallmarks of the Atlantic World experience in the eighteenth century—migration.[12]

Because they were adept at disseminating valuable information and securing money, these radical Pietists navigated the bureaucratic pitfalls of overseas travel, the corrupt and disease-ridden port cities of Philadelphia and New York, and the increasingly expensive and overcrowded backcountry with relative ease. Their deeply rooted collective identity, along with their careful decision making (evidenced by their securing their own ships and crews, rather than relying on exploitative captains and corrupt services) brought them safely to colonial shores. This propensity for organization and planning by the church leaders also made it possible for the immigrants to focus almost immediately on the challenge of joining new religious communities and congregation towns in this unfamiliar setting, and launching more missions. What the Moravians had not anticipated in their pious pursuit of the diaspora were the problems they would face living among such a large, diverse society, increasingly rife with cultural problems as complex in their own right as the ones they had left behind.[13]

Overview

Pious Pursuits invites readers to examine this eighteenth-century transatlantic Moravian world in all its complexity during a period of tremendous transformation from a variety of critical perspectives. The fifteen essays in this volume center on three key themes: the confessional nature of Moravian Pietism; the process of assimilation; and the question of Pietism's exceptionalism. Within these broad rubrics, the authors examine Moravian political culture and the character of communication in the transatlantic community; the meanings of Moravian dress and its evolution; commerce and early industry; medicine and health; gender and female authority; and slavery, Native Americans, and racism. The essays take us across a wide geographical range, from Saxony and Prussia to Bethlehem, Pennsylvania, Salem, North Carolina, the Cherokee lands in Georgia, and the Caribbean.

Part One analyzes structures unique to the Moravian confession, from the choir system to theology, and assesses the followers' respective roles in supporting this faith-based communal system in Europe and America. Here the term "confession" as an overarching rubric for the cultural elements of a specific denomination and its theology is especially significant. While American historians have tended to emphasize the distinctiveness of American Moravian communities as compared with their European brethren, this section underscores important confessional similarities, and the persistence of these similarities over time in these new places. Mack Walker's intriguing opening essay begins by comparing the Moravian choir system to the European guild system, to demonstrate many important resemblances and a few critical differences. It is his contention that Herrnhut and its Atlantic World settlements, ironically enough, strongly mirrored German civic community, with the exception of the critical patronage these communities received from aristocrats, beginning with Zinzendorf. The social systems of guild and choir served to "integrate, guard, and discipline the community," and thus exerted and enforced strict moral and economic sanctions on their carefully controlled membership.

Certainly, Walker points out, with respect to composition, size, shape, and architecture Moravians modeled their communities on German self-contained small towns and their attendant civic culture. But for him the key point of departure for these Christocentric communities was the preponderance of Pietist leaders from the noble class. While Baroque culture offered one avenue to eminence for the "underemployed" aristocrats, demonstrative piety, he posits, represented another and even more accessible path. Acknowledging the significance of these social structures in shaping these far-flung Pietistic communities invites important new questions. Walker suggests that future scholars, then, may want to examine the degree to which the social conditions that shaped early modern nobility in Central Europe may have retained their influence as shapers of "imperial communities" in America, well past the point at which historians traditionally mark the beginnings of American exceptionalism.

Like Mack Walker, Robert Beachy, in his essay "Manuscript Missions," underscores the critical continuities in Moravian culture not only across the Atlantic World but also over the course of the eighteenth century, despite the application of seemingly modern tenets and strategies. Beachy analyzes the history and function of the "Gemein Nachrichten," a handwritten Moravian church periodical first issued in 1747 and disseminated to Moravian communities, colonies, and mission outposts, and to other Pietist denominations in Europe and the Americas and among Central European nobility. He argues that this newspaper functioned as a purposeful counterpoint to the flourishing new print culture of the Enlightenment. Because it was handwritten and hence an intentionally scarce form, and was read aloud in churches, it fostered significant solidarity and loyalty. Its contents as well as its reception, limited to the Moravian community and its Pietist supporters, encouraged the uniquely confessional nature of the church and at the same time restricted critics' access to Moravian beliefs. Thus, while the "Gemein Nachrichten" resembled the periodical print of this period in that it transcended traditional boundaries of state and colony to connect widely dispersed Moravians through both spiritual and community renewal in an "imagined" church community, it did not encourage the dissemination of a variety of ideas, values, and beliefs, nor implicitly nurture secularization and individualism like its print brethren. Instead, the Moravian manuscripts throughout the second half of the eighteenth century reflected deliberate control of the world church community, as well as an inherent critique of print culture.

Craig Atwood, a scholar of Moravian theology, turns in his essay from outward manifestations of Moravian community to inward ones. Nonetheless, he too underscores the persistence of original Moravian theology in America through his examination of Zinzendorfian piety in Bethlehem, Pennsylvania, into the late eighteenth century. Unlike previous historians who have insisted upon American Moravians' intentional departure from Zinzendorfian theology in the wake of what they perceived as a fanatical expression of belief during the "Sifting" period, Atwood finds substantial evidence that they sustained their devotion to the blood and wounds of Christ, keeping it central to their piety, their community, and their mission long after the 1740s. He argues that the Zinzendorfian veneration of the wounds of Christ was not in fact unique to the Moravians but was rooted in the history of Christianity, as expressed in late medieval Catholic piety and even among seventeenth-century Lutherans. Not unlike the Elders' handwritten manuscripts, the blood and wounds theology worked as a spiritual discourse that defined the boundaries between Moravian piety and mission and the outside world. Atwood's argument suggests then that Zinzendorfian piety was not so much imposed by the European center upon its colonial periphery—although the "Gemein Nachrichten" would indicate it was certainly encouraged—as it was incorporated deliberately into the community's spiritual life by the Bethlehem settlement itself.

Renate Wilson, in her exploration of Moravian physicians in colonial North America, similarly reveals that while European models represented ideals for colonial communities to subscribe to, the realities of the colonial world necessitated a measure of self-determination and pragmatism. The medical men who served Moravian settlements in the mid-Atlantic and southern colonies were better educated (usually at the medical establishment in Herrnhut) and greater in number than other German physician émigrés. Expectations about their roles in both European and American settlements reflected close modeling after the medical institutions of the Francke Foundations at Halle. Zinzendorf understood the importance of providing medical care for domestic and outlying communities as far away as India, the Baltic territories, and also Suriname, but he remained committed to the Halle emphasis on minimal and frugal treatment. Perhaps ironically, Moravian communities in colonial North America, closed in structure, had to make room for these physicians while balancing their own closed community interests with the broader transatlantic professional interests of these medical men. These same men, however, privileged by their medical knowledge and therefore somewhat atypical members of the Moravian community, usually struggled to make a living and often lacked a substantive salary or even respect, even as they remained among the faithful themselves.

The four essays that constitute this first section of *Pious Pursuits* underscore how spiritual beliefs and social systems in new Moravian world communities remained circumscribed and familiar and therefore helped sustain these distinctive closed communities across time and place, even as they pursued transnational relationships and applied modern information and technologies. While these essays acknowledge tensions between the Central European origins and organization of Moravians' faith and its manifestations in other geographical contexts, be they London's Fetter Lane or North Carolina's Bethabara, they also highlight the structures and strategies Moravian leaders relied on to resolve them. The five essays in Part Two pay attention not only to how Moravians constructed their communal social identities in these wider worlds, but also to how those identities were challenged through cultural and economic assimilation pressures across generations.

Elisabeth Sommer opens this section by offering an intriguing examination of the evolution of Moravian dress as an expression of the tensions between gender, spiritual ideals, and the commerce of the wider world. She shows that Moravians developed a distinctive dress or *Tracht* beginning in the 1740s, but modified it with the death of Zinzendorf in 1760 out of a desire to be "less different." She finds that by mid-century, the sisters had adopted a peasant style of clothing, including a distinctive head covering—the *Haube*. Although the Moravians acknowledged significant social differences within their communities, including a largely aristocratic leadership, women's dress now downplayed class difference, emphasizing simplicity instead, and ultimately spiritual equality before God. If Moravian women were recognized at first for their unique rhetoric of dress by the outside world, after 1780 women's European fashions in general increasingly favored simple peasant attire, not only making it more difficult to distinguish Moravian women from their counterparts, but also giving the next generation of sisters less opportunity to use their fashion choices to challenge the Brethren.

Moravian men as well as women, Sommer insists, well understood that their fashions conveyed one set of symbols within their community but another beyond it. Clothing choice was encouraged by the Elders in an effort to reflect communitarian spiritual beliefs but was negotiated by individual Moravians as they defined themselves in their community and in the larger world. Later generations of young men, even more so than young women, constantly moved between these two worlds, were influenced by both, and did not necessarily embrace the Elders' preference for simple, workmanlike attire in a larger society that used dress to convey status and gender. Ironically, then, the loosening of Elders' attitudes about clothing choice encouraged the assimilation of Moravians. This was especially true in Europe, where social distinctions were greater and were more frequently displayed sartorially than in North America.

Like all the essays in this section, Scott Rohrer explores ways Moravians navigated the larger world beyond their community while retaining their faith. What makes Rohrer's "New Birth in a New Land" especially valuable is his insistence on the centrality of experiential conversion to the assimilation of ethnic groups in eighteenth-century America. Unlike most historians of evangelical religion in early America, he contends that evangelism brought distinct groups of people together in important new ways based on his case study of three *Landgemeinen* (farm congregation communities) in the southern section of the Wachovia tract in North Carolina. Unlike the better known *Ortsgemeinen* or Congregation towns of Bethania and Salem, where elders restricted residency to church members and expected residents to commit themselves fully to God, residents in the *Landgemeinen* could choose to become partial members and were not subject to the same rigorous control.

German-speaking Friedberg and Friedland and English-speaking Hope were populated by some 200 exceedingly diverse migrants eager for cheaper land and a special faith community. These new settlers had been recruited by Moravian missionaries from their homes in the mid-Atlantic settlements and New England. What resulted in their new locale, and in the wake of their life-altering experience of "new birth," was a high degree of ethnic intermixing as measured by friendships and marriages, which belied their significant cultural differences—and all within that first generation. Rohrer contends that the conversion experience and the values of their faith tightly bound these diverse people into a shared community, which was reinforced by their literally coming together in their frontier churches and stores, barn raisings, or trips to Salem for supplies, accelerating their assimilation as southerners, Americans, and evangelicals. This development marks a sharp contrast with non-Moravian German-speaking communities in Pennsylvania and elsewhere, whose communities were so tightly closed and nonevangelical that assimilation took many generations by comparison.

Whether creating Christian farm communities in the North Carolina backcountry, as Rohrer writes about it, or sanctioning young brethren for their "worldly fashion" in Central Germany, as Sommer has demonstrated, Moravians did not isolate themselves or their communities from wider engagement in Atlantic World culture or commerce, despite earlier historians' insistence otherwise, as the next three essays collectively covering the period from 1740 to 1860 make clear. Katherine Carté Engel, in her provocative analysis of Moravians' involvement in transatlantic trade, insists that the importance of religious faith to the Moravians did not preclude involvement in developing markets. In fact, she argues, Moravians purposefully married their need for safe and reliable transport for their migrants to their knowledge of markets in their newest missions at the edges of the Atlantic World by procuring their own ship carrying trade between the 1740s and the 1760s. Engel finds that Moravian finances, and the communities and missions they supported, were integrated in and dependent upon Atlantic market economies. Religion, then, played a far more critical role in eighteenth-century economic development than historians have acknowledged. Thus her essay fundamentally challenges the overly simplistic polarization of "market-driven" societies versus "moral economies" that scholars have touted so vigorously for several generations now.

Emily Conrad Beaver also highlights the interdependence of piety and profit in her examination of the transformation of the Salem economy over the course of the revolutionary era. New backcountry demand for their goods along with political pressures by patriots, Beaver suggests, melded these pacifist Moravians with their world community networks into something decidedly different—German-Americans. The small isolated religious community of Salem, self-sufficient in its earliest years of settlement, was transformed into a regional trade center of political importance by wartime patronage of its stores and the crafts of diverse backcountry settlers. The Aufseher Collegium, aware of the community's new economic dependence on outside trade, relinquished strictures and even permitted the development of new trades in the wake of the war. This loosening of economic regulations to sustain the valuable political and trade relations that Salem enjoyed during the Revolution marked the beginning of Salem's assimilation into the surrounding Southern society by the nineteenth century.

Michael Shirley picks up that thread a generation later to illustrate how Salem Moravians had become acculturated into the larger world by the sweeping market forces of the Jacksonian period. Whereas Beaver's revolutionary merchants remained committed to their piety even as they were drawn into the larger political economy, Shirley finds some Salem businessmen in the early republic choosing opportunities for personal success over commitment to their spiritual community and its beliefs. Salem leaders subsequently debated the role of the congregational order that sanctioned economic activity over the next few decades, putting it under full assault by the 1850s, at which time it ended. By this point, virtually all Piedmont farmers pursued cash crops, their daughters preferring "the latest" fashions over homespun. Salem merchants fought to sell local crafts to their customers, but the availability of Northern-made goods in neighboring communities compromised their wealth, in some cases leading them into bankruptcy, furthered by larger national economic downturns in the late 1820s and early 1840s. Shirley concludes that church dissolution of Moravian control over economic choices symbolized the death throes of Salem as a godly society of communitarians even as it signaled the residents' assimilation as Americans.

Together the essays in Part Two suggest the contours of a gradual decline of Moravian confidence in the gospel and the modification of Moravian godly communities into more commonplace locales. Moravians' global vision, once stoked so powerfully by their pietism, was being burned away by the new nationalism and capitalism of the nineteenth century, leaving parochial Protestants in its place.

The essays in Part Three tell an even more complex story. They highlight constructions of race and gender in the Moravian Church, and when read together make a compelling case for Moravian exceptionalism. Beverly Smaby conveys the nature of women's responsibility and spiritual leadership in the church under Zinzendorf, and the rapid dismantling of women's authority by male leadership upon his death. Although her task is made harder by the intentional destruction of those documents that conveyed the more "unorthodox" theologies and structures of the Moravian church during Zinzendorf's leadership (these perceived "unorthodoxies" included female leadership), Smaby mines women's personal writings, synod records, and paintings and prints to reconstruct women's positions in administrative and spiritual offices and to showcase the significance of feminine piety to the church. Her findings provide a sharp contrast to women's far more subordinate position as daughters and wives in the majority of households in Europe and America, and their absence from public roles in virtually all other Protestant churches. The demolition of Moravian women's authority after 1760, Smaby indicates, reflected male leaders' fear of outsiders' criticisms of their practices at a time when enormous debts made the Church eager to appear conventional before creditors. These women leaders transcended not only gender boundaries, by performing parts of the church service, but class ones as well, for working-class women were as likely to be advanced into these roles as noblewomen. Thus Moravian women leaders may well have been the most visible example of Zinzendorf's extremism, and therefore the most important to dethrone, much to the women's great discontent.

Marianne Wokeck's research on pastors' wives in German-speaking communities in the American colonies underscores Smaby's interpretation of the changing institutional role of women in the Moravian Church. Wokeck traces the emergence of the ideal of the virtuous parson's wife as helpmate to her husband, mother and educator of their children, domestic manager, and nurturing supporter of the pastorate in early modern Europe, to its manifestations in eighteenth-century America. She demonstrates that the *Pfarrfrau* was critical to a new clergyman's success by virtue of her family and community connections, (hence German-born clergymen's preference for local over German-born wives), her skillful household economy, and the degree to which she promulgated her spiritual and domestic values throughout the larger community.

By taking a comparative approach, Wokeck shows that the expectations of the first generation of Moravian women in America were not similar to those of Lutheran and Reformed *Pfarrfrauen* by a long shot. Zinzendorf insisted Moravians marry before departing from Europe to cut back on exogamous marriage in the colonies. Moreover, wives were not expected to serve the needs of their husbands and households, but instead the spiritual well-being of the whole community, underscoring the uniquely religious nature of Moravian marriage. Because Moravians were far more tightly organized throughout the Atlantic, and were supported by a structural system far more sophisticated than those of other denominations, their clergy proved far more self-reliant than their Protestant brethren, at least during the first generation of settlement. Intriguingly, however, Wokeck suggests that the gap between Moravian ministers' wives and Lutheran and reformed *Pfarrfrauen* closed over the next two generations, the former turning into more conventional helpmeets as Church author-ity began to wane. Both Wokeck's and Smaby's essays celebrate the inno-vativeness of Moravian women's roles, a unique situation that lasted for a little more than a generation. Both also point out, however, that women's authority was subsequently circumscribed formally by the Church and informally by colonial realities and the processes of assimilation just as the Enlightenment, with its secularizing bourgeoisie, advocated the rethink-ing of gender constructions.

Anna Smith's essay examines relationships between Moravian and Cherokee women in the early nineteenth-century American South, and finds that missionary work gave the Sisters some measure of independ-ence, although their authority as women remained restricted. Based on her interpretation of the records of the Springplace, Georgia, mission to the Cherokee and subsequent correspondence, Smith highlights the strong personal connections between these Pietists and Native Americans by virtue of their shared faith and work as women. Cherokee and Moravian women both lived in worlds separate from their men as reflected in divi-sions of labor that began almost at birth. Both shared the responsibilities of raising children, managing households, and producing and preserving foodstuffs, and both had measures of power within their societies. At Springplace, both sets of women engaged in exchanges of knowledge about herbs and healing, sewing and handicrafts. Although some Chero-kee women never converted, those who did convert appreciated the sim-ilarity in the matrilineal nature of the clan system and the female choirs, and found comfort in the degree of ritual that characterized church ser-vice. These shared experiences help explain why several of these Chero-kee families sent their daughters to attend boarding school in Salem, and why Cherokee women and Moravian Sisters remained lifelong friends and correspondents decades after the mission ended and the Trail of Tears began.

The reciprocity of the Cherokee-Moravian female relationships first forged in Springplace, Georgia, did not evolve with such relative ease be-tween African American slaves and Moravian missionaries in the Dutch colony of Suriname or the Danish colony of St. Thomas in the West In-dies. While Ellen Klinkers has found in her fascinating study of Suriname that seventy Moravian missionaries could boast some 27,500 slave con-verts by Emancipation (1863), the decades before and after were not nearly so successful. Although Moravian ministers had first reached out to Maroon and Indian communities deep in the interior in 1735, enjoying only slightly more success when they moved their missions into town in the late eighteenth century, it was not until planters recognized the im-plications for their profits created by the closing of the slave trade (1814), and later the announcement of Emancipation, that the Moravians made any real headway. Initially considered social instigators of slave rebellion, they became identified as pillars of white authority, social conservatives who supported imperial power.

The potential for winding up with too few laborers prompted planters, who had hitherto suspected the Brethren of inculcating ideas about freedom, to cast a favorable new light on their efforts; they wanted the Moravians' Christian rhetoric to tout marriage and family to increase the birth rate, as well as promote Western moral sensibilities and habits of industry to aid their disciplinary efforts. The Moravians, some of whom were slaveowners themselves until 1846, walked a thin line placating planters and wooing slave converts, especially as they came to understand the slaves' difficult circumstances and their longstanding commitment to the African-American *Winti*-religion, generations in the making and an inherent component of slave community and culture. Moravians, who had learned how planters used Christian values to maintain ideological constructions of race difference that served double duty by easing their consciences and increasing their wealth, were not always comfortable with these hypocrisies.

The abolition of slavery brought a quick halt to Moravians' increasingly successful conversion efforts. Although the Brethren had created opportunities for leadership, had mediated between planters and slaves in favor of the latter, and had accommodated slaves' *Winti*-religion to Christian conversion, they still represented white authority nonetheless in freedom. Nor did it help that Moravians were principle plaintiffs in an effort to criminalize freedpeople's "heathen practice" of African-American religion in 1872, a position they later regretted. The Moravians had spent the bulk of the nineteenth century negotiating between the strong Creole culture of Surinamese slaves and ex-slaves and the expectations of planters and the state as well as their own Christian beliefs about social institutions and behavior. Although the Moravians were finally "successful" by the century's end, building a lasting foundation for the Moravian church among the majority of African Americans in Suriname, it was not done exclusively on their own terms. Did that reality press Moravian missionaries, individually or collectively, to reexamine the inherently racist presumptions that had led them to embrace plantation economies and impose their Moravian tenets and theologies upon this black society?

Jon Sensbach casts his net even further in his examination of Moravian global outreach. Why, he asks, was the majority of the world's black Protestants Moravians at the end of the eighteenth century, and in what ways did the Moravians anticipate and shape the global outreach of evangelical Protestantism over the next two centuries and into today? For Sensbach, the Moravians offer a valuable means to understand how the encounters of Europeans with peoples from the Americas produced new systems of knowledge and language that blended both worlds. In his examination of Moravians' conversion of slaves in eighteenth-century St. Thomas, he finds (as did Klinkers in nineteenth-century Suriname), that the Brethren had to accommodate Afro-Caribbean religious beliefs in their teachings of the Christian faith. Sensbach argues that slaves themselves found that Moravian Christianity allowed slaves "to salvage a spiritual reckoning with enslavement" precisely because it gave Africans the extended spiritual family that had been destroyed by the Atlantic slave trade, as well as positions of responsibility and leadership (especially for slave women) in a hierarchical and brutal plantation economy that denied slaves such roles. Christian fellowship even allowed a few slaves a new mobility and in some cases outright freedom through their participation in congregant life in Herrnhut and North America. Moravian fellowship, Sensbach shows us, was not only transcultural but also transracial. Moravians consistently crossed ethnic and racial boundaries as well as religious and gendered ones, and offered important new opportunities to beleaguered peoples on a number of colonial and cultural frontiers. How significant were these opportunities in the long run, however, and how was Moravian fellowship transformed in the process?

A. G. Roeber's sweeping epilogue takes up that challenge by debating whether Moravians should be written into a global history of diasporic Christianity. He sees a critical need for greater and more imaginative examinations of Moravians' Christian "missions" to understand more precisely what they made of the "subalterns" they encountered, and the influence of these non-Europeans on their own faith and their understanding of the world. In taking this cue from Roeber, this collection as a whole invites reconsideration of Moravian founder Count Zinzendorf's own vision of a utopian Christian community, and the degree to which his ideals were realized in what became a far-flung network of Moravian colonies, from Saxony to the mid-Atlantic to the slave South to the West Indies.

One of the unique features of the Moravian Church was the gendered division of devotion and work, which segregated single men and women into choirs. An adaptation of the Pietist conventicle, the sex-specific choirs prevented courtship, romance, and even co-ed fraternization, and placed decisions regarding marriage in the hands of the community leadership. While often noted for the spiritual authority granted to women, this Pietism also frequently embraced patriarchy, an important tension with significant cultural and political consequences, which is also thoughtfully explored in several essays. Relations of gender also influenced the organization of labor and production, a central preoccupation of the Moravian Brethren. Most new communities forged a fascinating amalgam of German manorial and guild economies, but the demands of local production and commerce often impinged on this traditional organization. Several essays thus examine when and why these settlements began to permit private ownership and profit. These articles also address the relationship of Moravians to slavery, Africans, African Americans, and Native Americans in the American South and in the larger diaspora, as workers and as Christians.

The very category of "diaspora"—essential for the study of slave, immigrant, and minority identities—is recognized increasingly as a critical tool for considering the ethnic and confessional identities of German-speaking Protestants. Moreover, the term has a particularly rich application when analyzing the Brethren. Not only did Moravians embody contemporary social-scientific descriptions of diaspora—a sometime persecuted ethnic and/or religious group with a strong collective memory, maintained through the policing of communal boundaries, and through ties to a real or idealized homeland—but the Church actually incorporated the word into its own doctrine, evoking one of its original Greek applications in Christian Scripture, the "scattered" believers of the primitive church described in 1 Peter. This motivated the Moravians' formal theology of ecumenical evangelism, but it also provided a point of identification for the German-speaking colonists who built their confessional communities throughout the Atlantic World. The pieces in this volume implicitly acknowledge a diasporic consciousness and discuss the relationship of the new Atlantic World communities to the centralized Church administration in Herrnhut, Saxony. They point to those crucial moments of transformation when North American Moravians came to define themselves as "German-American" and eventually exclusively as "American."[14]

Pious Pursuits addresses key themes in the history of both early modern Germany and early America; ethnicity and identity; the integration of markets and regions; transatlantic production and exchange; immigration, migration, and patterns of settlement; the foundations and development of imperial policies; resistance, rebellion, and political thought; conceptions of gender, class, and race in colonization; and most especially, piety, confession, and religious expression. The volume contributes substantially to an understanding of diasporic communities by tracing how German-speaking Moravians negotiated an absolutely critical cultural exchange over place and time in the English-speaking world. It highlights transnational values and ideas, especially those steeped in Protestant Christianity in general and Protestant Pietism in particular, and how they played out across local terrains and contexts. This last set of themes in particular binds the volume together and helps pose new questions about Pietism's "uniqueness" in the Atlantic World. *Pious Pursuits,* from this perspective, is as relevant for understanding our world today as it is for understanding our past.

Notes

1. Katharine M. Faull, *Moravian Women's Memoirs: Their Related Lives, 1750–1820* (Syracuse, NY, 1997), 36–39.
2. Bernard Bailyn, *Atlantic History: Concept and Contours* (Cambridge, MA, 2005), 14.
3. J.G.A. Pocock, *The Machiavellian Moment: Florentine Political Thought and the Atlantic Republican Tradition* (Princeton, NJ, 1975); Bernard Bailyn, *The Ideological Origins of the American Revolution* (Cambridge, MA, 1967).
4. The literature is voluminous, and includes Bernard Bailyn, *The Peopling of British America* (New York, 1986); Stanley N. Katz, John Murrin, and Douglas Greenberg, eds., *Colo-*

nial America: Essays in Politics and Social Development, 4th ed. (New York, 1993); Anthony McFarlane, *The British in the Americas 1480–1815* (London, 1994); Jack P. Greene, "Beyond Power: Paradigm Subversion and Reformulation and the Re-Creation of the Early Modern Atlantic World," in Greene, *Interpreting Early America: Historiographical Essays* (Charlottesville, VA, 1996); J. H. Elliott, *Britain and Spain in America: Colonists and Colonized* (Reading, PA, 1994); Nicholas Canny, ed., *Europeans on the Move* (Oxford, 1994); Ida Altman and James Horn, eds., *"To Make America": European Emigration in the Early Modern Period* (Berkeley, 1991), 85–130; David Hackett Fischer, *Albion's Seed: Four British Folkways in America* (New York, 1989); Mary Beth Norton, *Founding Mothers and Fathers: Gendered Power and the Forming of American Society* (New York, 1996); Kathleen Brown, *Good Wives, Nasty Wenches and Anxious Patriarchs: Gender, Race and Power in Colonial Virginia* (Chapel Hill, NC, 1996); Peter Linebaugh and Marcus Rediker, *The Many-Headed Hydra: Sailors, Slaves and the Atlantic Working Class in the Eighteenth Century* (Boston, 2000); Ira Berlin, *Many Thousands Gone: The First Two Centuries of Slavery in North America* (Cambridge, MA, 1998); Allan Kulikoff, *Tobacco and Slaves: The Development of Southern Cultures in the Chesapeake, 1680–1800* (Chapel Hill, NC, 1986); Philip D. Morgan, *Slave Counterpoint: Black Culture in the Eighteenth-Century Chesapeake and Low Country* (Chapel Hill, NC, 1998); Eric Williams, *Capitalism and Slavery* (London, 1944); Robin Blackburn, *The Making of New World Slavery: From the Baroque to the Modern 1492–1800* (London, 1997).

5. Bailyn, *Atlantic History*, 48–49.

6. Important work that highlights the German-American Atlantic World includes A. G. Roeber, *Palatines, Liberty, and Property: German Lutherans in Colonial British America* (Baltimore, 1993); Aaron Fogleman, *Hopeful Journeys: German Immigration, Settlement, and Political Culture, 1717–1775* (Philadelphia, 1996); Jon S. Sensbach, *A Separate Canaan: The Making of an Afro-Moravian World in North Carolina, 1763–1840* (Chapel Hill, NC, 1998); Marianne S. Wokeck, *Trade in Strangers: The Beginnings of Mass Migration to North America* (University Park, MD, 1999); Sam Mustafa, *Merchants and Migrations: Germans and Americans in Connection, 1776–1835* (Aldershot, 2001); Colin G. Calloway, Gerd Gemunder, and Susan Zantop, eds., *Germans and Indians: Fantasies, Encounters, Projections* (Lincoln, NE, 2002); Hans-Jürgen Grabbe, *Vord der großen Flut: Die europäische Migration in die Vereinigten Staaten von Amerika 1783–1820* (Stuttgart, 2001); Frank Trommler and Elliott Shore, eds., *The German-American Encounter: Conflict and Cooperation Between Two Cultures, 1800–2000* (New York, 2001); and Hartmut Lehmann, Hermann Wellenreuther, and Renate Wilson, eds. *In Search of Peace and Prosperity: New German Settlements in Eighteenth-Century Europe and America* (University Park, PA, 2000).

7. Bailyn, *Atlantic History*, 96–101.

8. The best English-language narrative account of the Renewed Unitas Fratrum remains Kenneth G. Hamilton and J. Taylor Hamilton, *History of the Moravian Church: The Renewed Unitas Fratrum, 1722–1957* (Bethlehem, 1967). See also the essays in Martin Brecht, et al., eds., *Geschichte des Pietismus*, 3 vols. (Göttingen, 1993–2000).

9. Especially valuable are the essays on Pietism's influence on Zinzendorf by F. Ernest Stoeffler, *German Pietism During the Eighteenth Century* (Leiden, 1973) and *The Rise of Evangelical Pietism* (Leiden, 1965). See also the essays in *Geschichte des Pietismus*.

10. Gillian L. Gollin, *Moravians in Two Worlds: A Study of Changing Communities* (New York, 1967); Beverly Prior Smaby, *The Transformation of Moravian Bethlehem: From Communal Mission to Family Economy* (Philadelphia, 1988); Daniel B. Thorp, *The Moravian Community in Colonial North Carolina: Pluralism on the Southern Frontier* (Knoxville, TN, 1989); S. Scott Rohrer, *Hope's Promise: Religion and Acculturation in the Southern Backcountry* (Tuscaloosa, AL, 2005); Elisabeth W. Sommer, *Serving Two Masters: Moravian Brethren in Germany and North Carolina, 1727–1801* (Lexington, KY, 2000); J. C. S. Mason, *The Moravian Church and the Missionary Awakening in England 1760–1800* (Woodbridge, UK, 2001); Colin Podmore, *The Moravian Church in England, 1728–1760* (Oxford, 1998); Valdis Mezezers. *The Herrnuterian Pietism in the Baltic and Its Outreach into America and Elsewhere in the World* (North Quincy, MA, 1975).

11. A. J. Lewis, *Zinzendorf the Ecumenical Pioneer* (Philadelphia, 1962), 117–121; Horst Weigelt, *Geschichte des Pietismus in Bayern: Anfänge – Entwicklung – Bedeutung* (Göttingen, 2001), 288; Dietrich Meyer, "Zinzendorf und Herrnhut," in *Geschichte des Pietismus,* 2:65–66; John Weinlick, *Moravian Diaspora: A Study of the Societies of the Moravian Church within the Protestant State Churches of Europe* (Nazareth, PA, 1959), 20–35. Horst Weigelt, "Der Pietismus im Übergang vom 18. zum 19. Jahrhundert," in *Geschichte des Pietismus,* 2:701–705.

12. German Protestants generally, as Aaron Fogleman has argued, including Mennonites, Amish, and Schwenkfelders in addition to the Moravians, proved as expert at supporting emigration from Central Europe to colonial America as their successful secular counterparts. But the Moravians, with their extensive local support networks, fared especially well.

13. Fogleman, *Hopeful Journeys,* chap. 4.

14. For comparisons of German and other diasporic communities, see Richard J. Ross's "Intersecting Diasporas," and introduction to the forum "Jews and Pietists in Early America" *William and Mary Quarterly* 58, no. 4 (2001): 849–854. For a recent analysis of "Diaspora" see Khachig Tololyan, "Rethinking *Diaspora*(s): Stateless Power in the Transnational Moment," *Diaspora* 5 (1996): 3–36.

PART ONE

The Birth of Moravianism:
Confession and Culture

– Chapter 1 –

IMPERIAL COMMUNITIES

Mack Walker

A RECENT CHALLENGE TO Atlantic World historians is to explain the motives—or even obsessions—that induced Europeans to traverse an ocean and colonize a strange country. Accounting for the religious "imperialism" of the German Pietists, or more narrowly the Moravian Brethren, is that much the more pressing, in that sentimental hagiographic or ecclesiastical histories seem banal and unconvincing. Here I will attempt to develop a sociology both of the Moravian Gemeine, or community town, and of the cultural and political conditions in German Central Europe that supported the relative success of the imperial Moravian project. I propose to explain Herrnhut and its settlements, both in Europe and elsewhere, as reflections of the German civic community. The special twist in this story is the emphatically extracommunal or noble status of the most prominent sources of support for the Moravian project, a topic much neglected in most scholarship on the subject. Like the German civic community itself, this aristocratic patronage expressed a peculiarly German condition, namely the Kleinstaaterei or political fragmentation which fostered strategies of cultural compensation by an overabundant and often penurious social elite.

I begin with a comparison between the institutionally secular German communities, in the typified description I once offered of them, and the saved or Christocentric communities exemplified by Herrnhut and Ebersdorf in Germany and Bethlehem and Salem in North America, during the eighteenth century—or after, in the middle third, between the 1730s and the end of the Seven Years' War in the 1760s. This is to pose the "natural" civic community, "natural" in the religious jargon of the times, meaning unredeemed in Grace—the "home town," as I have called it[1]—

alongside the community of the redeemed, the "awakened" community possessed of Grace and the Spirit.[2]

I turn first to the principal and pervasive social institutions that bound individuals and families into the respective communities at large, namely the usual artisan and trade guilds of the preindustrial European towns, to be compared with the class or "choir" system of the communities of the redeemed. These parallel structures were, respectively, the main instruments for the indoctrination and admission of members into the confines of their settlement, their society, their economy. The guilds were restrictive organizations of butchers and bakers and chandlers and the rest, with their training systems of apprentices, journeymen, and masters, shop discipline and quality controls, civic ceremonies of induction and representation.[3] This was the "natural" home town. Parallel in the "redeemed" community was the choir system of a dozen or more elaborately defined and strenuously guarded categories of age, gender, and marital status (sexual potential seems to have been the common marker) with its hierarchy of "workers," their "helpers," their several choir ceremonies, and communal love-feasts.[4]

This elaborate choir organization sometimes strikes observers as a bureaucratic fantasy more than an operating social system, and no doubt it was full of gaps and elisions in practice, still more so probably than was the guild system. Both were meant, however, to integrate, guard, and discipline the community by ordering the specialized roles and interests according to categories deemed essential to its being—that is, the economic and kinship orders in the "natural" or home town. As for the "awakened" community, the choir system's special, indeed defining preoccupation with distinctions of gender and sexual roles reflects community organizers' awareness—quite explicitly Count Zinzendorf's—of the emotional overlap between religious and sexual passions, of which there were many examples in German Pietist experience.[5] These cropped up dramatically in the so-called Sifting Time to affect, for example, the otherwise stuffy German imperial jurist Johann Jacob Moser at Ebersdorf.[6]

The choir system of sexual segregation and controls was founded, to quote the Synod of 1768, "not on the grounds of our holiness but awareness of our human depravity and sinfulness."[7] For that matter the guild system, to pursue the comparison, was founded not on fraternal generosity and honor, but on awareness of human greed and selfishness. The choir system was, through age and gender segregation, in theory at least, a direct attack on the domestic family as the primary social unit for the nurture and civilization of children.[8] The guild system of economic orientation, by contrast, was *based* on the family: family indoctrination; family economic ties, favor, and status. The pairing of these contrasts—to control sinfulness by suppression of the family, to control greed by emphasis on the family—seems worth pondering. Civic integration by choir came at the price of radical segregation in everyday social life, with its elimination of domestic intimacy and privacy and of courtship, and imposed even where it did not reflect a preoccupation with sexual moral-ity. But guilds and guildsmen were deeply engaged too in what I have called "the mad morality of the guilds," which focused on legitimacy of birth and thus on the integrity of family and the inheritance of property and status. Notice, though, that the role of women was a more powerful one, or at least more prominent, in the choir system, with its exclusively female choir organizations and their parallel civic functions as workers and helpers and the rest. Women had important rights and functions in the guild system too, but informally and without political recognition, or else by derivation from family status as a widow or orphan.[9]

The Christocentric choir system of the "awakened" communities was probably the more effective one, when it was in place, at enforcing social discipline within subordinate groups, and also at transmitting the central authority of the community throughout its whole membership. The pa-triarchal guild system of the "natural" community, on the other hand, was probably better at economic organization and training, and survived the choirs apparently for that reason.[10] But even more striking than their differences are the parallels of the two systems, and the character of the analogies they present. They agreed that there had to be formal enforce-able systems of social organization including moral, religious, and eco-nomic sanctions. Both attached signal importance to the civic, social, and economic composition of their populations. They operated similarly in their selection, rendering, and control of membership—citizenship and brotherhood respectively—in their communities. Neither community al-lowed occupational freedom or individual choice of profession. Distribu-tion among the trades was closely controlled, in the interest of economic balance and the accommodation of supply to demand, administered by the Council of Elders in the redeemed community, and by the guildmas-ters and citizen magistrates in the natural home town. Moreover, when it comes to numbers, the actual distribution of occupations turns out to be markedly similar—quite evidently by design, and with an important ex-ception to which I shall turn below. Both systems featured a predominance of the artisanal trades, related services, and local commerce, set in a trib-utary environment of rural farms and village folk, the peasantry and the unredeemed respectively, deemed to be of inferior civic and moral status.

Controls over acceptance into full membership, despite different stan-dards of eligibility, produced markedly similar results. Beverly Smaby has figures in her 1988 book showing that whereas 87 percent of migrants coming into the Bethlehem community were already-saved Moravians, only 13 percent were admitted by conversion from outside the group. When I checked comparable figures for the town of Weissenburg in Fran-conia in my book of 1971, I found the figure for acceptance of new citi-zens there to be 84 percent from citizen or locally established families—a remarkable parallel in membership practices, with legitimacy of birth and proven economic viability required for membership in the unawak-ened natural home town, redemption into Grace for the awakened community.[11] And there can be no doubt that *exclusion* from the respective communities by their respective standards had similar consequences, for both the excluded and the excluding. Spangenberg's remark on the prudence of forfending potential disharmony that might corrupt the redeemed community—*Turpius eicitur quam non admittitur hospes*, it is harder to expel the stranger than not to admit him in the first place—might have served as epigraph for any or many a hometown charter.[12]

There are other parallels too, statistical, verbal, and visual, too many to pursue here; and from these it does appear that the framers of the Moravian communities had a model, knew what self-contained small communities were supposed to look like demographically, economically, even architecturally. But one *difference* in occupational distribution will matter a great deal for the comparison and the larger argument posed by my title. In the awakened communities of the German Moravians one finds large contingents of noble establishments: titled families with their retainers, household officers, servants, and *their* families. This noble presence was palpable in America too, if to a lesser degree. Alongside the noble presence was a substantial contingent of missionary occupations. Where there were nobles anywhere in or around the natural German home town, they normally stood in adversarial relation to the civic community itself here (distinct from unchartered rural villages under immediate noble jurisdiction or dependency).[13] Local clergy too were normally noncitizens, by custom and by ecclesiastical design. And if there were persons living there or nearby who were engaged outside the community in external commerce or manufacture for export, and thus were comparable to missionary clergy, then by mutual preference these too were unlikely to be community members (outside of large centers with dominant cosmopolitan interests),[14] let alone sponsors or officers or even chief administrators, as noble residents of German metropolitan cities might be. Zinzendorf's model statute of 1727 for Herrnhut might have served as the whole charter of a contemporary "home town" but for one factor: what Uttendörfer in 1925 called the "feudal" structure of authority led by a noble authority at the top with sovereign control over administration, police, and judicial powers.[15]

This noble participation is a difference that overrides similarities in the internal structures of government, such as the small central administrative councils and the smaller representative ones common to both systems. The political strategies of each incorporated a great number of constitutionally ordained public offices at all levels, so that nearly everybody—every member, that is, who was in a position to contribute, or to make trouble—was enmeshed in a system of appointive office or patronage.[16]

Of course, the main outward difference between the communities' political constitutions is that the redeemed community was a deliberate theocracy, with civic and ecclesiastical powers located in the same group or closely interlocking groups. In the German unredeemed community, ecclesiastical authority, including pastoral appointments, control over church properties and resources, and religious discipline, was situated in a wider ecclesiastical jurisdiction and hierarchy of an effectively sovereign, established state or extraterritorial church.[17] This is a reason why Count Zinzendorf worked so hard to obtain Lutheran ordination from some, from *any* German state church: to unite the religious with temporal authority under state sanction. And that ecclesiastical tradition and condition of German Protestantism was a necessary if not sufficient condition for the preeminent role of the German nobility, especially nobility of the middle or lesser rank, in the establishment, direction, promotion, and expansion of the Moravian communities in Germany, then Europe, and overseas. I turn now to the problem of noble underemployment in early modern Germany.

I started keeping track, as I looked through the histories of Moravian settlements, of the German comital houses—nobles, that is, with the rank of *Graf* or count—who engaged in the establishment of awakened or Moravian Brotherhood communities, *Colonien*, as they were commonly called, on their estates around the middle third of the eighteenth century.[18] I got this far: Counts Zinzendorf and Reuss, of course, but then Seidlitz, Promnitz, Gersdorf, Schaumburg-Lippe, Castell, Wolff-Metternich, Wittgenstein-Berleburg, Isenburg-Wächtersbach, Stollberg-Wernigerode, Isenburg-Büdingen, Isenburg-Meerholz, Isenburg-Birstein, Tenczin, Polzig, Erbach-Fürstenau, Saalfeld, Neuwied, Waldeck, and Wildenfels. What was going on here? What impelled and what characterized the Pietistical awakening of these particular noble ranks and their busy formation of Christocentric communities, on their own estates and eventually on others', at this time? What were they doing, and what *else* were they doing that might have accounted for this proliferation?

To pose the question this way predisposes one answer, toward which I cite an observation from another quarter that has been offered to explain the elaborate flowering and proliferation of the fine arts in Germany at this time, notably in decoration, architecture, and music. This answer invokes the political decentralization of the country together with a very large number of underemployed noble families competing for eminence commensurate with their names by the promotion of baroque culture, in place of the ways of war and politics lost, since the sixteenth century and especially since the Thirty Years' War, to the emergence of standing armies and territorial states. Demonstrative baroque culture and decorative arts offered one alternative way to the restoration of pride and dignity to these mediatized noble families.[19] Demonstrative piety offered another; and indeed, as seems to be the way of cultural phenomena, the two stimulated and provoked one another in a contest of mutual reciprocity and even repulsion. The tension appeared also as an alternation, over time and over generations, even within a single family. In Köthen, for example, we see the dialectic between chamber-music, and prayer circle: J. S. Bach, and the encounter group that succeeded him. Bach ornamented the cultural scene there as *Kappelmeister* in the 1720s when the Pietist prophetic pedagogue A. H. Francke came to call on one of his tours of Central German noble houses. Two years later Bach left for Leipzig, the next cohort at Köthen set up a community of the redeemed on the estate and court, and the musicians departed. Hans-Walter Erbe cites Köthen (though it was a territorial principality) as exemplary for his notion of the "contrasting" noble cultures of art and piety. What strikes me more in the present context is their analogy.[20] For the middle and lesser nobility, however, such as the comital houses I have mentioned that lacked the sovereign pretensions or the fiscal resources of the territorial princes, the path of exemplary acts of piety offered by far the readier opportunity.

Meanwhile there is something else going on, another mode of explanation that some readers may find more solid and persuasive, that is closely linked in any case with the foregoing. Many of these underemployed counts were also land-poor, especially in the thinly populated and relatively barren central and east central parts of Germany—the Hessens, Thuringia, and the little Saxonies. They inherited a lot of land but it was underdeveloped and unproductive, inhabited by a lethargic, unresponsive, and inefficient peasant labor force, if it could be got to labor, which it had little interest in doing, reasonably enough since whatever surplus it produced above subsistence was fair game for the landlord. Consequently the noble landlords were wanting in credit, in the broad significance of the term: status as well as money. Both cash and credit were scarce and in high demand, in that weakened but competitive early-modern noble culture; one way to reach for them was through the development of hitherto neglected and underused possessions by the attraction of a highly motivated, committed, energetic, God-fearing, and productive working population. Religious exiles offered an obvious multipurpose solution, especially since those of characteristically enthusiastic commitment could not go home again as more casual, undependable migrant labor or immature adventurers might. The dramatic example of this kind of reasoning and program was of course the successful settlement of the Salzburg refugees in East Prussia in the 1730s by the fiercely pious Frederick William I, who saw God's hand in this happy conjuncture of purposes and said so, and set his bureaucrats to busily setting up communal institutions on Prussian royal domains.[21]

A certain Count Zinzendorf came to East Prussia then and offered to assist in the enterprise, maybe with an ordination in the Prussian state church. However, the Prussians declined his help in both respects, named him a "Moravian bishop" instead, and sent him on his way back to Herrnhut, and to distant shores.[22] Count Zinzendorf is the link that returns this story to the themes of the volume and to the title I have set for the essay: the link between the imperial and the communal: as the representative of the stressed but awakened German nobility of the eighteenth century.[23]

At the age of ten, Nicolaus Ludwig Graf Zinzendorf had been sent to school with A. H. Francke at Halle, as was common among the country nobility of the region; he stayed until he was sixteen, dining at the table of the great Francke himself, placed among his peers as befit his rank. Besides possessing considerable homiletic, spiritual, and pedagogic powers, Francke was one of the most proficient pastoral entrepreneurs of his time in Germany or maybe in the history of European Protestantism. His special target was the Central European nobility, but his connections and the scope of his ideas were truly global. Consider his title to a proposal addressed to the king of Prussia in 1701 for the funding of a *Projekt:* "Project for a *Seminario Universali,* or, Laying out a Plantation, from which may be expected a general Improvement of all Estates of Society, inside and outside Germany, indeed everywhere in Europe and all other Parts of the World," followed by a still more elaborated and ambitious proposal (1704, revised and reissued in 1711) that historical convention has dubbed simply his "Great Treatise."[24]

So went the talk at Halle while Zinzendorf was growing up there, listening and connecting with schoolmates, then at the university at Wittenberg and on the travels customary among young noblemen. Another young count, of Reuss-Ebersdorf, came to be a special crony whose sister Zinzendorf married, and whom he tried to interest in an investment in John Law's Mississippi land-grant credit scheme ("Some Irishman has made 25 million with an investment of only ten thousand!") just before that famous "bubble" burst in 1720.[25] This Heinrich XXIX (sic) Graf Reuss-Ebersdorf would become, instead, founder and patron of the awakened community at Ebersdorf in the Vogtland, where for a time the aforesaid J. J. Moser took refuge from the aforesaid King Frederick William I of Prussia, until he was sifted out in the 1740s.[26]

In 1722 Zinzendorf got from his grandmother (his mother having married a Prussian general and moved to Berlin) a run-down estate at Berthelsdorf in the Oberlausitz. The place was in terrible shape, his overseer told him; the resident peasantry refused to work for any more than they needed to keep themselves alive. What was an enlightened landlord to do? The solution lay to hand: to recruit colonists, preferably religious refugees, to settle in and produce a margin of return above subsistence. These might come from a number of places infected by current religious instability, but conveniently could include disaffected Protestants from the Moravian estates of the Roman Catholic bishop across the border to the east.[27] The ensuing colonization at Berthelsdorf by the Moravian Brotherhood was the foundation of the Herrnhut community, which then was extended and expanded to include communal settlements of the redeemed elsewhere in Europe and also Bethlehem and Salem in North America, within a General Economy organized and directed from Herrnhut and the General Synod of the brotherhood.

Daniel Thorp and Aaron Fogleman have remarked on the colonial character of the Moravian communities in America, along with the presence and influence there of German petty nobility. Renate Wilson has recently documented the energetic engagement of German nobles in the organization and expansion of the international pharmaceutical trade via Pietist networks.[28] Zinzendorf himself claimed in 1752 that the North Carolina project he was then promoting should return £10,000 annual revenue by settlement of thousands of religious émigrés. This moreover would be a solution, Zinzendorf claimed, to an overbalance of unmarried young males and females for which the parent Herrnhut community could find no social space. Here exactly was a line of thought that reappeared in nineteenth-century German imperial theory and that critics in debate would dub "exporting the social problem."[29]

And here is where the comparison with which I began, between communities redeemed and unredeemed, has carried these remarks: through the social condition of early modern nobility to redundancy and exclusion, and so to a regeneration of domestic social forms in new places, and the fringes of imperial theory. Historians of the Moravian communities in America seem generally to agree that in the third quarter of the eighteenth century they departed from the Herrnhut orbit and evolved into "American" towns.[30] Americanization is a topic for historians of American society and culture; but I have been impressed, while preparing this essay, by Kathleen Conzen's imagery of "Phantom Landscapes of Colonization," a phrase she takes from Friedrich Kapp, sometime immigration commissioner of New York—and subsequently an active Progressive Party Member of the German Reichstag during those same imperialism debates—to define the place of ethnicity in American society. The phrase "phantom landscapes" resonates with the relation I have found here between the German Moravian settlements and their extension to America. Here Conzen is proposing a resolution to debates among American historians over immigration, melting pots, ethnic persistence, "contributions," and related issues of real and present concern.[31] So understood, the phrase suggests that a process of colonization has persisted, from the settlements of the eighteenth century into the massive migrations of the nineteenth, and maybe even to the ghettos and barrios of the twentieth and beyond, these colonizations of our times. Still, that may turn out to be another story altogether.

Notes

1. Mack Walker, *German Home Towns: Community, State, and General Estate, 1648–1871* (Ithaca, NY, 1971; repr. 1998). Note that this category excludes both large cities and peasant villages, a typology well known to contemporaries.
2. Elizabeth W. Sommer's "baptized community": *Serving Two Masters: Moravian Brethren in Germany and North Carolina, 1727–1801* (Lexington, KY, 2000).
3. Walker, *Home Towns*, chap. 3.
4. There are detailed comparisons in Gillian Gollin, *Moravians in Two Worlds: A Study of Changing Communities* (New York, 1967), 67–109, and in Otto Uttendörfer, *Wirtschafts-*

geist und Wirtschaftsorganisation Herrnhuts und der Brüdergemeine von 1743 bis zum Ende des Jahrhunderts (Herrnhut, 1926).

5. On this topic see especially Gottfried Beyreuther, *Sexualtheorie im Pietismus* (Munich, 1963).

6. On Ebersdorf see especially Hans-Walter Erbe, *Zinzendorf und der fromme hohe Adel seiner Zeit* (Leipzig, 1928), 172–209; Mack Walker, *Johann Jakob Moser and the Holy Roman Empire of the German Nation* (Chapel Hill, NC, 1981), 105–114, 162–172. The doubts I entertain in the latter about Moser's professed detachment from the erotic passions of that episode (see p. 169) I find confirmed by Erbe, *Zinzendorf*, 196.

7. Uttendörfer, *Wirtschaftsgeist*, 343.

8. But see Jacob J. Sessler, *Communal Pietism among Early Modern Moravians* (New York, 1933), 93–105, and Daniel B. Thorp, *The Moravian Community in Colonial North Carolina: Pluralism on the Southern Frontier* (Knoxville, TN, 1989), 58–59. Thorp also comments skeptically (passim) on the reality of these models in Wachovia.

9. Beyreuther, *Sexualtheorie*, passim; Thorp, *The Moravian Community*, 81–83; Walker, *Home Towns*, 83, 87–88.

10. Beverly P. Smaby, *The Transformation of Moravian Brethren: From Communal Mission to Family Economy* (Philadelphia, 1988); Gollin, *Moravians*, 198–215; Thorp, *The Moravian Community*, 58–64.

11. Smaby, *Transformation*, 64; Walker, *Home Towns*, 221. Note also the analogous use of the term "natural": being "naturally born," meaning illegitimate in civic discourse, or being "in a natural condition," as the absence of Grace was termed in religious discourse, were grounds for exclusion in the two systems respectively.

12. Hellmuth Erbe, *Bethlehem, Pa.: Eine kommunistische Herrnhuter Kolonie des 18. Jahrhunderts* (Stuttgart and Herrnhut, 1929), 52.

13. Compare Peter Blickle, *Kommunalismus: Skizzen einer gesellschaftlichen Organisationsform*, 2 vols. (Munich, 2000), esp. 1:76–86.

14. Compare Thomas J. Brady, *Communities, Politics and Reformation in Early Modern Europe* (Leiden, 1998) and his antecedent works.

15. Otto Uttendörfer, *Alt-Herrnhut: Wirtschaftsgeschichte und Religionssoziologie Herrnhuts während seiner ersten Zwanzig Jahre (1722–1742)* (Herrnhut, 1925), 19–34.

16. On organization of government and patronage see Gollin, *Moravians*, 25–49; Erbe, *Bethlehem*, 29–35; Thorp, *Moravian Community*, 81–104; and compare Walker, *Home Towns*, 44–59.

17. But I have a hunch that if I had better information and a way to generalize about the local office of deacon, I might be obliged to modify that dualist view.

18. The clue came from Friedrich W. Barthold, "Die erweckten im protestantischen Deutschland während des Ausgangs des 17. und der ersten Hälfte des 18. Jahrhunderts, besonders der frommen Grafenhöfe," in *Historisches Taschenbuch*, 3d series (Leipzig, 1853), 129–390. My pagination is to the 1853 Leipzig edition.

19. Walter H. Bruford, *Germany in the Eighteenth Century: The Social Background of the Literary Revival* (Cambridge, 1935), esp. 1–10, 45–105, 291–311; Adrien Fauchier-Magnon, *The Small German Courts in the Eighteenth Century* (London, 1958).

20. Erbe, *Zinzendorf*, 70–73.

21. Mack Walker, *The Salzburg Transaction: Expulsion and Redemption in Eighteenth-Century Germany* (Ithaca, NY, 1982).

22. Albrecht Ritschl, *Geschichte des Pietismus*, 3 vols. (Bonn, 1880–1886), 2:304–311.

23. A convenient biography for the present purpose is Dietrich Meyer, "Zinzendorf und Herrnhut," in *Geschichte des Pietismus*, ed. Martin Brecht, et al, 3 vols. (Göttingen, 1993–2000), 2:3–106; and see the general works cited there and in this essay.

24. A. H. Francke, *Projekt.: Zu einem Seminario Universale oder Anlegung einer Pflanz-Garten, von welchem man eine Verbesserung in allen Ständen in und ausserhalb Teutschlands, ja in Europa und allen Theilen der Welt zugewarten* (Halle, 1701), repr. in Francke, *Werke in Auswahl*, ed. Erhard Peschke (Berlin, 1969), 108–115; *Der Grosse Aufsatz (1711)*, ed. Otto Podczeck, *Abhandlung der Sächsischen Akademie der Wissenschaften zu Leipzig, Philologisch-Historische Klasse* 53, 3 (Leipzig, 1962).

25. Uttendörfer, *Alt-Herrnhut*, 144–145.
26. See Erbe, *Zinzendorf und der fromme hohe Adel seiner Zeit* (Leipzig, 1928), 172–209; Walker, *Johann Jakob Moser and the Holy Roman Empire of the German Nation* (Chapel Hill, NC, 1981), 105–114, 162–172.
27. Uttendörfer, *Alt-Herrnhut*, 147–148.
28. Aaron Fogleman, *Hopeful Journeys: German Immigration, Settlement, and Political Culture in Colonial America, 1717–1775* (Philadelphia, 1995), 107–112; Thorp, *The Moravian Community*, passim, esp. 90–92; Renate Wilson, *Pious Traders in Medicine: A German Pharmaceutical Network in Eighteenth-Century North America* (University Park, MD, 2000)
29. For Zinzendorf on overpopulation and colonization, Uttendörfer, *Wirtschaftsgeist*, 202–222, 254, 341; for imperialism and the social problem, Mack Walker, *Germany and the Emigration, 1816–1885* (Cambridge, 1964), 195–246; the quotation is from Karl Liebknecht (p. 243).
30. See for example Gollin, *Moravians*, 188–215; Smaby, *Transformation*, 40–42, 239–243 and passim; Sommer, *Serving Two Masters*, esp. 140–170.
31. Kathleen Conzen, "Phantom Landscapes of Colonization," in Frank Trommler and Elliott Shore, *The German-American Encounter* (New York, 2001), 7–21; see also Trommler's introductory comments, x–xix.

– Chapter 2 –

MANUSCRIPT MISSIONS IN THE AGE OF PRINT: MORAVIAN COMMUNITY IN THE ATLANTIC WORLD*

Robert Beachy

Introduction

A T A CONFERENCE HELD in Herrnhut, Saxony, in September 1780, Moravian Church leaders debated the distribution of the "Gemein Nachrichten," a Church periodical issued in manuscript form since 1747. The journal combined devotional literature with Church news in as many as thirty-five annual issues. By 1788 nearly forty copies were laboriously hand-drafted almost weekly and distributed throughout the Atlantic World. This broad circulation unnerved Church Elders, who demanded an exact accounting of its subscription. Who received the periodical, they asked, and who had access to it? If a single copy was shared by different groups, how long was it held by each and where was it finally deposited? The Elders also requested a description of how the "Gemein Nachrichten" was actually used: was it read aloud in formal services, or perused privately by individuals?[1]

Compiled in a questionnaire, these queries were directed to subscribers who responded from throughout Europe and the Atlantic World. This correspondence provides a fascinating glimpse into the character of communications within the Renewed Unitas Fratrum. Church Elders recognized the importance of maintaining institutional and emotional ties between the Moravian headquarters in Saxony and far-flung confessional colonies, diaspora communities, and missionaries. At the same time, the Church hierarchy worried that increased circulation of the paper would provide sensitive material for detractors and critics. The 1780 inquiry was thus an effort to control and carefully regulate access to the Church periodical.

The production, distribution, and use of the "Gemein Nachrichten" provide the focus of this chapter, whose analysis illustrates the implicit cultural values of Enlightenment print culture. Fundamentally, the manuscript periodical served to inform and link far-flung Moravian communities, missionaries, and supportive non-Moravians throughout the Atlantic World. In this light, the "Gemein Nachrichten" functioned as an instrument in the formation of an "imagined community" of Atlantic World Moravians. As Benedict Anderson's much-appropriated metaphor suggests, the broader Moravian community was constituted as a confessional diaspora that defied the face-to-face interaction of a traditional community. Membership in the larger Church was necessarily "imagined."[2]

Yet the "Gemein Nachrichten" poses a bewildering challenge to standard interpretations of communications and print media. As a manuscript, the journal was technically not an element of "print" culture. It was certainly not the direct product of "print capitalism," a force Anderson identifies in the emergence of national communities. Moreover, the journal fostered reading practices that contradict pervasive assumptions about the influence of eighteenth-century print culture. With the exponential growth of print, eighteenth-century readers increasingly skimmed, scanned, and browsed published materials, marking a dramatic shift from "intensive" to "extensive" reading practices. The related consequence of this "reading revolution" was a transformation in the content of printed materials. Whereas the literate once read a limited number of religious works, including scripture and devotional guides, by the late Enlightenment many indulged liberally in a wide range of secular publications.[3]

Like the thousands of new periodicals that shaped these eighteenth-century reading and print cultures, the "Gemein Nachrichten" incorporated elements of a newspaper with brief reports on contemporary political events, travel, and even weather patterns. Yet the manuscript functioned primarily as a communal devotional organ, circulating reports from Moravian missionaries and communities. And in manuscript form, the "Gemein Nachrichten" remained a restricted periodical, access to which was limited largely to Church members. Even this access was mediated by formal readings: in Moravian communities, the "Gemein Nachrichten" was incorporated into devotional ritual and read aloud in special services. For most eighteenth-century Moravians, separated from the mother Church by political borders or the Atlantic Ocean, reading services informed, inspired, and ultimately shaped a Moravian identity.

Moravian leaders understood these functions of the "Gemein Nachrichten" and maintained its scribal production, despite prohibitive costs. While the manuscript's limited access promoted an aura of secrecy and intimacy, enhancing group solidarity, it also reinforced the communal practice of reading aloud. In effect, the manuscript countered the phenomena that accompanied Enlightenment print culture: it curbed private reading and reflection, it circumscribed the "public" reception of a widely circulated periodical, and it fostered a distinct Moravian identity. While exploiting improved eighteenth-century transportation networks, the Church hierarchy also deployed the manuscript as an effective barrier to the secularizing and individualizing forces of print.

Communicating with the Faithful

The 1780 questionnaire was in part a stock-taking, an attempt to understand how the "Gemein Nachrichten" had developed, assess its distribution, and establish the most practical policies for its future management. As Church leaders suspected, the manuscript had a remarkable circulation that belied the modest number of distributed copies. The financial account from 1788 listed thirty-eight copies, together with their respective subscribers. These included the familiar Moravian communities *(Gemeinorte)* in Germany, Denmark, the Netherlands, Great Britain, Greenland, Russia, and North America. But an even larger number was sent to small groups or conventicles with informal ties to Herrnhut. Within German Central Europe, copies were distributed to Dresden, Leipzig, Berlin, Hanover, Königsberg, and Magdeburg, as well as the Duchy of Württemberg and the County of Holstein. Scandinavian subscriptions were dispatched to the Danish community of Christiansfeld, but also to the Danish capital Copenhagen, the Swedish capital Stockholm, and the western Swedish port city Gothenburg.[4] Separate copies were earmarked for Basel and Zürich, and the 1798 account listed copies for Estonia, Lithuania, Suriname, and Antigua.[5]

The subscribers' reports provide an even fuller portrait of the journal's circulation. The Basel copies were passed to groups in no fewer than thirteen separate towns and villages scattered throughout the canton, as well as to several dozen individuals.[6] The Gothenburg copy was shared by some two dozen groups, families, and individuals in Western Sweden.[7] A number of copies were also addressed to German nobility. The Dresden copy circulated among an elite circle of aristocratic Pietists with high-ranking positions as privy and court councilors in the Saxon state government.[8] The Leipzig manuscript was received by a Baron von Hohenthal, scion of an ennobled Leipzig merchant who shared his copy with a circle of Leipzig Pietists.[9]

Even those manuscripts sent to Moravian communities enjoyed a wide circulation far beyond the *Gemeinort* community. The colony of Zeist passed its copy along to at least ten Dutch cities, including Amsterdam, The Hague, and Rotterdam.[10] The Ebersdorf copy was forwarded to forty-five separate places, including the cities of Erlangen, Nuremberg, and Augsburg.[11] Neudiestendorf shared its "Gemein Nachrichten" issues with Erfurt, Weimar, Jena, Eisenach, Gotha, and Kassel.[12] The community in

Neuwied made its copy available to over fifty places and individuals within the Wetterau.[13] The American communities likewise shared their issues with a range of smaller congregations. In North Carolina's Wachovia, the periodical traveled between Salem, Bethabara, and Bethania.[14]

These patterns of distribution reflected both the institutional growth of the Moravian Church and the development of a Moravian theology. Most copies of the "Gemein Nachrichten" circulated in regions where Count Zinzendorf had traveled in his forty years of peregrinations. During a youthful Grand Tour from 1719 to 1721—before the founding of Herrnhut—the count visited the Netherlands, France, Switzerland, and close relatives in Franken and Bavaria, and from these early travels on he corresponded with Pietist conventicles throughout Western Europe.[15] Herrnhut had dispatched its first emissaries to England by 1728 and to Denmark in 1731. The first Moravian missionaries reached Greenland in 1733, Suriname and Georgia in 1735, Cape Town in 1737, Arctic Russia in 1738, and Algeria in 1740. Zinzendorf journeyed to Riga and then on to Estonia in 1736, and he made his first trip to London in 1737, and to Pennsylvania in 1741.[16]

Zinzendorf's own travels, coupled with Moravian missions' work, generated an overwhelming volume of reports and letters. By the 1730s, the peripatetic count is reported to have spent hours every day reading and responding to the missives of Moravian Church members and friends. Following his banishment from Electoral Saxony and Herrnhut in 1736, Zinzendorf found it difficult, not surprisingly, to maintain this correspondence. A practical solution was found with the creation of a manuscript bulletin in 1747, copied by scribes and issued periodically to the congregations of the Renewed Unitas Fratrum. Described variously as "Diarium der Hütten" (Diary of the Wanderers), "Pilgerhaus" (Pilgrims), or "Jüngerhaus" (Disciples), the bulletin reported the activities of the itinerant count and his associates, and included sermons and reports from the Moravian communities and missions of Central Europe and the Atlantic World.[17] By 1755 the manuscript had achieved the de facto status of an official Church organ, and the scribal work was assigned to students who worked for room and board at the Moravian Seminary in Barby, founded in 1754.[18]

The development of the "Gemein Nachrichten" also reflected the elaboration of Moravian doctrine and the conflicting ecumenical and sectarian impulses that animated it. A fundamental principle of this theology was the conception of *ecclesiolae in ecclesia*, which suggested, broadly, both a movement for Christian renewal within the larger Church *and* the Pietist activities of specific subgroups within local parishes. The formative influences for this doctrine were the Pietist leaders Spener—Zinzendorf's godfather—and Francke, whom Zinzendorf had encountered as a student in Halle. Both the early Pietist conventicles organized by Spener and, later, the position of Francke's Halle establishment within the Lutheran Church embodied aspects of this principle. The *ecclesiola* doctrine also animated the evangelical impulse of missionary work, promoted by the Halle Pietists.[19] Herrnhut, in Zinzendorf's initial vision, would represent an *ecclesiola* within the Lutheran Church, not unlike the Halle Pietists. Yet the Moravian self-consciousness of the first Herrnhut settlers and the constitution of the "Renewed" Unitas Fratrum in 1727 pushed Zinzendorf to conceive of his congregation as a distinct and separate denomination.[20]

The principle of *ecclesiolae in ecclesia* remained a creative tension for the Moravian Church. Zinzendorf's ordination as a Lutheran minister (in Tübingen in 1734) appeared to contradict his subsequent support for the ordination of a "Moravian" bishop, and clearly expressed this apparent conflict.[21] And despite the institutional growth of the Moravian Church, Zinzendorf developed an implicitly ecumenical doctrine. For one, Zinzendorf's conception of *Tropus* posited that the various Churches represented unique denominations within the larger Body of Christ. Elaborated at the Moravian Synod in Marienborn in 1744, the *Tropus* doctrine asserted that each confession possessed unique skills for fostering the faithful (in accordance with their respective customs). Accordingly, the range of Churches— whether Lutheran, Calvinist, Anglican, or ultimately Moravian—remained unified in essentials: ergo the modern Moravian motto.[22] Closely linked to this position was the notion of "diaspora," which, likewise, had a broad ecumenical character. Zinzendorf's religious outreach can be traced back to his days as a student in Halle, and the Herrnhut colony was involved in evangelism as early as the late 1720s. As mandated by the Moravian Synod in London in 1749, the Church undertook to provide spiritual mentorship for all Protestant Christians, regardless of denomination.[23]

This mandate sanctioned the "diaspora" work that the Moravians pursued assiduously throughout much of Western Europe well into the nineteenth century. But in contrast to the founding of colonies, the diaspora work had no specific institutional mission. Instead, lay Moravian ministers developed geographic circuits and then cultivated individuals and small groups through cycles of itinerancy, not unlike the American circuit ministers of the Second Great Awakening. In 1769, a reported 170 lay Moravian ministers or "diaspora workers" visited more than 800 German locations. Most of these "corresponding" Pietists never joined a Moravian congregation, however, and instead remained lifelong members of their own Protestant Churches.[24]

One of those touched by this itinerancy was Johann Wolfgang von Goethe, Germany's preeminent literary figure, who had a brief flirtation with Moravianism as a young man in his native Frankfurt in 1770. In his autobiography, Goethe recorded that the society "had survived in the crude world just by sending out its inconspicuous tendrils. Under the protection of an excellent, pious man [Zinzendorf] one single bud had now taken root and was spreading out again over the whole world from these obscure and seemingly random beginnings."[25] Goethe's metaphor suggests the impact of this itinerancy and the role of the "Gemein Nachrichten," which was used as a devotional guide by these largely non-Moravian groups between the periodic visits of lay ministers. This diaspora work also laid the groundwork for the German evangelical movements that emerged after the Napoleonic Wars, and ultimately, it explains the extensive circulation of the "Gemein Nachrichten" outside of the formal Moravian colonies and congregations.[26]

Composed in German, the "Gemein Nachrichten" was of limited value to non-German congregations. Once it had been established, however, the "Gemein Nachrichten" was translated in London and then distributed from there to the English-language congregations of England and Ireland. Referred to as the "Weekly Leaves," the "Gemein Nachrichten," as elsewhere in the German-speaking Moravian world, promoted the cohesion and Moravian identity of English-language congregations while fostering their ties to the rest of the Renewed Unitas Fratrum.[27] This not only apprised members of the Church's missionary work, it also inspired the interest of many non-Moravians. In their early years, the London Moravians were unique among English Protestants in their international scope, inspiring many to visit Moravian colonies on the Continent or embark on missions of their own.[28] Similarly, the Baltic communities prepared and distributed appropriate translations not only of the "Gemein Nachrichten" but also of other Moravian devotional literature.[29]

Reading Aloud and Communal Cohesion

The "Gemein Nachrichten" supported a particular set of communal reading and devotional practices, which reflected the incipient traditions of the Moravian Church. Not unlike the Moravian Love Feasts or *Singstunden*, developed since the 1720s by the original Herrnhut colonists, Moravian congregations devoted specific services to prayer and the reading of devotional literature, including the letters of distant missionaries, colonists, and Pietist friends. The "Prayer Day" or *Bettag*, inspired in part by Zinzendorf's prolific correspondence, was first organized in Herrnhut as a monthly festival in February 1728. By the 1730s, these reading services were used to share the growing volume of missionary reports that streamed into Herrnhut.[30]

The Moravian Prayer Days also influenced early revivalist figures, including George Whitefield and the Wesley brothers John and Charles, who made reading services a commonplace of the Anglo-American Great Awakening. A crucial venue for the diffusion of Moravian devotional practices was the Fetter Lane Society, organized in London in 1738. Never a Moravian organization, strictly speaking, Fetter Lane was founded by four German Moravians as well as John Wesley, who had encountered Herrnhut missionaries on his voyage to Georgia. The group attracted crowds of hundreds to its Sunday evening services, and also organized Moravian-style Love Feasts and Prayer Days. The Wesleys had left the society by 1740, yet the Moravians' influence on English Methodism is widely recognized. "In our [Methodist] literature," historian R. A. Knox has claimed somewhat patronizingly, "Moravianism will chiefly be remembered because our native enthusiasts have stolen its thunders."[31] Although never a member, George Whitefield read his own journal at Fetter Lane in 1738 and later organized monthly Letter Days in his own religious societies in Britain and North America.[32] These same revivalists attacked the Moravians in the 1740s and 1750s, yet Fetter Lane served as a formative nodal point shaping the broad network of Atlantic-world evangelicals, linked both by spiritual fellowship and religious contention.[33]

The "Gemein Nachrichten" maintained and extended these early networks of correspondence, while supporting the communal reading practices of Moravian congregations. An early set of directions, undated though probably drafted around 1760, outlined a set of editorial tips for compiling a more effective newsletter. These instructions, presumably authored by Church leaders, instructed scribes to work quickly so that the manuscript could be distributed with the greatest haste. The guideline also recommended that the "Gemein Nachrichten" needed to appeal to broad interests since it was read to different "choirs" or age groups. The inclusion of reports from Herrnhut was necessary, the instructions elaborated, but these needed to be short and concise while still maintaining accuracy; the annals, diaries, and journals from the colonies and diaspora groups were often too "dry" and required more careful editing to avoid repetition and tedium. The "children's diaries," the guideline acknowledged, were among the "cutest pieces" and should be solicited from correspondents and included more often in the manuscript.[34] But aside from the periodical's content, the instructions chided private reading of the paper.

> One notices a boredom in the reading services, and presumably because of the material, but also because the readings are rushed in an effort to finish more quickly. For this reason the productive application of the material and its comprehension suffer. This is because the paper passes through too many hands before the public reading, and many fail to understand the content. Consequently the public readings are neither enjoyed or attended with adequate diligence.[35]

These instructions were clearly followed, not only for using the "Gemein Nachrichten," as we shall see, but also for editing its content. By the 1760s the manuscript was divided into three sections: (1) Church and congregational reports, (2) diaspora and mission diaries, and (3) devotional materials including sermons, addresses, and autobiographical "memoirs."[36]

The memoirs evolved in tandem with the "Gemein Nachrichten" and became not only a unique Moravian institution but also a standard feature in the periodical. In the summer of 1747, Zinzendorf bemoaned the absence of any commemoration for the spiritual journey of a "passing" brother. In response, a short essay was composed and read, outlining the biography of the deceased.[37] This original memoir appears to have established what soon became a standard Moravian practice. Composed in old age or in the face of illness, the autobiography included a testimonial that was intended to be recited graveside. Zinzendorf clearly took inspiration from the genre of Lutheran *Leichenpredigten*. Luther had composed the first of these funeral orations, and they soon became a ritual element of Lutheran funeral services. By 1700 the Lutheran *Leichenpredigt* had become grossly formulaic and an ostentatious display for elites; printed and distributed, they sometimes exceeded eighty pages in length.[38]

About the same time that Lutherans dropped the practice in the mid 1700s, Zinzendorf adapted the *Leichenpredigt* for his own purposes. This version of the memoir was neither an expression of mourning nor a eulogy. Instead, it offered the faithful's witness and celebrated her union with God. At the Elders Conference of 1753, Church leaders demanded that "the memoir say nothing but the precise truth" about the life of the deceased.[39] Accurate autobiographies of the faithful were also considered the most effective form of evangelical witness, and by 1848 over 7,000 memoirs had been "published" in the manuscript pages of the "Gemein Nachrichten." In this fashion, the memoir served as both a communal funeral ritual and a devotional tool shared throughout the Moravian world.

The reception and uses of the "Gemein Nachrichten" by the various Moravian constituencies attest to the journal's effectiveness. One measure of the value placed on the manuscript periodical was its prohibitive cost, which was borne by subscribers. In 1760 the estimated expense of producing each annual subscription was 120–130 Reichsthaler, the annual wage of a middling master artisan.[40] This amount fell as the number of copies increased. The 1788 account listed a total cost of 2,488 Reichsthaler for thirty-eight subscriptions, an average of just over 65 Reichsthaler for each copy. This sum included 1,766 Reichsthaler for the student scribes in Barby and Niesky, 123 Reichsthaler for supplies, and salaries of 60 Reichsthaler for each of three full-time editors.[41]

The importance of the "Gemein Nachrichten"—as a connection to the Moravian world and an instrument of group solidarity—was most significant within those congregations isolated by great distance. For the Moravian colonists who settled in North Carolina, first in Bethabara and Bethania, and eventually in Salem, the weekly services devoted to reading the "Gemein Nachrichten" reinforced both the local community and a feeling of inclusion in the larger Moravian world.[42] "He has strengthened us through the reading of the Wochen," recorded one 1762 report, "and also by the correspondence with our dear ones in America and Europe, in sweet communion with His people."[43] But "sweet communion" depended on punctual mail deliveries, which became a constant concern of the North Carolina Moravians. In 1767 they arranged to have their own subscription sent directly, instead of waiting for a copy transcribed in Bethlehem. Ideally, increased efficiency would allow them to create the same devotional ritual as the home Church in Herrnhut, simply staggered by a year. The annual journal from 1769 reported that the "'Gemein Nachrichten' have come so promptly that on our Memorial and Festival Days we were able to use exactly the material used in the older congregations the same days in the preceding year; and we were thereby kept in touch with God's people everywhere on the earth."[44]

Mission reports copied in the "Gemein Nachrichten" were particularly welcome in the Carolina backcountry, providing an exciting vision of the Moravians' evangelical work. In 1772 the Wachovia brethren recorded, "we have heard, through the NR, of our congregations and Pilgrims in all the four corners of the earth, and hearts and eyes have been full ... especially as we have listened to ... news of the successful service of our Brethren among members of other Churches, and of the great work of God among the Heathen."[45] From the West Indies, Africa, the Indian Missions in North America, Greenland, and Arctic Russia, auditors received detailed accounts of conversions, and in other cases failures, but information, regardless, from exotic locales. The annual journal of 1792 reported,

> We express our deepest thanks for the happy and blessed use we have been able to make of the Nachrichten and the reports therein contained about the congregations and the foreign missions of the Unity of Brethren. We were particularly interested this year in the setting out of several Brethren for the Cape [of Good Hope], with the intention of renewing the mission begun there fifty years ago among the Hottentots; also in the enforced migration of our Indian congregations and their missionaries to the other side of Lake Erie, to find a resting place under English protection.[46]

These reports may have had even greater significance for the enslaved African members of the Wachovia fellowships. One African American in Salem, as documented by Jon Sensbach, was particularly taken by reports from the West Indies and likely "felt an affinity with blacks ... where he had lived before coming to NC. He seems to have seen himself as a member of a larger black Christian network."[47]

The "Gemein Nachrichten" cultivated a tremendous sense of community solidarity as well as a broad confessional identity embracing Moravians throughout the Atlantic World. An integral element of this was both its manuscript format and the practice of reading it aloud. With few exceptions, the "Gemein Nachrichten" was shared by communities or at least small groups of Moravian auditors. Church Elders clearly understood this and admonished congregations against circulating the "Gemein Nachrichten" for private reading. The Salem Diary confirmed this policy with a seemingly trivial entry from 1804 that Brother Miksch might be allowed to read the "Gemein Nachrichten" on his own, since he was unable to attend meetings.[48] Reading services—recounting aloud the trials, sufferings, and accomplishments of worldwide Church members—were clearly central to communal cohesion.

Censorship, Secrecy, and Confessional Solidarity

The communal use of the "Gemein Nachrichten" in reading services offers the best explanation for why Moravian Church leaders maintained its manuscript production into the nineteenth century. Not until the 1818 General Synod in Herrnhut did Church leaders seriously debate the additional expense of scribal duplication and sanction a printed edition. These deliberations provide tremendous insight into the perceived advantages of a manuscript. According to the "Gemein Nachrichten" editors, a printed edition would require as little as one third of the previous annual expense—the strongest motivation, apparently, for eliminating the manuscript. Publication would also permit the editors to prepare and distribute the journal more efficiently; the Moravian world would learn more promptly, ultimately, about the activities of the Church and its members. The printed edition could also prevent problems with false transcription or illegible writing, and copies lost at land or sea might easily be replaced.[49]

Yet the disadvantages of print were significant, and Church leaders understood these well. As a manuscript, the periodical fostered a sense of communal intimacy between the Moravian colonies, mission stations, and diaspora congregations. Moreover, the services devoted to declamation maintained an important ritual that strengthened the bonds of individual communities. At the 1818 Synod, Church Elders also faced the increased difficulty of maintaining control over their worldwide communities. They ultimately relinquished the practice of marriage by lot. They agonized, likewise, over the shift from manuscript to print:

> The "Gemein Nachrichten" as a manuscript has an exclusive character as product and property of the Brethren. The Sharing of news by <u>reading aloud</u> [underlined in document] remains in many places nearly the only bond that holds community members together. If one now has the opportunity without trouble or reflection to read at home what until now could only be heard with others in community, the services will be less well attended and the community could even lose members. ... In many locations in the Diaspora, some individuals read the Gemein Nachrichten at home, and know to value the blessings of the <u>community</u> [underlined in document] pleasure. Therefore we will not yet relinquish public reading in the Church. In the process, it will become reinvigorated and once again lively. The handwritten communications will not be entirely given up.

This compromise was realized beginning in 1819, when Part I, consisting of missions' reports as well as sermons and addresses, was issued in bimonthly printed editions. Parts II and III, devoted to memoirs, addresses, sermons, and congregational and diaspora reports, were distributed in manuscript form until 1848. While accepting economic realities, Moravian leaders maintained a limited manuscript edition to promote communal and confessional unity.

These deliberations also reveal a sophisticated understanding of the manuscript's significance in the context of a pervasive print culture. In contrast to published materials, the manuscript maintained an intimate and "exclusive character," creating a special aura of scarcity and value. Walter Benjamin's analysis, "Art in the Age of Mechanical Reproduction," offers a powerful insight for understanding this phenomenon. Just as the technology permitting cheap reproductions increased the "aura" of a work of art in the twentieth century, so too did the printing press increase the unique quality of the manuscript.[50] The curious survival of manuscripts as a mode of communication, well beyond the advent of printing, illustrates precisely this dynamic. According to Peter Burke, manuscript circulation was common within philosophical and literary circles in the early modern period and provided "a means of social bonding between the individuals involved, often a group of friends."[51] Although print allowed the inexpensive reproduction of a large number of texts, as Church Elders well understood, the manuscript enhanced the scarcity and intrinsic value of the "Gemein Nachrichten" by limiting circulation and access.

Yet issues of circulation and access were curiously absent in the discussion at the 1818 Synod. Throughout the eighteenth century, Moravian leaders had feared that the "Gemein Nachrichten" would fuel the attacks of critics. The editorial directions from the early 1760s warned of the "danger and damage" of both unauthorized transcriptions and the possibility of copies falling into the wrong hands. Beginning in the 1770s, the editors received pledges, apparently solicited, from diaspora subscribers promising never to share the "Gemein Nachrichten" with unauthorized individuals.[52] The directive from the 1780 Synod was an effort, in part, to control the precise circulation of the "Gemein Nachrichten." The extensive responses to the directive listed, in detail, the groups and individuals with access to specific subscriptions. The Zurich copy, for example, spent exactly a fortnight in the city before distribution to some forty villages within the larger Canton. According to the submitted report, it was delivered first to Brother Haeginer in the Oetenbacher *Gasse*. On Sunday, Tuesday, and Friday it was read out loud to the Zurich conventicle, and precisely six other individuals were allowed to keep the periodical overnight.[53] The 1780 questionnaire was followed up in 1786 with a list of precautions "published" in the "Gemein Nachrichten" and intended to prevent unauthorized access: those involved in posting or forwarding copies were enjoined to pay careful attention to the reliability of the postal service; addressees were required to check the contents of each packet and return a message confirming receipt; copies were to be handled with care and never soiled; and unauthorized persons should never have access to the "Gemein Nachrichten" as readers or auditors at communal services.[54]

If this discretion—perhaps paranoia—seemed a far cry from Zinzendorf's original ecumenical and evangelical vision, it was clearly a response to the sharp anti-Moravian attacks published since at least 1740. From the first, Zinzendorf and the Herrnhut colony had faced criticisms. The Moravians' break with Halle Pietists in 1733 and the count's exile from Electoral Saxony in 1736 signaled an extended period of religious contention. Certainly the Moravians enjoyed a growing reputation for their piety and missions, and exercised considerable influence in England, particularly through the activities of the Fetter Lane Society. But this exposure also fueled the criticisms of the English evangelicals John Wesley and George Whitefield, both of whom published attacks on the Moravians in the 1740s and 1750s.[55]

The Renewed Unitas Fratrum had similarly mixed relations with state governments. Perhaps the Church's greatest success was formal recognition by the English King and Parliament with the Moravian Act of 1749, which identified the Renewed Unitas Fratrum as an "Ancient Protestant Episcopal Church." This important concession not only conferred the same "Apostolic" status asserted by the Anglican Church but also facilitated Moravian activities in the English colonies.[56] Although Zinzendorf was banished from Denmark in 1735, the Moravians were finally invited to found the community of Christiansfeld in 1771, which enabled their mission efforts in the Danish West Indies.[57] In Central Europe, the Moravians' fortunes were as varied as the territorial states that constituted the Holy Roman Empire. While the religious pluralism of the Hohenzollern rulers, who recognized the Moravians as an independent Protestant Church in 1742, gave the Moravians a certain latitude in Brandenburg-Prussia; the conservative Lutheran orthodoxy of their home state Electoral Saxony limited their activities, at least until 1749, when authorities there finally recognized the Moravians as adherents of the Augsburg Confession, and therefore formally Lutheran.[58]

The vicissitudes of banishment *and* formal political recognition, or of ecumenical fellowship *and* hardnosed doctrinal conflict, certainly conditioned the Moravians' cautious and often conservative approaches to public exposure. These experiences clearly influenced the Moravian "diaspora workers" in the second half of the eighteenth century, who were carefully attuned to the religious and legal conditions of the state and local governments where they ministered and traveled.[59] But perhaps the Moravians' most formative influence was an episode for which they were solely responsible, the so-called "Sifting Time" of the 1740s, which generated the "blood and wounds" theology and left the Church all but bankrupt. Moravian leaders reacted to the "Sifting Time" after 1750 by attempting to avoid public scrutiny. Their policies of "damage control" even included a self-conscious revisionism of the Church's institutional history.[60]

These early struggles certainly clarify the Moravians' cautious self-censorship. Moreover, adherence to a manuscript format for the "Gemein Nachrichten" not only promoted confessional identity: its scarcity, at least with careful—if not paranoid—restrictions, also limited public exposure. Persecution and censorship further explain the conundrum of expensive scribal production in an age of print. Since the advent of moveable type, heretics, political dissidents, philosophers, and even pornographers had used manuscripts to evade detection or overt censorship. For example, Galileo, following his Papal reprimand in 1616, and especially after his house arrest in 1633, distributed manuscripts which were published much later or even posthumously. Thus, like some early modern scholarly communities, the Moravians evaded persecution through manuscript communications, which functioned ultimately to unify congregants and reinforce shared beliefs.[61]

Conclusion

The product of correspondence from itinerancy and evangelical missions, the "Gemein Nachrichten" offered a practical strategy for shoring up the communications of a growing Atlantic-world denomination. But the manuscript also provided critical protection from the corrosive attacks of political and religious opponents, by shielding the devotional culture and internal affairs of the Church from public view. From its inception, the "Gemein Nachrichten" was also a critical medium for supporting Moravian ritual. In its manuscript format, the journal supported communal reading practices and the evangelical culture of the Moravian Church. These devotional rituals and practices also reinforced both communal solidarity and the confessional identity of the worldwide Church. Moravian leaders strengthened communal and Church solidarity by restricting access to members and authorized readers. The original impulse for this discretion likely reflected the fear of exposure and persecution. Yet Church leaders clearly understood the sociological and psychological functions of scribal production and its cognate reading practices. Privileged access enhanced the bonds of membership and increased loyalty and solidarity.

The story of the "Gemein Nachrichten" also offers an incisive commentary on the characteristics of Enlightenment print culture. Demonstrating extraordinary sophistication, Moravian leaders relied on the technologies and improved transportation networks of the eighteenth century Atlantic World. Not until the end of the seventeenth century had ship travel made not only Atlantic travel but also regular communications into the practical possibilities that Moravian missionaries and colonists then fully exploited. Moravian leaders were no less hesitant to avail themselves of moveable type. As early as 1723, Zinzendorf engaged a printer in the Saxon town of Pirna, not far from his own estate, to publish literature for Herrnhut. Following the model of the English and German "moral weeklies," Zinzendorf actually published a Pietist magazine in Dresden in the mid 1720s. The Moravians also relied on the printing press for mass editions of their standard devotional literatures. The Ebersdorfer Bible appeared in 1723. Other important Moravian publications included the hymnbook (1729), the catechism, the daily *Losungen* or scriptural readings, and Zinzendorf's own writings. In conjunction with the seminary in Barby, the Moravians even established their own printing press in 1754.

Yet the Barby facilities also housed the scriptorium for producing copies of the "Gemein Nachrichten," and this commitment to a manuscript format reflects an acute understanding of the cultural significance of print. As many scholars have noted, the Enlightenment transformed both reading practices and the content of eighteenth-century print culture. When the percentage of religious titles among German-language publications plummeted in the eighteenth century, secular literatures came to predominate. This also marked a transformation in reading practices. The availability of periodicals and popular literature encouraged private reading and in turn a process of individualization. By the end of the eighteenth century, German observers frequently complained of a *Lesewut* or reading craze. In this light, eighteenth-century print culture signified more than a neutral, quantitative increase in published materials or the diffusion of print technology. Much more, it represented a set of cultural values, a preference for publicity, a taste for the secular, a rejection of the communal, and a valorization of the new.

The Moravians' use of the manuscript represented an implicit critique of that print culture and underlined its tacit cultural values. By insisting on the scribal production of the "Gemein Nachrichten" and enforcing strict rules for its circulation, Moravian leaders fostered a communal identity and the observance of Pietist spiritual ideals. Manuscripts also prevented exposure to public scrutiny, implicit in print culture. Following their negative experiences, Moravian leaders developed grave reservations about the utility of the public sphere for promoting their own mission. How could they respond to the attacks of George Whitefield and others without compromising their own ecumenical ideals? The publicity of print culture entailed contention and struggle. It rewarded aggression and conflict. From this perspective, the "Gemein Nachrichten," in its manuscript format, emblematized the Moravians' resistance to the implicitly secular values of Enlightenment print culture.

Notes

* For their helpful questions and comments I would like to thank Hartmut Lehmann and other participants at the conference "Religiosität in der säkularisierten Welt" (Frankfurt), where I presented this paper in March 2003. I would also like to thank Dr. Paul Peucker, curator of the Moravian Archives in Bethlehem and Professor Terence McIntosh of the University of North Carolina (Chapel Hill).
1. UA-Herrnhut, R.3.B.24.b, "Anzeigen, …" no. 5.
2. Benedict Anderson, *Imagined Communities: Reflections on the Origin and Spread of Nationalism*, rev. ed. (London, 1991), 5–7.

3. See Rolf Engelsing, "Die Perioden der Lesergeschichte in der Neuzeit," *Archiv für Geschichte des Buchwesens* 10 (1969): 944–1002; and also Roger Chartier, *The Cultural Uses of Print in Early Modern France* (Princeton, 1987), 222, 224.

4. A comprehensive list is in UA-Herrnhut, R.3.B.24.a.1, "Briefe, … 1780–98."

5. UA-Herrnhut, R.3.B.24.a.35.

6. UA-Herrnhut, R.3.B.24.b.17.

7. UA-Herrnhut, R.3.B.24.b.15, 16.

8. UA-Herrnhut, R.3.B.24.b.17.

9. Ibid.

10. UA-Herrnhut, R.3.B.24.b.22.

11. UA-Herrnhut, R.3.B.24.b.28.

12. UA-Herrnhut, R.3.B.24.b.30.

13. UA-Herrnhut, R.3.B.24.b.10.

14. *RMNC*, 2:689.

15. Dietrich Meyer, "Zinzendorf und Herrnhut," in Martin Brecht, ed., *Geschichte des Pietismus*, 3 vols. (Göttingen, 1993–2000), 2:13–17.

16. Kenneth G. Hamilton and J. Taylor Hamilton, *History of the Moravian Church: The Renewed Unitas Fratrum, 1722–1957* (Bethlehem, PA, 1967), 43–44, 52–59, 82–93; Valdis Mezezers. *The Herrnuterian Pietism in the Baltic and its Outreach into America and Elsewhere in the World* (North Quincy, MA, 1975).

17. *RMNC*, 1:106, footnote 12. See also the introduction to "Lists of Contents and Index to the Gemein-Nachrichten 1760–1848," compiled by Vernon Nelson in MA-SP, Sig: O50 G, pts. 1–4.

18. Hamilton, *History of the Moravian Church*, 113–14.

19. Especially useful are chapters on Spener, Francke, and Zinzendorf in Ernst Stoeffler's *German Pietism During the Eighteenth Century* (Leiden, 1973).

20. On early struggles to determine whether the Herrnhut colonists would remain within the State Lutheran Church, or embrace a distinct Moravian denominational identity, see Hamilton, *History of the Moravian Church*, 40–41; and John Weinlick, *The Moravian Diaspora: A Study of the Societies of the Moravian Church within the Protestant State Churches of Europe* (Nazareth, PA, 1959), 7–19.

21. Ibid., 60–63.

22. "In essentials unity, in non-essentials liberty, in all things charity." See Hamilton, *History of the Moravian Church*, 101–102; Joseph Mueller, *Zinzendorf als Erneuer der alten Brüderkirche* (Leipzig, 1900), 84–95; Bernhard Becker, *Zinzendrof im Verhältnis zu Philosophie und Kirchentum seiner Zeit* (Leipzig, 1866), 496–506.

23. A. J. Lewis, *Zinzendorf the Ecumenical Pioneer* (Philadelphia, 1962), 117–121; Horst Weigelt, *Geschichte des Pietismus in Bayern: Anfänge – Entwicklung – Bedeutung* (Göttingen, 2001), 288; Meyer, "Zinzendorf und Herrnhut," 65–66; Weinlick, *Moravian Diaspora*, 20–35.

24. Meyer, "Zinzendorf und Herrnhut," 66.

25. *Goethe: The Collected Works*, ed. Thomas P. Saine, 12 vols. (Princeton, NJ, 1994), 4:465.

26. Horst Weigelt, "Der Pietismus im Übergang vom 18. zum 19. Jahrhundert," in *Geschichte des Pietismus*, 3 vols. (Göttingen, 1993–2000), 2:701–705.

27. J. C. S. Mason, *The Moravian Church and the Missionary Awakening in England 1760–1800* (Woodbridge, UK, 2001), 24–25.

28. Colin Podmore, *The Moravian Church in England, 1728–1760* (Oxford, 1998), 123–124.

29. Mezezers, *The Herrnuterian Pietism in the Baltic*, 77–85.

30. Hamilton, *History of the Moravian Church*, 37.

31. R. A. Knox, *Enthusiasm* (Oxford, 1950), 404.

32. Frank Lambert, *"Pedlar in Divinity": George Whitefield and the Transatlantic Revivals, 1737–1770* (Princeton, NJ, 1994), 91, 141.

33. Podmore [*The Moravian Church in England, 1728–1760, 29–71*] uses Moravian sources to revise older Methodist historiography by emphasizing the influence of the Moravian presence in London. On relationships between Moravian, Wesleyan, and Whitefieldian groups, consider Arnold Dallimore, *George Whitefield: The Life and Times of the Great*

Evangelist of the Eighteenth-Century Revival, 2 vols. (Edinburgh, 1980), 2:235. For the influence of Continental Pietism on New World revivalism generally, see Timothy Hall, *Contested Boundaries: Itinerancy and the Reshaping of the Colonial American Religious World* (Durham, NC, 1994), 37–38, 129–139. For the role of religious controversy in shaping an American public sphere, consider Michael Warner, *The Letters of the Republic* (Cambridge, 1990).

34. UA-Herrnhut R.4.E.3 "Die Geschäfte auf Zinzenzendorfs Schreibstube ... " (unfol.).

35. Ibid.

36. By 1765 the journal was divided into Parts I and II with a third "Supplement" section consisting largely of devotional material. This organization was changed in 1802 and the journal was then issued in Parts I, II, and II. Generally Parts I and II consisted of Church and congregational reports, while Part III was devoted to evangelical diaspora reports, mission diaries, and the memoirs or autobiographies. Section II was devoted exclusively to sermons and addresses. All three sections were produced as manuscripts until 1819, when Part I was finally printed. Parts II and II were printed beginning in 1849. See the introduction to the English-language index by Nelson, "Lists of Contents and Index ...," MA-SP, Sig: O50 G, pts. 1–4.

37. UA-Herrnhut, J.H.D. Ex. A. 1747. I.-LII. Woche, 244–246.

38. The single best introduction to the *Leichenpredigt* is F. M. Eybl's entry, "Leichenpredigt," in *Historisches Wörterbuch der Rhetorik*, ed. Gert Ueding, 5+ vols. (Tübingen, 1992-), 5:124–151. See also the three essay collections edited by Rudolf Lenz, *Leichenpredigten als Quelle historischer Wissenschaften*, 3 vols. (Marburg, 1975–1984). On Lutheran funeral ritual see Craig Koslofsky, *The Reformation of the Dead: Death and Ritual in Early Modern Germany, 1450–1700* (London, 2000).

39. UA-Herrnhut, R.2.A 33.c.1–4 [Ratskonferenzen].

40. See the last folio sheet in UA-Herrnhut, R.4.e.3, "Die Geschäfte auf Zinzenzendorfs Schreibstube ...," dated 2 February 1760 (the other materials in this file are undated).

41. UA-Herrnhut, R.3.B.24.a.1, "Briefe, das Copieren der Gemain Nachrichte betrefft ... 1780–98."

42. *RMNC*, 1:418, 420. See also Elizabeth Sommer, *Serving Two Masters: Moravian Brethren in Germany and North Carolina, 1727–1801* (Lexington, KY, 2000), 145–148, 155. Jon Sensbach, *A Separate Canaan: The Making of an Afro-Moravian World in North Carolina, 1763–1840* (Chapel Hill, NC, 1998), 119.

43. *RMNC*, 1:239.

44. *RMNC*, 1:384.

45. *RMNC*, 2:659.

46. *RMNC*, 5:2349.

47. Sensbach, *A Separate Canaan*, 122–123.

48. *RMNC*, 6:2782.

49. UA-Herrnhut, R.2.B.50.f. Beilagen 3: VI. Gemeinschriften, no. 62.

50. This important essay appears in *Illuminations: Essays, Reflections*, ed. Hannah Arendt (New York, 1969), 217–252.

51. Peter Burke and Asa Briggs, *A Social History of Media: From Gutenberg to the Internet* (Cambridge, 2002), 45.

52. UA-Herrnhut, R.3.c.1–24, "Reverse Communication ... 1774–1807."

53. UA-Herrnhut, R.3.b.6.

54. MA-SP, "Gemein-Nachrichten," 1786, Week 51, Part I, "Pro memoria wegen der Gem. Nachrichten."

55. On the conflicts between the Moravians and other German Protestant groups in colonial North America, see John B. Frantz, "The Awakening of Religion among the German Settlers in the Middle Colonies," *William and Mary Quarterly* 33, no. 2 (1976): 266–288. George Whitefield's anti-Moravian diatribe, published in 1753, is reprinted in Dallimore, *George Whitefield*, 2:325–332.

56. Podmore, *The Moravian Church*, 228–265; and Hamilton, *History of the Moravian Church*, 119–131.

57. Anders Pontoppidan Thyssen, "Christiansfeld: Die Herrnhuter im Spannungsfeld zwischen Pietismus und Aufklärung," in *Aufklärung und Pietismus im dänischen Gesamtstaat 1770–1820*, ed. Hartmut Lehmann (Neumünster, 1983), 151–158; Hamilton, *History of the Moravian Church*, 191–194.
58. Hamilton, *History of the Moravian Church*, 94–95, 103–104.
59. Weigelt, "Der Pietismus im Übergang vom 18. zum 19. Jahrhundert," 702.
60. Paul Peucker, "'Blut auf unsre grünen Bändchen:' Die Sichtungszeit in der Herrnhuter Brüdergemeine," *Unitas Fratrum. Zeitschrift fur Geschichte und Gegenwartsfragen der Brudergemeine* 49/50 (2002): 41–94.
61. Consider Wolfgang Hardtwig, *Genossenschaft, Sekte, Verein in Deutschland: Vom spätmittelalter bis zur Französischen Revolution* (Munich, 1997), 183, 304–327.

– Chapter 3 –

DEEP IN THE SIDE OF JESUS: THE PERSISTENCE OF ZINZENDORFIAN PIETY IN COLONIAL AMERICA

Craig D. Atwood

Introduction

A UGUST GOTTLIEB SPANGENBERG ARRIVED in Bethlehem, Pennsylvania, on 30 October 1744, bringing with him the newly written *Litany of the Wounds*. One observer wrote that when it was first read, "An aura of blood prevailed, refreshing our hearts."[1] About once a week for more than twenty years the residents of Bethlehem recited this litany and offered worship to the wounds of Christ. In addition to the *Litany of the Wounds*, the Moravians venerated the side wound in the *Pleurodie* litany, and in dozens of hymns. Moreover, this adoration of the wounds of Christ in Bethlehem influenced other Moravian communities in Pennsylvania, New Jersey, and North Carolina, as well as the Native American missions.

In the *Litany of the Wounds*, Jesus' physical injuries are described as "juicy" and "succulent" because they provide nourishment for the soul. The worshiper is strengthened by sucking at the side of Christ: she "licks it, tastes it." The wounds also provide a warm and soft bed in which to lie and protect children from the cold. The worshiper recites, "I like lying calm, gentle, and quiet and warm. What shall I do? I crawl to you." The believer longs to crawl inside the "deep wounds of Jesus" and lie there safe and protected. The wounds spread the power of salvation over the believer: "Powerful wounds of Jesus, So moist, so gory, bleed on my heart so that I may remain brave and like as the wounds." The brothers and sisters of Bethlehem joined the "many thousand kinds of sinners" who sat in the "treasure hoard" of the "cavernous wounds of Jesus."[2] As we shall see, this adoration of the wounds has been widely misunderstood and, contrary to prevailing interpretations, was ultimately central to the life and success of the Moravian communities in America.

The Idea of *die Sichtungzeit*

The *Litany of the Wounds* is so graphic and compelling that later genera-tions of Moravians tried to dismiss it as part of the so-called *Sichtungzeit* or Sifting Time. This term—familiar to anyone who has read about the Moravians in Europe and America—refers to a period of fanatical ex-cess originating in the German Herrnhaag community in the 1740s.[3] The term originated during the time of Zinzendorf, but the idea of *die Sich-tungzeit* grew in the retelling until it became a prominent heuristic tool for understanding Zinzendorf and the Moravians. Nearly every history of the eighteenth-century Moravians uses *die Sichtungzeit* as a way to make sense of Zinzendorf and his piety.

The standard interpretation of *die Sichtungzeit* is that Zinzendorf al-lowed his theological imagination to roam too far. Like Icarus, he flew too close to the sun, and catastrophe followed. One influential Victorian-era Moravian historian, James E. Hutton, argued that

> As long as Zinzendorf used his own mental powers, he was able to make his "Blood and Wounds Theology" a power for good; but as soon as he bade good-bye to his intellect he made his doctrine a laughing-stock and a scandal. Instead of concentrating his attention on the moral and spiritual value of the cross, he now began to lay all the stress on the mere physical details. He composed a "Litany of the Wounds"; and the Brethren could now talk and sing of nothing else.[4]

Influenced by Hutton, John Jacob Sessler blamed Zinzendorf's theology for the financial crisis that threatened to bankrupt the *Brüdergemeine* and the Bethlehem community in the early 1750s. The Brethren were too en-thralled by the wounds theology and too trusting in God's grace to actu-ally work or plan for the future.[5] Similarly, American sociologist Gillian Gollin maintained that Moravians in Bethlehem in the late 1740s pre-ferred devotion to industry.[6] This was in fact a period in which the Beth-lehem Moravians constructed many large buildings and dramatically increased their mission.[7] But despite this productive activity, these and later histories of Bethlehem accepted the argument that wounds piety led to laziness and irresponsibility.

An additional feature of this standard interpretation of the *Sich-tungzeit* is the salutary roles ascribed to prominent Moravian figures, es-pecially August Gottlieb Spangenberg and Peter Böhler, who allegedly exerted a counterforce to Zinzendorf's evocative theological style. Both Spangenberg and Böhler are credited for shielding the Moravians in North

America from much of Zinzendorf's influence.[8] Accordingly, they acted as rationalists and realists by assuming control in 1749 and thus ending the Sifting, which allowed the church to recover from Zinzendorf's outlandish theology. In the judgment of Moravian bishop and historian Kenneth Hamilton, the "Moravian" element eventually reasserted itself and restored proper biblical theology: "The discipline so characteristic of the refugees of 1722 to 1727 was revived. The unhappy features of the time of Sifting disappeared; the hymnals and liturgies which had been instrumental in promoting them were suppressed."[9] This is a simplistic and flawed approach to a controversial period of Moravian history. For one, it ignores the fact that the first so-called Sifting occurred between 1725 and 1727. More important, it denies the fact that most of the litanies and hymns of the 1740s continued to be used in America long after *die Sichtungzeit* and ignores the persistence of Zinzendorfian piety, particularly blood and wounds theology, for decades after the count's death (1760). It also obscures the deep involvement of Spangenberg, Böhler, and others in Zinzendorf's theology and piety.[10]

Before attempting to make sense of Zinzendorf's piety, we first need to address the question of why this misleading understanding of *die Sichtungzeit* has been so influential. Simply put, it has served a convenient apologetic purpose. Most of what historians, Church leaders, or theologians have considered bizarre or unorthodox about the eighteenth-century Moravians has been identified as part of *die Sichtungzeit* and thus dismissed.[11] This process began after the death of Count Zinzendorf with the works of David Crantz, August G. Spangenberg, and Benjamin La Trobe.[12] Typically, in English-language Moravian scholarship Zinzendorf has been treated primarily as a patron and an inspirational leader whose theological experiments had a brief but minor effect on the "true" Moravian Church. This traditional view of *die Sichtungzeit* has exerted great influence and continues to serve political and ecclesiastical purposes, though it is clearly contradicted by the evidence. I would go so far as to say that the dominant understanding of *die Sichtungzeit* in Anglo-American scholarship is a historical fiction.[13] This does not mean that there was no "Sifting," particularly in the Herrnhaag community, but that our present understanding of this term distorts the history. Moreover, since many of the crucial original sources related to *die Sichtungzeit* at Herrnhaag were destroyed, we cannot establish definitively what the Sifting Time was.[14] Despite the prevailing assertions, I think that we can say what it was *not* about—namely, Zinzendorf's blood and wounds theology, his understanding of the Trinity, or even his idea of the mystical marriage.[15]

In their efforts to invent both a Moravian Church and a Zinzendorf unaffected by the real Zinzendorf's more creative ideas, scholars have distorted rather than illuminated our understanding of the entire Zinzendorfian era and the evolution of Moravian theology and piety. This is most evident in the way American historians portray the colonial American Moravians as distant from or even opposed to the Brethren in Europe.[16]

Die Sichtungzeit has been used to distance the Moravian Church from the blood and wounds theology of Zinzendorf and the eighteenth-century Moravians, but for decades that theology was in fact central to their life in America as well as in Europe.

Blood and Wounds Piety in the United States

Examples from the Bethlehem records demonstrate the persistence of evocative blood and wounds language even after the end of the so-called *Sichtungzeit*. We read, for instance, that at a communion service the "corpse bees enjoyed the sacrament."[17] In another service, "After those who are sick had also received their portion of the body, Br. Nathanael [Seidel] sang the corpse-bees completely to sleep with the late Christel's corpse liturgies for a blessed rest in His grave!"[18] Based on the standard periodization of Moravian history, we would date these entries to the late 1740s or perhaps the period when Spangenberg was in Europe. They actually come from the late 1750s, however, when *die Sichtungzeit* was over and Spangenberg himself was fully in control in Bethlehem. These references to the "corpse bees" are not an echo from *die Sichtungzeit*; they represent a deeply felt Zinzendorfian piety that was shared by Spangenberg and the Bethlehem community.

It is true that Spangenberg did not talk about "corpse bees" in his later apologetic works, but he certainly used such expressions when he was the "Vicar General of the Ordinary [Zinzendorf] in America" in the decade following *die Sichtungzeit*.[19] This has been overlooked for two centuries because of the influence of the traditional interpretation of *die Sichtungzeit*, but we simply cannot understand the Brethren in colonial America unless we face the fact that devotion to the blood and wounds of Christ was central to their piety, their mission, and their communal existence well beyond the 1740s. Moreover, we must understand them in connection with Zinzendorf and the Brethren in Europe.[20]

When the single Brothers built their choir house in Bethlehem in 1748, shortly after arriving from Germany, they inscribed the core of the doctrine of the *Brüdergemeine* on the lintels front and rear. On the south side of the building was a sundial with the superscription *"Gloria Pleurae"* (Glory to the Side) with a star beneath and the year in Roman numerals. An inscription in the wall on the north side said "Father, Mother, and dear Husband, honor the young men's plan."[21] Their house was thus suitably dedicated to the divine family and to the side wound of Christ, two key Zinzendorfian concepts. This was not a passing fancy; it was carved in stone.

Bethlehem celebrated the wounds of Jesus in numerous hymns, the most popular of which was *Seitenhölgen, Seitenhölgen, du bist mein!* ("Little side hole, little side hole, you are mine!") This was a hymn that could revive the spirits of the dying and was a source of joy to children. The great missionary to the native tribes, Christopher Pyrlaeus, translated this hymn into Mahican soon after beginning work among that tribe in the early 1740s, but the fascination of the *Seitenhölgen* hymn was not confined to the 1740s. When Spangenberg was leader of Bethlehem in 1752, the community observed the birthday of the *Seitenhölgen* hymn, "which was very joyful to us."[22]

Six years later the children held a Love Feast that impressed upon them "the account of the opening of the pleura and the Spirit born from it." Later in the day the adults declared their own "devotion to the holy side, as the Mother-place of *our* spirit." The congregation sang the familiar hymn "Sidehole, Sidehole, you are mine."[23] Clearly, wounds theology was not a brief expression of fanaticism in Bethlehem that Spangenberg worked to overcome. Even when use of the *Litany of the Wounds* declined in the late 1750s, it was replaced by the *Pleurodie*, a litany devoted entirely to the side wound.[24] This represents a strengthening rather than a weakening of wounds devotion in Bethlehem after *die Sichtungzeit* and during Spangenberg's tenure. At least until the end of the communal economy in 1762, the Brethren continued to crawl inside the side of Christ.

The history of the *Litany of the Wounds* that has so offended Hutton, Sessler, Sawyer, and other Anglophone scholars illuminates how historians have allowed the theory to determine the evidence.[25] Once one accepts as fact that the *Litany of the Wounds* is a piece of *Sichtungzeit* nonsense, one then fails to notice its persistent use after 1750, particularly since the name of the litany was changed to something more traditional. The *Litany of the Wounds* did not disappear after 1750; it became, with minor revisions, "The Litany of the Life, Sufferings, and Death of Jesus." The second part of the litany became a separate piece called "Hymns of the Wounds." In this form, most of the old *Litany of the Wounds*, including the petitions to the wounds quoted earlier ("so moist, so gory") remained in publication until the end of the eighteenth century, fifty years after *die Sichtungzeit*.[26]

The Moravians in Bethlehem asserted that the *Litany of the Wounds* was the centerpiece of their theology.[27] Historians would be wise to believe them and examine this wounds theology as part of a long tradition of Catholic devotion. Indeed, the Zinzendorfian veneration of the wounds of Christ is hardly unique in the history of Christianity. Gerhard Reichel has shown that seventeenth-century Lutheran hymnody had a great impact on Zinzendorf.[28] Moreover, it should be noted that the most popular "wounds hymn" among the Moravians was *O Haupt voll Blut und Wunden* (Oh Sacred Head, Now Wounded), by Bernard of Clairvaux. Late medieval piety was replete with literary, musical, and visual imagery focusing on the wounds of Christ. By some accounts, there were as many 6,666 wounds of Christ to worship.[29] By focusing on just five wounds, the Moravians were rather restrained.

Caroline Walker Bynum's insight into the wounds' imagery of the late Middle Ages applies to Zinzendorf's theology as well.

> The cult of the wounds, the blood, the heart of Christ expresses not solution or resolution but the simultaneity of opposites: life and death, glory and agony, salvation and sin. ... The wounds, the blood of Christ, are present then even in heaven; they are access, condemnation, and recompense.[30]

According to the Moravian litanies, Christian victory came not in the crucifixion but in the piercing of Christ.[31] Human creatures are more blessed than the angels because the Church as the bride of Christ is at home in the side wound and can adore it without shame or fear. All true believers, like the prophet Isaiah and the apostle Thomas, are drawn to the open side of Christ. Salvation, sanctification, community life, and divine protection are all brought together into a single striking symbol, that of "the Prince with an open side."

In his sermons, Zinzendorf connected the physical hole in the body of Christ to the gates of heaven. Since there is no way to the Father except through Jesus, there must be a doorway through Jesus, namely the side hole of Jesus: "No one is directly adopted by the Father, he passes first through the Savior; no one is directly born through the Holy Spirit, he goes first through the Canal of the Savior."[32] The side wound of Christ becomes the organ of spiritual birth in Zinzendorf's theology. It is the birth canal through which souls pass on their way to a new life in Christ. In other words, the sidehole is the womb of rebirth.[33]

It is important to note that in referring to the side wound of Christ as an organ of birth, Zinzendorf did not turn Jesus into a woman as Aaron Fogleman has claimed in a recent article.[34] Jesus remains a wounded male, and the principle liturgical piece was the *The Litany of the Wounds of the Man* (or husband). Zinzendorf compared the birth of the Church to the creation of Eve from the side of Adam. Like Adam, Jesus fell asleep on the cross, and his side was opened. God took the Bride of Christ (human souls) from the opened side of Jesus, just as God "took out [Adam's] future wife from his side."[35] Centuries earlier, Cistercian authors made similar connections between the side wound and the womb, even portraying Christ as a male mother.[36] More research is needed to determine the precise connections between Zinzendorf and late medieval piety, but for now it is important to note that Zinzendorf was not unique in viewing the side wound as a womb.[37]

In the *Pleurodie*, the Church, as the bride of Christ, is portrayed as being doubly flesh of his flesh. Not only did he become human, but the Church was born from his side. Moreover, since the Church was born from the Spirit that flowed out of the side wound with the blood, it shares "God's nature." As Caroline Walker Bynum argues for the case of thirteenth- and fourteenth-century devotions, "Concentration on the eucharist and on Christ's suffering in the passion ... is not primarily a stress on the sacrifice needed to bridge the enormous gap between us in our sin and God in his glory; it is rather an identification with the fact that Christ is what we are."[38] This insight applies equally to the Moravians, and Zinzendorf naturally connects his blood and wounds symbolism to the Holy Communion, the most "palpable" way for Christians to experience union with Christ.[39] Zinzendorf frequently cites John 6:53 ("unless you eat the flesh of the Son of man and drink his blood, you have no life in you") as a eucharistic text that supports his own blood and wounds theology. Holy Communion is a form of union with God in which "through the tormented body of Christ we are united with the divine nature and come into a condition which foreshadows something of the resurrection."[40] This union with the divine occurs when the worshiper approaches the person of Christ and sets his mouth to his side and drinks of the blood from the wound that ever opens anew.[41] Here Zinzendorf depicts Christ as a nursing mother whose side wound is the breast from which pours nourishment for the believer. Again, this has a precedent in Catholic devotion. Aelred of Rievaulx, a twelfth-century monk, also urged Christians to drink from the bleeding side of Christ: "… wounds have been made in his limbs, holes in the wall of his body, in which, like a dove, you may hide while you kiss them one by one."[42] This image of being a dove flying into the side wound of Christ was used frequently in Moravian litanies.

Holy Communion for the Moravians was a ritual of both spiritual and community renewal. Every month difficulties within the community were addressed through the process of confession known as "speaking" and then resolved through absolution and communion. Communion also provided a controlled environment for the release of intense personal emotions as the brothers and sisters dissolved into tears and experienced near-ecstasy through the effect of the prayers, hymns, and partaking of the body and blood. Devotion to the bleeding wounds of Christ brought the Moravians into intimate connection with God, their creator and savior. In communion the Brethren physically enjoyed the corpse and blood of Jesus that they conjured every day in their liturgies. During communion, the congregation lay prostrate before the communion table, which often had a painting of Christ hanging on the wall behind it, and prayed silently while the liturgist offered a corporate prayer of confession. Following the absolution and reconciliation through the kiss of peace, the elements were consecrated. This in itself could produce a type of religious ecstasy, as when Böhler was "transported" in a communion service in 1758.[43] The communion hymns listed in the Bethlehem Diary revolve around the same core group of images: the mystical marriage, the atonement for sins, the presence of Christ, the wounds and corpse of Jesus, and the life flowing through the blood.[44]

The blood and wounds of Christ and the mystical marriage are joined in many verses such as "Draw us to thee, and we will come / Into thy Wounds' deep Places / Where hidden is the Honey-comb / Of thy sweet Love's Embraces."[45] At the point of partaking of the bread, the communicants sang, "Pale lips, kiss us on the Heart! Open arms, take us!" The blessing of the cup was preceded with verses about the blood and the side wound, such as "On Heart and Mouth, O Lamb, do Thou bleed, We smiling look to thy holy side: To thy Heart now put us, on thy Wounds press us, In these blest Sacrament-Hours so precious, Lamb, Lamb, O Lamb!"[46]

Interpreting the Wounds Cult

It has been easier to view the colonial Moravians' blood and wounds theology as an expression of some type of deep pathology. Sessler, for one, accepted this argument and concluded that "Zinzendorf suffered from a pathological condition which broke out in demonstrations of emotionalism, phantasies, and morbidity. In place of the pious exhortations of earlier days, his speech now resounded with word pictures of the merits of Christ's blood and wounds and an excess of sensual symbolism."[47] At least one twentieth-century psychologist, Oskar Pfister, concluded that Zinzendorf transferred his severely repressed sexual drive to Jesus and found sexual release in fantasizing about sucking and licking the ersatz vagina of the side wound.[48] It is undeniable that the body of Jesus has been eroticized in the blood and wounds theology, and familiarity with Freud is not required to recognize that the side wound is a vaginal symbol, especially since Zinzendorf himself repeatedly identified it as a womb or birth canal.[49]

There are problems, however, with the Pfister thesis. The most sophisticated refutation has been offered by Wilhelm Betterman, who argues convincingly that Zinzendorf's blood and wounds theology is a form of the Lutheran "theology of the cross," which was vital to Zinzendorf's theology.[50] Although very useful, this theological analysis does not answer all of the questions related to Zinzendorfian piety and its persistence in colonial America. There are still psychological and anthropological questions to address, even if we reject Pfister's conclusions. Aside from the difficulties of psychoanalyzing the dead, we should keep in mind that the unusual is not necessarily pathological. No matter how bloody or outlandish, fantastic imagery may have served important functions in the Moravian communities of the eighteenth century.

Indeed, explanations that invoke individual or group pathology are obviously belied by the incredible leadership of Zinzendorf himself and the impressive achievements of the Moravian Church. As a figure of European renown, Zinzendorf earned the admiration and devotion of thousands of supporters from dozens of countries. He had a prodigious capacity for work and fathered several children. Theories of group pathology are likewise difficult to sustain, when we consider that *die Sichtungzeit* in the 1740s was a time of the *Brüdergemeine*'s most vigorous and expansive growth.[51] In 1749 the Moravian Church was validated as "an antient and Protestant Episcopal church" by the British Parliament, and Zinzendorf's order of banishment from Saxony was repealed. During this time, the Moravians built some two dozen communities that were models of rational organization and aesthetic charm. With a few notable exceptions, contemporary observers were more impressed with the Moravians' industry and harmony than with any deviant behaviors. In an age when witch hunts were recent memory and messianic prophets were active in Europe and America, Zinzendorf and the Moravians seem rather conventional.

Theories of pathology fail to account for the presence, persistence, and power of Zinzendorf's blood and wounds piety, but so do theories that minimize blood and wounds theology as a brief aberration. It is no accident that blood and wounds theology thrived during the period of the General Economy in Bethlehem. In fact, the preservation of that communal system depended in part on the emotional, graphic, and disturbing language of the cult of the wounds.[52] The adoration of the wounds and corpse of Jesus served to sublimate a variety of personal needs and fears that would have otherwise destroyed the community. As long as Bethlehem remained a carefully regulated communal society, wounds theology was useful and vital. It strengthened the community boundaries by providing an internal discourse, yet allowed a point of entry for new members. Moreover, it also helped the community sublimate sexuality and aggression and even overcome the fear of death.

One function of the wounds cult was to provide an internal discourse for the *Gemeine*. As Zinzendorf puts it, the brides of Christ have their own "jargon," which the unconverted do not know and should not attempt to speak. It is a language for intimate moments with the Bridegroom, an erotic language based on the Song of Solomon and the cross of Jesus, which identifies its users as brides of Christ.[53] This internal discourse helps individuals identify with the community and its mission, marks the boundary with the outside world, and keeps people within the society by marking them as "strange" to the outside world. As early as 1747 American Moravians were urged to keep some of their language secret from the world. "Such books, letters, and hymns should be handled carefully and not communicated so freely because it is unbearable for the wounds of Jesus and similar things to be prostituted to the ridicule of the world."[54] This remained a concern long after *die Sichtungzeit*. In 1760 the members were informed that:

> Everyone who has a liturgy book should take care that it does not fall into strange hands. The word of the Lord applies here, "You shall not throw holy things in front of dogs nor pearls before swine." The deep, divine truths that are in the *Büchlein* must never become material for controversy, and therefore no one should get hold of it, than who will use it with an inner feeling.[55]

Aaron Fogleman has shown that vigorous opposition to Zinzendorfian piety by the Moravians' neighbors even led to violence at times.[56]

However, the Moravian communities were not completely separated from the world. In fact, they were engaged in aggressive missionary activity. Daniel Thorp has identified the Moravian tension between seclusion and evangelization in his study of the Bethabara community (North

Carolina) and shown that the Moravians had clear but permeable boundaries.[57] Residence within the community was rigidly controlled, and visitors were isolated as much as possible. Far from stagnating, however, the Brethren actively sought new members.

Entrance into the community, by birth or conversion, was literally an act of violence to the social structure, and the Moravians ritualized this by means of the side wound. According to Mary Douglass, social structure affects attitudes toward the body. Societies that stress group identity and feel threatened by the outside world (like the Moravians) are usually concerned with maintaining control of the body's orifices.[58] Following Douglass's theory, I propose that the violence experienced by the Moravian communities when new members joined was ritualized as violence to Christ himself. The metaphorical body was forced to yield a new and unique orifice by which persons could enter. The boundary was provided with a bloody hole that allowed the flow of people in and out that was necessary for survival.

Life in a communal society such as Bethlehem had many personal benefits, including security and intimacy, but it also involved a tremendous personal cost. Individuals were required to give up much of their privacy and autonomy. The cult of the wounds, I believe, helped to mediate this tension in Bethlehem. Here Pfister's insight into the sexual nature of the blood and wounds theology is most helpful, but one must transpose his personal psychological theory about Zinzendorf to a social key.

The wounds cult provided an outlet for sexual energy that was community enhancing rather than community destroying. Release came in worship when "the whole *Gemeine* fell before its bloody husband and his *pleura,* and lay there trembling in the presence of the side hole."[59] The adoration of the side wound of Jesus, with its compact symbolism (womb, vagina, breast, bed, etc.), could incite and satisfy the erotic desires of the whole community:

> Our Morning Blessing was especially bloody and juicy. The Married People sang from its place in the pleura, its "Ave," and the youthful flock trembled behind in the side hole, whose new manifestation they observed today with a blessed sensation of shaking from love's fever.[60]

It was important to tie the erotic to the wounds of Christ because an overt sexualizing of religion in Bethlehem would have brought the *Gemeine* under legal censure and made it more difficult to keep members from acting physically on their mental imagery. Thus the erotic was combined with the repulsive. The side wound could be a sexual image only so long as it remained a wound. If it were to become too clearly a vagina, the ability of this symbolism to sublimate sexuality would have been lost.

Another psychological toll paid in a communal society is the repression of aggression, particularly that directed against fellow members. René Girard theorizes that the origin of religion itself was violent sacrifice that was performed in order to prevent outbreaks of unrestrained violence that could destroy a society. He calls this the "scapegoat mechanism," and concludes that "Violence is the heart and secret soul of the sacred."[61] The need to control violent impulses was compounded for the Moravians since they were functionally pacifist and theologically called to love their enemies.[62] Thus the ritualized torture and murder of Jesus served to transfer violent emotions out of the *Gemeine* and into the mythical realm. Night after night they witnessed the dying of Jesus, often in gory detail. Frequently we are given descriptions of cathartic release as a result. Violence was imaginatively expressed and at the same time forgiven. The worshiper participated in the act of violence while receiving absolution for his sins from the one who was wounded. Thus Jesus served as the ultimate theological and sociological scapegoat for the *Gemeine*. The community could imaginatively act out destructive and self-destructive impulses in a safe environment.

The wounds cult also helps us understand the ability of the *Brüdergemeine* to repress the natural fear of death. For centuries Christian doctrine has taught that death should not be feared by those with faith in Christ. During the communal period in Bethlehem, there was an overwhelming sense of joy and celebration, and even a longing for death.[63] This reflected in part the severing of traditional family emotional ties that was achieved with the choir system, but it is also related to the wounds cult. In short, the dying were comforted by the contemplation of the wounds. It was not unusual that Caspar Boeckel enjoyed hymns such as "My wounds of Jesus, Yes mine!" as he was dying: "He faded away nicely and happily with the words, 'At the end of all need.'"[64] Brother Steifel was similarly comforted by verses about the side wound that were sung by the Single Brothers as he died.

> They formed a circle around him and sang him many beautiful side hole stanzas with music for going home; and then his spirit was revived and he came back to himself because his soul lives so entirely in the material of the side hole, so that he babbled much along with them, as well as he could, and raised up his hands in joy, which, for such an old Separatist, was a quite nice sight.[65]

The death of a community member was announced by the brass ensemble, which played the familiar tune about the wounds of Christ.

This contemplation of the wounds of Jesus at the time of death was in part an expression of the desire for union with God and a sense of the assurance of salvation through the atonement. But it also reflects the scapegoating function described above. The horrors of dying, the bleeding, smell, agony, sweat, and filth that were central to the medieval *danse macabre* were not denied in Bethlehem, but they were transferred from the dying individual to his or her Savior-God. Christ endured all of these things and, in so doing, removed their horror. This overcoming, at least partially, of the fear of death helped the community to survive and thrive.

Its members could give themselves entirely to the mission of the Church without denying their own mortality.

Conclusion

The vivid imaginative life of the eighteenth-century Moravians was not pathological; it was rather a critical factor in the success of the Moravians' communities in both Europe and the Americas. It provided a mythology and ritual that allowed the members of the society to sublimate a variety of personal drives and fears to the mystical realm for the good of the community and its mission. The sense of ecstasy and joy so often reported in Moravian sources was real. It was a religious experience inextricably connected to a deep psychological experience of catharsis. The brothers and sisters in Bethlehem did indeed sleep in the arms of their Creator and were drawn into his side wound; there, they found both ecstasy and security.

This changed gradually after Zinzendorf died. The Moravian communities in the United States slowly became industrial cities where value was measured in terms of commerce rather than communion. As long as Zinzendorf's followers found inexpressible joy in the wounds of Christ, they were nourished for their worldwide mission and inspired for their communal lives. As they turned away from that communal mission, they also turned away from the Zinzendorfian piety that nurtured and sustained it.

Notes

This article is a synopsis of my book *Community of the Cross: Moravian Piety in Colonial Bethlehem* (College Station, PA, 2004). Portions of this article also appear in my article "Understanding Zinzendorf's Blood and Wounds Theology," *THMS* 32 (2002).

1. MAB, 7 November and 19 December 1744, *Bethlehem Diary*; also published as *The Bethlehem Diary: Volume 1, 1742–1744*, trans. Kenneth Hamilton (Bethlehem, PA, 1971), 210, 214.

2. The litany first appeared in *Anhang XII* of the *Herrnhuter Gesangbuch* in 1744. A modern English translation of the complete text of the litany appears in Atwood, "Zinzendorf's Litany of the Wounds," *Lutheran Quarterly* 11 (1997): 189–214, and in *Community of the Cross*, 235–237.

3. See Atwood, "Interpreting and Misinterpreting the Sichtungzeit," forthcoming in *Neuen Aspecte in Zinzendorfforschung*, ed. Martin Brecht and Paul Peucker. The single best work on the Sifting Time is Hans-Walter Erbe, ed., *Herrnhaag eine religiöse Kommunität im 18. Jahrhundert* in *Unitas Fratrum: Zeitschrift für Geschichte und Geganwartsfragen der Brüdergemeine* 23/24 (1988): 4–222. See also Paul Peucker, "'Blut auf unsre grünen Bändchen': Die Sichtungzeit in der Herrnhuter Brüdergemeine," in *Unitas Fratrum: Zeitschrift für Geschichte und Geganwartsfragen der Brüdergemeine* 49/50. Most American work on the Moravians follows John R. Weinlick, *Count Zinzendorf* (New York, 1956) and Kenneth G. Hamilton and J. Taylor Hamilton, *History of the Moravian Church: The Renewed Unitas Fratrum 1722–1957* (Bethlehem, PA, 1967), who reproduce the basic arguments of German Moravian scholars, including Hermann Plitt, whose three-volume

history of Zinzendorf's theology separates the "Sifting Time" from the rest of Zinzendorf's theology: *Die ursprüngliche gesunde Lehre Zinzendorfs (1723–1742); Die Zeit krankhafter Verbildungen in Zinzendorfs Lehrweise (1743–1750); Die wiederhergestellte und abschließende Lehrweise Zinzendorfs (1750–1760)* (Gotha, 1869–1874). Otto Uttendörfer followed this same pattern in *Zinzendorf und die Mystik* (Berlin, 1952). Likewise in Erich Beyreuther and Gerhard Meyer's edition of Zinzendorf's work, *Hauptschriften*, 6 vols. (Hildesheim, 1962), Zinzendorf's sermons on the *Litany of the Wounds* are in volume 3 *(Reden während der Sichtung Zeit in der Wetterau und in Holland)*. Erich Beyreuther's classic biography of Zinzendorf, *Die Grosse Zinzendorf-Biographie* (Marburg, 1957–1961) is likewise divided into three sections with the middle one dealing with the Sifting Time.

4. J.E. Hutton, *A History of the Moravian Church*, 2d ed. (London, 1909), 274.
5. John Jacob Sessler, *Communal Pietism Among Early American Moravians* (New York, 1933).
6. Gillian Lindt Gollin, *Moravians in Two Worlds: A Study of Changing Communities* (New York, 1967), 19.
7. Helmut Erbe estimated that the average workday was nearly sixteen hours long during the period routinely dismissed as *die Sichtungzeit*. According to one visitor there were as many trades in Bethlehem in 1751 as in a major city. See Erbe's *Bethlehem, Pa.: Eine kommunistische Herrnhuter-Kolonie des 18. Jahrhunderts* (Stuttgart and Herrnhut, 1929), and also Beverly Prior Smaby, *The Transformation of Moravian Bethlehem: From Communal Mission to Family Economy* (Philadelphia, 1988), 87–91.
8. Sessler, *Communal Pietism*, 153.
9. Hamilton and Hamilton, *History of the Moravian Church*, 105 and 106.
10. For more on Zinzendorf's theology, see Arthur Freeman, *An Ecumenical Theology of the Heart: The Theology of Nicholas Ludwig von Zinzendorf* (Bethlehem, PA, 1998), and Peter Zimmerling, *Gott in Gemeinschaft: Zinzendorfs Trinitatslehre* (Giessen, 1991).
11. This apologetic approach has affected German scholarship as well. German scholars have used *die Sichtungzeit* to separate the "real" Zinzendorf from the piety of the 1740s that provided so much fuel for polemical attacks in his day and latter.
12. J. C. S. Mason, *The Moravian Church and the Missionary Awakening in England, 1760–1800* (Woodbridge, UK, 2001), 5–28.
13. Atwood, "Interpreting and Misinterpreting the Sichtungzeit," *Neuen Aspecte in Zinzendorfforschung*, and Atwood, "Zinzendorf's 1749 Reprimand to the *Brüdergemeine*," *TMHS* 29 (1996): 59–84.
14. Paul Peucker, "'In Staub und Asche': Bewertung und Kassation im Unitätsarchiv 1760–1810," in *"Alles ist euer, ihr aber seid Christi": Festschrift für Dietrich Meyer*, ed. Rudolf Mohr (Cologne, 2000). In a forthcoming article, "'Inspired by Flames of Love': Homosexuality and 18th Century Moravian Brothers," Peucker demonstrates that one of the central issues of *die Sichtungzeit* was probably homoeroticism among the single Brothers in Herrnhaag.
15. Atwood, *Community of the Cross*, 14–19. See also Atwood, "Sleeping in the Arms of Christ: Sanctifying Sexuality in the Eighteenth-Century Moravian Church," *Journal of the History of Sexuality* 8, no. 1 (1997): 25–51; and Atwood, "The Mother of God's People: The Adoration of the Holy Spirit in the Eighteenth-Century Brüdergemeine," *Church History* 68 (1999): 886–909.
16. Gollin's *Moravians in Two Worlds* is particularly noteworthy in this respect.
17. MAB, 19 January 1760, *Bethlehem Diary*.
18. MAB, 27 November 1756, *Bethlehem Diary*.
19. Atwood, *Community of the Cross*, 130.
20. See Elisabeth W. Sommer, *Serving Two Masters: Moravian Brethren in Germany and North Carolina, 1727–1801* (Lexington, KY, 2000). For a contrasting view, see Gollin, *Moravians in Two Worlds*.
21. 13/24 June 1748 (¶ 3), *Bethlehem Diary*, MAB. On the Moravian understanding of the Holy Spirit as the Mother, see Atwood, "The Mother of God's People" and Gary S. Kinkel, *Our Dear Mother the Spirit: An Investigation of Zinzendorf's Theology and Praxis* (Lanham, MD, 1990).

22. MAB, 10 March 1752, *Bethlehem Diary.*
23. MAB, 24 March 1758, *Bethlehem Diary.*
24. Atwood, "Understanding Zinzendorf's Blood and Wounds Theology," includes a modern translation of the *Pleurody.*
25. Consider Hamilton and Hamilton, *History of the Moravian Church,* 104.
26. This includes both German and English hymnals: *A Collection of Hymns Chiefly Extracted from the Larger Hymn-Book of the Brethren's Congregations* (London, 1769); *A Collection of Hymns, for the Use of the Protestant Church of the United Brethren* (London, 1789); *Liturgic Hymns of United Brethren: Revised and Enlarged* (London, 1793).
27. MAB, 8/19 November 1748, *Helpers Conference Minutes.*
28. Gerhard Reichel, *Zinzendorfs Frömmigkeit im Licht der Psychoanalyse* (Tübingen, 1911), 71.
29. Caroline Walker Bynum, "Violent Images in Late Medieval Piety," *German Historical Institute Bulletin* 30 (Spring 2002): 5.
30. Bynum, "Violent Images," 23.
31. English translations of many of the most common litanies can be found in Atwood, "Theology in Song," in Peter Vogt and Craig D. Atwood, eds., *The Distinctiveness of Moravian Culture: Essays and Translations in Honor of Vernon Nelson,* (Nazareth, PA, 2003).
32. "Ein und zwanzig diskurse," in Beyreuther and Meyer, *Hauptschriften,* vol. 6, discourse 4, 102.
33. "Ein und zwanzig diskurse," in Beyreuther and Meyer, *Hauptschriften,* vol. 6, discourse 2, 73.
34. Fogleman, "Jesus is Female: The Moravian Challenge in the German Communities of British North America," *William and Mary Quarterly* 60 (2003): 295–332.
35. "Gemein Reden," in Beyreuther and Meyer, *Hauptschriften,* vol. 4, sermon 19, 286; "Ein und zwanzig diskurse," in Beyreuther and Meyer, *Hauptschriften,* vol. 6, discourse 4, 102.
36. The classic study of this is Caroline Walker Bynum, "Jesus as Mother and Abbot as Mother: Some Themes in Twelfth-Century Cistercian Writing," in Bynum, *Jesus as Mother: Studies in the Spirituality of the High Middle Ages* (Berkeley, CA, 1984), 110–169.
37. Katharine M. Faull, "Christ's Other Self: Gender, the Body and Religion in the Eighteenth-Century Moravian Church," *Covenant Quarterly* 62 (2004).
38. Bynum, "Jesus as Mother," 130.
39. Beyreuther and Meyer, *Hauptschriften,* vol. 4, 43, 49.
40. Zinzendorf, *Nine Public Lectures on Important Subjects in Religion Preached in Fetter Lane Chapel in London in the Year 1746,* trans. and ed. George W. Forell (Iowa City, 1973), 20.
41. "Kinder Reden," in *Ergänzungsbände zu den Hauptschriften* (hereafter ZE), ed. Erich Beyreuther and Gerhard Meyer (Hildesheim, 1964–1985), sermon 56, 282. "Ein und zwanzig diskurse," Beyreuther and Meyer, *Hauptschriften,* vol. 6, sermon 3, 89.
42. From *De instituione,* chap. 31, *Opera omnia* 1:667, as quoted by Bynum, *Jesus as Mother,* 123.
43. MAB, 25 November 1758, *Bethlehem Diary.*
44. The following verses were used in a communion service led by Spangenberg in 1760: "Bloody Redeemer of the *Gemeine* servants, if a thousand times I wet your feet with my tears and kiss them before this lovefeast, it is still not accomplished; So we live and rejoice these cry so good to suffer"; "Your body has fed us, your blood has been our drink." "Now I thank you from the heart, for your soul's pains." MAB, 31 August 1760, *Bethlehem Diary.*
45. *The Litany-Book, According to the Manner of Singing at present mostly in Use among the Brethren … Translated from the fourth German Edition* (London, 1759), 232.
46. *Litany-book,* 240.
47. Sessler, *Communal Pietism,* 162.
48. Oskar Pfister, *Die Frömmigkeit des Grafen Ludwig von Zinzendorf: Ein psychoanalytischer Beitrag zur Kenntnis der religiösen Sublimierungsprozesse und zur Erklärung des Pietismus* (Leipzig, 1910), 5, 57–64. Gerhard Reichel has refuted Pfister's charge that Zinzendorf was psychologically unbalanced in *Zinzendorfs Frömmigkeit im Licht der Psychoanalyse.*

49. Atwood, *Community of the Cross*, 111; cf. Fogleman, "Jesus is Female."

50. Wilhelm Bettermann, *Theologie und Sprache bei Zinzendorf* (Gotha, 1935).

51. Colin Podmore, *The Moravian Church in England 1728–1760* (Oxford, 1998).

52. Atwood, *Community of the Cross*, 216–221.

53. "Gemein Reden," Beyreuther and Meyer, *Hauptschriften*, vol. 4, sermon 41, 208.

54. MAB, 24 February/7 March 1747 (¶ 7) *Engere Conferenz Minutes*.

55. MAB, 28 June 1760, Verlass des von 26ten bis 29ten June 1760 in Lititz gehaltenen Brüder-Synodi (¶7), 605, *Bethlehem Diary*.

56. Fogleman, "Jesus is Female."

57. Daniel B. Thorp, *The Moravian Community in Colonial North Carolina: Pluralism on the Southern Frontier* (Knoxville, TN, 1989).

58. Mary Douglass, *Natural Symbols: Explorations in Cosmology* (New York, 1973); and Douglass, *Purity and Danger: An Analysis of the Concepts of Pollution and Taboo* (New York, 1989).

59. MAB, 31 December 1748, *Bethlehem Diary*.

60. MAB, 29 April/10 May 1748, *Bethlehem Diary*.

61. Renè Girard, *Violence and the Sacred*, trans. Patrick Gregory (Baltimore, 1972).

62. Threatened by Native Americans in the 1750s, the Brethren were often in danger, but the fear and desire for revenge could be channeled through the wounds cult, as when Spangenberg applied the Hymns to the Wounds to a community member, Seidel, who had barely escaped hostile natives. MAB, 31. October 1756, *Bethlehem Diary*.

63. Atwood, "The Joyfulness of Death in Eighteenth-Century Moravian Communities," *Communal Societies* 17 (1997): 39–58.

64. 9 August 1758, Beilage, 131–132, *Bethlehem Diary*, MAB.

65. MAB, 2/13 October 1748 (4), *Bethlehem Diary*.

– Chapter 4 –

MORAVIAN PHYSICIANS AND THEIR MEDICINE IN COLONIAL NORTH AMERICA: EUROPEAN MODELS AND COLONIAL REALITY

Renate Wilson

T HIS ESSAY EXPLORES THE EIGHTEENTH-CENTURY transatlantic transfer of medical care, using a variety of Moravian sources in the US and Germany. This German influence developed from the juncture of religious mission and colonial medicine and corresponded closely to the goals and ambitions of eighteenth-century evangelical movements. In the German sphere, first the Halle Pietists and then the Moravian brotherhood established their missions and outposts not only on this side of the Atlantic but also in the East Indies and the Ottoman Empire. In previous work, I have linked the structure and mechanisms of this transatlantic evangelicalism to the practice and teaching of medicine and to the use of medical care and medicines. The linkage of religion and medicine had been a practice of the Jesuit missions to Africa and India. Likewise it provided the incentive for the eventual pharmaceutical trade of the Halle Orphanage, one of the eighteenth-century centers of German evangelical reform, which was a predecessor and model for the Moravian transatlantic movement of Count Zinzendorf.[1]

For the history of North American medicine in the eighteenth century, a wider perspective that encompasses German contributions has yielded far more detailed and historically useful information than previously available. During the colonial period and beyond, there were trained physicians and surgeons (many of whom dispensed medicinals), clergy practicing medicine, trained and untrained midwives, barber surgeons, and dispensers of single remedies. Many if not most practiced alone and were paid for their services and the medications they provided. A very few held salaried positions.[2] Moreover, the range of medical services among German-language communities in eighteenth-century North America and the providers who offered them were probably at least as wide and heterogeneous as those among other immigrant groups.[3] For the German language practitioners, however, we have few coherent sources that illustrate both practice and patients, with the exception of the settlements sponsored by or ministered to by clergy from the Francke Foundations in Halle.

Another much more closely defined group of immigrants and potential patients came from the Moravian brotherhood, which enjoyed both continuous guidance and early financial support from the German mother institution. The movement is documented in large archives both in Europe and on this continent. This chapter represents an initial attempt to mine more systematically some of the sources in the rich literature on the Moravian brotherhood for the history of medicine. Its objective is to place the Moravian plans for German community and mission care within the context of late eighteenth-century American medical practice. In particular, we can contrast European expectations based on principles of brotherhood and sisterhood but governed by a hierarchical relationship between the European center and the colonial periphery with the realities of transatlantic medical practice in missionary and frontier communities.

In addition, our sources offer a rare glimpse of direct involvement in the philosophy of medical care by the founder of the eighteenth-century Moravian movement, Count Nicolaus Ludwig von Zinzendorf. His fragmentary views on medicine and medical care and the responses to those—both during his lifetime and after his death in 1760—are of particular interest for what they reveal not only about Moravian medicine but also about the numerous physicians and other medical providers who were drawn into or engaged with the Moravian network of North American immigrants over the period from 1740 to roughly 1810.[4]

Medical Care in German-Language Settlements

Apart from medical supplies and recipe collections and the presence of some midwives, there was little medical expertise in most American frontier settlements, regardless of language or national background. But physicians often appeared within the first five or ten years of a community's growth, once the patient population could support one or more trained practitioners. In areas of German settlement from New York to Georgia, itinerant trained medical providers were often former French, Swiss, or German military personnel. These onetime field apothecaries or army surgeons sometimes remained in the colonies after the European campaigns of the early part of the eighteenth century, if there was a catchment area sufficiently prosperous to generate income.[5]

In many communities, a major source of medical care was the clergy. In German settlement areas, these were usually Lutheran and Reformed ministers who practiced medicine as an adjunct to their clerical office. A specifically Pietist medical practice and along with it access to the medications from the Halle Orphanage were brought across the Atlantic to Germanophone Lutheran and Reformed congregations by several generations of Pietist ministers beginning in the 1730s. They practiced side by side with other German and English medical men and women of very different levels of training in a geographic area extending from the East Coast below New England to the backcountries of Pennsylvania, Maryland, Virginia, and North Carolina. In combining medical and clerical functions, these ministers resembled their Congregationalist colleagues in New England, the Presbyterians in the middle colonies, and their brethren from the Anglican "Society for Promoting the Gospel in Foreign Parts," who had all practiced medicine since the early colonial period.[6] Clergy were willing to join medical and clerical practice for reasons of community cohesion and out of the need to augment their incomes. Moreover, they enjoyed some measure of respect and the confidence of their congregations.

In the eyes of the colonial authorities, there can have been little doubt that clerical medical practice would not only provide medical services but also help to block itinerants of doubtful religious persuasions trying to peddle their messages. Given the religious tolerance prevailing in at least the middle colonies, practitioners of more radical religious beliefs, like the Schwenkfelders or the Moravian physicians in their closed communities, rarely posed a danger other than by attracting the parishioners of the more conservative denominations.

The medical communities of colonial Eastern Pennsylvania illustrate the prevalence of quite sophisticated medical practitioners, who often had been expelled from Silesia, Huguenot areas of France, the Palatinate, and Protestant Hungary.[7] Many came from private colleges—the Continental dissenting academies that stood in opposition to the academic monopoly.[8] Some could not have practiced either their religion or their profession in Europe, like the Schwenkfelder Abraham Wagner and the French Universalist George de Benneville. In North America, these nonconformists provided a level of rural medical practice and pharmaceutical dispensing that, except for the academic trappings that many rejected for religious reasons, probably differed little from European models.

The medical men attached to the Moravian settlements in the middle and southern colonies form an intriguing group, in terms both of their number and the timing of their arrival.[9] Most came to North America in the latter half of the eighteenth century, and they were more numerous and far better trained on average than earlier German medical immigrants. With few exceptions—the Salzburger settlement in Georgia being the one best known to me—they seem to have been the only German-language medical contingent that formed part of an explicit settlement structure supported from Europe. In this respect, they resembled the medical staff of the Catholic missions in Louisiana and Canada more closely than the individual German practitioners who had drifted across the Atlantic. Of various levels of training but often with full medical degrees and supplied with advice from the medical establishment in Herrnhut and Barby (where Zinzendorf had planned to erect a medical college), the Moravian practitioners were intended to be in a position to concentrate on their medical mission, in contrast to Pietist and other clergy, who combined their clerical duties with charity practice and the sale of the Halle medications.

However, the Moravian physicians and their patients soon faced questions of professional independence versus social status within the *Gemeinen*. The realities of finding and securing adequate financial resources for salaried reimbursement, which most physicians demanded instead of un-reimbursed community work, quickly forced most Moravian medical men to extend their work beyond their sectarian communities, many opening pharmacies and offering services to outsiders. In this respect as well, the obstacles to unfunded community practice resembled the course of the closed Salzburger settlement in Georgia. Founded in 1733, that settlement always had at least one, and for most of the time two, medical providers sent from Germany, although they were never fully salaried. They were expected to provide charity or community care to the settlers in return for housing, firewood, and in-kind payments, and to make an additional living by selling the Halle Orphanage medications and providing care to people in the surrounding communities. Insufficiently remunerated and chafing under clerical supervision, the senior of these medical men, Ernest Thilo, was in constant conflict with his superiors in Europe and the settlers' expectations of free care and ample medications. He eventually created a profitable and extensive fee-for-service practice for which we find evidence in numerous orders for medical supplies from Halle.[10]

As in other spheres, the planning for communal medical services in Moravian settlements both in Europe and abroad was closely modeled on the institutions of the Francke Foundations at Halle.[11] Unpublished documents at the central Herrnhut archives and at Bethlehem reflect the intention to provide institutionalized medical systems, including the famous Halle hospital conferences. We have protocols of regular if not daily medical conferences in Marienborn (1744), in Lindseyhouse (Chelsea-London, 1754), and Bethlehem (1756–1760). There are reflections by Zinzendorf on medicine dating to 1744 and 1755, as well as more formal medical instructions for congregations and missions (e.g., those sent to Bethlehem in 1773). There were also plans early on to set up a pharmaceutical trade centered in Holland and based on the immensely successful Halle model, but like plans for the medical college at Barby, these remained unrealized.[12] It remains an intriguing question whether medical care in the Moravian communities reflected the principles of a gentle and more frugal Pietist medicine developed by famous Pietist physicians (including Johann Samuel Carl and Johann Junker, both students of Georg Ernst Stahl), or if frugality was in fact economic prudence.

The Role of the Moravian Physician: Instructions from the Center

The need to provide medical care in domestic and outlying communities was specifically recognized in one of the general Moravian synods of 1739, which contemplated missions from Russia and its Baltic territories to India to Suriname. People were designated for a variety of community functions (usually referred to as *Diener*), with alternates proposed for all posts. A Native American mission was envisaged, as were missions to Greenland and Lapland.[13] Physicians or medical staff were assigned to various positions at these synods, although it is not clear that all of these appointments were posted. For example, Adolph Meyer, known to be practicing in Pennsylvania by 1757, was noted as available to go to Livland as a community physician in 1739. He was not linked to the *Gemeine* as a *Diener*, however, and we thus lack further administrative information.[14]

During one of Zinzendorf's stays in England, resident *Diener* Dr. Johann Friedrich Schmidt was recommended to serve in New York as both a community physician and a Moravian Church organist. Since Schmidt's financial and other obligations in Livland (where he was then practicing) were sufficiently settled, he "accepted the proposal with great joy."[15] There is no evidence of his practice in North America, however. Here and elsewhere, questions of physician payment and their integration into the fully dedicated Moravian community structure continued to be raised, both in the planning stages and for more settled German communities.

Apparently these medical concerns were driven in part by the original preferences of Count Zinzendorf. During his sojourn in the Wetterau, a hotbed of radical thinking in the first half of the eighteenth century, Zinzendorf was strongly influenced by the more radical wing of Halle Pietist physicians, who tended to be minimalist and frugal in treatment. Zinzendorf himself wrote a rambling discourse on medicine and disease at Barby in 1755, which reflected his preference for noninterventionist medicine and mingled his own medical philosophy and considerations of financial prudence.[16] In this essay, Zinzendorf followed well established spiritualist and reformist trends by attacking physicians and their systems of disease entities, as well as their excessive use of Latin nomenclature. Noticeable too was his concern with medically justified absenteeism on the part of community members, which would deprive the economy of worker contributions. "Where there is no doctor," Zinzendorf claimed, "one finds fewer sick brothers." He continued:

> No physician working in the *Gemeinen* should make a living taking care of the ill but should instead receive a general salary. Nor should a pharmacy be

included in the social services budget and medicines dispensed for a price. ... It has been noted that once physicians receive a stipend, they become less inclined to work. Clearly the answer is that in such a case, they would not be worthy of being a Brother.[17]

Issues of medical governance were similarly addressed by Johann Wilhelm Tralles and by Peter Svertner, a Dutch Moravian who received a medical degree from Göttingen University in 1772. Svertner and Tralles were among the fully academically qualified members of the Moravian medical community, and they left a number of medical writings that deal with the role and place of the proper *Gemeine* physician, both echoing and expanding on Zindendorf's positions.[18] Reflecting pervasive professional concerns, Svertner wrote in the 1770s while at Barby and, later, as owner-manager of the pharmacy at Herrnhut and lecturer at its college. Tralles practiced likewise in Herrnhut in the 1770s. Both commented on the place of the physician in a closed Moravian community, attempting to balance community against the professional interests of physicians.

On the one hand, Svertner noted, most physicians' interest in fame and income in the outside world was deleterious to service in the *Gemeine*. But if no proper salary were allocated for physician support, the doctor would resort to acting as the apothecary and doing work not appropriate for a professional physician. Smaller *Gemeinen,* required some medical staff who could perform other tasks as well. However, Svertner was not enamored of lay prescribing based on manuals and recipe books. "Since I have been entrusted with the *Praxis medica* in this community," he wrote, after his appointment in Barby in 1773, "I have been concerned with a better, Christian provision of services, also for distant brothers and sisters." Svertner felt obligated to share his views, although these were largely re-statements of previous pronouncements on mission synods. All the same, Svertner's concern for the proper role of the professional in a religious hierarchy was clear. "For those *Gemeine* workers scattered throughout the world," Svertner proposed training in basic medical skills, reflecting an undefined "medical essence of our medicine."

> For my own person, I do not care much if a *medicus* in a *Gemeine* should be considered an *Arbeiter* |worker| and is a member of this or that conference. Least of all, his office should not be defined by others. But I strongly feel that he must be a servant of the Savior ... although as a physician he does not belong among the workers. In small communities, however, there should be a double function. In matters of his competence, he should be able to assert his views. I propose a medical conference for each *Gemeine,* where the helpers, the physician, surgeon, midwives, and caretakers congregate and discuss matters of their concern, for there is no one in the community who must work in such a broad capacity and carry such a burden other than the physician, who is isolated and needs moral support.[19]

This scheme for a medical conference had in fact been discussed since the late 1730s but apparently was not everywhere a fully workable model, even before Zinzendorf's death. We have some documentation for such conferences in larger American settlements like Bethlehem, but they seem to have been sporadic. One reason may have been that even where instituted, many of the physicians did not particularly appreciate keeping "rounds," for, as Svertner noted, they preferred their independence. Physicians may have felt that this used up time needed for other duties. Svertner's conclusion, therefore, remained ambivalent and resigned: "The *medicus* is defined not by his place, whether as a worker or by receiving a salary, but he should work as a servant of the Lord."[20]

In his lengthy and heavily annotated *Medizinalordnung,* Tralles cast a wider net, questioning, like many religious-medical reformers and Zinzendorf himself, both the premises of medical science and the qualifications of his peers. In principle, Tralles asked whether one might not forego entirely the practicing or "physical" physician *(leiblichen Ärzte).* On the other hand, it seemed to be taken for granted that both physicians and surgeons were needed in the fully constituted communities *(ordentlichen Gemeinen)* and that their absence caused much embarrassment. At the same time, there remained much suspicion among the brethren of the medical profession. Indeed, Tralles claimed, "we still know so little of this science of medicine as a whole and thus of what should make the essential character of a man whom one calls physician, his duties, his relationship with the people, and of that indispensable, and necessary independence ... accompanied by an awareness of insufficiencies ... that is the foundation of his office."[21]

Following this general preamble, Tralles launched into the by now familiar problems of Moravian community practice. The *medicus* could not be a worker, but in many instances he lacked a proper salary and respect—a demoralizing situation. Payment was inadequate in most cases. On the other hand, few *Gemeinen* were so poor that they could not afford a physician, and there was much waste in other areas. It had been argued, Tralles noted, that it might be best if the *medicus* were to be paid by the sick for each service rendered, and this alternative had in fact been mentioned in one of the provincial synods. But would this not be the end of a Christian physician, Tralles asked, for which Brother could with a clear conscience ask a poor patient for his pennies?

> And the rich, where are they? Where we find any, they give less than anyone else, and even if they act reasonably when in the eye of the world, they will be impertinent, coarse and ungrateful in dealing with a brother. Overall, the financial constitution of the communities is such that there is not a ducat left to pay the physician and the medical men remain ill paid throughout.[22]

Of course, neither Svertner nor Tralles had served abroad; their reflections were those of the Moravian *Gemeinarzt,* who apparently took the place of the customary German *physicus* and his sources of payment.[23]

Both Tralles and Svertner, and other Moravian physicians as well, compiled drafts of self-help manuals from various sources suited for small domestic and outlying missionary communities. None of these seems to have been published in Germany or abroad, however. Bishop August Spangenberg, Zinzendorf's major American deputy, summarized their reception and actual usefulness in the North American communities. Writing at the end of his life in the late 1780s, Spangenberg related the somewhat quixotic effort to produce a practical medical manual:

> He [Zinzendorf] consulted many physicians and commissioned several to draft a medical compendium to be used in the communities. Blessed Dr. Schmidt from Jena was to my knowledge the last whom he charged with this task.[24] Brother Schmidt did furnish a outline . . . which I was given along with the book by Dr. Richter [likely an edition of *Die höchst nöthige Erkenntnis vom Leibe und natürlichen Leben*] to take to America … But Dr. Schmidt's work turned out to be quite useless for our communities. He had set himself too wide a scope and wrote more in a learned than in a practical manner. In the 1764 synod, the blessed Brother Hocker was then charged with this task.[25] He made a good try and provided us with a nice essay. But our *Doctores* did not advocate printing this work, since they were of the opinion that this would only encourage quacks in the *Gemeinen*, and there were already more than enough of those. Moreover, Hocker had copied most of the content from Tissot. Next Brother Peter Hesse was commissioned to make an excerpt from this manuscript, but he too died before completing the work. There is also a practical and useful book by Brother Gebhard.[26] But it is written in too much of a Brotherly [*brüderische*] style and thus not appropriate for publication.[27]

Thus the writing of a useful manual for physicians and lay brothers and sisters took considerable practical skill, and at least in North America, the works of these men, including so eminently successful a text as the Richter manual, were trumped by the enormous popularity of Samuel Auguste Tissot's *Advice to the People in General* and by the preference of local physicians for their own decision-making. In more ways than one, however, the American preference for Tissot likely reflected a difference in medical resources, and social stratification between European centers, colonial missions to the East, and American diasporas.

This American affinity for Tissot was actually elucidated by Hocker in his introduction to the *Medicinische Unterricht*.[28] Here Hocker noted that he had been charged to provide practical medical instruction for those brothers and sisters in the colonies who lacked a physician and were forced to rely on their own skills. Hocker had recognized the difficulty of making simple but extensive instructions, and wanted to suggest either the Richter manual or another guide. Upon inspection, however, Hocker noted that these texts, while good, were compendious and contained too many medications, and therefore could not be recommended. His remarks make for an astute critique of the Richter treatise, which advertised the Halle Orphanage medications throughout and thus provided relatively little in the way of simple self-help remedies.

At the same time, Hocker disparaged Tissot for concentrating too much on the rural or common people. What Hocker perceived as a defect in Tissot's work, however, ensured its usefulness for a larger market in North America—namely a concentration on the common man and on a simpler approach. Hocker had served in the aristocratic arenas of the Moravian brotherhood in the Baltics and Leuwen and had moved in the rarefied circles of medical missionary work in the Ottoman Empire, which was peopled by diplomats, foreign agents, and high Church officials.[29] He clearly lacked, and would have frowned on, a consciously American and populist perspective, although, as noted by his German-American peers, he seems to have appropriated at least some of Tissot's material.[30]

An Account of Moravian Medical Providers in North America

By the 1750s, a sufficient number of medical providers had arrived from Central Europe for a regional medical culture to arise in North American areas of German settlement. Heinrich Melchior Mühlenberg maintained that there was in fact an excess of medical providers of all backgrounds, particularly in more densely settled areas.[31] A growing number of secular physicians and surgeons arrived over the next decades, and among these were now a cadre of academically trained Moravian physicians, many of whom became dispensing pharmacists and served the Moravian communities from Bethlehem to Betharaba.

Of course the best provisioned communities included the central and generally northern *Gemeinen* like Bethlehem, which commanded a fairly large and continuous medical and caregiver staff, including women *Diener,* who met to discuss patients and patient care issues. The relatively few examples of these conferences yield instructions by the attending physician concerning diet and motion. In the absence of patient records, the patient census at the Bethlehem hospital remains unknown, although it was probably no more than five to ten patients at a time. The existing Bethlehem records indicate common pediatric and adult chronic complaints, though there is no evidence of epidemics.

But as reflected in the concerns raised in Europe, the medical provision for Moravian communities was quite uneven. In contrast to Bethlehem and the northern settlements, outlying communities and missionary settlements lacked adequate provision of doctors. In the southern communities, a single physician, Johann Martin Kalberlahn, one of the first settlers of Betharaba (North Carolina), planted a famous herbal garden that helped to establish an extensive practice and attract patients from far and wide.[32] Indian missionary settlements further west are known to have requested medical materials and preparations among orders of goods to be purchased in centers like Lancaster and Philadelphia. Yet, trained physicians were generally scarce in these outlying settlements.[33]

By the 1770s, however, the Moravian medical community was sufficiently strong and apparently offered rewarding placement for intergenerational training and continuity. For example, Johann Adolph Meyer (mentioned at the 1739 synod), who came to Pennsylvania in 1742, was the son of a pharmacist from Halberstadt. In midlife, Meyer practiced outside the closed Moravian communities but within the Eastern Pennsylvania German medical community. By the time of the Revolutionary War, he had returned to the Moravian community at Lititz, where he died in 1781. The brothers Johann Friedrich and Johann Mattheus Otto were famous for their long Bethlehem practice. Johann Friedrich Otto had studied at the Universities of Jena and Halle, obtaining his medical degree in Halle. He had arrived with the first large Moravian contingent in 1743, practicing in Bethlehem, Lititz, and Nazareth from 1750 to his death in 1779. His brother Johann Mattheus Otto had been apprenticed to their surgeon father in Meiningen and to two physicians in Augsburg. He ran both hospital and pharmacy in Bethlehem, assisted by his wife, Johann Sophia Magdalena, née Dressel, and for a good thirty years by the American born Timothy Horsefield, a native of Long Island and the son of English Moravians who had been reared in the children's home in Bethlehem. The pharmacy was a community-owned enterprise until the 1790s, when it was privatized by another dispensing physician, Johann Eberhard Freytag. It remained a going concern until the end of the nineteenth century.

Other Moravian physician families included Johannes Ettwein, Jr. (son of Bishop Ettwein), who trained under Timothy Horsefield but died at the age of twenty. Christian Friedrich Kampmann learned his medicine at the Barby seminar and served in Germany, in Gnadau, before following a medical call in 1778 to Hope, New Jersey, where he served in British territory. He also had a son who followed in the medical tradition. The Otto family represented another Moravian medical "dynasty." Joseph Otto studied first with his uncle Mattheus and then in Philadelphia for a few years, before returning to a practice in Nazareth in 1774 where he worked until his death in 1820. Heinrich Benjamin Schmidt, despite a full medical degree from Göttingen, married into the Otto family and ran the Nazareth pharmacy from 1804 to 1826. Gottfried Henrich Thurnhard, son of a surgeon and a surgeon himself, went first to St. Thomas and then became an assistant at the Freytag pharmacy until receiving an appointment to Lititz in 1791.

Before attempting to copy a European academic medical hierarchy—such efforts being unsuccessful until the late nineteenth century—American medical practice clearly required a pragmatic approach. As Heinrich Melchior Mühlenberg wrote to his superiors in Germany in the 1750s,

> One who wishes to practice as a doctor of medicine among the English must, first, be experienced in the English manner of surgery; second, he must be sufficiently advanced in the apothecary's art or in chemistry that he can prepare medicinals for internal and external injuries; and third he must be sufficiently knowledgeable in medicine and its constituent disciplines that he can practice on his own. In this manner, a real English doctor is at one and the same time a phlebotomist, surgeon, apothecary, chemist, and physician. A

young fellow who also has some Latin can learn the whole course in this country in about three years, for a fee of about 100 pounds current. Then he can settle here and practice his art without any further examinations or license being necessary.[34]

While this agenda may not have been attractive to well-situated European physicians, it clearly did not deter most Moravian physicians. Not all of these medical immigrants practiced all forms of medical care, ranging at the time from surgery to bloodletting to the compounding of medicines, but most did engage in a wide form of practice, according to their preference and in response to the expectations of their patients. Brother Kalberlahn had both an herbal garden and a little laboratory, but according to de Schweinitz and Siewers, he was also famous as a phlebotomist. Georg Ernst Thilo and George de Benneville, who trained under famous professors in Halle and elsewhere, mixed their own botanical medications and engaged in careful bloodletting, the sine qua non of traditional humoral practice. Similar procedures seem to have been followed by the brothers Otto in Bethlehem.

Conclusion

Over the course of the eighteenth century, German-language practice in the colonies and the new republic followed many of the trends and economic requirements of the larger medical culture of the colonies. Most if not all trained American practitioners laying claim to the title of doctor or physician, regardless of national background or academic training, prepared and dispensed their own medications. Colonial fee bills and custom usually attest to fees for the medication but not the visit, unless surgery or delivery was involved.[35] Even in the 1760s, when a younger cohort of American-born physicians returned from Europe and attempted to de-commercialize the medical profession, most of the reputable and even famous among the American physicians ran their own pharmaceutical businesses, including John Morgan, the Shippens, the Say family, William Brown, and, among the German contingent, Adam Simon Kuhn in Lancaster (the father of Adam Kuhn, later professor at the University of Pennsylvania), Abraham Wagner, and George de Benneville.[36]

In this paper, we can observe similar paths of practice for the fairly large and continuous contingent of Moravian medical providers. These providers from Central Europe were numerous and heterogeneous in background and training, but tended to have increasingly academic levels of medical education. They occupied a solid place in the open medical structures of the colonial and postcolonial period. Together with the services of other trained and untrained laymen and clergy, they probably provided a fair degree of access to medical care for potential patients of

German-language origins. They benefited from religious tolerance, medical markets divided by region, language, and denomination, and the lack of providers in rural areas. Until the end of the eighteenth century and beyond, there was no integrated hierarchical network with academically trained physicians at the center, as did exist in Germany, England, and France, where colleges of physicians, medical councils, and universities ensured a fair amount of top-to-bottom interdependence and control.

Moreover, denominational competition and distrust kept even the German-language practitioners apart from each other, so that we find little specific documentation on whether and how they interacted. The Mühlenberg writings are a good example of this. While there are few sources providing a richer German perspective on the religious, political, and local state of the Commonwealth of Pennsylvania and adjoining colonies, the important community building role of the Moravians is not documented in Mühlenberg's journals and letters, nor are there blow-by-blow accounts of the fierce competition between the followers of Count Zinzendorf and the German Pietist Lutherans for pride of place in German congregations. Likewise, important medical men like the Schwenkfelder Abraham Wagner, who was close to the medical establishment at Mühlenberg's home base, the Pietist Orphanage at Halle, received only cursory mention. Prominent practitioners like George de Benneville, a friend of the Sauer clan, do not feature in Pietist diaries or correspondence at all. And even Georg Thilo, who was part of the Halle network, fell out of favor and was therefore largely ignored.

The newly renascent Moravian literature offers some insight into the structure of medical care in their settlements. Further work with sources both here and in Europe will shed light on our understanding of how therapeutic resources and medical practice developed in North America, from and within a European context. Operating within a humoral system of health and disease, some of these physicians tended toward safety and against heroic treatments of continuous depletion. Like their increasingly secular Scottish and English colleagues, the Moravian and German physicians still drew on a traditional and eclectic reservoir of therapeutic resources that remained the mainstay of America physician practice until the rise of the botanical movements in the early nineteenth century. What remains to be demonstrated is both whether and how the practitioners from Central Europe contributed to the evolution of the eclectic practices of many nineteenth-century American physicians and where they stood with regard to the homeopaths who came over from Europe beginning in the early 1800s. In the longer view, exploration of these and related issues may contribute to a more layered and discriminating understanding of the links between religious and medical traditions in their historical and social contexts.

Notes

1. W. R. Ward, *The Protestant Evangelical Revival* (Cambridge, 1992). For a summary of my own work on transatlantic movements of philanthropy and trade, see most recently Renate Wilson, *Pious Traders in Medicine: A German Pharmaceutical Network in Eighteenth-Century North America* (University Park, MD, 2000).
2. Whitfield Bell, *The Colonial Physician and Other Essays* (New York, 1975), 229; and Bell, "Medicine in Boston and Philadelphia, 1750–1820: Comparisons and Contrasts," in *Medicine in Colonial Massachusetts, 1620–1820* (Boston, 1980); David L. Cowen, *Medicine and Health in New Jersey: A History* (Princeton, NJ, 1964); John Duffy, *The Healers: The Rise of the Medical Establishment* (New York, 1976); J. Worth Estes, "Therapeutic Practice in Colonial New England," in Colonial Society of Massachusetts, ed., *Medicine in Colonial Massachusetts, 1620–1820* (Boston, 1980).
3. Renate Wilson, "The Traffic in Eighteenth Century Medicines and Medical Ideas and the Medicina Pensylvania of George de Benneville," *Pharmacy in History* 44, 4 (2002): 141–151; R. Wilson and W. J. Savacool, "The Theory and Practice of Pharmacy in Pennsylvania: Observations on Two Colonial Country Doctors," *Pennsylvania History* 68, no. 1 (2001): 31–65; R. Wilson, "Eighteenth-Century Practitioners of Medicine from Central Europe: The Pietist Connection," in *Apothecaries and the Drug Trade: Essays in Celebration of the Work of David L. Cowen*, ed. Gregory J. Higby and Elaine C. Stroud (Madison, WI, 2001), 29–55.
4. There is little published work on the medical planning that went into the Moravian missions, although the Unitäts Archiv in Herrnhut contains a range of fascinating sources, some of which I draw on in the following. I thank Paul Peucker, former chief archivist in Herrnhut and now director of the Moravian Archives in Bethlehem, for his generous help and support during a visit to Herrnhut.
5. A French surgeon practiced in Purysburg in South Carolina, for instance, and an army apothecary from Hungary, Andreas Zwifler, served in Ebenezer. See John I. Waring, *Medicine in South Carolina* (Charleston, 1964), and Renate Wilson, "Die Halleschen Waisenhausmedikamente und die 'Höchst-nöthige Erkenntnis' im Kolonialstaat Georgien, 1733–1765," *Schriftenreihe für Technik, Naturwissenschaften und Medizin*, 28 (1991): 108–128.
6. For New England, see in particular Patricia Watson, *The Angelical Conjunction: The Preacher-Physicians of Colonial New England* (Knoxville, TN, 1991); Norman Gevitz and Micaela Sullivan-Fowler, "Making Sense of Therapeutics in Seventeenth-Century New England," *Caduceus: A Humanities Journal for Medicine and the Health Sciences* 11, no. 2 (1995): 87–102.
7. Louis Meier, *Early Pennsylvania Medicine: A Representative Early American Medical History, Montgomery County, Pennsylvania, 1682–1799* (Boyertown, PA, 1976); Andrew Berky, *Practitioner in Physick: A Biography of Abraham Wagner, 1717–1763* (Pennsburg, PA, 1974); J. Woodrow Savacool, "Illness and Therapy in Two Eighteenth-Century Physician Texts," *Caduceus: A Humanities Journal for Medicine and the Health Sciences* 13, no. 1 (1997): 51–66.
8. Christa Habrich, "Untersuchungen zur pietistischen Medizin und ihrer Ausprägung bei Johann Samuel Carl und seinem Kreis" (Habil. diss., Ludwig-Maximilians-Universität, Munich, 1982).
9. It is not clear from the available secondary sources if the Native American missions also had their own medical staff. See the recent work by Carola Wessel, "'We Do Not Want to Introduce Anything New…': Transplanting the Communal Life from Herrnhut to the Upper Ohio Valley," in ed. Hartmut Lehmann et al., *In Search of Peace and Prosperity: New Settlements in Eighteenth-Century Europe and America* (University Park, MD, 2000).
10. Renate Wilson, "Die Halleschen Waisenhausmedikamente"; Renate Wilson and Hans Joachim Poeckern, "A Continental System of Medical Care in Colonial Georgia," *Medi-*

zin, Gesellschaft und Geschichte: Jahrbuch des Instituts für Geschichte der Medizin der Robert Bosch Stiftung 9 (1992): 99–126.

11. Wilson, *Pious Traders;* Jürgen Helm, "Der Umgang mit dem kranken Menschen im halleschen Pietismus des frühen 18. Jahrhunderts," *Medizinhistorisches Journal* 31 (1996): 67–87.

12. The Bethlehem instructions are in UA-Herrnhut, R.2.A.35.2.d. I owe this information and access to Dr. Paul Peucker and Vernon Nelson. For the Catholic medical structures in colonial North America, see Ronald L. Numbers, ed., *Medicine in the New World* (Knoxville, TN, 1987).

13. The synod is recorded in UA-Herrnhut, R.2A.1–3.

14. *Diener* bound to the *Gemeinen* are documented in the so-called *Dienerblätter,* which provide relatively complete information on dates of birth, marriages, training, and other matters.

15. UA-Herrnhut, R.2.A.35.A, Lindsey House conference, 1 January 1754, p. 2.

16. UA-Herrnhut, R.20. D.7, no. 84. "Zinzendorfs theologische Bedenken betr." 30 September 1755. I have not yet been able to identify the texts from which Zinzendorf drew his inspiration.

17. Ibid.

18. UA-Herrnhut, R.28.45, "ein paar lesenswürdige Aufsätze von unserem Bruder Medico Peter Schwerdner and von dem sel. Dr. Tralles (Joh.Wilhelm, d. 1781)." Added by another hand: "Die medicin betr." The *Medizinalordnung* is unpaginated and undated, though the cover date is 1757.

19. Ibid., fol. 1r.

20. Ibid.

21. Ibid., *Medizinalordnung,* n. p.

22. Ibid.

23. Mary Lindemann, *Health and Healing in Eighteenth-Century Germany* (Baltimore, 1996).

24. According to his *Dienerblatt,* Schmidt studied medicine in Jena, his place of birth (b. 1722, d. 1756), and established a pharmacy in Ebersdorf in 1747. In 1748 he went to London, where he was the medicus of the Jüngergemeinde (disciples commune), and then he returned to Herrnhut in 1755. He seems to have been instrumental in the attempt to establish an independent provision of medicinals. A balsam bearing his name was recommended for export to and manufacture in North America as early as 1743 by Zinzendorf, who suggested to Spangenberg that he bring along a "Menschen, der ihm distillieren hilft" (someone who could help him distillation). Protocol of a conference with Zinzendorf, March 1743, in MAB, Zinzendorf Collection, NZ XI, 1.

25. Frederick William Hocker studied theology at Jena and medicine in Helmstedt, and then alternated between medical positions in the Moravian communities in Germany and repeated self-selected missions to Persia and Egypt. During a six-year stay in Herrnhut and Zeist between 1761 and 1768, he authored *A Medical Introduction for Missionaries and Pathology,* before returning to Christian missions with Copts and Greeks and medical practice in Cairo, where he died in 1770. UA-Herrnhut, R.28.43 and 65, and the Hocker *Dienerblatt.*

26. Heinrich Philipp Ludwig Gebhard was a trained surgeon and apothecary who ran the Ebersdorf pharmacy and practiced medicine there for forty years.

27. UA-Herrnhut, R.21.A, no. 168.z, Spangenbergiana, 4–7 ("P. mem. Die medic. Bedienung der Gemeinde betreffend," is here quoted in full).

28. UA-Herrnhut, R.28.33, "Br. Hockers medicinischer Unterricht."

29. Renate Wilson, "Heinrich Wilhelm Ludolf, August Hermann Francke und der Eingang nach Russland," in *Halle und Osteuropa,* ed. J. Wallmann and U. Sträter (Halle, 1997), 83–108.

30. For a similar and apparently common American dilemma, see Renate Wilson, "The Traffic in Eighteenth-Century Medicines and Medical Ideas and the Medicina Pensylvania of George de Benneville," *Pharmacy in History* 44, no. 4 (2002): 141–151. The first American English imprint of Tissot dates to 1771 [Samuel Auguste Tissot, *Advice to the*

People in General, with Regard to Their Health... (Philadelphia, 1771)]. The Richter title is Christian Friedrich Richter, *Seeligen Hn. D. Christian Friedrich Richters Höchst-nöthige Erkenntnis des Menschen, sonderlich nach dem Leibe und natürlichen Leben, oder ein deutlicher Unterricht, von der Gesundheit und deren Erhaltung; ...* (Halle, 1708).

31. Letter to G.A. Francke and M. Ziegenhagen of 9 October 1760, in Kurt Aland, ed., *Die Korrespondenz Heinrich Melchior Mühlenbergs: Aus der Anfangszeit des Deutschen Luthertums in Nordamerika,* 4 vols. (Berlin, 1986–1993), 2:429.

32. Ralph De Schweinitz Sievers and Christiane Maria Sievers, "The Dear Brother Kalberlahn: A Glimpse at Medicine in Colonial North Carolina," *North Carolina Medical Journal* (March 1964): 109–116; Dorothy Long, "Native and Imported Medicines in Eighteenth Century North Carolina," *North Carolina Medical Journal* (January, 1954): 37–38.

33. Wessel in Lehmann et al., "We do not want to introduce anything new."

34. H. M Mühlenberg to G. A. Francke, 14 March and 26 July 1754, letters 145, and 153 in *Korrespondenz Heinrich Melchior Mühlenbergs,* vol. 2.

35. Cowen, *Medicine and Health in New Jersey,* 10–11; Waring, *Medicine in South Carolina.*

36. For Shippen and Morgan, see John Morgan Bell, *Continental Doctor* (Philadelphia, 1965). For the attempt to specialize in medicine only, see Toby Gelfand, "Origin of a Modern Concept of Medical Specialization," *Bulletin of the History of Medicine* 50 (1976): 511–535. More recently on Brown, see David Cowen, "The Letters of Dr. William Brown to Andrew Craigie," *Pharmacy in History* 39 (1997): 140–147.

PART TWO

Moravian Culture and Society:
Identity and Assimilation

– Chapter 5 –

FASHION PASSION: THE RHETORIC OF DRESS WITHIN THE EIGHTEENTH-CENTURY MORAVIAN BRETHREN

Elisabeth Sommer

People, where they are not known, are generally honor'd according to their clothes and other accoutrements . . . from the richness of them we guess at their wealth, and from their ordering of them we guess at their understanding.

Bernard de Mandeville (1714)

No man is ignorant that a tailor is the person that makes our clothes; to some he not only makes their dress, but, in some measure, may be said to make themselves.

The London Tradesman (1747)[1]

IN HIS *LIFE OF JOHNSON*, Robert Boswell remarked, "Dress, indeed, we must allow, has more effect even upon strong minds than one should suppose."[2] Referring to the eighteenth century, fashion historian Christopher Breward argues that clothing came second only to food "as a medium for the display of informed choice by the middling sort."[3] Few articles of material culture have held more power of speech (if only suggestive) than clothing. Indeed, Roland Barthes identified a "fashion system" based on the model of linguistic analysis.[4] Barthes' application of semiotics to fashion has generated a brisk response, both positive and negative. It says much about the relationship between clothing and identity that no one questions whether clothes make a statement; the discussion centers on how they make it. Sociologist Fred Davis put the analysis of dress squarely in the historians' court by insisting on the importance of time and context within the "clothing code." In his view, this "code" is never fully realized because its use of symbols is ever shifting, depending on where and when they appear.[5]

Most analysis of fashion, historical and otherwise, has focused on the relationship between dress, economic development, and social status. While this relationship is undoubtedly important, particularly in the eighteenth century, it threatens to diminish the richness of the concept of dress as symbol. More recently, gender has played an increasingly dominant role in the discussion of dress in response to the semiotic possibilities of fashion. It is worth noting, however, the existence of lacunae in the literature; the relationship between religion and dress has received little attention, yet no aspect of culture is more connected to the use of symbol. The world of the eighteenth-century Moravian Brethren provides the ideal laboratory in which to explore faith and fashion. They formed their communities in a period of significant economic development, intellectual change, and rapid dissemination of fashion along the social scale.[6] Moreover, because the Brethren believed that the daily life of the inhabitants directly reflected their spiritual state, their records give insight into the ways in which they saw dress as a spiritual matter. Women's dress in particular became a powerful signifier of the ideals of the Brethren. By the century's end, however, the desire of the Brethren's leadership to avoid any appearance of socially suspect "uniformity" in dress opened the door to new rhetorical battles with fashion at their center. In this new conflict, the "fashion passion" of younger members of the Brethren became an indicator of their growing restlessness with their parents' expression of piety. The tension over proper dress appeared on both sides of the Atlantic, although its driving force centered in Europe.

As Davis argues, in order to understand the rhetoric by which the female members of the Brethren clothed themselves, we must first understand the context in which they dressed. The development of eighteenth-century fashion, both in "the world" and among the Brethren, can be divided roughly into two periods, with the transition occurring between 1750 and 1770. The first period saw the development of a distinctive dress (or *Tracht*) on the part of the female Brethren (referred to as Sisters), and the second saw the beginnings of a modification in this dress that led to its decline in the nineteenth century. The corresponding development in European fashion generally saw a shift from extreme ornamentation to a greater simplicity. The ironic result put the Sisters in the vanguard of fashionability and robbed their dress of much of its rhetorical power.

As indicated, the eighteenth century was a volatile one, especially in the areas of commerce and fashion. The "middling sorts" became more prosperous and increasingly sought out the newest fashions. Historian Neil McKendrick argues that with the advent of scaled-down fashion dolls and fashion prints a broader audience had access to what was considered fashionable; urban centers and resorts provided additional sources for the spread of fashion across socioeconomic lines.[7]

Although contemporary comments on dress in the eighteenth century ring with laments over the breakdown of sartorial lines of status, the first half of the century was still dominated by clear class distinctions. This was particularly the case in Germany, where the Brethren's communities originated. The enforcement of sumptuary legislation there until the mid century resulted in a slower pace of fashion change among the lower classes, reinforced by a strong tradition of regional dress.[8] These traits came to be reflected in the dress of the Sisters.

The basic wardrobe of the working woman consisted of a shift, stays, a heavy petticoat, skirt, and a fitted jacket; for ornamentation and modesty she might wear a linen or silk neckerchief and an apron.[9] Upper-class dress was characterized by the use of large amounts of highly decorated fabric, especially for court gowns, which could take up to 30 ells (37 yards). Ornamentation often took the form of gold and silver lace, which had to be replaced frequently. Even as fabrics grew lighter toward the mid century, the use of ruffles, lace, ribbons, and jewels increased. The two primary dress forms, the mantua and the sack, were both designed for maximum display of fabric, boasting trains, and overskirts that were often split to reveal a decorative petticoat. The stomacher, which was pinned to the bodice, afforded another surface for display—lace and ribbons by day, jewels by night. Every element worked with the others for maximum impact, whether for the flirtation of the boudoir, or the ceremony of the court.

In many ways, the world that the Brethren made for themselves rested uneasily between the culture of the aristocracy and that of the artisan. Ideally, all of the Brethren were united by devotion to Christ and to the common good, and they referred to each other as "Brother" or "Sister." In effect, the Brethren formed a type of subculture that rejected the standards of "the world" even as they modeled their institutions on worldly ones.[10] The distinctiveness of the Brethren's culture emerged most clearly in the peculiar social arrangement known as the choir system. Within their communities, members of the Brethren were divided not just into biological families, but also into spiritual families, or choirs, according to age, life status, and sex. A choir thus united people from a wide range of social and economic statuses, and within the various choirs the emphasis was on mutual support and harmony. This blend reflected the social makeup of the Unity, with its largely artisan and middle-class membership and heavily aristocratic leadership. This same social blend shaped the development of female dress.

The mixing of social ranks within the devotional life and the choir houses created an atmosphere that posed a real challenge to the social distinctions of dress still prevalent in the German lands. The Brethren's emphasis on spiritual equality enhanced this challenge. As early as 1733, Zinzendorf complained that the women looked like so many "colored birds" and threatened to impose a clothing ordinance.[11] Years later Heinrich von Damnitz remarked that if the Brethren did not want to enforce sartorial distinctions in rank it was "better that the nobility be brought completely to heel, than that the imitation by Brethren of lesser birth be tolerated."[12]

Ironically, this "dressing down" on the part of the nobility was the essence of the *Tracht* (costume) of the Sisters, which was probably in place by the time that von Damnitz made his observation in 1752. The dress that became distinctive among the female Brethren drew heavily on the clothing characteristic of the lower classes. It also embodied the ideal of simplicity that stood in stark contrast to the complex decorative surfaces of upper-class dress. This simplicity and utilization of lower-class forms puts the Sisters' dress in the category of "anti-fashion," characterized by an "oppositional stance" to current fashion.[13] The Brethren recognized the distinctive nature of the dress worn by the Sisters in their use of the term *Tracht* rather than *Kleidung* (clothing) when discussing it.

Most of the discussion of the formation of the Sisters' costume focuses on the cap *(Haube)*. This cap was the most uniform part of their dress, and the most dramatic expression in their antifashion rhetoric. There are at least two versions of the adoption of the cap as the representative headgear of the female Brethren, both written years after its first appearance.[14] Both narratives agree on the basic facts; the cap was first worn by a widow in 1728, who simply adapted the plain white linen cap that was the "ordinary head-covering of the Berthelsdorfer peasant women." Berthelsdorf was the village just over the hill from Herrnhut, and the original settling place of the exiles. The cap itself was a close fitting piece of linen or cotton that came to a peak over the forehead (hence the later term "beaked cap"), and was secured by a separate band that tied at the nape of the neck and ribbons that tied at the chin. Gradually several of the other women in Herrnhut began to wear similar caps, because they found the style to be "something exceedingly simple and dignified." It is worth noting that this description expressed a blend of simplicity and nobility not usually associated with peasant garb. A royal princess (the narrative does not specify of which house or whom) enabled the spread of this fashion when she gave all the Sisters cap fabric, so that the caps could all be made the same. Significantly, the narrative identifies her gesture as "allowing" the upper-class Sisters to "take up this fashion" despite the disapproval of Countess von Zinzendorf, who kept to her usual dress. Since all the visual records of the Brethren, including portraits of Zinzendorf's daughters, show the women in the cap, it must have been in place by the 1740s.[15]

The potential shock value of this headgear when worn by non-peasant women, particularly noblewomen, cannot be overstated. Indeed, the aristocratic leadership of the Brethren was never entirely comfortable with the social challenge implied by the use of the *Haube* as the distinctive headdress of the Sisters. In an intriguing talk in 1747, Zinzendorf imbued the cap with a decidedly spiritual meaning.

> And just as the men have an invisible Shekinah and diadem, … the Sisters
> have a comparable visible diadem, which is modeled on the men's invisible

diadem, the diadem of the high priest, Jesus' burial cloth that covered his head ... Now one sees nothing in the world more similar to Jesus' grave cloth than the Sisters' simple, although orderly and proper, headband.[16]

In this speech, Zinzendorf likened the Sisters' cap to some very powerful sacred symbols. It thus took on multiple meanings, at least among the Brethren. It is unlikely, however, that this sacralization had much rhetorical power outside of the communities. In "the world," the social expression undoubtedly dominated.

Within the communities, the cap served as a platform for further sartorial symbolism in the colors of the ribbons that tied it under the chin. The evidence suggests that these ribbons evolved from a perceived threat to simplicity into a visible sign of the Choir to which the Sister belonged, and that they probably originated among the Sisters themselves. The notation of an exchange of ribbon color between the little girls' and single sisters' choirs supports this view. The colors designated for each choir shifted some over time, but settled into red or green for the children, white with red edging for the teenaged girls, deep pink (rose red) for the single Sisters, deep pink with white edging for the older single Sisters, blue for the married Sisters, blue with white edging for the younger widows, and white for the older widows. In the latter part of the century these divisions were simplified, and the age distinction among the single Sisters' and widows choirs were removed, reducing the choir colors to deep pink for the former and white for the latter.

The colors of the ribbons reflected a long-standing liturgical tradition of color symbolism in which green stood for hope, red for Christ's blood, blue for devotion, and white for purity. The deep pink of the single Sisters, which replaced green in 1750 and had no established liturgical meaning, stood for the rose of the valley from the Song of Solomon, an ironically erotic choice of symbol for the virginal choir.[17] For a period of time, the ribbon colors also played a type of disciplinary role similar to the sumptuary laws that required prostitutes to wear distinctive clothing. In a "Summary Instruction" of 1755, Zinzendorf stated that previously "[t]he Mary Magdalenes, i.e. such female persons who have lived bad lives ... wore a black ribbon," but added that subsequently this practice came to be seen as "ignoble and ungenerous."[18]

Although the documentary evidence suggests that the Brethren's leadership was most concerned with explaining the *Haube*, it only formed one element of the total costume. Pictorial evidence reveals a definite uniformity in the basic dress worn by the Sisters in the eighteenth century, at least by the late 1740s. The costume depicted in almost all portraits and illustrations consists of a jacket laced up the front, with three-quarter length sleeves, a shift, a petticoat, a white neckerchief, and a white apron. The jacket was usually laced with ribbons matching those of the cap. Occasionally small bows were attached to the cuffs of the shift and/or a larger one to the bodice. The colors varied, but no surviving evidence of printed fabric has surfaced. This outfit appears to have been worn by all ranks, including Zinzendorf's daughters. The one clear exception was the countess, who continued to wear the mantua or sack dress. It is worth noting that Zinzendorf's daughters all held official positions within the Brethren, while their mother acted as lord of the manor for her husband's holdings. Her position thus required the signs of secular authority in a way that her daughters' did not.

The dress that completed the costume of the Sisters was essentially that of the working woman. As with the cap, anyone looking at this dress would have immediately associated it with the lower classes. Even a detail such as the white apron held specific meaning, since upper servants in a household typically wore white aprons. The use of open front lacing was quite old-fashioned and, although a regional characteristic of Eastern European dress, also formed a deliberate contrast to the use of highly decorated stomachers. Overall, the elements of the costume combined to signify servanthood, yet when worn by those who were anything but servants in the eyes of the secular world, the message took on a spiritual meaning.

There were other ways in which the elements of dress rhetoric could be tweaked. The various qualities of clothing, such as fabric, color, cut, weave, and transparency, can all be signifiers.[19] As such, these details of dress often act as bricolage to transform one meaning into another, or to mix metaphors.[20] For example, in her history of eighteenth-century dress, Aileen Ribeiro points out that informal styles can be formalized by the use of rich fabric.[21] This frequently happened within the context of fashion development. The mantua began its career as an informal gown, as did the sack dress. In the case of the Sisters' costume, portraits suggest that members of the upper class wore silk and velvet, and their neckerchiefs and aprons were of fine, sheer linen (or perhaps silk in the case of the neckerchief). The intended message was one of spiritual equality, not social equality. It is easy to see, however, how it might have become confused.

As in the case of the cap, some variations on the dress had special meaning only within the community. Most paintings of the Sisters show brown as the predominant color. This is especially the case for Sisters shown in positions of spiritual service, such as helping to distribute the cake and beverage at the Love Feasts. It seems likely that this most humble of colors was worn as the sign of service among the Brethren. Written as well as visual evidence reveals the development of special dress for festival days. In 1749 the Brethren specified that for what they designated as "small celebrations" the Sisters should wear striped jackets and petticoats (usually gray striped), while the Sisters who held office were to wear white. At "great celebrations" (such as Easter Sunday) all the Sisters could dress in white.[22] For members of the community, dress signaled special events within their daily rhythm of devotion, but beyond this, the use of white clothing by the Sisters for high festivals may have been linked to their use of the image of Christ as bridegroom. It would also have enhanced their spiritual presence, since the male officiants wore white robes.

After Zinzendorf's death in 1760, the records of the Brethren show an increasingly practical bent in their decisions, and a desire to reemphasize social distinctions. One manifestation of this was the declaration of the Synod of 1769 that the Sisters should not insist on maintaining the special festival dress. They cited the expense of frequent laundering necessary to keep the light striped and white dresses in good condition as the primary concern. The passage just before this one, however, suggests a general discomfort with the whole notion of "costume" and its signification: "the uniformity or equality [*Gleichheit*] in dress and clothing that has taken such a strong upper hand, so that strangers often think that we are almost all people of one rank and wealth, is unmistakably to be reckoned as a ruinous spirit that has spread among us."[23] This observation indicates that despite the use of bricolage within the elements of dress, the overriding message came from the style of the garment.

The explanation of the development of the Sisters' cap mentioned above comes from a set of instructions for traveling Brethren issued in 1753, which indicates that the leaders were aware that the cap held potential meaning for "strangers" who might see it outside of the *Gemeine*. Evidence also suggests that the Sisters' dress was distinctive enough to be recognized as particular to the Brethren. In a diary entry from 1798, Elizabeth Drinker, a Pennsylvania Quaker, remarked that, "M[ary] Penry sent Peter this morning to M. Stockers for her picture which was drawn forty years ago … in the Moravian dress."[24] By the time Drinker made her observation, however, the discomfort with *Tracht* evident in the Synod Report of 1769 had led to a sustained effort to discourage its use, except for the *Haube*. In part, this campaign formed part of a general move among the Brethren to become more "mainstream" in their activity and theology. It coincided with the growth of a second generation, many of whom apparently found little meaning in the spiritual rhetoric of their elders.

The power of dress to express social and spiritual ideals made it a primary target for commentary in the move toward the mainstream. The language used in 1770 in a section of the newly revised community statutes, or "Brotherly Agreement," connected outward signs with spiritual and moral propriety when it stated, "the godly order in the difference of ranks ought never to be out of sight even in the *Gemeine*."[25] In listing the various elements of this visible "godly order," the "Agreement" included "clothing or the mode of dress" and specified that "at the very least … uniformity in clothing [*Kleidertracht*]" was not to be made a necessity. The "Household Ordinances" of the Herrnhut single Sisters' Choir, revised in 1779, repeated the same theme but expressed attachment, although "merely for order and cleanliness," to the general grammar of simplicity that formed the basis of the *"Gemein-Tracht."*[26] This tension between the discomfort with costume and the desire to avoid vanity in dress grew over the following decades.

Ironically, this same time period saw the beginning of a fashion shift that soon robbed the costume of much of its threatening rhetorical power. Beginning around the 1770s, fashionable dress became increasingly simplified. Flowers and feathers frequently replaced jewels; jewelry was pared down to a few striking pieces; elements of working women's dress, such as the jacket and petticoat, were adopted by members of the nobility; printed linens and cottons overtook silks and brocades for all occasions except appearances at court. This transition began with rather transparent imitations of working dress by members of the French court, prompted by Marie Antoinette. As the mood in France became more revolutionary, so did the use of sober dress styles typical of the middling and working classes. England led the way in the move toward what Breward calls the "bourgeoisation" of fashionable dress, which he attributes to a deliberate "reconstruction" of the aristocratic image in response to criticism of excess.[27] The English aristocracy sought to forestall revolutionary fervor by identifying themselves with reform.

Much of this new "respectable" appearance of the fashionable woman centered on the use of the jacket and petticoat. These items slowly "rose in the social scale," and by the 1780s they dominated fashionable day dress.[28] It became increasingly difficult to tell the lady from her maid, a fact continually lamented by contemporary commentators. The replacement of silk with cotton and linen undoubtedly added to the potential for social confusion. The last decades of the century also saw the gradual triumph of subtle earth tones over the bright colors popular in the early and middle decades.[29] The notable exception to the move to simplicity lay in the hairstyles, which literally grew upward during this period, often reaching perilous heights. Some sign of status needed to be maintained.

The result of these shifts in the language of fashion was to place the costume of the Brethren in a context entirely different from the one in which it originated. As Davis observes, the fluidity of fashion means that "the very same ensemble that 'said' one thing last year, will 'say' something quite different today…"[30] Fashion did not change quite so rapidly in the eighteenth century (although by the end of the century it was coming close), but certainly the costume of the Sisters in the 1780s indeed said "something quite different" from its radical rhetoric in the fashion world of the 1740s. Rather than being antifashion, it stood squarely in the vanguard of fashionability. One element, however, retained its rhetorical strength. The *Haube* remained staunchly opposed to the truly "big hair" favored in the 1780s and early 1790s. Significantly, although the leadership of the Brethren expressed discomfort with the uniformity of the Sisters' costume, they never criticized the cap. The impetus for modification of the *Haube,* and its ultimate restriction to church functions, came from the Sisters themselves in the nineteenth century.

The downplaying of a "spiritual" dress after 1760 did not mean that the Brethren became indifferent to fashion. The records of the 1780s and 1790s contain plenty of fulminations on fashion, but that is precisely the point. By the late century the leadership of the Brethren appears to have been fighting a losing battle against the lure of the new. The danger they risked in discouraging "costume" was to open the door to a greater awareness of, and interest in, fashion. The leadership did continue to use "simplicity" as the ideal measure for dress, and put a spiritual spin on their admonitions. The Synod of 1769, for instance, cited the Old Testament as evidence of divine concern about clothing. The leadership's remarks about dress indicate, however, that they were not thinking of specific sacred clothing, but rather of criticisms of "vanity."

Remarks about dress in the Compendium of Synod Reports for synods held between 1764 and 1789 show two dominant themes: discomfort with uniformity of dress among the Sisters, and a concern for vanity. Both of these themes touch on an underlying motif of anxiety about social order. The term *Gleichheit*, for example, can contain a double meaning of physical "uniformity" and social "equality." The minutes of the single Sisters' committee at the synod of 1789 reveal a connection between clothing and the potential challenge to the social order that other historians of dress have noted as representative of the eighteenth century. The committee remarked that Sisters in service were often "spoiled" by presents of money and "pieces of clothing" given by their employers.[31] In the same context, they also observed, "many citizens [*Bürcher*] of lesser origin and wealth do not want to allow their daughters to go into service." Remarks such as these suggest that the leadership of the Brethren perceived a dangerous social ambition on the part of their lower-class members that was being fostered, at least in part, by the ability to dress up. This concern remained active to the end of the century. On a visitation to Herrnhut in 1797, Jacques Christoph Duvernoy expressed dismay that the daughters of families on poor relief went about in gowns, and told the Herrnhut Aufseher Collegium (Board of Economic Overseers) to refuse to give such people more help from the poor chest.[32]

One of the most detailed discussions of dress took place in 1785 within the chief governing body of the Unity. In the minutes of this meeting, the Unity Elders Conference declared women to be at fault "when they do not cover their neck [read bosom] sufficiently; as to them, <u>otherwise</u> often much vanity shines out from <u>their</u> clothing."[33] They went on to specify (among other things) "neckerchiefs and English gowns of striking colors and patterns." It would seem that uniformity had been sufficiently discouraged. By discouraging the spiritual use of dress as an expression of equality and dedication to Christ, the leadership left only the secular use of dress as an expression of social ambition and success. For the younger Brethren, it also became a means of emphasizing their individuality within the confines of the *Gemeine*.

The new material rhetoric of dress took aim not at the world, but at the older generation among the Brethren. One of the bulwarks of the older generation, Bishop August Gottlieb Spangenberg, wrote a rather blistering letter to the head of the Herrnhut single Sisters in 1780 in which he identified the visual nature of the new threat to the Brethren's spiritual ideal.

> If you ask me what I mean by the horror that has entered into the *Gemeine;* I will say that I mean thereby the worldliness *[Weltsinn]* that the people allow to rule them—I mean the spirit of the world that has the upper hand among them ... I mean the wanton eyes that always look to the world, and would gladly learn something from it—thus it calls in their hearts—Oh, this and that look pretty! Could we not also have it? Thus one increasingly seeks to dress up...[34]

Spangenberg clearly viewed this vanity as focused in the desire to make a visual statement, and to wear what was pleasing to the external rather than the internal or spiritual sense. This same visual component surfaced in the 1785 reference to vanity "shining out" from the clothing of the Sisters.

Despite Spangenberg's focus on the Sisters, the problem with "fashion passion" *[Modesucht]*, as it was often called by the Brethren, was not confined to women. Indeed, much of the debate over new and "striking" modes of dress centered on the Brothers, and suggested a challenge to gender/sexual boundaries within the *Gemeine* in addition to the social challenge already noted. The stage for the incorporation of male dress within the concern for "fashion passion" was set by some dramatic changes in men's clothing beginning in the 1780s. While the changes in women's dress brought the *Gemeine Tracht* within the bounds of fashion, the changes in male fashion posed a stark contrast to the sober coverings favored by the Brethren. In a nutshell, the contours of the male body came to be revealed in a manner not seen since the 1500s (and some contours not even seen then). The record of the discussion within the Unity Elders Conference (UEC) in 1785 contains a detailed description of "obscene" male clothing that indicates just how shocking the new fashion could be to older eyes, as well as the extent to which it had penetrated the Brethren. The UEC identified the offending fashion as the following:

> when the fastening of the jacket ... is too narrow at the bottom, the vests made without fastenings or too short, and (the jacket) so broadly cut out in front that the lower part of the body is not decently and properly covered on either side; further, when Brothers wear an open shirt furnished with a shirt frill under an unbuttoned vest so that the bare breast is visible.[35]

The leadership of the Brethren appear to have been very bothered by what they "read" in the rhetoric of the short, tight jacket and open shirt that characterized the new fashions for men. It is noteworthy that they found the bare male breast potentially provocative. Of course, some aspects of the new male fashions sprang from the same emulation of the lower classes as did the new female fashions. This may have included working men's tendency to go jacketless with unbuttoned shirts, at least in the workplace, thus the shocking nature of the fashion may have been social as well as sexual. In the case of the women, the UEC focused on the increasingly low necklines that, in their minds, absolutely required a proper, but not strikingly colored or patterned, neckerchief.

The leadership took both sexes to task for "vanity," which the UEC seemed roughly to equate with anything that drew attention or appeared exaggerated. For the Sisters, this meant using all sorts of "fashionable ribbons," shoes with high heels "that are indeed harmful," and the aforementioned "striking colors and patterns." The men were criticized for "large fashionable shoe buckles," and the new round, wide-brimmed hats (again, taken from working men's dress). The UEC resolved to instruct the tailors in the *Gemeinen* to refuse to make any of the offending garments, and to expressly forbid them "as being against the *Gemeine* ordinances." This latter move allowed the local ruling bodies of the communities to discipline members for sartorial infractions. No indication of members being disciplined specifically for clothing violations exists in the records; however, the move to include it indicates that the leadership wanted to shine a spotlight on the problem. It also seems likely that a number of the Brethren who were disciplined for "worldliness" and "improper conduct" dressed the part.

The Sisters left no record of their reaction to the 1785 dictate of the UEC, but the minutes of the January 1786 UEC meetings contain a discussion of points raised by the local Elders Conference in Barby, which then served as the seat of the Unity's seminary. The tenor of these suggests that the Brothers desired to be allowed as much leeway as they could manage. For example, the Barby Elders asked whether all round hats were forbidden, and suggested that they should be permitted as long as they were "of proportional size and without [decorative] cords."[36] The UEC decided that even modest round hats were not proper to the sartorial "language" of the *Saal* (assembly hall), and confined them to use on walks. The Barby Elders made a more practical and successful argument regarding white stockings. They pointed out that white ones promoted cleanliness since they had to be changed often, while colored ones were more expensive and did not hold their color. They did, however, allow that silk stockings of any color were not proper for the Brethren. It is worth noting that by 1789, the synod meeting that year decided to move the seminary away from Barby, which they considered too close to the corrupting influence of universities in the area.

Evidence of the continuing struggle to contain the "fashion passion" of the youth in the *Gemeine* surfaced throughout the 1780s and 1790s. The 1789 synod of the single Sisters' committee recommended more vigilance to prevent the older girls and young Sisters from being "so very inclined to outward finery [*Putz*]" and lamented the fact that this tendency "already began with the children."[37] In 1792 the Neuwied Elders Conference observed that in general Church discipline was being neglected, but noted "especially that our young people are not opposed emphatically enough regarding the increasing fashion passion and pride in clothing [Kleider-thorheit]."[38] The next year, the Herrnhut Elders Conference noted the fruit-lessness of all admonitions about "the striking clothing in which many young people make themselves so conspicuous," and later specified "high pointed hats" and "extraordinarily tied cravats."[39] On a visitation to Gnadenberg in 1795, Jonathan Briant referred to the "clothing folly" that he found prevalent among the younger members and noted that after being expelled one young man had openly ridden through the town "in a jacket with yellow lining and a yellow vest."[40] In each of these cases, the disturbing factor was the attention that the mode of fashion called to the individual who indulged in it. The type of fashion that came under fire also strongly suggests that some of the young men within the German *Gemeinen* were skating dangerously close to the English "macaroni" style with its emphasis on flamboyance, a trait that was increasingly associated with effeminacy.

In general, the Brethren in North Carolina appear to have been less inclined to "fashion passion" than were their Continental counterparts. To some degree this may reflect a different cultural environment. In a let-ter to a member of the UEC, Salem official Ludwig Benzien remarked, "The dear Brothers will be surprised that *in North Carolina, where even well-off people take care to dress entirely simply,* that vanity of clothing should have slipped in among the Brethren, and yet this matter has caused us much concern for several years."[41] As implied in this remark, however, the records of their ruling bodies echo the opinions and concerns from across the Atlantic. A circular on dress sent from the UEC in 1781 gave rise to a discussion of "all sorts of costly, unnecessary, and wondrously striking clothing" worn by the local Brethren.[42] Two years later the Elders Conference of Salem resolved to issue an admonition regarding clothing "[s]ince several Brothers use a new improper fashion in their dress."[43] Again, the men were singled out for pushing the fashion envelope. The same pattern surfaced in 1787, in response to a second, and more urgent, circular from Europe. The discussion in Salem closely echoed that of the UEC in 1785, and defined "the desire for fashionable dress" as "a wish to wear something different … and so become noticeable and attract at-tention."[44] The eight specific fashionable infractions listed as having ap-peared among the North Carolina Brethren include only two aimed at the Sisters.

This apparent gender difference in the pursuit of fashion, or at least in the level of concern expressed by the leadership, raises some intrigu-ing questions. Perhaps women felt less driven to mark themselves out by dress. After all, their traditional "simple" dress now appeared very fash-ionable. More probably, men had more options at their disposal, espe-cially since they usually had control of more disposable income. In 1788 the Salem Aufseher Collegium (Board of Economic Overseers) implied a connection between economic ambition and fashion indulgence when they commented that Franz Stauber, who wanted independent power over the sale of his wares in pottery, "dressed in a worldly and expensive fashion which was beyond his means."[45]

For all the concern over vanity in dress, "fashion passion" formed only one element within a general tendency on the part of many younger members of the Brethren to defy the behavioral standards set for them. It is telling, however, that amid the many fronts on which the Unity waged a battle over proper godly behavior, the leadership viewed what members wore as a significant visible indicator of their allegiance, or lack thereof, to Christ and the *Gemeine*. This sign seems to have held more power among the German Brethren than among the Americans, probably because dress in America generally did not display social distinctions to the degree that it did in England or on the Continent.

Over the course of the eighteenth century, the Unity of the Brethren developed and then "deconstructed" a rhetoric of dress that reflected their spiritual ideals. The early "spiritual" dress was largely confined to the women and contained a social challenge in its use of elements of lower-class clothing that were worn by all the Sisters regardless of their rank. After Zinzendorf's death, the leadership of the Brethren grew increasingly uncomfortable with the implications of "uniform" dress and discouraged its use, while seeking to retain the ideal of simplicity. Many of the younger Brethren, however, took the opportunity to express their individualism in their clothing. The fashions of the late eighteenth century gave the men, in particular, a host of "shocking" ways to mark themselves out. The rhetoric of dress that triumphed at the turn of the century was twofold, a visual decoration on the part of the youth designed to draw attention to their person as well as a responsive attempt on the part of the leadership to condemn sartorial indulgence while avoiding any hint of "equality of dress." Everything old is new again.

Notes

1. Quoted in Aileen Ribeiro, *Dress in Eighteenth-Century Europe* (New York, 1984), 43.
2. Ibid., 115.
3. Christopher Breward, *The Culture of Fashion* (Manchester, 1995), 136.
4. Roland Barthes, *The Fashion System* (New York, 1983).
5. Fred Davis, *Fashion, Culture, and Identity* (Chicago, 1992), 5–8.
6. On fashion and the economy see Neil McKendrick, *The Birth of a Consumer Society: The Commercialization of Eighteenth Century England* (Bloomington, IN, 1982).
7. McKendrick, *The Birth of a Consumer Society*, introduction; Breward, *The Culture of Fashion*, 133.
8. Ribeiro, *Dress in Eighteenth Century Europe*, 70.
9. Ibid., 64 and 41.
10. Elisabeth W. Sommer, *Serving Two Masters: Moravian Brethren in Germany and North Carolina 1727–1801* (Louisville, KY, 2000), 16–18.
11. UA-Herrnhut, Herrnhuter Diarium, 24 Oct. 1733.
12. Quoted in Sommer, *Serving Two Masters*, 83.

13. Davis, *Fashion, Culture, and Identity*, 121.
14. The discussion of the development of the *Haube* comes from various sources, which have been compiled with their respective references in UA-Herrnhut, Mappe III/28.
15. Excerpted in Hans-Christoph Hahn and Helmut Reichel, eds., *Zinzendorf und die Herrnhut Brüder* (Hamburg, 1977).
16. UA-Herrnhut, Jünger Haus Diarium, 1747, v. 2, 681.
17. Ibid., 1750, 711.
18. Hahn and Reichel, *Zinzendorf und die Herrnhut Brüder*, 255.
19. Davis, *Fashion, Culture, and Identity*, 13.
20. For a discussion of bricolage see Claude Lévi-Strauss, *The Savage Mind* (Chicago, 1966), 16–36.
21. Ribeiro, *Dress in Eighteenth-Century Europe*, 38.
22. UA-Herrnhut, Mappe III/28.
23. UA-Herrnhut, Harmony of the Four Synods, 1764, 1769, 1775, 1782, v. 1, 430–431.
24. Elaine Forman Crane, ed., *The Diary of Elizabeth Drinker* (Boston, 1991), 1053.
25. Excerpted in Hahn and Reichel, *Zinzendorf und die Herrnhut Brüder*, 315.
26. UA-Herrnhut, R4.C.IV.10.a, Hausordnungen der ledigen Schwestern Herrnhut 1779, no. 14.
27. Breward, *The Culture of Fashion*, 134.
28. Ribeiro, *Dress in Eighteenth-Century Europe*, 105.
29. Ibid., 143.
30. Davis, *Fashion, Culture, and Identity*, 6.
31. UA-Herrnhut, R2.B.48.e, minutes of the single Sisters' Committee from the Beilagen der Synod 1789.
32. UA-Herrnhut, Minutes of the Unity Elders Conference, 23 May 1797, 207–08.
33. Ibid., 20 October, 1785, 151.
34. UA-Herrnhut, R4.c.IV.10.a, August Gottlieb Spangenberg to Henrietta Louisa von Hayn, 1 November 1780.
35. UA-Herrnhut, R3.B.4.f, Minutes of the Unity Elders Conference, 20 October 1785, 150–152.
36. Ibid., 16 January 1786, 138–139.
37. UA-Herrnhut, Minutes of single Sisters' committee, 1789.
38. UA-Herrnhut, R7.G.b.4.b, Extracts of the Minutes of the Neuwied Elders Conference, 29 December 1792, no.2.
39. UA-Herrnhut, Extracts of the Minutes of the Aufseher Collegium Herrnhut, April–June 1793, pt. 6, no. 1; Extracts of the Minutes of the Elders Conference Herrnhut, 24 August 1793, no. 5.
40. Jonathan Briant to Johann Christian Geisler, 28 February 1795. Quoted in Sommer, *Between Two Masters*, 84.
41. MA-SP, Ludwig Benzien to Christian Gregor, 28 February 1787.
42. MA-SP, Minutes of the Salem Elders Conference, 28 August 1781, no. 7.
43. Ibid., 17 April 1782, no. 3.
44. The Minutes of the Helper Conference, 1 Feb. 1787, *RMNC*, 5:2177.
45. Ibid., 5:2231.

– *Chapter 6* –

NEW BIRTH IN A NEW LAND: EVANGELICAL CULTURE AND THE CREATION OF AN AMERICAN IDENTITY

S. Scott Rohrer

AFTER A LIFETIME OF SEARCHING, George Soelle believed he understood the answer to a mystery that Christians had been pondering for centuries: how to achieve eternal salvation. Open your heart to Jesus, Soelle told anyone who would listen, and He will come into your life. Soelle was hardly bashful about delivering this message of eternal life. An energetic missionary who came to Wachovia, North Carolina, in 1770 in the twilight of his career, Soelle traveled extensively throughout the backcountry, spreading the word.[1]

Soelle's eagerness to deliver the joyful message of the new birth was hardly unusual among evangelicals. His spiritual journey was remarkably similar to that of other pilgrims searching to find communion with Jesus Christ, and of those missionaries seeking to help them find it. In an evangelical world, the striking fact was not the differences expressed by leading theologians of the day, but the commonality of the conversion experience among the faithful. In the South, the leading denominations—Baptist, Methodist, Presbyterian, and Moravian—shared a loose kinship based on experiential conversion. This conversion experience transcended race, nationality, and ethnicity, and it helped to create a community of believers that deemphasized differences along denominational and cultural lines.

The role that evangelical religion played in acculturation was complex and fascinating. Fervently reformist, bent on energizing Christian life, evangelism became a rumbling force on the South's social landscape, especially in the inchoate communities of the backcountry. In many places, evangelism helped overcome ethnic barriers and reduced the psychological distances between diverse settlements. The doctrine of that transforming moment known as the "new birth" created a community of believers and helped change how people looked at each other. The results were far reaching, fostering the assimilation of ethnic groups and influencing the interactions of diverse groups in multiple ways.[2]

Few studies, however, have explored how evangelism worked on the community level to foster cultural adaptation. Instead, a majority of historians have interpreted this religious movement as an assault on the values of the gentry and mainstream churches. For historian Rhys Isaac, the radicalism of evangelicals produced a cultural clash in Virginia as the Baptists confronted the gentry with a spirited challenge to their worldly lifestyle centered on tobacco, horse racing, gambling, and drinking. For Nathan O. Hatch, evangelism helped democratize American society by giving power to ordinary people. Countless other historians have likened the explosive growth of the Baptists and Methodists in the nineteenth century to an invasion, with circuit-riding evangelicals putting older churches on the defensive in a cultural war.[3]

Certainly, such scholarship has proved fruitful, illuminating the tensions in Southern society and the radicalism of religion. But this paradigm of cultural conflict continues to dominate historians' understanding of evangelism, with new works merely showing how upstart revivalists made accommodations with the aristocratic elite in the nineteenth century.[4] Few, as a result, have explored the evangelicals' influence on acculturation in early America. By turning to the community and away from the elite, a whole new set of questions emerges. How did evangelism influence settlers' community life? In what ways did people change as a result of these countless encounters between the saved and the unsaved? What did evangelism mean in the lives of ethnic groups that flocked to the Southern backcountry in the late colonial period?

Evangelism's impact can be seen clearly by examining the Moravian *Landgemeinen*, an obscure and little understood part of the Brethren's movement. The Moravian colony in North Carolina was populated in 1800 by about twelve hundred pilgrims from some nineteen countries. Non-German speakers came to comprise at least 12 percent of Wachovia's population. Colonization of the tract began in 1753, when the Unity founded Bethabara. Two church-founded settlements known as *Ortsgemeinen*, or congregation towns, followed: Bethania in 1759 and Salem in 1766. In the *Ortsgemeinen*, elders restricted residency to Church members and expected inhabitants to fully devote their lives to Jesus and the Church.[5]

But there was a second, equally important component to the Moravian mission. Outside the *Ortsgemeinen*, individual groups of former Lutheran, Reformed, and Anglican colonists gathered in Wachovia for spiritual sustenance and economic opportunity. These settlers founded three settlements known as *Landgemeinen*, or farm congregations: German-

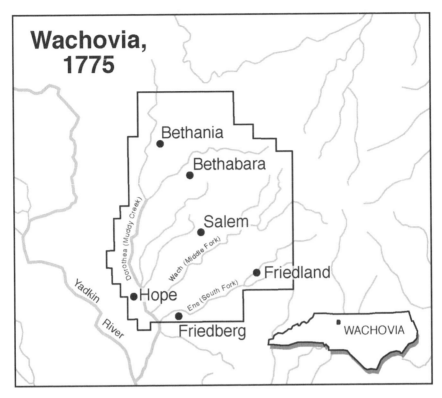

Figure 6.1 The Wachovia Tract and Settlements, 1775 (Map courtesy of Jodie Morris)

speaking Friedberg in the 1760s, German-speaking Friedland in 1771, and English-speaking Hope in 1772. In these farm communities, inhabitants lived with far less oversight from Elders, and they had the option of becoming Society, or partial, members.[6]

Count Nicolaus Ludwig Zinzendorf placed the Moravians at the forefront of a nascent ecumenical movement. He wanted to carry the message of Christ's salvation to all parts of the globe, and in 1727 the Unity began sending missionaries to the Caribbean, Africa, and North America for work among blacks, Indians, and whites. Besides trying to Christianize the "heathen," Zinzendorf established the Diaspora, where Moravian missionaries sought to introduce Christians of other faiths to "heart religion." The goal was not to convert Christians to Moravianism but to awaken hearers to the glory of Jesus Christ and thus revitalize staid church life. The awakened had the option of joining Moravian Societies while remaining members of their home churches. In Pennsylvania, Maryland, and Maine during the 1750s and 1760s, Moravian missionaries not only encouraged settlers to embrace Zinzendorf's heart religion but also to consider moving to Wachovia, where land was cheaper and they could join a unique Christian community based on the new birth. More than two hundred settlers responded before the Revolution, a migration that led to the founding of the three *Landgemeinen*.

The life-altering experience known as the new birth helps to explain how two interlocking aspects of religion and assimilation worked in the late colonial and early national periods. The first aspect was the most fundamental: in the North Carolina backcountry, evangelism helped create the conditions that made intermixing between ethnic groups possible. The conversion experience allowed individuals from different backgrounds to find common ground. Intermixing among evangelicals often resulted in swift and decisive cultural change in the first generation, a corrective to those studies that posit assimilation in generational terms. Evangelical values predisposed immigrant followers to a second and overlapping phase of acculturation. The impulse to reform a worldly culture and revive Christian life meant that evangelicals were engaging the outside world on several fronts, ranging from the frontier store to the meetinghouse—an engagement that ultimately accelerated the process by which German speakers and other immigrants became "American."[7]

A "Sinner's" Rebirth

The new birth was both personal and ritualized, and consisted of a three-step process that varied in length: *vocation*, where one was in a lost spiritual condition; *justification*, where one experienced the liberating power of Jesus Christ; and *sanctification*, where this new relationship with Jesus was cemented. George Soelle's conversion was typical in its intensity and difficulty. He was born in Denmark in 1709 and raised as a Lutheran. But, as Soelle recalled, he did not truly know Him despite his years of church attendance. At age twelve, "I was overcome with such an alarm and fear of God that I went into the church, threw myself on the floor, and besought the dear God with many tears to forgive my sins. My fear passed, and I felt safe, but for twelve more years, I went my own way." As was the case with countless others of the "unsaved," Soelle's rebirth did not come easily or quickly. The tearful Dane recognized he was unsaved, but he did not know what to do about it. Such helplessness led to even deeper feelings of self-loathing. While in school, "I felt how terrible sin was…. For several years, I was greatly oppressed and miserable." Soelle, in short, was rudely experiencing that first terrifying step in the conversion process that all pilgrims had to undertake—vocation, the feeling that one was utterly worthless and corrupt.[8]

Getting to the second stage of the conversion process—justification, where Jesus offers assurance for the pardon of sins—proved to be as daunting for Soelle as it was for others. He credited two sources for putting him on the path to salvation, one mystical and the other earthly. In a series of dreams, Soelle learned of the Savior and, more mysteriously, of the Unity of Brethren, whom he had never heard of. Soelle could make no sense of these nightly visions: "it seemed that I was one of the men who were carrying the body of the Savior, and as it disappeared from our hands, I heard a voice say three times, 'The Brethren have overcome.'" These dreams led to a great deal of soul searching. While true conversion remained beyond his grasp at this point, Soelle decided at the age of thirty-two to become a Lutheran minister. The earthly help came a year later, in 1742, in the form of a Moravian missionary. Brother Grasmann was the first Moravian Soelle had ever met, and his appearance apparently fulfilled the vision that Soelle had had years earlier. Through this chance meeting with Grasmann, Soelle said he "first learned of the sin of all sins, the lack of faith in the atonement of the Savior, which I had not hitherto felt in my heart. Now at last my lost condition was evident to me, and it was hard for me to speak and to preach of the Savior, for I did not yet know Him." Grasmann's plain but persuasive words had struck Soelle with great force and set the stage for Soelle's rebirth. For Soelle, Grasmann's words reinforced his belief that he was lost and corrupt. What he finally came to understand was that he had to open his heart to Jesus. Only then did "the crucified Savior appear to me, as He died on the cross for my sins."[9]

Soelle's difficult journey to salvation was a lonely one, but he was not alone in taking it. Other evangelicals underwent similar and equally difficult journeys. As one historian of Southern evangelicalism has noted, "If the paramount issue was conversion, then all those who shared this experience in some way were members of a vast spiritual community." Soelle intuitively understood that his experience as a sinner was typical, and that he had much to offer to those trying to find spiritual peace. Having successfully been reborn, this Lutheran asked to join the Unity in 1747 and to become a Moravian missionary. The Brethren advised him to serve the Lord in his old post. But Soelle rejected this advice: "I had no rest in my heart until I preached my farewell sermon and set out for the Unity." Soelle reached the Moravian community of Herrnhaag in October, then moved to Marienborn, where he was received into the Moravian congregation in December.[10]

In seeking converts, Soelle brought to his task an empathy for those struggling to achieve a new birth and a certain toughness that the unsaved needed to confront sinful ways. In 1771, Soelle was both patient and stern with George Lang of Friedland who was trying to find the "light." Soelle explained to Lang during repeated visits that no one could be saved until he took that first step to vocation and admitted his worthlessness. On 24 July Soelle reported that he was making progress: "Grace is becoming more and more active in [Lang] and makes him more conscious of his misery and ruin."[11] Moravian views of salvation reflected Count Zinzendorf's Christ-centered philosophy. For the count, a love of Jesus was at the core of an experiential heart religion. The locus of one's faith was to be the heart and not the head. The essence of true belief, the count preached, was an individual's loving relationship with God and Jesus.[12]

The conversion experience facilitated a closeness among Wachovia's diverse population. *Landgemeinen* and *Ortsgemeinen* members may have lived on scattered farms or in congregational towns, hailed from different countries, grown up in different faiths, and descended from different ethnicities, but they were all evangelical cousins who struggled together to achieve a new birth and to maintain it. The new birth also encouraged extensive contact with outsiders, influencing acculturation on a second important level. Konrad Lange, a Diaspora worker in eighteenth-century Europe, noted that Moravian missionary efforts entailed working through other denominations in an attempt to awaken Christians "to the merits and death of Jesus, through which all sectarianism disappears by itself." Such a belief remained paramount into the nineteenth century. Central Elders summed up this philosophy in 1818: "We claim fellowship with all true children of God in other Christian denominations—wishing to live in brotherly union with them all."[13]

With the mandate to carry the gospel to all, Wachovia's congregations welcomed outsiders to its services. Congregational diaries were peppered with references to "strangers" attending services. An entry of 1802 was typical: "In Hope, a large number of persons gathered, of all religious persuasions, so that the Saal could not hold them." The Moravians thus built up a sizable following west of Wachovia that resulted in many outsiders affiliating with the Unity.[14]

Mixing so extensively with English speakers because of their religious values, German-speaking Moravians began to absorb Southern mores on social, economic, political, and even religious levels. This interaction began as early as 1753, when Wachovia was founded, and accelerated in the Early Republic as more "creole" families were created under the first stage of the assimilation process. The brethren grew cash crops for the market, came to embrace slavery, and participated in the "consumer revolution" of the late eighteenth century. They also cast their lot with the Patriot cause in 1776. Such an identity with an Anglo-American political revolution meant that American Moravians were further distancing themselves from their Germanic origins. All of this contact with the wider Anglo-American world produced a wave of change that picked up speed after 1800.

The changes in the early republic can be seen most clearly in evolving religious practices. Striving to be good Americans after 1800, Southern Moravians formed Bible societies, joined the temperance crusade, and celebrated the Fourth of July. They also embraced the burgeoning Sunday School movement that had its roots in the Northern middle-class reform movement of the 1820s. Inside their meetinghouses, Wachovia's Brethren abandoned worship practices that were originally intended to link them with original Christians but had tended instead to separate them from more conventional Christian worship. In the early 1800s, Moravians ceased to prostrate themselves in prayer during communion and knelt instead. In 1818, they no longer exchanged the kiss of peace. For the

Unity, the kiss was meant to signal a moment of union with Christ. Congregation members received new members with the kiss of peace, an act that signaled admission into God's society. Now, like other mainstream churches, the Brethren extended the right hand of fellowship. All these changes meant that Moravians were moving away from radical practices that had attempted to emulate primitive Christianity but that had tended instead to make them "different."[15]

Intermixing in Hope

Because of extensive intermixing among Moravians in Wachovia, equally momentous change was occurring simultaneously on the individual level. The workings of this cultural interaction among Moravians can be seen most clearly by looking at Hope, the only English-speaking settlement in predominately German-speaking Wachovia. Anglo-American emigrés from Frederick County, Maryland, began arriving in Wachovia in 1772, and they established a small but resilient congregation that soon totaled some 150 people.

The inclusive foundation of the new birth smoothed the way for Hope. Indeed, the settlement achieved full congregation status within eight years, the fastest of the three *Landgemeinen*. The language barrier proved to be one of the practical obstacles for Hope to overcome. There is no evidence that Hope's Anglo-American settlers spoke German or bothered to learn it (unlike another group of outsiders who lived in Wachovia–African-American slaves). Instead, Wachovia administrators assigned an English-speaking missionary named Richard Utley to pastor to the new arrivals in 1772.

Besides sharing the new birth, German- and English-speaking brethren came into daily contact in church, farm field, and parlor. From the settlement's earliest days, choir life played a significant part in bringing German and English speakers together. In December 1780, the board overseeing the *Landgemeinen* began making plans to hold *Anfassung* or "speakings" in Hope once a month "in order that one may discuss spiritual topics" with the "young male and female persons" in the congregation. The choirs were organized not by ethnic group but by age, sex, and marital status. The effect of these pietistic conventicles was to break the congregation down into smaller groups that usually met once a month for fellowship to discuss matters of mutual concern. In Hope, the choirs served another function as well: they helped to establish psychological links with the German-speaking Brethren in Salem and elsewhere through the mutual exchange of members. Choir life, in short, helped make Hope part of Wachovia's Church family, narrowing the divide between German- and English-speaking Brethren.[16]

Other community-wide events served the same function. Salem's leaders constantly reminded residents that they were part of not only the

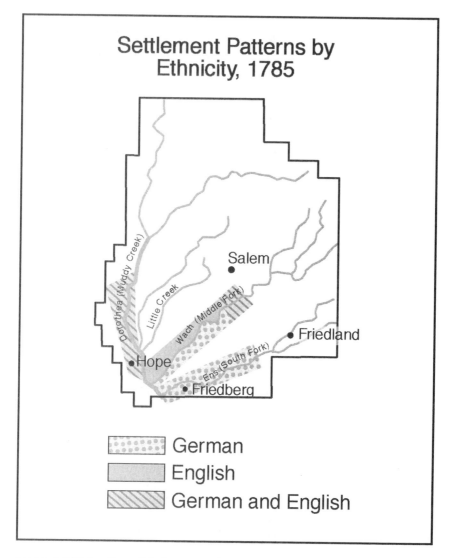

Figure 6.2 In southern Wachovia, English and German speakers lived in close proximity; the intermixing was most pronounced in Hope and along the Middle Fork. (Map courtesy of Jodie Morris)

Wachovia community but a worldwide Church. New Year's Eve festivities especially reinforced this sense of community and brotherhood among far-flung Moravians. All of the settlements gathered at their *gemeine Hauses* for the reading of the Memorabilia of Wachovia congregations that recounted the highlights of the past year. In Hope and the other settlements, the year consisted of an endless round of festivals that ranged from the married people's festival to the older girls' covenant day to the congregation festival. Except for language, little distinguished Hope from its German neighbor to the south, Friedberg. Both settlements developed a strong sense of community despite a backcountry landscape of dispersed, individual farms.[17]

All of these close religious contacts helped lead to close social contacts among German- and English-speaking Moravians. German-speaking members from all settlements mixed easily with their English brethren. One obvious indicator of the amount of intermixing between English and German is the number of German speakers who decided to affiliate with the Hope congregation. By 1810, identifiable German speakers in Hope constituted 32 percent of the population. This was especially significant considering that the settlers who arrived in 1772 were all Anglo-Americans who came with the express purpose of starting an English-speaking settlement. Moreover, the intermixing came relatively rapidly. By 1780, less than eight years after the first Marylanders arrived, the settlement was 12 percent German. Such a swift rise in the German population indicates that intermixing was not merely a generational phenomenon, where second- and third-generation Moravians were less concerned with ethnic divisions. Intermixing began with first-generation settlers.[18]

The close proximity of Friedberg to Hope helped ensure that its German and English members enjoyed especially close ties. This was particularly true from 1772 to 1780, when Hope's members attended services at Friedberg because their settlement did not have a full-time pastor. Hope bordered Friedberg to the north, but there were no firm geographic boundaries between the settlements. Muddy Creek and its two main forks determined where people set up farms.[19]

Friedberg's members lived mainly along the South Fork, but its upper farms spilled over into territory occupied by residents of Hope near the Middle Fork, also known as Salem Creek. More than half of Hope's Society members lived outside of Wachovia. But those residents who chose to reside within this Moravian enclave lived along Muddy Creek and the Middle Fork. Only one German-speaking family lived along the north bank of the Middle Fork—this was strictly English country. Whereas the south bank contained a pronounced ethnic mixing. Settlement patterns on Muddy Creek, near Hope's meetinghouse, also reveal a mix of the two groups. German speakers lived to the south, near Friedberg, while English speakers grouped near Hope's meetinghouse. But the tracts north of the meetinghouse show a variety of German and English. One can discern an English enclave only on the north bank of the Middle Fork, and even there they had German-speaking neighbors directly across the river. In all other parts of Hope, Germans and English lived side by side.

The presence of so many German speakers in Hope, combined with the extensive religious and social contacts between settlements, ensured that the English-speaking Moravians got to know their fellow Brethren intimately. German and English, as a result, forged strong friendships, as baptismal records indicate. Parents who had their children baptized chose their most trusted and respected friends to be their children's godparents or baptismal sponsors. While choirs tended to diminish this role in congregation towns, baptismal sponsors played an important role in social relationships in the *Landgemeinen*. In Hope, the number of English and German choosing sponsors outside of their ethnic groups corresponded to the number who intermarried. In farm communities, such close friendships ultimately influenced marital patterns. Thirty percent of first-generation settlers in Hope married outside their ethnic group— English took German spouses and vice versa. That figure rose in the second generation to 38 percent.[20]

It would be tempting to conclude that close geographic proximity alone was enough to reduce the gap between ethnic groups. Yet, studies of other communities in early America have not found that to be the case. Historian Laura Becker examined Reading, Pennsylvania, a heterogeneous town founded in 1751 northwest of Philadelphia. Like Wachovia, Reading was predominantly German: 83 percent German and 12 percent English. Despite the shared landscape, Becker finds that only 0.6 percent of English and German taxpayers intermarried. She concludes that ethnic divisions were pronounced in Reading because Germans and English married within their own groups. In Germantown, Pennsylvania, 18 percent intermarried—a figure historian Stephanie Grauman Wolf considers high.[21]

What distinguished Wachovia from Germantown and Reading was religion. The Moravian version of evangelism and the strong sense of community broke down the walls of ethnicity in Wachovia. Reading and Germantown lacked such a cohesive religious force. Wachovia's sense of brotherhood and Christian commitment ensured that its members regularly met and mixed. These members shared the bond of the new-birth experience and more. Commitment to heart religion overcame language and cultural barriers to an impressive degree.

A closer look at intermarriage shows how evangelism succeeded in blurring ethnic lines. Among the first generation in Hope, 66 percent of those intermarrying were English men taking German-speaking wives. In the second generation, as more "creole" families were created and ethnicity became even less important, more German-speaking men married English speakers—60 percent versus 33 percent in the first generation. Unity doctrines did not discuss ethnicity. They, instead, advised the Brethren to marry not only out of love for their spouses, but also out of concern for the Savior, the community, and the welfare of their souls. The Unity saw all four as inseparable. Pastors in the North Carolina *Landgemeinen* stressed to parents that they should encourage their children to follow religious considerations and not economic ones in choosing a spouse. Love for their mate and their Savior should guide members' selections, not the desire for a bigger and better farm. Parents, the pastors advised, were to avoid *Kuppeleien*, or matchmakings, that try to set up "their son or daughter … in the material sense."[22]

The evidence is mixed as to how seriously the Brethren took these admonitions. Clearly, young people in the *Landgemeinen* went to great

Figure 6.3 At Hope's meetinghouse, Moravians of different ethnicities interacted in settings that ranged from worship services on Sundays to community
gatherings during the week. (Collection of the Wachovia Historical Society:
Photograph courtesy of Old Salem Museums and Gardens)

lengths to select the partner of their choice. Yet, other evidence indicates
how important religion was to Society members in selecting a mate. For
Adam Spach Jr. of Friedberg, marriage represented a chance to remain
true to his religious principles. Like other evangelicals, this German
speaker struggled mightily to achieve a new birth and to sustain it. Adam's
background was typical of second-generation *Landgemeinen* settlers. He
was born in Maryland in 1753, the year his family moved to Wachovia,
and he grew up in Friedberg, where his father was a founding member of
the congregation. Young Adam felt the first religious stirrings when the
Brethren came to preach at his house in the early 1760s, before Friedberg's
meetinghouse had been built in 1767. It was these sessions that planted
the seeds of his faith.[23]

But Adam did not know what to make of these stirrings. He wan-
dered in a spiritual wilderness for more than four years, until the death
of his sister in 1777 forced him to confront his beliefs. Adam, at last, was
experiencing vocation: "Oh, how wholly reprehensible I felt myself to be!
I had become an enemy even toward my dear Saviour.... I now acknowledged that I was completely dead and cold toward him." After taking this
momentous step—acknowledging his sinfulness—justification followed.[24]

Adam was only twenty-four when he experienced this new birth, but
it represented a lifetime of searching. He well understood that his next
challenge was equally daunting—to avoid backsliding, or "how I might
remain in His possession," as he put it. His solution was an interesting
one: he would find someone to marry. Adam reasoned that his chances of

staying true to his religious principles would improve if he married a de-vout woman. That way, they could battle the forces of sin together. To find such a woman, this German-speaking brother cast his eyes across the meetinghouse benches—and upward. "I prayed without ceasing," he recalled. "I asked: 'Dear Saviour, bring me a person with whom I can live in love and joy, someone with whom I can follow you in my progress through life.'" His prayers were answered in the earthly form of Catharina Tesch, a Friedberg congregant.[25]

Such a shared belief in Christ made it easy to bridge the ethnic divide that separated German from English in Wachovia. Ethnicity was not important to these pilgrims; religious commitment was. In Hope, those English men taking German-speaking wives were, with two exceptions, Society members who lived outside of Wachovia. As Society members, they had the freedom to marry whomever they wanted. And because they lived outside of Wachovia, they had a wide choice of potential partners. Yet, they chose to marry German-speaking Moravians. Obviously, the attraction of this religious world proved to be powerful; they opted for marriages built on the foundations of evangelical experience. For these "outsiders," marriage to a Moravian represented something more; it was a way for them to achieve closer ties with the Unity. Economic motivations appear to have been absent from their considerations.[26]

For German-speaking Moravians entering into Anglo-American unions, religious motivations also predominated. Evangelism was so strong a force that the possible loss of their ethnic identity seemed to matter little to them. From Unity boards on down, Wachovia's inhabitants appeared to be little concerned with preserving their Germanic heritage. Salem's elders, for instance, did not require that schooling be conducted in German, nor did they insist that church services be in German, although they did prefer the use of their native language. Language, to them, was a practical instrument of the Lord—it was a tool that enabled them to take the gospel to more hearers. The attitude of Herrnhut's Board of Unity in 1766 was typical: it instructed a mixed company of English- and German-speaking brethren leaving for Wachovia that "our German Brethren should learn English, & our English Brethren German" so that they could more readily converse with each other and with outsiders. Such an attitude meant that all of Wachovia's settlements were conducting services in English at least once a month by 1803, including in Salem.[27]

German Lutherans, by contrast, saw language as an important marker of their faith and identity. In 1813, a German magazine cautioned North Carolina's Lutherans, "Teaching Children only English is a sign of religious indifference. Children are thus deprived of German religious literature, which, because of the poverty of the English language, cannot be translated." For many German-speaking Anabaptist groups, language helped set them apart from the Anglo-American world and enabled them to maintain a degree of distinctiveness. As historian Harry S. Stout has noted, ethnicity and religion reinforced each other, enabling minority groups to maintain a group identity in a strange new land. Church services, Stout concludes, "become a symbolic rite of affirmation to one's ethnic association and a vehicle for preserving the ethnic language." The maintenance of language and culture, in turn, resided on the twin pillars of church and school. These interlocking institutions inculcated the young in the ways of religion and Germanic culture, allowing German sects to maintain their religious and ethnic identity. Even for Lutheran and Reformed settlers, maintaining their membership in the church of their homeland was an act of allegiance to their heritage. "To belong to a church," historian Stephanie Grauman Wolf points out, "was to accept its cultural orientation along with its doctrine."[28] Ecumenical evangelism worked far differently. The Moravian Diaspora produced a union of diverse people based not on ethnicity but a shared religion. Religion, in effect, became the most important glue in both creating a community and holding it together. Evangelism's broad emphasis on the new birth dampened ethnic identity among Moravian leaders and followers alike.

Wachovia's "Triple Melting Pot"

Extensive intermixing with both outsiders and Moravians of different ethnicities meant that German speakers were increasingly exposed to "American" values, and English-speaking Moravians were exposed to German. Both sides changed as a result. This amalgamation of values can be seen most clearly in the German and English approach to family and testate practices. As A. G. Roeber and other historians have shown, colonists from southwest Germany and Prussia showed an attachment to land and family that rivaled their English counterparts. In Pennsylvania and elsewhere, German speakers devised testate practices whose purpose was to protect the family and keep the family farm running smoothly and efficiently. Anglo-Americans' attachment to family was equally strong, but they followed different strategies to achieve the goal of family protection. English-speaking colonists tended to devolve all of the family land to one or two sons in an attempt to protect the family line; German colonists, by contrast, tended at first to follow southwestern German practices of partible inheritance, where heirs shared equally in family property. In the late colonial period, as acculturation proceeded, the initial German pattern of devolving land equally gave way to the Anglo-American system of favoring sons.[29]

This same process was at work in Wachovia but with a significant difference: an examination of extant wills in Hope and Friedberg shows that German values achieved inroads as well among these former Anglicans. In the late eighteenth century, German speakers in Friedberg and Hope generally followed the ways of southwest Germany. "Share and share alike" was a common phrase in these wills, as they instructed that their property be sold and divided equally among sons and daughters. The

English-speaking settlers in Hope, by contrast, showed a disposition toward rewarding favorite sons. By the early nineteenth century, change can be detected on both sides. In the period from 1760 to 1800, 42 percent of Germans in Hope and Friedberg divided their property equally, but only 33 percent did from 1800 to 1830. While these German speakers in southern Wachovia were absorbing Anglo-American values, English-speaking Moravians were absorbing German: 43 percent of the Anglo-Americans in Hope made an unequal distribution of property in the eighteenth century; only 22 percent did in the later period.[30]

Such a two-way acculturation was also evident in the treatment of sons. German speakers in Wachovia and elsewhere tended to grant land to sons before their passing to ensure a more rational and equitable distribution of family property; Anglo-American fathers did the opposite. Before 1800, no English member of Hope passed on land to their sons before their deaths. But after 1800, 46 percent of first- and second-generation English fathers followed the German practice of bequeathing land while they were alive. At the same time, 53 percent of Germans in Hope and Friedberg in the 1800–1830 period followed Anglo-American practices of waiting to pass on land.[31] Historians of the German immigrant experience typically cite economic factors in explaining such changes in testate practices, especially for the greater use of impartible inheritance: a growing shortage of land combined with rising familiarity with the Anglo-American commercial system caused German colonists to adopt Anglo-American ways. But the experience in Hope shows the importance of cultural contact: intermarriage and close friendships changed both sides on the most basic levels.

This was not simple "assimilation," where an ethnic minority gave way to a culturally dominant group, such as the absorption of French Huguenots into American Protestantism. Instead, a melting pot was at work in Wachovia that, in its early stages, resembled sociologist Ruby Jo Reeves Kennedy's "triple melting pot" theory: two ethnic groups meet, mingle, and coalesce around a shared religion into a new ethnicity.[32] The impact of religion was most pronounced among first-generation settlers in Wachovia, when the cultural differences between English and German were widest. As German and English marriages produced "creole" families, these distinctions blurred even more. Acculturation proceeded at different paces in different settlements. It moved the fastest in Bethania, Friedberg, and Hope, which had the most contact with outsiders, and the slowest in Bethabara and Friedland, which had the least. But in all of Wachovia's settlements, pietistic values and the conversion experience helped propel Moravians toward a unique, and ultimately American, identity. This meant that by 1830, Moravian identity was a complex amalgam. Heart religion remained paramount, and many members still spoke German, but the Brethren now saw themselves as Southern, American, and evangelical.

Notes

1. *Lebenslauf,* or memoir, of George Soelle, reprinted in *RMNC,* 2:804–07.
2. Historians have defined "evangelism" and "evangelicalism" in different ways, the former often meaning the winning of converts in a common faith and the latter the ethos emanating from the revival movement. I define evangelism as a broad reform movement shared by Pietists, Baptists, Methodists, revivalists, and others. It is based on a belief in salvation by faith in Jesus Christ. "Ethnicity" is another troublesome term; I define it as a sense of peoplehood that arises from common heritage, language, and folkways.
3. Rhys Isaac, *The Transformation of Virginia, 1740–1790* (Chapel Hill, NC, 1982); Nathan O. Hatch, *The Democratization of American Christianity* (New Haven, CT, 1989); and Larry E. Tise, *The Yadkin Melting Pot: Methodism and Moravians in the Yadkin Valley, 1750–1850* (Winston-Salem, NC, 1967).
4. See for example Christine Leigh Heyrman, *Southern Cross: The Beginnings of the Bible Belt* (New York, 1997).
5. Birthplaces for Wachovia's inhabitants are derived from biographical cards on file at MESDA, Winston-Salem.
6. S. Scott Rohrer, "Searching for Land and God: The Pietist Migration to North Carolina in the Late Colonial Period," *NCHR* (October 2002): 409–439. For background on the *Landgemeinen,* see S. Scott Rohrer, *Hope's Promise: Religion and Acculturation in the Southern Backcountry* (Tuscaloosa, 2005).
7. Jerry Lee Surratt, for instance, argues that American individualism undermined the religious values of Salem in, "From Theocracy to Voluntary Church and Secularized Community: A Study of the Moravians in Salem, North Carolina, 1772–1860" (PhD diss., University of North Carolina, 1968). Daniel B. Thorp offers the most sophisticated view of Moravian assimilation by arguing that Moravian leaders sought to selectively assimilate while preserving the purity of their faith. Thorp, "Assimilation in North Carolina's Moravian Community," *Journal of Southern History* 52, no. 1 (1986): 19–42; and Thorp, *The Moravian Community in Colonial North Carolina: Pluralism on the Southern Frontier* (Knoxville, TN, 1989). For a fuller treatment of my model and its importance, see introduction to *Hope's Promise.*
8. Soelle, *Lebenslauf.*
9. Ibid.
10. John B. Boles, *The Great Revival: Beginnings of the Bible Belt* (Lexington, KY, 1996), 129; Soelle, *Lebenslauf.*
11. MA-SP, Diary of the Reverend Soelle, 24 July 1771, translation by Kenneth G. Hamilton, F228:3.
12. Ernest F. Stoeffler, *German Pietism During the Eighteenth Century* (Leiden, 1973), 143–150.
13. Lange quote is from John Rudolph Weinlick, "The Moravian Diaspora" (PhD diss., Columbia University, 1951), 31; MA-SP, "Conclusion of the Synod of the United Brethren assembled at Herrnhut in the year 1818 as addressed to the Country Congregations in Wachovia."
14. MA-SP, Hope committee minutes of 8 January 1804 and 11 March 1804.
15. The changes in religious practices are drawn from memorabilia, congregational diaries, and other sources.
16. MA-SP, Land Arbeiter Conferenz (hereafter LAC) of December 1780, Frances Cumnock translation; *RMNC,* 4:2466–2467.
17. *RMNC,* 6:2839.
18. Memoirs and other church records; for details, see Rohrer, *Hope's Promise,* 75–80.
19. Conclusion is based on an 1804 map of Wachovia by Frederick C. Meinung.
20. Memoirs and Hope Church Book; for details on methodology, see Rohrer, *Hope's Promise,* 75–80.

21. Laura Becker, "Diversity and Its Significance in an Eighteenth-Century Pennsylvania Town," in Michael Zuckerman, ed., *Friends and Neighbors: Group Life in America's First Plural Society* (Philadelphia, 1982), 196–221, figure on 203; and Stephanie Grauman Wolf, *Urban Village: Population, Community, and Family Structure in Germantown, Pennsylvania, 1683–1800* (Princeton, NJ, 1976), 132.

22. Gillian L. Gollin, *Moravians in Two Worlds: A Study of Changing Communities* (New York, 1967), 117; and MA-SP, LAC minutes of 14 November 1785, Cumnock translation.

23. *Lebenslauf* of Adam Spach Jr. Between 1802 and 1811, not one marriage proposal was put to the lot in the *Landgemeinen*. See MA-SP, "Book of the LAC concerning Lot votes, 1802–1805 and 1805–1811." For a rare example of an arranged marriage in the *Landgemeinen*, see LAC minutes of 16 September 1785.

24. Spach Jr. *Lebenslauf.*

25. Ibid.

26. See for example Deed Books 2:196 and 4:196, Stokes County, Forsyth County Library.

27. *RMNC*, 2:592, and congregational diaries.

28. William H. Gehrke, "The Transition from German to the English Language in North Carolina," *NCHR* (January 1935), 1–2; and Harry S. Stout, "Ethnicity: The Vital Center of Religion in America," *Ethnicity* (June 1975): 207.

29. A. G. Roeber, *Palatines, Liberty, and Property: German Lutherans in Colonial British America* (Baltimore, 1993), 157. Also see Daniel Snydacker, "Kinship and Community in Rural Pennsylvania, 1749–1820," *The Journal of Interdisciplinary History* (summer 1982), 41–61; and Barry Levy, "The Birth of the 'Modern Family' in Early America: Quaker and Anglican Families in the Delaware Valley, Pennsylvania, 1681–1750," in Zuckerman, *Friends & Neighbors*, 26–63.

30. Will of Matthew Markland, Book 1:81$^{1}/_{2}$, Stokes County Will Book. The figures are derived from an examination of fifty-eight wills in the two settlements. Friedberg is included because of its close relations with Hope and to increase the sample of German speakers; only six wills of German speakers in Hope are extant. Several German families had members in both congregations, and others switched congregations.

31. None of the English Moravian wills from the period 1772 to 1800 indicate that fathers gave land to sons while they were alive, and six wills decreed that sons receive land after their passing. From 1800 to 1830, six of sixteen wills show that fathers gave land while they were alive, and five bequeathed land after their death. In the earlier period, for Germans in Hope and Friedberg, four of fourteen gave land before they died; six gave land after. This percentage who bequeathed land before their deaths is lower than that for the rest of Wachovia—further evidence of intermixing's impact on the first generation in Hope. In the later period, six of twenty-eight gave land before their deaths and fifteen after.

32. Ruby Jo Reeves Kennedy, "Single or Triple Melting Pot? Intermarriage Trends in New Haven, 1870–1940," *American Journal of Sociology* 49 (January 1944): 331–339.

– Chapter 7 –

"COMMERCE THAT THE LORD COULD SANCTIFY AND BLESS": MORAVIAN PARTICIPATION IN TRANSATLANTIC TRADE, 1740–1760

Katherine Carté Engel

THE "ATLANTIC WORLD" HAS BECOME, in recent years, an important construct for early American history, pushing historians to consider traditional stories in new and broader perspectives. The image is compelling. During the seventeenth and eighteenth centuries, tens of thousands of people, both free and enslaved, brought languages, religions, cultures, and diseases to a "New World," where they encountered native languages, religions, and cultures. Multiethnic "contact points" in America reflected these influences and slowly—sometimes violently—developed creole societies unfamiliar to any European, African, or Native American ancestral memory.[1] The spread of evangelical religion and the growth of the early American economy were two important facets of this historical Atlantic World, and each now sports its own body of scholarship. Ministers and congregants corresponded with their counterparts across the ocean, keeping each other informed of their efforts to do God's work in far off places. Revivals (and the techniques for encouraging them) moved from east to west and back again, as did sermons, tracts, and other printed material.[2] Commercial connections were equally deep and lasting. Scholarly emphasis on the "staples model" of colonial economic development has long made clear the link between American agricultural production and European consumption. More recently, studies of the "consumer revolution" have pointed to complex economic and cultural relationships between colonists, native peoples, and European producers.[3]

But despite the importance of religion and the economy to the Atlantic World, the two fields rarely overlap—though the subjects of both types of scholarship lived in the same cities, shopped in the same markets, and worshiped in the same churches. Two notable exceptions to this historiographic segregation, however, indicate that an intricate relationship existed between the religious and the economic in the eighteenth-century Atlantic World, a relationship that deserves further elaboration. Historian Frank Lambert has connected the Great Awakening, and particularly the astonishing career of George Whitefield, to the consumer revolution, demonstrating how Whitefield used new forms of publication and publicity to shape religious revivals. Similarly, and moving beyond the Anglo-American world, Renate Wilson argues that the Halle pietists used the pharmaceutical trade to support their religious endeavors, a system that served both the spiritual and the corporeal needs of thousands of German immigrants in British North America. These two works point to some of the myriad ways religious and economic trends influenced one another in the developing Atlantic economy.[4]

The study of Moravians, with their far-flung missions and tightly-organized communities, benefits greatly from an Atlantic perspective, which links the religious and the economic. First, the community's extensive missionary work demanded ready cash, forcing the group to use economic opportunities creatively. Second, current historiography on the group has created an untenable contradiction. Specifically, scholarship on European Moravian economics has emphasized the group's facile market engagement, while American scholars have created an image of anti-capitalist communitarians confined to the congregation towns of Bethlehem, Pennsylvania, and Salem, North Carolina.[5] Such a discrepancy might be possible in a less tightly organized community, but since in this case the same individuals were involved on both sides of the Atlantic, it is unlikely. Moreover, this division reflects a larger paradox in early American historiography: on the one hand, historians accept the significance of market-driven economic structures in the transatlantic sector, but they simultaneously question the influence of market economies on colonial societies, particularly those with a strong religious current. In other words, it appears that the identification of Moravians with opponents of economic change reflects historiographical assumptions more than it does the results of research.

By restoring the Atlantic dimension of Moravian economic activity, this article addresses these contradictory literatures and argues that Moravian finances—and thus the missions and communities they supported— were integrated in and dependent upon Atlantic market economies. Such a study has implications beyond the sectarian history of the Moravians, a sophisticated and well-placed but small community. It argues that religion played a significant role in the eighteenth-century American economy, a fact that should lead scholars to soften the divide between "market driven" or "profit driven" and "communal" or "moral" economies.

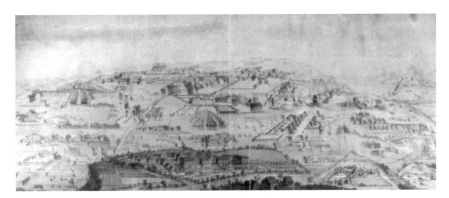

Figure 7.1 The Moravian World. This painting places towns from around the Atlantic World in close proximity, reflecting the Moravians' perception that their dispersed towns were intimately joined. (Moravian Historical Society, Nazareth, PA)

Moravian engagement in the Atlantic World began almost immediately after the community's rebirth in Herrnhut in 1727, under the leadership of the Saxon Count Nicolaus Ludwig von Zinzendorf. The renewed *Brüdergemeine* swiftly attracted newcomers from around Europe, and the vibrant community saw the entire Atlantic World as their missionary field. The first Moravian "pilgrims" headed for the sugar plantations of the Danish West Indies in the early 1730s. Soon afterward, they turned their attention to British North America. Meanwhile, other Moravians established substantial projects throughout the Caribbean, in South America, and in Greenland.[6]

Such expansive missionary and settlement projects proved as expensive as they were successful. During the 1730s and 1740s, a large portion of the necessary financing for these projects came from the Zinzendorf family's own reserves and from funds raised through the group's many connections to wealthy and titled Europeans. Nonetheless, finding sustainable sources of additional funding was crucial. In Pennsylvania, plans for a Moravian town capable of supporting the material needs of North American missionaries developed in the early 1740s in tandem with new missionary schemes. In Herrnhut, merchant Abraham Dürninger eventually brought the Church's business ventures, originally modeled on the Halle enterprises, into the black. No matter how successful these efforts were, however, all the money that came into Church coffers quickly went back out again to fund religious work—chiefly missions, schools, and new settlements. The Church paid for travel by members, the printing of religious literature, the construction of new buildings and communities, and even postage costs for the endless series of meticulous reports that held together this increasingly dispersed and international community. Moravian religious work required Moravian businesses to succeed, and financial success led to greater missionary expansion. Religious fervor and economic necessity thus joined in an inextricable nexus.[7]

Spiritual needs first set the stage for direct Moravian engagement in the Atlantic economy, beginning with a series of ships either purchased or built to transport members across the Atlantic. The missionary opportunities presented by Pennsylvania and the rest of British America were immense, but their plans required hundreds of workers to migrate westward. August "Joseph" Spangenberg, the leader of Moravian work in America before 1760, described Pennsylvania's potential:

> Thus, there are two tasks for the <u>Brethren</u>, who will perhaps go [to Pennsylvania], according to the will of God: The Gospel must be preached to the many thousands [of Europeans] who know nothing of it, or who have an indescribable hunger for it; and the Awakened, who are eager for <u>Fellowship</u>, must be assembled into *Gemeine* [congregations].

Providing pastoral care for the unchurched and newly "awakened" was only the first of the two jobs for the Moravians, however, and even that was "not the work of one, but rather of many." In addition, "there are [also] the <u>Indians</u>," continued Spangenberg, "who would prefer not to live near the Europeans, and for whom perhaps the blessed hour [of salvation] has come."[8]

If the Moravians had been the only ones crossing the ocean, the journey might have been simple, but the sheer number of people who migrated to North America during the eighteenth century created, in the Moravians' eyes, financial and moral dangers to safe passage. During the single decade of the 1730s, over 75,000 people moved to British North America. More than half that number, 40,500, were African slaves suffering forced migration, while the majority of the free migrants, around 25,000, came from Germany and Ireland. German migration alone totaled almost 30,000 individuals during the 1750s, despite the disruptions caused by war in the second half of that decade.[9] The process of immigration was frequently grueling. Lacking funds for the trip, many immigrants indentured themselves to captains to pay for their passage and then found themselves on crowded and filthy ships for a trip that could last for months. Some did not survive, and many others faced years of forced labor in their new country; one third of German migrants between 1720 and 1760 served time as indentured servants, a percentage that increased across that period.[10]

Since transatlantic transportation was a prerequisite to all their American plans, the Moravians decided that owning a vessel was a good way to minimize the perils of the passage and avoid the immigrant trade altogether. Their first ship, the *Catharine*, bought in 1742, aided the American project in two important ways. First, with their own ship the Moravians sidestepped the cycle of debt and servitude that formed such a prominent part of German migration and avoided the individual indentures that could have divided the group upon arrival in America and interfered with their religious plans. Second, migrating as congregations—organized groups with pastoral care—shielded the Moravians from the dangerous and chaotic influences of rough port cities and irreligious fellow passengers. The regular rhythms of daily worship that prevailed on land continued at sea. The Moravians enjoyed a third advantage, but one they would benefit from only later: the ownership of a vessel gradually decreased the price of any single journey and created the potential for profit.[11]

Though the idea of using ships as long-term investments took time to develop, the Moravians made good use of the capital they invested in the *Catharine*, which they sold after her initial journey and whose proceeds they reinvested in their North American projects. On this maiden voyage, the *Catharine* transported the "First Sea Congregation," made up of fifty-six individuals, mainly married people and single Brethren, from London to Philadelphia, arriving on 7 June 1742. Peter Böhler, the minister in charge of the on-board congregation, then sold the ship in that city. His instructions dictated that the *Catharine* be disposed of for no less than £400. From that amount, the crew and captain were paid, and £200 went to the Society for the Furtherance of the Gospel (the Moravian organization that collected money for missionary work from both inside and outside the Moravian community). Any amount left over was to support the new settlement at Nazareth, Pennsylvania. In this way, the capital used to buy the ship immediately went to fund the work the new migrants were doing in America.[12]

The Moravians next decided to procure a ship for more permanent use. Unfortunately, luck did not smile on their first attempt. Nicholas Garrison, a Moravian ship's captain, bought the *Little Strength*, which transported the Second Sea Congregation safely from Rotterdam to New York via London, in September 1743. On the return voyage in the spring of 1744, Spanish privateers captured the ship and temporarily imprisoned Garrison and the rest of his crew. This loss did not deter the Moravians, however, and for their next venture they decided to commission the building of their own ship, the *Irene*, at a Staten Island shipyard.[13] The *Irene* turned out to be the community's most successful investment in Atlantic shipping, both in terms of the number of transported Moravians and the return on the capital investment. The *Irene* first sailed for Amsterdam on 8 September 1748. The ship made thirteen roundtrips over the next decade, most between New York and London, many transporting new Moravian migrants to America or Church workers to Europe, and always carrying letters and news between distant congregations.[14]

The *Irene* represented an investment on the part of the Moravians in their transatlantic community and in the religious security of their members, but when she was not needed in her primary capacity as a *Gemeinschiff* [Congregation ship], the church leased cargo space to both Moravian and non-Moravian merchants. Between 1750 and 1752, and then again from 1755 and 1757, the ship made a total of six transatlantic roundtrips, never with more than sixteen Moravian passengers, and sometimes with no Moravians other than the crew. Captain Nicholas Garrison imported bricks from Holland, for example, which he sold upon arrival in New York. Non-Moravian merchants likewise contracted to transport a wide range of goods on the ship. In 1752, the *New York Mercury* carried ads from Dirck Brinkerhoff, Gerard W. Beekman, William Cockroft, and Garrat Noel for goods "Just imported in the *Irene*[.]" While the first two reported only "A neat assortment of European and Indian Goods," Noel, a bookseller, included a lengthy list of his volumes to entice New York readers. Five years later, in October 1757, five different merchants sold goods imported on the *Irene:* Bernard Lintot, John Smith, David Clarkson, Andrew Barclay, and Francis Lewis. Thus, while the Moravians purchased the ships in order to protect the souls of their travelers and to connect their distant congregations, the prospect for profit from owning such ships did not escape them, and with the *Irene* they made a substantial investment in the Atlantic economy as well as in their own society.[15]

Profiting from the *Irene* required connections to the transatlantic merchant community; examining the individuals who made use of the Moravian investment reveals a further role of religion in the Atlantic economy. The Moravians were not the only religious group with ties to international trade, of course. Jews and Quakers, to name only two groups, depended heavily on their coreligionists for information and trading partners. As the transatlantic economy grew in complexity and size during the eighteenth century, cultural factors such as personal reputation and religious community played a large part in how merchant networks—the backbone of the Atlantic economy—developed and functioned.[16] For the Moravians, who had only a few representatives around the Atlantic rim in cities like London and Amsterdam, each individual merchant played a key role for the Church. Managing the *Irene* on the American side of the ocean fell to New Yorker Henry Van Vleck. His shipping business reached from New York to London, Bristol, and Amsterdam and included both Moravian and non-Moravian connections. Newspaper notices tie Van Vleck to at least seven ships in the transatlantic trade between 1748 and 1762, including the Moravian vessels, *Irene* and *Hope,* for which he was a trustee. The *Concord,* a non-Moravian ship linked to Van Vleck, was captained by Christian Jacobsen, one of the Moravian sailors who worked on the *Irene.* Although he may only have contracted to import goods on some of these ships, he owned part of another boat as well, the *Mercury,* with Samuel Broome & Co.[17]

We can reconstruct at least the outlines of Van Vleck's business from available sources by tracing the web of threads that connected his religious and economic lives. Like many other merchants, Van Vleck's business had several parts, including arranging for cargo to fill his outgoing ships, importing goods from Europe, and selling them in his store on Wall Street. He advertised goods for sale "cheap for cash or short credit."[18] Van Vleck used the *Irene* extensively in his business, making the ship a central part of his trade. He also managed her on behalf of the Church. The ship made thirteen round trips between 1748 and 1757. On many, if not all, of these journeys, Van Vleck imported fabrics, thread, tools, and spices on his own account. His access to the Church's ship thus provided him with an economic advantage. Yet, on the other hand, he also paid for the privilege of using the *Irene*, charging himself over £200 for freight in 1757. Van Vleck also used the Moravian network in his business, relying on ship's captains and coreligionists Nicholas Garrison and Christian Jacobsen to handle much of his trade on the other side of the Atlantic. This trade went both ways, however. When the *Irene* arrived in New York, Van Vleck took charge of the incoming cargo for the captains, including goods sent on consignment. For example, on 29 January 1755, shortly before the ship sailed on its tenth voyage, Van Vleck paid Jacobsen "Fifty Four Pounds Currency being in full for a Trunk of Hose delivered him. I Say Rec'd in behalf of Mr. Thomas Lateward of London." Jacobsen later reported that he paid the money to Mr. Lateward that May. Completing the cycle of exchange when the *Irene* was in the harbor, waiting for a full load, Van Vleck arranged for both "freight and passage" from his shop.[19]

Europe's imperial wars made the Moravians' (and everyone else's) shipping difficult. The *Little Strength* was lost to the Spanish during King George's War, and the *Irene* made half of her voyages after the outbreak of the French and Indian War in 1754. She sailed from New York for the last time on 20 November 1757. Van Vleck estimated her worth full of cargo, including a "Large parcell of Indigo & Coffee," at £40,000. He

Figure 7.2 The *Irene*. Benjamin Garrison, ca. 1750. (Unitätsarchiv Herrnhut, TS.Bd.2.1.)

instructed Captain Jacobsen to "Ransom her as Cheap as he possibly Can but not to Exceed £2000 Sterling" if they were taken by privateers. Andrew Schoute, a Moravian sailor, "will goe as Hostage."[20]

The loss of the *Irene* in 1757 signaled a new era in Moravian commercial enterprise. Although the group made plans to replace her, new avenues for profit deriving directly from the group's missionary network emerged with a new institution, the Commercial Society, which formally combined private and Church capital in transatlantic commerce. Whereas initially shipping had been an afterthought to religious needs, and Van Vleck had combined Church work and his personal business in various ways, the Commercial Society structurally and legally connected religious work and transatlantic commerce. Importantly, while the Moravian merchant network owned and operated the Commercial Society, it was the brainchild of Church leaders, whose discussions provide an important window on the melding of religious and economic interests within the community.

By the mid 1750s, the Church's presence around the Atlantic rim provided it with unusual commercial prospects. Its representatives on the ground—mission workers who were familiar with local markets in places like Pennsylvania, St. Thomas, and Suriname—provided crucial information to merchants in New York, London, and Amsterdam. The communication network built to sustain the religious community also served to transmit economic information, and had done so for years. Indeed, Church leaders in Herrnhut had recognized the economic potential of their network a full decade before the Commercial Society's founding. In 1749, Jonas Paulus Weiss posed the question "whether or not, for the maintenance of the affairs of the Savior, a permissible, honest, upright commerce, manufactures, etc. is to be regarded as a proper thing for the *Gemeine* [Congregation] of the Savior, particularly because, with our extensive establishments in all provinces, the nicest opportunities would be there."[21] As a Moravian leader looking for new enterprises to support his cash-starved Church, Weiss thought it wise to capitalize on the Atlantic World's growing economy. Such endeavors would be "for the maintenance of the affairs of the Savior" (Moravian parlance for missionary work), and therefore the profits would go to the best possible ends.

Over the next decade, the *Irene*'s commercial expeditions went some distance towards answering Weiss's question in the affirmative. But by 1758, after the loss of the *Irene*, there was a new urgency for creating a formal Moravian trading system. Missionary outposts on the western side of the Atlantic, particularly in Suriname, were including goods for trade in their requests for supplies. But Church leaders feared that mingling religious and economic activities too closely might become problematic for the missions. Even Weiss argued that piggybacking trade onto missionary work might cause confusion and adversely affect charitable collections for the missions, since potential donors might think their gifts funded commerce rather than the saving of souls. In May 1758, Weiss proposed that the Moravian Church construct an independent Commercial Society whose profits could fund missionary work. In other words, the group's merchant network would engage in commerce on its own behalf, using information gained from the Church's missionaries. Weiss intended to "find Brethren who, at their own risk and solely for their account, [will] take care of the buying and conveying of wares, and who will freely dedicate half of the profits found therein to the [mission] establishments, and make do for themselves with the other half." The Church could (and did) buy shares in the project, but would be protected from the risk of direct involvement in transatlantic trade. With such an arrangement, "neither the [international Moravian Church] nor the [missions] can or should ever be harmed" by the trade, but they would benefit greatly.[22] Obviously, the plan would appeal only to those merchants who wished to support the Church's religious work (since, as we have seen, most were already engaged in informal joint projects).

Getting approval for the Commercial Society from the Church's bureaucracy required the community to examine its ideas about commerce and trade. That the Moravians accepted transatlantic commerce as useful did not mean that they failed to worry about problems arising from wealth or greed. Indeed, Weiss felt it necessary to reject explicitly such motives for his pet project: "It is not my idea to erect a great company from which one has to fear danger and disadvantage over time, or [to build such a company] out of the intention of becoming rich or otherwise making great profit, where one could be seduced to serve oneself with unequal advantages, or to do someone harm[.]" Quite the contrary, Weiss believed that the Moravians should seize the opportunity in front of them: "one should no longer hesitate, if [the project] were also at first very gentle and small, to start a commerce that the Lord could sanctify and bless." Going a step further, Weiss also dismissed the idea that the commerce he proposed was more dangerous than any other, more "traditional" business:

> The objection, that through commerce the Brethren have so much to do in this work that it could bring their hearts damage, has no more ground than with cobbler's and tailor's work or with other Professions, or from beer and spirit making, or by the sale of natural goods, where the people can also suffer damage, but always, when it happens, are themselves responsible for it, not the commerce or the industry. In this, however, one will try to erect [the Society] in the best way possible so that all damage will be avoided.[23]

Avoiding damage meant ensuring that those who participated in transatlantic commerce kept their eyes on God, guaranteeing that the motive force behind the Society was ultimately to benefit the Moravian Church but in a manner that was in keeping with its values. In essence, however, this moral charge to Society members did not differ from that placed on all Moravian economic actors. As Zinzendorf said in 1754 when addressing what had been perceived as his ambivalence to those engaged in commerce: "It's all the same what one does. When the Savior has given one what is necessary, one takes the talent and uses it." This attitude—that it was the spirit with which one carried out economic endeavor and not the specifics of the enterprise that mattered—lay at the heart of Moravian involvement in the Atlantic economy and in Bethlehem's communitarian workshops and farms. It permitted Moravians to engage in the most profitable sectors of the entire Atlantic economy and to continually innovate in response to new opportunities, provided their motives and the uses to which they put their earnings were pure.[24]

Shortly after Weiss introduced the proposal, the Directorial College (the international Church's governing body) and Count Zinzendorf gave their approval for the Commercial Society, essentially as it had been proposed.[25] The Society offered definite benefits to the Unity. Beyond the obvious profits, it placed the community's commerce in a distinct arena, separate from mission finances yet still able to lend crucial financial support. That level of remove protected the Unity from the financial risks that inevitably accompanied trade, risks the Moravians understood well after having lost two ships at sea. Weiss believed the Society would even help bolster the Church's credit, "[b]ecause when such things [trade] are handled orderly and right (I might almost say with grace), it will support the Brethren's reputation more than when they are only pursued half and half, as it has been going before now."[26]

The Commercial Society was bound up inextricably with the Moravian Church and its religious work and, during the ten years when Church leaders supervised its activities, it was the fullest expression of Moravian integration into the Atlantic economy and of the intermingling of religious and economic networks and goals. It connected Moravian merchants to one another financially, depended on the Church's religious networks for its markets, and turned a third of its profits over to missionary work. Yet, despite its subservience to the Church, its members used it to seek profits as they would any secular trading network. William Smalling, the Society's agent, managed the commerce of the Moravian community, but like Van Vleck before him, he also received a monetary fee for his services. He performed tasks for "the usual Commissions allow'd in the common course of Trade[ ]"[27]

In three distinct ways—through capital, the private activities of members, and the Commercial Society—the Moravians engaged in and profited from the Atlantic economy. In doing so they combined their religious needs with their economic ones. Transatlantic travel and communication were both essential to their religious lives, but individuals and the community as a whole profited from the opportunities created by the Moravians' transatlantic network. The Commercial Society could not have existed without the work of missionaries, and certainly the economic needs generated by the missions gave rise to the project in the first place. Conversely, Moravian missionary work would not have been as successful—arguably would not have existed—without the Atlantic economy and the Moravians' willingness to exploit it.

Moravian engagement in Atlantic trade demonstrates something beyond mission financing, however. It suggests that the religious movements of the eighteenth century and the development of the market economy were intertwined, and that these connections ran considerably deeper than just a few individuals, like George Whitefield, who were directly involved in commercial ventures. Furthermore, taking an Atlantic perspective on the Moravian story indicates that the intersection between religion and economic practice in early America was complicated and fluid. Rather than simply resisting economic innovation, as some historians have suggested was typical of the group's American settlements, the Moravians retained the institutional flexibility and creativity to build communitarian settlements and also invest their capital in profit-making transatlantic commerce. On that base, the group succeeded in building one of the most dynamic early evangelical communities. In short, economic growth fed religious growth in a continuing cycle, not unlike a ship traveling endlessly between Atlantic ports.

Notes

The author would like to extend her sincere thanks to the McNeil Center for Early American Studies, the members of the Harvard Atlantic World Seminar, Michele Gillespie, Robert Beachy, and Jeffrey A. Engel for support and comments during many stages of writing.

1. The literature on the Atlantic World is substantial. For recent treatments, see David Armitage, *The British Atlantic World, 1500–1800* (New York, 2002), and Bernard Bailyn, *Atlantic History: Concept and Contours* (Cambridge, MA, 2005). For the German-speaking world, see Hartmut Lehmann, Hermann Wellenreuther, and Renate Wilson, eds., *In Search of Peace and Prosperity: New German Settlements in Eighteenth-Century Europe and America* (University Park, PA, 2000). For intercultural exchange, see Andrew R. L. Clayton and Fredrike J. Teute, eds., *Contact Points: American Frontiers from the Mohawk Valley to the Mississippi, 1750–1830* (Chapel Hill, NC, 1998).

2. For transatlantic treatments of religion, see, for example, W. R. Ward, *The Protestant Evangelical Awakening* (Cambridge, 1992); Michael Crawford, *Seasons of Grace: Colonial New England's Revival Tradition in Its British Context* (New York, 1991); and Susan O'Brien, "A Transatlantic Community of Saints: The Great Awakening and the First Evangelical Network, 1735–1755," *American Historical Review*, 91 (1986): 811–832.

3. John J. McCusker and Russell R. Menard, *The Economy of British America, 1607–1789* (Chapel Hill, NC, 1991) support the "staples model." Marc Egnal has challenged the traditional synthesis as too difficult to quantify and as unnecessarily obscuring other sectors of the economy. All the same, Egnal places an aspect of the commercial relationship between Britain and her colonies, the terms of trade, at the fore of the factors determining economic growth. Marc Egnal, *New World Economies: The Growth of the Thirteen Colonies and Early Canada* (New York, 1998). For discussions of the "consumer revolution" and its effects, see Carole Shammas, *The Pre-Industrial Consumer in England and America* (New York, 1990); and T. H. Breen, "'Baubles of Britain': The American and Consumer Revolutions of the Eighteenth Century," *Past and Present*, 119 (1988): 73–104. For native peoples and European trade goods, see Daniel K. Richter, *Facing East from Indian Country: A Native History of Early America* (Cambridge, 2001), 42–53.

4. Frank Lambert, *"Pedlar in Divinity": George Whitefield and the Transatlantic Revivals, 1737–1770* (Princeton, NJ, 1994); Renate Wilson, *Pious Traders in Medicine: A German Pharmaceutical Network in Eighteenth-Century North America* (University Park, MD, 2000). See also Harry S. Stout, *The Divine Dramatist: George Whitefield and the Rise of Modern Evangelicalism* (Grand Rapids, MI, 1991).

5. Recent historiographical surveys of Moravian economic life include Peter Vogt, "Des Heilands Ökonomie: Wirthschaftsethik bei Zinzendorf," *Unitas Fratrum*, 49–50 (2002): 154–172; and Gutram Philipp, "Wirtschaftsethik und Wirtschaftspraxis in der Geschichte der Herrnhuter Brüdergemeine," in M.P. Van Buijtenen et al., eds., *Unitas Fratrum: Moravian Studies* (Utrecht, 1975). For Halle's financial organization, see Wilson, *Pious Traders in Medicine*. Works on Moravian economic history emphasizing Europe include, most importantly, Otto Uttendörfer's two books: *Alt-Herrnhut: Wirtschaftsgeschichte und Religionssoziologie während seiner ersten Zwanzig Jahre, 1722–1742* (Herrnhut, 1925); and *Wirtschaftsgeist und Wirtschaftsorganisation Herrnhuts und der Brüdergemeine von 1743 bis zum Ende des Jahrhunderts* (Herrnhut, 1926). Gillian Gollin, *Moravians in Two Worlds: A Study of Changing Communities* (New York, 1967), compares Herrnhut and Bethlehem. Works that emphasize Moravian economic life in North America include: Jacob John Sessler, *Communal Pietism Among Early American Moravians* (New York, 1933), 188; and Michael Shirley, *From Congregation Town to Industrial City: Culture and Social Change in a Southern Community* (New York, 1994). See also Hellmuth Erbe, *Bethlehem, Pa.: Eine kommunistische Herrnhuter-Kolonie des 18. Jahrhunderts* (Stuttgart and Herrnhut, 1929). Several other works have addressed Moravian economics and community in America, although without focusing on economics directly. For Bethlehem, see Craig D. Atwood, *Community of the Cross: Moravian Piety in Colonial Bethlehem* (University Park, PA, 2004); and Beverly Smaby, *The Transformation of Moravian Bethlehem: From Communal Mission to Family Economy* (Philadelphia, 1988). For North Carolina, see Elisabeth Sommer, *Serving Two Masters: Moravian Brethren in Germany and North Carolina: 1727–1801* (Lexington, KY, 2000); Jon F. Sensbach, *A Separate Canaan: The Making of an Afro-Moravian World in North Carolina, 1763–1840* (Chapel Hill, NC, 1998); and Daniel Thorp, *The Moravian Community in Colonial North Carolina: Pluralism on the Southern Frontier* (Knoxville, TN, 1989).

6. For early Moravian missions to the West Indies, see Jon F. Sensbach, *Rebecca's Revival: Creating Black Christianity in the Atlantic World* (Cambridge, 2005). For a brief summary of early Moravian missionary work and its role in the Church's development, see Kenneth G. Hamilton and J. Taylor Hamilton, *History of the Moravian Church: The Renewed Unitas Fratrum, 1722–1957* (Bethlehem, PA, 1967), 34–59.

7. On the practical aspects of Moravian financing, see Edmund de Schweinitz, *The Financial History of the American Province of the Unitas Fratrum and of Its Sustentation Fund* (Bethlehem, PA, 1877). See also Hamilton and Hamilton, *History of the Moravian Church*, 34–59, 76–81, 140–142.

8. Quoted in Joh. Plitt, *Denkwürdigkeiten aus der Geschichte der Brüderunität*, 1828–1841, Volume II, § 205, Manuscript, MAB.

9. John W. Jordan, "Moravian Immigration to Pennsylvania, 1734–1767, with Some Account of the Transport Vessels," *TMHS*, 5 (1899): 40–90. For eighteenth-century immigration figures, see Aaron Fogleman, *Hopeful Journeys: German Immigration, Settlement, and Political Culture, 1717–1775* (Philadelphia, 1996), Table 1.1, p. 2, also passim. See also Fogleman, "From Slaves, Convicts, and Servants to Free Passengers: The Transformation of Immigration in the Era of the American Revolution," *Journal of American History*, 85 (1998): 43–76.

10. Fogleman notes that only one of 830 Moravian immigrants died in transit: "This figure was sixteen times less than the death rate of the northern Kraichgau immigrants and thirty-eight times less than that of all German-speaking immigrants who arrived in Philadelphia." See *Hopeful Journeys*, 126, 1–12. See also Fogleman, "From Slaves, Convicts, and Servants to Free Passengers," 72; and Marianne Wokeck, *Trade in Strangers: The Beginnings of Mass Migration to North America* (University Park, PA, 1999).

11. Jordan, "Moravian Immigration"; Fogleman, *Hopeful Journeys*, 113–126; Joseph Mortimer Levering, *A History of Bethlehem, 1741–1892* (Bethlehem, PA, 1903), 105–127, 166–169.
12. Deed for the Catharine, Box: Peter Böhler Collection, MAB.
13. Jordan, "Moravian Immigration," 58–62. Those on board the *Little Strength* survived and eventually reached their destinations. Garrison's adventures aboard the *Little Strength* represented his second encounter with the Spanish. For his vivid descriptions of his earlier captivity, and his spiritual development while there, see Garrison's *Lebenslauf*, MAB.
14. Jordan, "Moravian Immigration," 63–81.
15. *New York Gazette Revived in the Weekly Post Boy*, 18 June 1750; *New York Mercury*, 8 October 1752, 24 September 1752, 15 October 1753, 3 October 1757.
16. For treatments of religion and merchants' communities, see Thomas Doerflinger, *A Vigorous Spirit of Enterprise: Merchants and Economic Development in Revolutionary Philadelphia* (New York, 1986); Frederick B. Tolles, *Meeting House and Counting House: The Quaker Merchants of Colonial Philadelphia, 1682–1763* (Chapel Hill, NC, 1948); Bernard Bailyn, *The New England Merchants in the Seventeenth Century* (Cambridge, 1955); Nuala Zahedieh, "Making Mercantilism Work: London Merchants and Atlantic Trade in the Seventeenth Century," *Transactions of the Royal Historical Society*, 9 (1999): 143–158; J. F. Bosher, "Huguenot Merchants and the Protestant International in the Seventeenth Century," *William and Mary Quarterly* 52 (1995): 77–101; and Jonathan Howes Webster, "The Merchants of Bordeaux in Trade to the French West Indies, 1664–1717" (PhD diss., University of Minnesota, 1972).
17. The ships were, the *Irene; Hope; Two Brothers* [*New York Gazette*, 17 January 1757]; *Concord* [*New York Mercury*, Supplement, 21 July 1760]; *Charming Rachel* [*New York Gazette*, 18 June 1750]; *Prince of Wales* and *Lamb* [*New York Gazette*, 5 December 1757]. For business connections, see Henry Van Vleck Receipt Book, New-York Historical Society (hereafter NYHS); James A. Scoville, *Old Merchants of New York*, Third Series (New York, 1865), 182–83; Virginia D. Harrington, *The New York Merchant on the Eve of the Revolution* (New York, 1935), 185.
18. Cathy Matson, *Merchants and Empire: Trading in Colonial New York* (Baltimore, 1998), 141. For Van Vleck's business, see advertisements and notices, *New York Gazette Revived in the Weekly Post Boy*, 11 September 1749, 18 September 1749, 18 June 1750, 5 December 1757, 19 December 1757; *New York Mercury*, 19 September 1757 (p. 3 and p. 4), 26 September 1757, 3 October 1757, 21 July 1760 (supplement).
19. *Irene*'s account printed in William C. Reichel, "A Register of Members of the Moravian Church and of Persons Attached to Said Church, in this Country and Abroad, Between 1727 and 1754," *Transactions of the Moravian Historical Society*, no. 1 (1876): 330. Henry Van Vleck Receipt Book, NYHS. Jordan, "Moravian Immigration," 63–86. *New York Gazette*, 17 January 1757. See also newspaper advertisements listed above.
20. Van Vleck to Horsfield, 17 November 1757, Horsfield Collection, MAB. On its previous journey, the captain of the *Irene* was instructed to ransom her for £800 sterling. On that trip, she was underwritten by "R. Livingston and David Van Horne," and paid as much as 15 percent for the insurance, a rate that was not uncommon in that wartime year. Although the *Irene* was most likely insured on her final journey, no record of the terms remains. Van Vleck to Horsfield, 7 March 1757, Horsfield Collection, MAB. For marine insurance, see Matson, *Merchants & Empire*, 268, 419–20, note 9.
21. Quoted in Otto Uttendörfer, *Wirtschaftsgeist*, 37. For discussion of Zinzendorf's position on economic development, see ibid., 36ff.
22. Proposal presented to the Directorial College by Jonas Paulus Weiss, May 17 and 20, 1758, R.04.A.41.1, UA-Herrnhut.
23. Ibid.
24. Quoted in Uttendörfer, *Wirtschaftsgeist*, 48. For discussion of Moravian economic innovation in Bethlehem, see Katherine Carté Engel, "Of Heaven and Earth: Religion and Economic Activity in Moravian Bethlehem, 1741–1800," (PhD diss., University of Wisconsin, 2003).

25. Approval from the Directorial College, R.4.A.41.2; Approval from Zinzendorf, R.4.A.41.4; Artickel des Londonischen Brüder *Commercien* Collegii, UVC I 45, UA-Herrnhut.

26. Proposal presented to the Directorial College by Jonas Paulus Weiss, May 17 and 20, 1758, R.04.A.41.1, UA-Herrnhut.

27. Artickel des Londonischen Brüder *Commercien* Collegii, UVC I 45; Balance sheet from July 58 to June 59, R.4.A.41.12; Balance sheet from July 59 to June 60, R.4.A.41.17, UA-Herrnhut. See also discussions about the Society in the synodal commerce committee records, esp. June 13, 1765, R.4.A.51.1b, UA-Herrnhut. The details and scope of the Commercial Society's trade, and thus its ultimate profitability, are difficult to discern, as no account books have been found either in the United States or in Germany and annual balance sheets do not include sufficient detail. For present purposes, however, its existence, rather than its success or failure, is the key factor.

– Chapter 8 –

PIETY AND PROFIT: MORAVIANS IN THE NORTH CAROLINA BACKCOUNTRY MARKET, 1770–1810

Emily Conrad Beaver

FOR RELIGION MUST OUT OF NECESSITY produce both industry and frugality, and these cannot but produce riches, but as riches increase,
so will pride, anger, and love of the world in all its branches," penned
Methodist evangelist John Wesley. Inspired by the Moravians he met in
England during the 1750s, Wesley grasped the central paradox between
wealth and piety that would plague successful Moravian settlements like
Salem, North Carolina, by the late eighteenth century. In both Old and
New World Moravian communities, the Church controlled every aspect
of life, including the economy. These deeply religious and tightly moni-
tored Moravian settlements almost always thrived because of the frugality
and hard work expected of each member, yet success could undermine
the spiritual commitment Church leaders sought. This tension, apparent
by the mid eighteenth century in the Moravian towns of Herrnhut, Germany, and Bethlehem, Pennsylvania, became increasingly evident deep
in the backcountry in Salem, North Carolina, during and after the American Revolution.[1]

Self-sufficient by 1770, Salem soon developed into an important
source of supplies and goods for backcountry settlers during the American Revolution.[2] Patrons traveled over one hundred miles to buy necessities like pottery, clothing, and salt, often paying in goods since cash was
scarce. This wartime patronage helped transform Salem into a regional
trade center. As the Moravian town increasingly relied on outsiders for
business, Salem's self-sufficient nature waned. When the economy stabi-

lized after the war, trade resumed elsewhere in the backcountry, and Salem's importance diminished. Brethren realigned their merchandise to compete in the widened market, in hope of returning to wartime profits. They disregarded Church controls and flooded the Aufseher Collegium (Board of Economic Overseers) with petitions asking for modifications of regulations that restricted their economic freedom. The Aufseher Collegium, recognizing the need to retain customers and develop new trade, relinquished traditional economic controls intended to maintain Salem's communal culture.

Michael Shirley has written extensively on the breakdown of the congregational system and the loosening of economic controls in Salem during the second quarter of the nineteenth century. He has argued that the process of industrialization and economic expansion, which occurred in much of the burgeoning nation at this time, first affected Salem in the 1820s.[3] But as this essay will show, the relaxing of economic policies, the transformation to a trade economy, and the breakdown of the Moravian community actually began during the American Revolution.

Salem, like other Moravian communities in Europe and the United States, was organized as a theocracy. Every aspect of daily life, from marriage to trade to spiritual wellbeing, was controlled by Church leaders.[4] Each decision and policy was deeply rooted in Moravian religious ideology, including economic sanctions and community control within each *Gemein Ort,* or central congregational town.[5] Moravian ideology turned on a powerful community identity. Founder Count Nicolaus Ludwig von Zinzendorf believed that the practice of religion had to include a social experience in which the faithful could be bound together in brotherly love.[6] While communal religious experience was intended to enhance personal salvation, it also provided an economic crutch for less able members of the community. "Every resident shall work, and eat his own bread," Zinzendorf stated, "but when he is old, sick, or destitute, the community shall take care of him."[7] This mutual support system manifested itself in an community economy controlled by the Church.

In most eighteenth-century Moravian towns in America, including Salem, businesses such as the tavern, the pottery, the tanyard, the store, and some mills were owned by the community as a whole but managed by salaried individuals. Strict prices were set based on the cost of raw materials and labor. Any profits secured went to the Church and eventually back into the community.[8] While surpluses allowed the Church to provide for members in need, other ideological reasons shaped Church regulation and price control as well. Because Moravians believed that Christ was the sole owner of man's possessions, Church Elders and the community were expected to act as the administrators of God's wealth.[9] A 1754 Brotherly Agreement from Bethlehem, Pennsylvania, where the Church controlled property under a system of proprietorships, stated that "what we have, that all belongs to [the Saviour], and He shall dispose of it as pleases Him."[10] While Moravians believed that all their worldly possessions were at the disposal of the community, the Church nonetheless upheld some sanctity of private property by renting Church-owned land to individual members. Church leaders allowed these Moravian tenants to keep all money and goods necessary for themselves and their families before giving any surplus from their labors to the Church.[11]

Moravians considered themselves an elite group of God's chosen people, whose intensely private relationship with God necessitated withdrawal from the outside world.[12] Separation from non-Moravians encouraged the closeness of this spiritual community, and along with the choir system of gender separation, helped avert those ideas, situations, and experiences that might encourage Moravians to lose focus on their spiritual lives. While Church leaders promoted isolation for spiritual reasons, trade with outsiders was nevertheless essential to economic survival in both Europe and America. In an effort to impede the negative influence of worldly ideas gleaned through economic interaction, Church leaders implemented specific economic regulations.

Moravian communities like Salem were regulated so that they produced essential goods without competition. During the first twenty years of Salem's existence, the Aufseher Collegium discouraged personal initiative among artisans by formally sanctioning all businesses, even those privately owned.[13] Each artisan or businessman received a monopoly on his trade to prevent competition.[14] The Aufseher Collegium also discouraged making luxury items like fancy clothes, silver belt buckles, and elaborate pottery, which might draw attention away from God and toward materialism.[15] Instead, the Church encouraged production of simple goods essential to everyday life, like buckskin breeches, everyday pottery, and beeswax candles. While religious reasons prompted the Church to create isolated communities and implement strict economic regulations, it was their self-sufficiency that allowed Moravians to survive in relatively remote settings like the North Carolina backcountry. This economic stability proved both blessing and burden, as shown by Salem's experiences during the Revolution and the early years of the new republic.[16]

More than a decade before Salem was founded in 1767, Moravian settlers in North Carolina had already established a reputation for honest trade, high quality products, and successful settlements.[17] They had come to the North Carolina Piedmont in 1753 as a part of the larger Moravian exodus from Herrnhut that brought missionaries to many other parts of the world, including Sweden, Greenland, and the Caribbean.[18] Lord Granville, a British official well aware of the Moravians' good reputation, proposed to Count Zinzendorf in 1750 that he purchase a large tract of land in the western North Carolina Piedmont.[19] This backcountry appealed to Moravians because of its physical size and limited population. They would be able to settle many Church members here and remain removed from outside threats. A new settlement could also provide a vital source of income for Church leaders as Herrnhut's prosperity declined and political tensions in Saxony grew.[20] The Church purchased one hundred thousand acres of land from Lord Granville in 1752. Two years later Bishop August Gottlieb Spangenberg brought fourteen men from Bethlehem to search for a suitable place to establish a town. In 1753 these settlers established Bethabara, a temporary post, eventually expected to give way to a central congregational town, or *Gemein Ort*, that could support trade with surrounding Moravian settlements and serve as a commercial outpost for backcountry settlers.[21] This *Gemein Ort*, named Salem, was established in 1767 and became the largest town in Wachovia, with 125 residents on the eve of the Revolution.[22]

Even before construction of Salem had begun, Moravians at Bethabara had established economic prominence in a backcountry otherwise peopled by a few hundred Scotch-Irish and German settlers on small family farms.[23] Salisbury, fifty miles south of Salem, marked the only other town in the region, with a mere 150 residents in 1762.[24] This sparse population discouraged the development of widespread economic networks.[25] Bethabara artisans, as well as those in Salisbury, looked elsewhere for large-scale trade opportunities, like markets for thousands of pounds of deerskins. Treacherous mountain passes, the absence of roads, and the northwest to southeast flow of the rivers posed significant problems for the development of east-to-west trade routes within the state. The difficulty of navigating the North Carolina coast discouraged eastern markets. Few ships chanced the dangerous waters around ports like Brunswick and Wilmington in Cape Fear, North Carolina.[26]

Not surprisingly, Moravians and other backcountry traders in the 1750s and 1760s ignored intracolonial markets, pursuing intercolonial markets with Charleston, South Carolina, and Petersburg, Virginia, instead. Safe, widely traveled roads led from Bethabara and Salisbury to Charleston, and the prices paid for frontier exports like deerskins far surpassed the prices paid at Cape Fear. Imported goods like molasses, rum, and sugar, moreover, were sold at a much lower cost in Charleston. In general, Moravian merchants could sell all of their products, including pottery and leather, in Charleston, and at the same time acquire imported goods at reasonable prices.[27]

The Moravians were virtually the only backcountry merchants and businessmen who produced enough goods and possessed the necessary transportation to establish long-distance trade networks at this time.[28] Most settlers relied heavily on local trade networks, fostered by small-scale tavern and shopkeepers, for everyday necessities. Backcountry shopkeepers, with the exception of the Moravians, sold goods on credit to local farmers unable to raise hard cash. As a result, most shopkeepers exacted a significant markup, (one that almost always exceeded 100 percent, and at times rose as high as 400 percent) on the price of their goods.[29] Such high prices made it harder for local farmers to purchase necessities. Moravian merchants like Traugott Bagge, who ran the store at Bethabara and then at Salem, never negotiated prices, however, and were instructed by Church Elders to seek only a marginal profit.[30] Moravian shopkeepers quickly gained the trust of backcountry patrons, which ultimately brought them more trade.[31]

During the 1760s Cape Fear merchants and Governor William Tyron, who knew of the good reputation of these Moravian businessmen, made repeated attempts to facilitate trade with them but failed until better coastal markets and safe, direct roads began to appear.[32] Once Scottish immigrants settled around Cross Creek during the early 1760s, they began establishing sound trade networks in the central part of the state. This development prompted the provincial assembly to open roads that converged at Cross Creek and connected various parts of North Carolina. By 1773 these roads reached from the Cape Fear River into the backcountry and into parts of Virginia and South Carolina. Moravian traders began to send more wagons to Cross Creek, although Cross Creek often had fewer goods.[33] As Moravians took advantage of improved transportation to extend their trade networks within the state, their good reputation made it possible for them to continue to participate in the Cross Creek market once the war was underway.

Salem quickly emerged as the economic center of Wachovia and the Piedmont on the eve of the war.[34] Salem, the center of artisan production among the Moravians, was going full tilt.[35] The other Moravian settlements, Bethabara, Hope, Friedland, and Bethania, reverted to farming.[36] Salem provided Moravian and non-Moravian backcountry settlers with quality goods and services such as watch repair, grain milling, medicine, and access to colonial newspapers imported from Pennsylvania.[37] The fair business practices of Moravians still drew surrounding settlers, and trade with Charleston and Salisbury, as well as eastern North Carolina, continued to grow. The Church continued to provide economic security and a cohesive community that all members could rely on during hard times, and especially during the war.[38] Furthermore, the Moravian community extended far beyond the Wachovia tract. Communications and travel between Wachovia and other Moravian settlements, primarily in Pennsylvania, continued despite the Revolution, allowing Salem's Moravians to use their widespread brotherhood for commercial purposes and communication.[39]

In contrast, non-Moravian merchants and storekeepers suffered during wartime because they had no way to replenish their stock. Imports at the coast, mostly from France since trade with the British declined as tensions mounted, rarely made it to backcountry markets like Hillsborough and Salisbury.[40] In 1777, merchants who had traveled from Philadelphia to Charleston desperately seeking goods made such high bids on imports that backcountry merchants were unable to match them.[41] Moravians, on the other hand, were able to sustain trade in Salem, because of its economic self-sufficiency, and the Church was able to acquire sufficient funds from Moravian artisans and merchants to obtain goods from places like Cross Creek. Indeed, trade in everyday goods in Salem allowed artisans and merchants enough profit to contribute to the Church, as required by the

Aufseher Collegium. Because all artisans and merchants were an extension of the Church community, Church funds were used to purchase items for the stores and supplies for Salem's artisans. As early as September 1774, wagonloads of goods purchased in Cross Creek by Traugott Bagge, manager of the community store, sold out in only a few days due to their scarcity, brining in profit.[42] Moravians like Bagge were allowed to purchase goods in Cross Creek, even though they did not possess the necessary "Liberty Men" certificate because of their refusal to become directly involved in the war.[43]

Opposed to bearing arms, Moravians remained neutral during the American Revolution, although the services they did provide during the war were often more beneficial to the cause than armed men on the front would have been.[44] Moravians often furnished both British and Continental troops with valuable medical services and supplies. This neutrality worked to their economic advantage. Moravian men continued to trade and produce goods while men from other communities were away at the front. Not surprisingly, however, Moravians' refusal to bear arms for either side sparked rumors from Patriots. Some suspected that Moravians in Wachovia were undercover agents for the British crown, or were secretly hiding former royal governor Josiah Martin.[45] These allegations were accentuated by memories of Moravian refusal to join other backcountry settlers against British Governor William Tyron during the Regulator movement of 1771.[46] Suspicions led to threats to destroy Wachovia towns and execute all Moravians so that they could no longer aid the British.[47]

To allay some of these rumors and threats, Moravian leaders attempted to develop positive relationships with local leaders through economic alliances. In 1775, Traugott Bagge became a major purchasing agent for the Continental Army, supplying them with buckskin shirts and moccasins produced in Salem, lead, and guns, all on a "public account."[48] The economic stability of Salem and the Moravians' sound business practices appealed to local military leaders, who soon relied on Moravian artisans and merchants for goods and supplies. Because of their reliability, military leaders like Colonel Martin Armstrong from Surry County typically chose to purchase goods rather than appropriate them. Moravian leaders were able to develop a reciprocal relationship with local leaders. They provided supplies like guns and clothing in exchange for tickets redeemable from the state, and military leaders afforded them protection against threats and "in general...ma[de] things as convenient as possible for [them]."[49]

Advantageous connections with Continental leaders even provided protection against the draft. Political assistance from prominent local officials allowed Moravians to avoid sending drafted men to the front by paying fines or hiring replacement soldiers.[50] As a result, Moravian artisans remained at home to produce much-needed goods, including supplies for the Continental army and local militias, while other backcountry

artisans were required to fight. Thus a mutually dependent economic relationship developed between the Moravian community and local leaders to whom they appealed for political protection during the war.

This continued production allowed Salem to remain economically via-
ble, unlike other backcountry settlements, despite a cessation in British
imports by mid 1776.[51] Salem was so prosperous, however, that skeptics
accused the Moravians of illegally trading directly with the British, as they
had before the war.[52] These suspicions, combined with false accusations
that Bagge and other Moravians had offered arms to Lord Cornwallis,
prompted outside threats from local militia, particularly from Wilkes
County. In 1775, before the war began, the accusations had already become so bad that Bagge actually decreased the stock in his store so that
Salem's supply of goods would not seem so radically different from that
of other backcountry settlements.[53] While the Moravians in Salem were
no longer trading with the British once the war was well under way, it is
a testament to their relative prosperity that even their limited supplies of
goods aroused suspicion.

The economic hardships of war eventually affected Salem, but for the
first few years of the American Revolution, its ability to obtain goods and
maintain production made it the economic hub of a struggling Carolina
economy. Growing numbers of strangers came to rely on Traugott Bagge's
ability to stock his store with essential goods, on artisans' abilities to maintain the production of domestic items such as pottery and clothing, and
on tavern discussions as a source of news and information.[54] In 1775,
Elders recorded that Virginians came to "buy in the store" and gather in
the tavern for "much disputing over the strife of the land."[55] In the same
year, Church Elders remarked that many people came to the Salem store
and workshops for "almost nothing [could] be bought in the stores elsewhere in [their] neighborhood."[56]

Moravian Church records and colonial records attest to economic reliance on Salem not only by soldiers, but by settlers in both the Virginia
and North Carolina piedmonts. In several instances, settlers traveled
more than one hundred miles to Salem to purchase salt. When the supply
sold out, people left weeping.[57] In 1776, the Salem tavern often fed more
than a hundred strangers a day, lodging more than sixty overnight. In fact
the store, the tanyard, and the pottery had more trade than they wanted.[58]
Rumors that pottery was available in Salem brought desperate backcountry settlers, many of whom could pay only in butter, and "an entire burn-
ing [of pottery] was sold in one morning."[59]

By 1776 Salem was one of the only functioning trade centers in North
Carolina. In June that year, Bagge supplied a South Carolina merchant
who usually imported goods to sell inland with linseed oil he was unable
to import at the coast. Elders commented that there were "other occasions
when the Brethren sold to merchants in seaboard towns articles which
were formerly supplied by the seaboard towns to the interior."[60] Salem
was so prosperous and connected that not only could Bagge provide

coastal merchants with otherwise unavailable items, but Brethren noticed increasing "jealousy" among neighboring towns that could not obtain their own goods.[61] Despite Salem's economic stability during the Revolution, the lack of hard currency and the issue of paper money made fair trade difficult.[62] The excessive issue of paper currency in North Carolina and other states prompted massive inflation, until the currency collapsed in 1781.[63] Since hard cash was scarce but paper currency was plentiful, patrons insisted on buying goods with paper money, yet refused to accept it as payment for produce.[64] Produce was virtually the only area in which Salem was not self-sufficient. Townspeople relied on exchanges of goods and money with nearby farmers to supply the town with produce. While this mutual interdependence bolstered Salem during the war, Church leaders feared the worldly influence of these outsiders on the spiritual mindset of Moravian Brethren and often commented that the "passing of people through town was sometimes more than desirable."[65]

Just as Moravians' dependence on outsiders grew over the course of the American Revolution, so did the involvement of Moravians in the affairs of the outside community. Both the Continental army and Lord Cornwallis's troops (who appropriated supplies) increasingly relied on Bagge to supply them with munitions, food, and lodging when they passed through the area. Salem merchants and overseers made it a point to maintain good relations with military leaders like Colonel Martin Armstrong and Captain Joseph Graham, and political officials like the leaders in Richmond, the Surry County seat.[66] As the Revolution came to a close, new political entities like Richmond, created in 1781 and located just five miles north of Wachovia, began to emerge. Church Elders realized that the Revolution had enhanced Salem's place in the Piedmont economy, and as a result, state and local leaders took more interest in its affairs. They responded by taking an interest in the outside world too.

The North Carolina state legislature met in Salem in 1781 and 1782, and Salem hosted the North Carolina General Assembly in 1783.[67] A new state government and increased attention from outsiders could threaten the ability of Church leaders to maintain a distinct religious community.[68] To retain as much control as possible over Salem's future, Moravian leaders sought involvement in the newly developing local governments in Richmond and Brethren ran for and won seats in county offices.[69] This outside political involvement, coupled with the economic needs of Salem after the war, created a conflict with the regulations set forth by Church leaders in order to make Salem a closed community.

After the Revolution the backcountry economy began to stabilize as other artisans returned home and the supply of goods increased. In 1789, Church leaders remarked that more potters had moved into the neighborhood, and though they "ma[d]e little good ware," their presence hurt trade in Salem.[70] Business began to decline when other trading centers like Salisbury drew customers away from the four dozen Moravian artisans in Salem and from Traugott Bagge's store.[71] Because necessities like needles, thread, soap, salt, and pottery had been scarce during the war, Bagge had realigned his merchandise to carry more of these items and fewer indulgences like coffee, sugar, silver, snuff boxes, and fine cloth. At the same time, Moravian artisans typically produced only necessities and not luxury goods. As trade stabilized in the 1780s and 1790s, demand increased not only for luxury items like fine ceramics, clocks, silks, and educational materials, but also for goods not necessary for daily survival, like paper.

The Aufseher Collegium discouraged the mass production of goods that might encourage Moravian Brethren to divert attention from God. Prior to wartime hardships, however, fancy clothes, silver shoe and belt buckles, and fashionable pottery were still produced, though not used, by Moravian artisans.[72] When trade in Salem began to decline after the war and luxury items could be found in nearby Salisbury and Fayetteville, the Aufseher Collegium faced a problem. Although Salem now relied on outsiders for its economic prosperity, it no longer held a monopoly on necessary goods. Patrons were taking their business elsewhere. Church leaders and businessmen would have to look further than daily wares and watch repairs to enjoy the economic success brought on by the Revolution.

Church leaders relinquished provisions made for an ideal community separated from outsiders, and more importantly brought in new trades. The development of the pottery industry, the 1799 arrival of Johann Eberhardt, a professional clockmaker, and the construction and advertisement of the paper mill by Gottlieb Schober illustrate the significant changes the leaders allowed within the greater system of economic controls. Each case signified a shift toward the production of luxury items as the Aufseher Collegium began to cater to the changing local economy and reevaluate economic policies that had been established for communal and spiritual reasons. Its development of new trades meant Salem could provide exclusive goods to Piedmont patrons and thus sustain its significance as an economic center in the North Carolina backcountry despite postwar challenges.

The emergence of the pottery trade, which included importation and production of finer pottery, began during the first few years of Salem's existence, but was not fully realized until the Revolution. In the early 1770s, Bagge obtained the latest imported British ceramics to sell to neighborhood patrons with affluent tastes. When imports decreased with the outbreak of war, Salem could not afford to lose the business brought in by luxury ceramics. Frederick Marshall, a community leader in Salem, after noting the poor selection of imports available at Cross Creek in 1774, reported it would soon be necessary for Moravian artisans to make the wares themselves.[73] Thus when a potter from Pinetree, North Carolina, came to Salem in May of 1774 to demonstrate making "queensware and stoneware," Elders concluded his work represented a "sideline for pottery which can be further developed."[74] The production of imitation British imports and finer ceramics not only developed as the Revolution progressed, but exploded when artisans catered to a more selective back-country populace after the war, many of whom were rising political leaders who came from Richmond and wished to showcase their new wealth and importance.[75]

In addition to encouraging broader product lines, the Aufseher Collegium sought greater varieties of artisans after the Revolution. In 1786, Church Elders wrote to the Unity Elders Conference in Germany that Salem would welcome the arrival of "a clock-maker, a coppersmith, a pewterer, and a book binder, although he would have no work at present."[76] While the single Sisters were producing leather gloves and linens in addition to plain cloth, there was "barely enough work" for the tanners and tinsmiths, who produced more common goods.[77] Although the Elders in Salem had assigned the gun and lock smith, Adam Koffler, to handle simple watch repairs and the town clock, the town needed someone to take on the job full time, sell clocks to the Moravian community, and cater to the surrounding market.[78] This request was answered in 1799 when clockmaker Johann Eberhardt was sent from Germany to Salem.[79] Yet Eberhardt entered the community with more personal initiative than the Aufseher Collegium desired. He was less interested in repairing watches and small clocks than in making them.[80] By 1805, Eberhardt had more work than he could handle and was unable to attend to repairs on the Hillsborough town clock, for which he was responsible, due to his workload.[81]

Because Eberhardt brought in valuable business by providing Salem and the surrounding communities with clocks and large-scale clock repairs, the Aufseher Collegium allowed him to continue otherwise prohibited trade practices rather than permanently exclude him from the community.[82] In opposition to the longstanding theory that trade monopolies discouraged personal competition, the Aufseher Collegium allowed Eberhardt not only to take over the sale of watch supplies from Traugott Bagge, but also allowed John Vogler to handle watch repairs, and, in 1816, to compete with Eberhardt when he could not meet the demand for clocks.[83] In addition, and perhaps more surprising, the Aufseher Collegium allowed Eberhardt to sell watch pieces at a much higher price than Bagge. He was also allowed to expand his business to specialized trades such as piano repairs and scales, and to advertise his products as far east as Raleigh.[84] The reaction of the Aufseher Collegium to Eberhardt's practices, and its acceptance of his numerous breaches of economic regulations, show that Church leaders valued the business Eberhardt attracted and were willing to relinquish some economic controls to increase it.

An even more striking example of the Aufseher Collegium's willingness to tolerate hitherto undesirable economic practices is that of Gottlieb Schober and the Salem paper mill. Schober came to Salem in 1769 at the age of twelve to learn to make deerskin breeches.[85] A shrewd businessman early in his career, he constantly broke community economic regulations to supplement his income. When Schober became a master craftsman in

1780, he was severely reprimanded for purchasing supplies outside Salem to avoid the local tannery markup.[86] His tendency to violate economic sanctions was not, however, curtailed by the admonitions of the Aufseher Collegium even after his petition to work in the Salem store with Traugott Bagge was granted. In 1781, Schober became the assistant manager of the community store, under Bagge, and while he consistently took orders for goods, he also began to trade merchandise on his own.[87] Schober was never excluded from the community although the Aufseher Collegium was well aware its reprimands never convinced him to curtail his activities. Subsequently, in 1789, the Aufseher Collegium allowed Schober to construct a paper mill on the outskirts of town, believing it would bring much needed business as the only paper mill in the Western part of the state.[88] Initial negotiations between Schober and the Aufseher Collegium required he curtail his illegal practices or approval of the mill would be denied.[89] Schober did not cease his side ventures, yet was allowed to proceed because the prospect of the mill's success was so great.

Paper was one of the most sought after commodities in the years following the war. In 1789, North Carolina boasted only one small paper mill in Hillsborough.[90] That same year, the North Carolina legislature granted funds for the construction of mills within the state. These factors provided an added incentive for approving Schober's proposal.[91] The Aufseher Collegium even allowed Schober to advertise to "economical housewives," eager to "serve their country" by providing the rags and worn-out clothing necessary for producing paper in the *Fayetteville Gazette* in 1789.[92] The Aufseher Collegium also permitted Brother George Stockburger, a farmer who had fallen on hard times, to travel the countryside in search of rags, which he exchanged for small articles like needles, buttons, and tape.[93] During his journeys, Stockburger took orders for tinware, to be paid for in rags, and traded in luxury items like snuff boxes, silk, knives, beads, scissors, reading primers, coffee, and tea spoons, all brought in illegally by Schober.[94] The Aufseher Collegium preferred that Schober pay for the rags with hard cash or with paper, but was willing to accept his merchandizing in order to facilitate the paper mill.[95]

By 1791, Schober was advertising his paper as far as Knoxville, Tennessee, and his product was considered equal to that of any paper manufactured in America.[96] The mill brought more business and a wide range of customers to Salem including merchants and printers from Fayetteville, Halifax, Salisbury, and Charlotte, in North Carolina, as well as from Lynchburg, Virginia, and Lancaster, South Carolina.[97] The success of Schober's economic venture relied in part on the fact that the Aufseher Collegium allowed him to conduct business in a manner generally out of line with Moravian ideals.

The development of the mill and the reaction of the Aufseher Collegium reflect Moravian recognition of a changing economy and the need to readjust economic practices to keep up, even if that meant religious compromise. The mill also represented the initial phases of a greater economic change taking place at the turn of the nineteenth century. The communal system in Salem and the provisions in place to enhance Church control were already beginning to break down by the late eighteenth century. Historians like Michael Shirley have argued that the move towards a more industrialized economy, rooted in the Salem paper mill and the textile mill constructed in 1837, led to a capitalist economy based less on personal specialization and more on mass production.[98] Changes, however, were well underway before the antebellum period.

Eventually Salem was subsumed by the larger national economy, and the closed community that leaders strove to maintain gave way to outside forces. The period during and directly following the Revolutionary War represents an important transitional phase in Salem's economy. Its centrality as an economic center during the war generated reliance on outsiders for business, and subsequently, political involvement in the Piedmont, even as it underscored Salem's religious autonomy as a distinct group within a larger community. When the war was over, the Elders in Salem readjusted economic control in order to retain outside business and maintain good political relations with the new American government.

To survive, let alone thrive, Salem had to participate in an outside economic and political system and facilitate interaction with the outsiders that Church leaders so feared. Regulations were ignored and exclusionary rules were bent to adapt. While other historians have documented such a change from the turn of the nineteenth century on, citing shifts in the treatment of slaves, the favoring of Anglican as opposed to German architecture, and the change into a more industrial town, larger economic shifts and Church understanding were already in motion between 1770 and 1810. These changes indicate a conscious effort on the part of Moravians to dispel their reputation as a strange and separate people within the community.[99] They may also reflect the realization that outsiders could influence Moravians to abandon their religious beliefs in favor of more worldly opportunities. Most likely, the changes in economic practices, social ideas, and cultural conventions reflect a little of both.

The economic transition Salem underwent between the Revolutionary and Civil wars can be more fully understood through the changes in Moravian economic practices from the American Revolution through the early nineteenth century. During that time Moravians in Salem were faced with difficult questions about the nature of their tightly regulated lives that would define the future of their community. To maintain the good political and trade relations that Salem enjoyed during the Revolution, Church leaders compromised strict exclusionary and economic regulations, marking the beginning of a steady loss of religious, economic, and community control within Salem that intensified during the first half of the nineteenth century and led to its integration into the larger Anglo-American society by the Civil War.

Notes

1. Gillian L. Gollin, *Moravians in Two Worlds: A Study of Changing Communities*, (New York, 1967), 197.
2. *RMNC*, 2:842.
3. Michael Shirley, *From Congregational Town to Industrial City: Culture and Social Change in a Southern Community*, (New York, 1994), 2.
4. Jerry L. Surratt, "The Role of Dissent in Community Evolution among Moravians in Salem, 1772–1860," *NCHR*, 52, no. 3 (1975): 236.
5. Gollin, *Moravians in Two Worlds*, 15; David R. Morris, "Permanence for the House of Passage: The Establishment of Historic Bethabara Park, Winston Salem, North Carolina," MA thesis, Wake Forest University, 1994), 13–14.
6. Gollin, *Moravians in Two Worlds*, 15.
7. Ibid., 132.
8. Surratt, "Dissent in Community Evolution," 240.
9. Gollin, *Moravians in Two Worlds*, 217.
10. Ibid., 140.
11. Ibid., 140; and Surratt, "Dissent in Community Evolution," 239.
12. Gollin, *Moravians in Two Worlds*, 14–15.
13. Jerry L. Surratt, *Gottlieb Schober of Salem: Discipleship and Ecumenical Vision in an Early Moravian Town* (Macon, GA, 1983), 2.
14. Ibid.
15. Surratt, "Dissent in Community Evolution," 239.
16. See Gollin, *Moravians in Two Worlds*.
17. Morris, "Permanence for the House of Passage," 6.
18. Ibid., 5; Morris, "Permanence for the House of Passage," 5–6; Aaron Fogleman, "Moravian Immigration and Settlement in British North America, 1734–1775," *TMHS*, 26 (1996): 23; John R. Weinlick, "The Moravians and the American Revolution: An Overview," *TMHS*, 23, (1977): 2.
19. Morris, "Permanence for the House of Passage," 6–7.
20. Ibid., 7.
21. Daniel B. Thorp, "Assimilation in North Carolina's Moravian Community," *The Journal of Southern History*, 52, no. 1 (1986): 19–42, 27; Brian W. Thomas, "Inclusion and Exclusion in the Moravian Settlement in North Carolina, 1770–1790," *Historical Archaeology*, 28, no. 3 (1994): 17; Morris, "Permanence for the House of Passage," 13; Jerry L. Surratt, "The Moravian Businessman: Gottlieb Schober of Salem," *NCHR*, 60, no. 1 (1983): 1. In addition, Surratt suggests in "The Role of Dissent in Community Evolution among Moravians in Salem, 1772–1860" that Salem's emphasis as a commercial center was intentional.
22. Thomas, "Inclusion and Exclusion," 17; and Morris, "Permanence for the House of Passage," 14, 16.
23. Daniel B. Thorp, "Doing Business in the Backcountry: Retail Trade in Colonial Rowan County, North Carolina," *William and Mary Quarterly* 48 (1991): 389; Johanna Miller Lewis, *Artisans in the North Carolina Backcountry* (Lexington, KY, 1995), 89; Marjoleine Kars, *Breaking Loose Together: The Regulator Rebellion in pre-Revolutionary North Carolina* (Chapel Hill, NC, 2002), 15–16.
24. Roger A. Ekirch, *Poor Carolina: Politics and Society in Colonial North Carolina, 1729–1776* (Chapel Hill, NC, 1981), 177; Kars, *Breaking Loose Together*, 17.
25. Charles C. Crittenden, *The Commerce of North Carolina: 1763–1789*. (New Haven, CT, 1936), 86.
26. Ibid., 87.
27. Ibid., 69–70, 90, 93, 93.
28. Estate inventories in Orange County from the 1750s and 1760s show a lack of wagons in backcountry households. Moravian Bishop August Gottlieb Spangenberg traveled

140 miles in 1752 and saw "no wagon or plow, nor any sign of one." Alice Hanson Jones, *Colonial Wealth: Documents and Methods* (New York, 1977).

29. Ibid., 403, 405.
30. Well educated and fluent in several languages, Traugott Bagge came to Wachovia in 1768, having traveled extensively in Europe before joining the Moravian congregation. Bagge served as shopkeeper in Salem, public spokesman for the community during the war, and as *Fremden Diener* (the servant to strangers). Hunter James, *The Quiet People of the Land: A Story of the North Carolina Moravians in Revolutionary Times* (Chapel Hill, NC, 1976), 3, 15, 26.
31. Ibid., 404.
32. Crittenden, *The Commerce of North Carolina*, 94.
33. Ibid., 94, 95.
34. Shirley, *From Congregational Town to Industrial City*, 9.
35. *RMNC*, 2: 589, 658; Lewis, *Artisans in the Backcountry*, 82. In 1762 Bethabara had a population of 147, thirty-two of whom were artisans.
36. *RMNC*, 2: 589; Morris, "Permanence for the House of Passage," 16.
37. Frank P. Albright, *Johann Ludwig Eberhardt and His Salem Clocks*, (Chapel Hill, NC, 1978), 9.
38. Johanna Miller Lewis, "The Use of Water Power on the Wachovia Tract of North Carolina by the Moravians during the Eighteenth Century," *Communal Societies*, 9 (1989): 11.
39. Crittenden, *The Commerce of North Carolina*, 138.
40. Ibid., 133–134.
41. Ibid.,139.
42. *RMNC*, 2: 818.
43. Crittenden, *The Commerce of North Carolina*, 137.
44. Weinlick, "The Moravians and the American Revolution," 1.
45. James, *The Quiet People of the Land*, 41–43.
46. Kars, *Breaking Loose Together*, 121.
47. Ibid., 43.
48. *RMNC*, 2: 842, 850; James, *The Quiet People of the Land*, 41–42.
49. Ibid., 49–51.
50. Surratt, "Dissent in Community Evolution," 243, 244.
51. Crittenden, *The Commerce of North Carolina*, 118–120.
52. Ibid., 137.
53. James, *The Quiet People of the Land*, 41.
54. Crittenden, *The Commerce of North Carolina*, 137.
55. *RMNC*, 2: 881.
56. Ibid, 2: 891.
57. Crittenden, *The Commerce of North Carolina*, 137.
58. *RMNC*, 3. 1033.
59. Ibid., 3: 1210.
60. Ibid., 3: 1038.
61. Ibid., 2: 851.
62. Crittenden, *The Commerce of North Carolina*, 139.
63. Ibid., 134–135; *RMNC*, 4:1596.
64. *RMNC*, 3:1214.
65. Ibid., 3:1040.
66. Thomas, "Inclusion and Exclusion," 23.
67. Surratt, "Dissent in Community Evolution," 242; and James, *The Quiet People of the Land*, 119.
68. Thomas, "Inclusion and Exclusion," 27.
69. *RMNC*, 5:2269; Thomas, "Inclusion and Exclusion," 15; Surratt, "Dissent in Community Evolution," 242.
70. *MRNC*, 5:2283.

71. *MRNC*, 5:2393–2394.
72. Surratt, "Dissent in Community Evolution," 239.
73. Thomas, "Inclusion and Exclusion," 26.
74. *RMNC*, 2:817.
75. Thomas, "Inclusion and Exclusion," 17–18, 24. British styles made up more than half of all shards recovered in Richmond, whereas only one fifth of the shards found in Salem were of British styles. Excavation reports on Richmond, and of the Fifth House and pottery in Salem were compiled by Stanley South.
76. *RMNC*, 5:2148.
77. Ibid., 5:2148.
78. Albright, *Eberhardt and His Salem Clocks*, 9.
79. Ibid., 3.
80. Ibid., 59.
81. Ibid., 62.
82. Ibid., 14.
83. Ibid., 59, 62, 63; *RMNC*, 7:3302.
84. Albright, *Eberhardt and His Salem Clocks*, 62, 95–97.
85. Surratt, *Gottlieb Schober of Salem*, 3.
86. Ibid., 5.
87. Ibid., 8.
88. Ibid., 10; Ellin Lee Rogers, "History of the Paper Mill at Salem, North Carolina, 1789–1873," (MA thesis, Wake Forest University, 1982), 7.
89. Ibid., 7.
90. Rogers, "Paper Mill at Salem," 4-5, Jerry L. Surratt, *Gottlieb Schober of Salem*, 49.
91. Roger, "Paper Mill," 7; *RMNC*, 5:2271; Surratt, *Gottlieb Schober of Salem*, 50–51.
92. *RMNC*, 5:2402, Surratt, *Gottlieb Schober of Salem*, 12.
93. Rogers, "Paper Mill at Salem," 9, 11.
94. Ibid., 1.
95. Ibid., 11.
96. Ibid., 15; Surratt, *Gottlieb Schober of Salem*, 16.
97. Rogers, "Paper Mill at Salem," 16.
98. Shirley, *From Congregational Town to Industrial City*, 63.
99. Thomas, "Inclusion and Exclusion," 19.

Chapter 9

MORAVIANS, THE MARKET, AND A NEW ORDER IN SALEM

Michael Shirley

IN JANUARY 1834 HENRY LEINBACH surveyed the personal wreckage wrought by his father's bankruptcy and recorded in his diary, "It appears there is little love among us any more." Leinbach believed that money was leading many of his Brethren to abandon the congregational principles he held dear because where money was involved, "brotherly love" among the congregation "forsakes us immediately." The change Leinbach perceived in the congregational community was much larger than his father's dire financial condition. For years, Leinbach had witnessed growing numbers of neighbors challenging the Moravian congregation's regulation of business activity in Salem. The Moravian shoemaker could see in their behavior the impending demise of his cherished community. Believing that many of his neighbors did not "do as they wish others to do unto them," he concluded his Moravian communion would not continue.[1] Though Leinbach's perceptions may represent a sentimental attachment to a community that never existed, his words hint that a different and, in his mind, troubling ethos was emerging to guide Moravians in Salem.

But Henry Leinbach's diary tells only one side of the Salem story. While Leinbach expressed regret at the turn of events in Salem others saw opportunity to increase their wealth. William Fries, a joiner by trade, clashed often with Church authorities. He continually asserted his private economic interests in the face of a traditional community ethos under which no one would profit at the expense of another and everyone would enjoy the necessities of life.[2] William Fries, and later his son Francis, were in the vanguard of the Salem artisans and shopkeepers who transformed the Moravian community. Father and son departed from the congregational spirit, promoting self-reliance and the pursuit of individual interests, not the Christian brotherhood the Moravians valued. Fries, in his words, "relied on myself, I depended upon myself, I took care of myself."[3] Yet his claims for absolute independence to pursue his private business came at a price many Moravians like Leinbach could not imagine paying.

Salem Moravians lived on the edge of cultural and economic change between tradition and modernity, where contradictory demands were made on the individual. They attempted to reconcile their identity as Moravians with these new demands. For them, it was a quest to understand their place on this shifting ground in a congregational community where their way of life was threatened. The choices that Henry Leinbach and the Frieses made, and their consequences, reveal in human terms the impact of impersonal economic forces reshaping American communities during the transition to capitalism in the nineteenth century. Unwittingly, Leinbach and Fries expressed in their words the essence of the transformation that was breaking over the Moravian congregation in Salem and in the North Carolina Piedmont before the Civil War. Their words and actions reveal the struggle of Americans in the early nineteenth century to define the nature of social relations and order as their communities were transformed during these years by the expansion of a market economy.[4]

Americans like Henry Leinbach, William Fries, and Francis Fries witnessed during their lifetimes the development of many of the elements of modern capitalism, including a flexible currency, banking, corporations, transportation infrastructure, industrialized production, and a pervasive consumerism. After the Revolution, Americans plunged themselves into the pursuit of making money. This obsession fueled the pursuit of individual interests, fundamentally altering American society and culture in the early nineteenth century as capitalism became a part of the American consciousness. But the transition to a capitalist society was complex and uneven, and included a variety of changes: increased agricultural productivity, an increasing proportion of wage laborers in the work force, greater social differentiation, increasing purchasing power, proliferation of retail stores, and the growth of consumer demand. Capitalism fostered and rewarded a set of behaviors and core values based on individual free choice and action and competition. It involved people in new relationships and dissolved deeply rooted patterns of behavior and belief in communities that it touched.[5]

Over the first half of the nineteenth century economic forces operating beyond the town's boundaries fueled the emergence of a new order that transformed the economy and congregational government of Salem. Personal relations were reshaped. The greater commitment among most Salem shopkeepers to individual freedom, private property rights, and the pursuit of personal economic opportunities free of external restraints facilitated this development. By the eve of the Civil War most Moravian shopkeepers in Salem had adopted a worldview at odds with the traditional congregational ethos, transforming the community order of Salem. But as the experiences of the Moravians at Salem demonstrate, the march toward a capitalist society and culture was contested. Not everyone in Salem embraced the new order.

Salem was the center of a local economy where craftsmen and farmers in the neighboring countryside and villages created a vibrant trade with their neighbors. In the early nineteenth century few markets existed beyond the local community since no deep rivers ran from the Piedmont to the coast. A limited commerce moved the few marketable commodities down the primitive roads of the Yadkin and Catawba river valleys into South Carolina and on to Charleston, through the Shenandoah Valley to Philadelphia, and east to Fayetteville and then down the Cape Fear River to Wilmington. Salem occupied a central location along these trade routes, but roads in those years were little more than paths. The movement of goods and people was "slow, difficult, and expensive." Out of necessity, the settlers in the North Carolina backcountry turned to each other to acquire necessary goods and services, and a diversified economy of farming and crafts wove neighbors together into networks of local exchange.[6]

In relative isolation in their early years, the Moravians attempted to live a life of simple Christian discipleship with religion at its center. They hoped to be a community of brotherly love guided by a spirit of cooperation. Friedrich Marshall described the congregation town as "like one family, where the religious and material condition of each member is known in detail, where each person receives the appropriate ... oversight and assistance in consecrating the daily life." The congregational government, through the Aufseher Collegium and the Elders Conference principally and its system of authority, forged bonds of community by bringing everyone under the auspices of congregation rules that governed virtually all aspects of life. A key to the congregation's success was the preservation of exclusivity and homogeneity in the community. To this end the congregation regulated the conduct of business, entrance into the trades, apprenticeship, and the prices and quality of work.[7]

Artisans and shopkeepers were the central characters in the economic life of the town during the eighteenth and early nineteenth centuries. Salem's master craftsmen like Leinbach, working alongside their journeymen and apprentices, produced articles for trade in the local community and in the surrounding countryside. In this economy, Salem's shopkeepers were relatively secure. With competition restricted and quality maintained by congregation regulations, prices for Leinbach's shoes remained tied to the costs of production, leaving little threat to his status as a skilled artisan in Salem. In this regulated local economy, the work routine of Leinbach and other artisans remained quite casual. Work in the shops was done by hand with the artisan crafting raw materials into a finished product. Leinbach's daily work routine reveals the preindustrial character of craft production. On Mondays, he usually spent the day cutting out the leather for shoes that his apprentices and journeymen as-

Figure 9.1 Henry Leinbach home. The home and workshop of shoemaker Henry Leinbach on Main Street in Salem. The original house was erected by Leinbach in 1822. His shoemaker's shop and store were located in the room with the two windows immediately to the right of the front door. (Library of Congress, Prints and Photographs Division, Historic American Buildings Survey, Reproduction Number HABS, NC, 34-WINSA,7)

sembled. On other days, Leinbach spent the morning in his shop, and the afternoons fishing, hunting, walking, playing "corner-ball," or, in wintertime, ice skating. During the day's work, Salem's master craftsmen and journeymen artisans often gathered at the local tavern or a store like Winkler's bakery for beer or brandy, conversation, and companionship.[8]

The second quarter of the nineteenth century saw the steady improvement and expansion of transportation facilities in the North Carolina Piedmont, which enabled Salem to develop trading relations with northern cities and western towns. Shipments traveled from Boston, New York, and Philadelphia by steamboat to Petersburg and by wagon from Petersburg to Salem. Salem's two textile mills, established in the late 1830s, shipped their cloth and yarn north to consignees in New York and Philadelphia and west to Mississippi, Louisiana, and Texas. By mid-century railroads and plank roads linked the Piedmont countryside with the fall-line commercial towns that provided gateways to national and world markets.[9]

An improving transportation infrastructure transformed Piedmont agriculture. Easier access to markets prompted once self-sufficient Piedmont farmers to produce commodities for exchange in a wider market. Production of cotton, tobacco, and wheat expanded many times over between the 1830s and 1860s. In Stokes and Forsyth counties between 1839 and 1859 production of wheat increased 300 percent, tobacco 340 percent, and cotton 115 percent. At the same time corn production showed only a modest increase of 31 percent. During the 1850s per capita corn production actually dropped from 29 bushels to 23 bushels. The turn to market production between 1839 and 1859 becomes even clearer upon examination of the ratio of market crops like tobacco and wheat to subsistence crops like corn. In 1839 the ratio of tobacco output to corn output in Stokes County was 1.4, but in 1859 when tobacco cultivation expanded, the ratio for Stokes and Forsyth counties was 3.7. The ratio of wheat output to corn output during these years reflected a significant change also, but its impact is not as dramatic as that of tobacco cultivation, 0.17 in 1839 and 0.43 in 1859. As Piedmont farmers shifted an increasing share of their effort and resources to produce tobacco and wheat for the market, more households around Salem went into the market to acquire needed goods as well as those articles that made life more comfortable and enjoyable. With cash earned from the sale of market crops or through the trade of corn, beef, or fruit many households acquired needed goods like cloth, molasses, books, shoes, and whiskey. The countryside around Salem witnessed a steady decline in the per capita value of household manufactures between 1810 and 1860, from $2.40 to $1.64.[10]

By the eve of the Civil War households around Salem were embracing an economic orientation that contrasted sharply with that of households sixty years earlier. Piedmont farmers pursued opportunities in the market, selling or trading their surplus wheat, corn, and orchard products for cash, other commodities, or articles produced by local artisans or manufactured in distant factories. When conditions allowed, these farmers produced for the market to realize profits and achieve family financial strategies. At mid-century, farms were producing more, and farmers were able to get their crops to market much more easily than at any time in the past. Economic life was expanding in the countryside around Salem during the second quarter of the nineteenth century. The improvement of transportation facilities and the consequent easier access to markets made the northwest North Carolina Piedmont, with its small-farm, mixed agriculture economy, an attractive region for settlement. From 1820 to 1860 population growth in Stokes and Forsyth counties increased from 14,033 in 1820 to 23,094 (including Forsyth County) in 1860, a 64.6 percent jump. The number of enslaved African Americans also grew spectacularly as farmers and others sought more labor. Between 1820 and 1860 the number of slaves in the two counties increased 92 percent, and, between 1840 and 1860 their numbers jumped 57 percent.[11]

The effect of these developments on Salem's artisans was profound. From the late 1820s onward Moravians increasingly recognized that economic circumstances were changing. While access to wider markets opened new opportunities for the region's farmers, it presented both opportunity and challenges for Salem artisans and shopkeepers. Some of Salem's artisans suffered losses from the competition of lower-priced goods arriving from outside the community. The increasing availability of cheaper goods from manufacturers in Philadelphia and other northern industrial centers discouraged many in Salem and the nearby countryside from purchasing custom-made articles by local craftsmen. Increasingly, quality- and fashion-conscious young Moravian women like Louisa Belo were attracted to goods from the North that they believed were better made or more appealing in style. Louisa asked her friend Julia Jones in nearby Bethania to order shoes for her when she placed her own order with a certain shoemaker at 59 New Street in Philadelphia because his shoes "wear and fit better than any I have ever owned."[12]

Salem's shopkeepers also confronted increased competition from the many artisans who poured into the surrounding countryside. These artisans were not constrained in their economic activities by the congregation regulations that governed Salem artisans. John Conrad, a Stokes County farmer and shoemaker, made shoes for neighboring farmers who might otherwise have gone to Salem and patronized its shoe shops.[13] Changing circumstances meant Salem's artisans and shopkeepers had to adapt to survive and prosper as craftsmen. Henry Leinbach observed in the early 1830s that demand for custom work in his shoe shop had fallen off, and he increasingly relied on retail trade instead of custom-made shoes, producing shoes that were not "spoken for." Leinbach recognized that to prosper he had to adapt to new market conditions and change the way he conducted business in his shoe shop, such as "exposing shoes to view induces people to buy, otherwise they would not have thought of buying." By merchandising his wares he might stimulate consumer desire for his shoes.[14] Despite the efforts of Salem craftsmen like Leinbach to lure customers into their shops, residents of Salem and neighboring communities continued to develop a taste for goods made in the North.

An economy tied to national and international markets brought greater financial risks to those living in the North Carolina Piedmont as the periodic downturns in the economy in the late 1820s and early 1840s threatened their well-being. Many Moravians in Salem found themselves in tight financial circumstances and some went bankrupt, including John Leinbach, Henry's father and a prominent member of the Salem congregation. John Leinbach was involved in several business enterprises and by 1833 had accumulated property worth about $2,400, including an oil mill, a saw mill, a cotton gin, and 228 acres of land. But in the new economy the margin for error was slim. Leinbach had made some bad business decisions as well as overextended himself, incurring more debt than his income could cover. Leinbach lost all of his property in a sheriff's sale. His son Henry noted that while his father's case unfolded other members of the congregation found themselves in the same circumstances.[15]

William Fries also found himself ensnared. Fries arrived in Salem in the fall of 1809 from Herrnhut and, after a year and a half as a joiner in the Brothers' House, became the master of the shop. In 1811, Fries, at the age of thirty-five, married and became a member of the congregation as a head of household. Quickly becoming a respected member of the congregation, he was elected to the Congregation Council in 1815 and to the Aufseher Collegium in 1819 and in 1821. William Fries prospered: by 1819 he had acquired a 32-acre farm and a town lot in Salem, and four years later his farm had grown to 162 acres. Branching out, in 1826 Fries acquired the congregation's tobacco shop, which he ran in addition to his joiner's shop. By the late 1820s William Fries had accumulated enough capital to make some investments, putting himself in a precarious financial situation that left him strapped for cash in the late 1820s when one of his investments, the Cape Fear Bank, failed. Fries wrote to his son Francis about conditions in Salem: "the times are very bad with us. Our business goes very slowly because money is so scarce."[16]

Rising tensions in the 1830s and 1840s affected all areas of community life in Salem but most noticeably economic affairs, as challenges to the congregational regulation of the trades escalated. Some of the ambitious shopkeepers perceived new entrepreneurial possibilities in the wider market, but their conduct provoked antagonisms among their neighbors. Some pursued their own interests and profits, and often engaged in activities that did not conform to congregational regulations. Seeking a competitive edge, some shopkeepers joined into partnerships, while others hired slaves. Still others engaged in what the Aufseher Collegium (Board of Economic Overseers) called "secret trading," selling articles that the congregation authorities deemed illegitimate. Recognizing the increased incidence of illegal trading, the Aufseher Collegium took action to maintain the congregational economic order and attempted to convince the Brethren of the congregation that the established economic order in Salem worked to the benefit of the congregation and all of its members.[17]

William Fries was a constant nuisance to many in Salem, including the Collegium. In the late 1820s and 1830s, he was deeply involved in the secret trading controversies that engulfed the whole community and prompted serious doubts that the congregation and its special way of life would survive. To find a way out of his financial troubles, Fries expanded the inventory in his tobacco shop, violating congregation rules by selling glass, coffee, and sugar, among other goods, to increase his income. Fries hoped to make his activities legal, petitioning the congregation authorities for permission to operate a small store in conjunction with his tobacco shop in 1829. His request exposed tensions that for years had festered under the surface. The Collegium considered Fries's petition, but it also heard numerous charges against other individuals engaged in illegal trading in their shops. Attempting to justify his own behavior, William Fries accused Elizabeth Rights of operating a dry-goods store in her deceased husband's toy shop. Others in town criticized David Clewell for selling items not usually associated with a shoemaker's trade, including toys, coffee, sugar, and dry goods. Papermaker Gottlieb Schober complained that Clewell sold stationery that competed with his paper mill. Schober in turn was said to be selling a variety of goods in addition to the paper he manufactured. Like William Fries, Gottlieb Schober continually challenged the congregational regulation of trade in Salem. The situation was frustrating for the Aufseher Collegium because all of the shopkeepers justified their illegal activities by pointing to the illegal activities of others.[18]

As William Fries waited for a response to his petition to operate a dry goods store, the Aufseher Collegium considered the trades. Acting to regain control of the conduct of business in the community, the Collegium reached agreements with Elizabeth Rights, Gottlieb Schober, and David Clewell, who promised not to sell items that infringed on other shopkeepers' business. The Collegium refused to be intimidated by Fries's threat that he would rather leave the Salem congregation than be continually troubled by the Collegium's meddling. Fries's petition was denied, and he was ordered to sell only tobacco and glass. When Fries protested that he had to sell a wider selection of goods to live and that the Collegium's demands were excessive, the Collegium spoke bluntly to Brother Fries. It expressed its confidence that Fries could make a good living if he ran his tobacco shop "expediently" and engaged in his actual trade as a joiner. The Collegium then reminded him that he could sell his house and move from Salem to do as he pleased if he were so unhappy in the congregation. It regretted that Fries did not examine his true motives in his behavior and "seek the cause of this troublesome situation of his with himself." The Collegium believed that if Fries could not control his ambition, then he and the congregation would benefit if he left Salem. Congregation leaders recognized that the only weapon they possessed to address the matter effectively was moral suasion, especially appeals to brotherly love and loyalty to the community and its special ideals. But William Fries was unrepentant. In a letter to his son Francis, he laid bare the situation as he saw it. Many artisans in Salem no longer placed confidence in the authorities to regulate economic affairs in Salem: "We are well and have nothing to complain of if it was not for the silly Collegium that wants to quarrel with us and others all the time." Fries continued, "They are ridiculed in the village and think they are the only wise ones." Disregarding the Collegium, William Fries went ahead with his plans to expand his business endeavors. Fries surreptitiously offered patrons of his tobacco shop a variety of "small wares" including coffee, sugar, molasses, spices, nails, glass, and paints.[19]

The congregation authorities were unable to rein in the ambition of those in Salem who violated the rules. Some members of the governing boards of the congregation, such as William Fries, David Clewell, and John Christian Blum, frequently violated those rules and even advocated the abolition of restrictions on business. The 1830s meetings of the Aufseher Collegium were often contentious, as the issue of "free trade" in the village continually demanded attention. After one meeting, Leinbach exchanged "warm words" with fellow Collegium member John C. Blum over the trade issue. Blum opposed the continued regulation of business. Out of frustration and in a fit of rage, Blum, who felt out of touch with other Collegium members on this issue, left the meeting saying that he should resign from his office. For Blum this was a serious matter that touched his heart as a faithful member of the congregation because to violate the rules alienated him from his community. It meant not only risking the loss of his trade and home in Salem, along with membership in the community, but also his status as a communicant of the Unitas Fratrum. The regulation of trade was reinforced by spiritual sanctions that cast severe penalties for a faithful member of the congregation. Still, many Salem shopkeepers continued to challenge the congregation rules by engaging in illegal trade.[20]

In July 1840 Belo, a joiner, petitioned the Aufseher Collegium for permission to open a dry goods store. The Collegium recognized Belo's difficulty making a living at his trade, but was concerned that if Belo opened a store he would compete with already established shopkeepers who, in self defense, would begin to sell articles reserved for the artisans. Such a development would further undermine the congregational system. Yet it was believed that the town could support another store, and because Belo would not have to borrow much capital to begin business, the authorities consented. They stipulated, though, that Belo had to give up his joiner's trade and not enter into a partnership with any stranger or person living outside of the community.[21]

A growing number of Moravians understood that the trade regulations would have to be modified or abandoned if the town's economy was to adjust to the emerging market economy. The majority of adult male members of the community were ready to change the rules that governed the congregation's regulation. During the late 1820s and 1830s many young Moravians were forced to leave Salem. The Elders Conference lamented that many of the congregation's young men who had completed their apprenticeships found it difficult to find a position as a journeyman in a Salem shop and were forced to "go out into the world and are lost to the congregation." Many of the congregation's young men believed that the trade rules impeded their opportunity to establish themselves as proprietors and householders in the congregation. Shopkeepers like William Fries and John C. Blum who challenged the congregational rules that regulated trade won increasing support from those who saw few prospects for themselves in Salem. Their frustration erupted into open opposition to the elders. In 1834 the young men of the congregation caucused, putting together a slate of candidates they supported for election to the Aufseher Collegium. Their ticket carried the day, with the exception of Henry Leinbach the incumbents were turned out, and new men like Francis Fries were put on the Collegium.[22]

A new generation in the congregation confronted the changing economic conditions that made Salem's special way of life difficult to maintain. In January 1849, the congregation council recognized that the rules governing the trades had been broken repeatedly in recent years. The council also recognized that new economic circumstances made it difficult to enforce the rules without causing hardship for the community. This situation resulted from the increased availability of manufactured goods, which could be sold more cheaply than local artisans could produce them. When a citizens' committee proposed the abolition of the trade regulations the Congregation Council took up the matter, and forty of the fifty members of the congregation present voted to abolish all of the rules regulating the conduct of the trades. Complete freedom of trade was guaranteed. Now individuals who wished to open a shop in Salem no longer needed the permission of the Aufseher Collegium and the Elders Conference.[23]

The abolition of the trade rules allowed some Salem craftsmen to turn to the more profitable business of merchandising. The number of merchants in Salem had doubled, from three in 1840 to six in 1850. Increasingly, by mid-century, the people of Salem and the neighboring countryside patronized merchants who offered a wide variety of goods that satisfied a growing sophistication in consumer tastes and an increasing demand for more luxury goods. Salem merchants Boner and Crist, Edward Belo, and A. T. Zevely offered residents and the neighboring countryside a wide assortment of goods that once would have been acquired from local artisans like Henry Leinbach or made in the home.[24]

Francis Fries represented the new generation in Salem at home in the market economy. He owned and operated a textile mill and employed forty-seven operatives, as well as a paper mill, a tannery, and a general store. He also owned real estate in Salem and nine slaves. In 1859 the R. G. Dun Company reported Fries to be worth between $75,000 and $100,000. Mindful of the opportunities in commercial enterprise and the need to expand the infrastructure of commerce, he took a leading role in promoting transportation improvements that bound Salem to regional and national markets, including the Fayetteville and Western Railroad connecting Salem to Fayetteville on the Cape Fear River.[25]

Francis Fries's attitude of self-interest and individualism reveals a way of thinking that challenged the communal ethos of Christian brotherhood the Moravians valued. He attributed his success to "economy, unceasing perseverance and industry in giving to every detail my personal attention." According to Fries, he never paid attention to "anything that I did not consider my own business." He was not concerned with public matters or the concerns of others unless they were connected to his own affairs. But there was a price to be paid by some Moravians who embraced this ethos, and Francis Fries found himself alienated from many of his neighbors who questioned the motives behind his private ambition. During the early years of the Civil War, as hardship and loss darkened the lives of so many of his neighbors, Francis Fries was accused of profiteering by his contracts to equip North Carolina soldiers. In 1864, townsfolk hard pressed by the sacrifices and shortages of war took to the streets when US troops entered the town. When the doors of the Fries woolen mill were thrown open by troops, a crowd of men, women, and children swarmed the mill, taking finished goods as well as cutting cloth still on the looms. A member of the Fries family observed that these goods were found in the possession of persons who were thought to be "good and friendly neighbors." After his early death in 1863, Francis Fries was eulogized in the *Western Sentinel* as a man of boundless enterprise who "breathed the soul of energy and success into everything he touched … he was a model—whatever opinions men may have entertained of his motives, we are sure they were ever the dictates of good conscience."[26] However, in these final words about the quick remarkable life of Francis Fries lies the acknowledgement that some in Salem doubted his purpose and did not share his vision of what life in the Moravian community meant.

Despite the congregation's move toward deregulating business activity, some members of the community remained loyal to the ways of the congregation and the life it promoted. Some Moravian artisans were uncomfortable with the market economy and the ethos of risk-taking private acquisitiveness that drove men like Francis Fries. They remained faithful to the Moravian congregation's values of harmony, brotherhood, and the subordination of private interests to the common wellbeing. These Moravians believed that too many Brethren were guided by their own interests in their objections to any rules that limited their freedom to pursue private opportunities. They hoped that through God's grace their neighbors would not forget Jesus' call to be a congregation that acts "according to the kingdom of God and his righteousness" and not be led merely by worldly interest.[27]

In contrast to the Frieses, Henry Leinbach and others represented a commitment to the old order. Leinbach remained a shoemaker, working alongside his journeymen and farming his fifty-one acres outside of Salem. A man of modest wealth, he never owned a slave. He continued to hold on to his identity as a member of the Moravian congregation and his commitment to its religious ideals and social ethos. Mindful of his father's experience with a risk-taking quest for speculation and profit, Leinbach may have clung to an ethos that valued security and independence and abhorred unnecessary risk. It may be said that Henry Leinbach valued the love and harmony of the congregational community more than the profits and wealth of capitalist business endeavor that drove Francis Fries. But it was much more than this to Leinbach: for him, the congregation and its ethos represented a particular way of life guided by an ethos that gave his life meaning.[28]

By the late 1840s, most in Salem agreed that fundamental changes were due. Salem's shopkeepers were ready to remove economic activity from congregational regulation so that they might utilize capital, land, and labor as economic conditions demanded, a freedom essential for capitalist economic development. They questioned the efficacy of the traditional congregational way of life in this emerging market economy. Ambitious shop owners and entrepreneurs like William Fries, Francis Fries, and Edward Belo led a transformation that created a new moral economy with new ways of behavior. They were not less Moravian in their religious faith, but their identity as Moravians was complemented by an awareness of themselves as autonomous individuals driven by ambition to acquire private wealth. By mid-century, the market had assumed greater importance than congregational agencies as an instrument of social discipline and character modification, producing individuals who were rational and calculating, and who took their cue from the market as they sought new moneymaking ventures.[29]

The controversies within the Moravian community over congregational regulation of the trades and constraints on business activity, and the tensions and debates regarding the retention or dissolution of the congregational order in the 1850s, reveal the specific impact of the market revolution on one community. By sweeping away the congregational order in the 1850s the Moravians of Salem unleashed entrepreneurial energies to participate in the market economy and bring about the postwar economic expansion of the community. The experience of the Moravian community reveals in bold detail the profound impact of economic change on community culture. The essence of the congregation community was its relative homogeneity, its single vision and way of life. Emotional bonds among the faithful and a mutuality that grew out of the religious mission of the Moravians characterized social relations in the congregation. Hence, in Salem, community was synonymous with the experience of being Moravian.

In contrast, the advent of a capitalist economic and social order created a distinctive culture of self-realization in which the individual was released from traditional restraints so that he could make of himself whatever he wanted. In this transition the autonomous individual achieved freedom by becoming self-determining. Consequently, the common ends of the Moravian congregation yielded to the individual choices made by William Fries and others in Salem. The experiences of the Moravians in Salem demonstrate how capitalism in the United States had to fight its way to supremacy by breaking down the traditional order. Henry Leinbach, William and Francis Fries, and their neighbors lived the struggle between tradition and modernity in the Moravian congregation. It was a contest between different standards of life, even different identities, with each claiming ethical sanctions.[30] But most of Salem's residents still looked to their Moravian faith and its traditions as an anchor in a world of rapid change. New ways of life and work emerged in Salem, but old patterns persisted—though overlaid with the new—as Salem became an arena in which competing individuals pursued private opportunities and interests.

Notes

1. MA-SP, John Henry Leinbach, Diary, January 14, February 9, 1834, John Henry Leinbach Family Papers.
2. Kenneth G. Hamilton and J. Taylor Hamilton, *History of the Moravian Church: The Renewed Unitas Fratrum, 1722–1957*, (Bethlehem, PA, 1967), 169.
3. MA-SP, Francis Fries to J. F. Shaffner, 30 June 1861, Shaffner-Fries Correspondence.
4. Ronald Hoffman, Mechal Sobel, and Fredrika J. Teute, eds., *Through a Glass Darkly: Reflections on Personal Identity in Early America* (Chapel Hill, NC, 1997), 1–6, 157–162.
5. Michael Shirley, *From Congregation Town to Industrial City: Culture and Social Change in a Southern Community* (New York, 1994); Gordon Wood, *Radicalism of the American Revolution* (New York, 1992), 305, 325–326; Charles Sellers, *The Market Revolution: Jacksonian America, 1815–1846* (New York, 1991), 3–33. Paul Gilje, "The Rise of Capitalism in the Early Republic," in *Wages of Independence: Capitalism in the Early American Republic*, ed. Paul Gilje (Madison, WI, 1997), 1–2; Walter Licht, *Industrializing America: The Nineteenth Century* (Baltimore, 1995), xiii–xviii; Allan Kulikoff, "The Transition to Capitalism in Rural America," *William and Mary Quarterly* 52 (1989): 120–144.
6. *RMNC*, 1:143, 352, 400, 404; 7:3045–3046; and 8:3755, 3788; Harriet Martineau, *Society in America*, 2 vols. (London, 1837), 2:2; Leinbach, Diary, 16–18 April 1830.
7. Hamilton and Hamilton, *History of the Moravian Church*, 169; Gillian Lindt Gollin, *Moravians in Two Worlds: A Study of Changing Communities* (New York, 1967), 9–18; John Sessler, *Communal Pietism Among Early American Moravians* (New York, 1933), 32, 100–101, 106–108, 138–154; *RMNC*, 1:313.
8. Leinbach, Diary, 3, 4, 5 March, 10 May, 20 November 1830; *RMNC*, 8:3746, 3847, 3939; Susan Hirsch, *Roots of the American Working Class: The Industrialization of the Crafts in Newark, 1800–1860* (Philadelphia, 1978), 9.
9. *RMNC*, 8:3864, 4252; Adelaide Fries, "One Hundred Years of Textiles in Salem," *NCHR* 27 (1950): 12–13; MA-SP, Salem Manufacturing Company, Minutes of the General Meetings, 44, 50, 55–58, Fries Mills Collection; MA-SP, Salem Manufacturing Company, Minutes of the Board of Directors, 95–96, 103, Fries Mills Collection; F. and H. Fries Company, Daybooks 11 and 12, F. and H. Fries Collection, MA-SP; George R. Taylor, *The Transportation Revolution, 1815–1860* (New York, 1964), 74–103, 203; Douglass C. North, *The Economic Growth of the United States, 1790–1860* (New York, 1966), 204–207; Hugh T. Lefler and Albert Ray Newsome, *North Carolina: A History of a Southern State* (Chapel Hill, NC, 1963), 348–349, 360–362, 378.
10. Cornelius O. Cathey, *Agricultural Developments in North Carolina, 1783–1860* (Raleigh, NC, 1956), 105–139, 202–205; *Compendium of the Sixth Census, 1840; Statistical View of the United States, Compendium of the Seventh Census, 1850; Report of the United States in 1860; Compiled from the Original Returns of the Eighth Census*, Volume 2; *RMNC*,10:5088–89; John Henry Leinbach, Diary, 14 July 1843; Gavin Wright, *The Political Economy of the Cotton South: Households, Markets, and Wealth in the Nineteenth Century* (New York, 1978), 166; Lacy K. Ford, *Origins of Southern Radicalism: The South Carolina Upcountry, 1800–1860* (New York, 1988), 54–88, 375–377; Edmund Blum, Daybook, 1857–1864, Manuscripts Department, Duke University Library, Durham, North Carolina; Salem *People's Press*, 8 February, 29 March, 14 June 1851, 1 July 1854, 18 April 1856; Rolla Milton Tryon, *Household Manufactures in the United States, 1690–1860: A Study in Industrial History* (Chicago, 1917), 176.

11. *Census for 1820*; *Compendium of the Sixth Census, 1840*; *Report of the United States in 1860*, vol. 2.

12. Taylor, *Transportation Revolution*, 74–103, 203; North, *Economic Growth of the United States*, 204–207; Louisa Belo to Julia Jones, n.d., 1847, February 1, 1849, Jones Family Papers, Southern Historical Collection, University of North Carolina at Chapel Hill, Chapel Hill, North Carolina.

13. *RMNC*, 9:4479; John Conrad, Ledger, 16 May 1823–28 September 1827, Conrad Family Papers, Manuscripts Department, Duke University Library.

14. Leinbach, Diary, 17 February 1831, 2 January, 19 March 1832, 26 January 1834.

15. *RMNC*, 7:3087; 8:3398, 3617, 3768, 3794, 3841, 4074, 4087, 4128–4129, 4131, 4135; 9:4590, 4685, 4713, 4741, 4758; Salem *Weekly Gleaner*, 25 November 1828; Leinbach, Diary, 20–22 July, 28 October 1833; 4 January, 19 March 1834; 14 July 1843; Stokes County, List of Taxables, 1833, NCDAH.

16. *RMNC*, 7:3086, 3095–3097, 3112, 3138, 3144–3145, 3254, 3398, 3466; 8:3839, 3841; Stokes County, List of Taxables, 1819, 1823, NCDAH.

17. *RMNC*, 8:3809; MA-SP, Minutes of the Aufseher Collegium, 23 February 1829, Salem Congregation.

18. *RMNC*, 8:3929; MA-SP, Minutes of the Aufseher Collegium, 9, 25 February, 31 August, 7 September 1829, Salem Congregation.

19. *RMNC*, 8:3841, 3876, 3929.

20. *RMNC*, 8:3994–3995; Leinbach, Diary, 19 March 1830; 17 February, 7 November, 28 November 1831; 2 January 1832.

21. *RMNC*, 9:4541–4542.

22. *RMNC*, 9:passim; 1850 Census, Population Schedule manuscript microfilm, Forsyth County, North Carolina; Leinbach, Diary, 24 January, 9 February 1834.

23. *RMNC*, 10:5399–5401.

24. *RMNC*, 9:4541; 1850 Census, Population Schedule manuscript microfilm, Forsyth County, North Carolina; Salem *People's Press*, 27 September, 1851; 11 December 11 1852.

25. 1850 Census, Population Schedule manuscript microfilm, Forsyth County, North Carolina; 1850 Census, Manufactures Schedule manuscript microfilm, Forsyth County, North Carolina; 1850 Census, Slave Schedule; 1860 Census, Slave Schedule manuscript microfilm, Forsyth County, North Carolina; North Carolina, 10:463, 465, 502, R. G. Dun and Company Collection, Baker Library, Harvard University Graduate School of Business Administration; Samuel A. Ashe et al., eds., *Biographical History of North Carolina from Colonial Times to the Present*, 8 vols. (Greensboro, NC, 1917), 3:129–134.

26. MA-SP, Francis Fries to J. F. Shaffner, 30 June 1861, Shaffner-Fries Correspondence; Francis Fries to Capt. C.W. Garrett, 5 December 1862, Thomas Marrit Pittman Papers, NCDAH; John Fries, "Remembrance of Civil War Times," 10–15, Fries Papers, NCDAH; *Western Sentinel*, 6 August 1863.

27. *RMNC*, 9:4527; Leinbach, Diary, 28 October 1833; 24 January 1834.

28. Stokes County, List of Taxables, 1847, NCDAH; James Henretta, "Families and Farms: Mentalité in Pre-Industrial America," *The William and Mary Quarterly* 35 (1978) 5, 14–29.

29. Thomas Haskell, "Capitalism and the Humanitarian Sensibility," *American Historical Review* 91 (1985): 550; Joyce Appleby, *Capitalism and a New Social Order: The Republican Vision of the 1790s* (New York, 1984), 22.

30. Daniel Bell, *The Cultural Contradictions of Capitalism* (New York, 1976), 12–16; Max Weber, *The Protestant Ethic and the Spirit of Capitalism*, trans. Talcott Parsons (London, 1930; reprt. 2001), 18–23.

PART THREE

Race and Gender
in the Moravian Church:
A Protestant Exceptionalism?

– *Chapter 10* –

"NO ONE SHOULD LUST FOR POWER ... WOMEN LEAST OF ALL.": DISMANTLING FEMALE LEADERSHIP AMONG EIGHTEENTH-CENTURY MORAVIANS

Beverly P. Smaby

UNDER THE LEADERSHIP OF Count Nicolaus Ludwig von Zinzendorf, mid-eighteenth century Moravian women held responsibility and power in the realms of spiritual care and governance in the Moravian Church. After Zinzendorf's death in 1760, however, his successors began to dismantle his intricate system of female leadership. Detailed general synod records of the 1760s, including the minutes of the ad hoc committees, show how these successors analyzed perceived problems and made real decisions, often confidential, that reshaped Moravian women's roles.

Anna Johanna Piesch's life helps illustrate the administrative and spiritual responsibilities Zinzendorf accorded Moravian women. A niece of Anna Nitschmann, the leading woman in the Moravian Church of the eighteenth century, Piesch played significant roles in the Moravian Church in her own right. Church leaders, having noticed her talents, named her General Eldress of Children at age fifteen, leader of all children in the Church. At nineteen she became a *Pflegerin* (caretaker or leader) of Single Sisters Choirs, first in Herrnhaag and then in London. Piesch handled her offices with such distinction that she was named the General Eldress for all Single Sisters Choirs, at 21. She subsequently lived in Zinzendorf's household (*Jüngerhaus* or House of the Disciple) along with his other close co-workers and was a member of the central governing body of the Moravian Church. In this role, she traveled often throughout not only

Germany, but also America, Holland and England, writing candid reports informing Zinzendorf and Nitschmann about single Sisters Choirs and Moravian settlements elsewhere. Her duties were ministerial too—ordaining deaconesses, giving sermons in the worship services held by Single Sisters Choirs, and holding interviews (*das Sprechen* or Speakings) with individual Single Sisters before an upcoming Communion celebration to evaluate their spiritual condition. She usually took part in synods as a lead delegate. Piesch married Nathaneal Seidel, at 34, in order to assume joint leadership of Bethlehem, Pennsylvania. Together they led this settlement through its difficult transition from a purely communal economy into a largely private one. She described their efforts as "a difficult piece of work ... that caused my good husband and me many sleepless nights."[1]

Thus, Anna Nitschmann was not the only woman who played a major role in the eighteenth-century Moravian Church. While no one knows the actual number of leading Moravian women, probably between 100 and 150 held administrative and spiritual offices in the settlements and central Church, based on their attendance at synods. Such representation in public office was unusual for European and European-American women. With the exception of nuns, some aristocratic women, and widows, most women lived as daughters, wives, or servants in families governed by men. With the exception of the Quakers, no other groups allowed women to hold positions of such high authority in Church or local government.[2] Moravian women had to learn to govern, because they lacked role models and had so little experience. Their many spiritual biographies express their industry and commitment to their new roles and how much joy these new roles brought them.

Many illustrations and paintings from the Zinzendorf period, produced to document events in the Moravian Church and socialize young people and converts to Moravian beliefs, provide a lively picture of Moravian women's roles. Artist Johann Valentin Haidt commemorated an important session at the Herrnhut Synod of 1750, distinguished by the rigid separation of the genders characteristic of Moravians, with women on one side of the room and men on the other. A closer look makes it apparent that leading Moravians sat at the center table, including Zinzendorf, flanked by leading men on one side and leading women on the other. Despite the significant presence of women, this painting indicates that hierarchy was preserved. Women represented just six of the twenty-five people at the center table, while the height of chair backs indicated importance, with Zinzendorf, at the table's center, having the highest chair back, and those leaders flanking him, the second highest. While non-Moravians would have taken this hierarchy for granted, they would have been surprised by women's participation in Church governance. Haidt also painted individual portraits of leading Moravians, many women among them, all depicted as spiritual, fulfilled, and happy, including Anna Johanna Piesch.

Figure 10.1 The typical seating arrangement at Synods, c. 1750. (Moravian Archives Herrnhut, GS 171)

Likewise, a set of black and white prints, used in a contemporary book (called *Zeremonienbüchlein*) to illustrate various ceremonies among the Moravians, convey women as active in worship services, helping to serve Communion to the entire congregation. Two male ministers actually serve Communion, one to men and the other to the women. Behind each minister is a person identified as the one "who is carrying the bread," and that person is a woman on the women's side of the room.[3] Another Haidt painting, titled the *Jungfernbund* or *Covenant of the Virgins*, was intended to remind Moravians, especially the Single Sisters, of the important covenant that took place on 4 May 1730 between eighteen Single Sisters and the Savior. Anna Nitschmann, the initiator of the covenant sits in the middle, holding the Savior's body in her lap, surrounded by seventeen other Sisters. Zinzendorf stands at the edge looking on. This painting not only commemorates this event, but also conveys the special piety of women in the Church. Zinzendorf believed that members of each choir had a fitting path to the Savior. Children, for instance, would best find the Savior by focusing on his childhood, while Single Brothers could best identify with the Savior as a single man. The Sisters could best understand the Savior through Mary, whose body was the vessel through which he became human.

The single Sisters could identify with the Incarnation because Mary had been a virgin. This painting underscores this feminine piety by placing Anna Nitschmann where we are accustomed to seeing Mary. Here is a Pieta (the Savior on Nitschmann's lap) blended with a manger scene (visiting worshipers all around Nitschmann and Zinzendorf as Mary and Joseph). It was used for the Festival of the Single Sisters Choir on 4 May each year to remember the original covenant and strengthen the Single Sisters' special piety.[4] The themes of both these prints and paintings, and of the many others in existence, convey women's importance in the administrative and spiritual circles of the eighteenth-century Moravian Church.

Zinzendorf was responsible for the unusual amount of female leadership among the Moravians. Although Moravian policy under Zinzendorf was officially developed by groups of leading Moravians (at synods and in the extended household—*Jüngerhaus* or Disciple's House—that Zinzendorf led), synod minutes show how his charismatic leadership, with its explorations in theology, piety, and social theory, set the direction. But why did Zinzendorf award so much responsibility to so many women? Certainly several women in his life influenced him greatly, providing him with models of capable women who balanced religious commitment with an ability to govern large households. These women included his grandmother Henrietta von Gersdorf and his wife Erdmutha Dorothea née von Reuss.[5] But these two women, a baroness and a countess, represented a long tradition whereby women held positions of some power on their family estates.[6]

In Zinzendorf's Moravian world, women of *all* social classes held leading positions. Anna Nitschmann was the daughter of a carpenter. Anna Johanna Piesch's father was a shoemaker. Others came from peasant or burgher families. Indeed, the great majority of leading Moravian women did not carry the "von" in front of their last names, yet held positions at the head of choirs and on governing councils in Moravian settlements around the world. Outside the Moravian Church, such German women might have hoped to marry peasant farmers, master craftsmen, or merchants, giving them authority within their households and garnering the respect of neighbors, but they could never have held governing positions in their communities or Churches.[7]

Such participation, however, lasted little more than a generation, because only Zinzendorf introduced and defended such extensive female participation. After his death, not a single leading man was willing to argue that women should continue to hold these unusual roles. Zinzendorf's successors strove with breathtaking speed to remove women from offices and responsibilities they had held while he still lived. Three weeks after Zinzendorf's death, and just one week after Nitschmann's, Johannes von Watteville (Zinzendorf's son-in-law and intimate co-worker) called together a council of Moravian leaders *(Ratskonferenz)* to discuss the Moravian Church's future. The role of Sisters in the Church was second on the agenda only to the future "constitution of our cause in general."[8]

In the General Synod of 1764, the first after Zinzendorf's death, delegates again took up the issue of women's roles by discussing appropriate membership in the General Directorate, the highest governing body. They decided that "The Brothers shall keep [their membership in] the General Directorate, and the Sisters don't desire it; rather they are assistants and advisors [to the Directorate]" and added that "general offices [for women] were not thought to be good," although women like Anna Nitschmann and Anna Johanna Piesch had held them previously.[9] The delegates also decided the Single Sisters and the Widows Choirs in each Moravian settlement required a male "curator" to administer their secular affairs. Finally, they concluded that Single Sisters should no longer hold the "oversight over the education of the children in the Girls' House" in Moravian settlements, but that a Married Couple should play that role.[10] Through these three measures, the Synod of 1764 revoked significant female responsibility in the central administration of the Church and the settlements as well.

The leading men also helped curtail women's previous involvement in spiritual care by determining that ordained men in Moravian settlements, rather than deaconesses, should be responsible for intimate spiritual interviews with each individual Sister, known as "Speakings." To avoid any untoward relationship between a minister and a Sister, delegates required the presence of another woman (such as the minister's

Figure 10.2 Woman assisting at Communion. (Moravian Archives, Herrnhut)

wife) during the interview, but denied the witness a role. Although the
Elders Conferences in each settlement specified precisely how this system
worked in their jurisdiction, this central change marked a clear limitation
of women's spiritual caretaking roles.[11] Delegates also expressed concern
about possible reactions by outsiders to Moravian women's assistance at
Communion services, concluding that women would assist only when
"necessary" and only in Communion services where outsiders were not
likely to be present.[12]

The General Synod of 1769 (the second after Zinzendorf's death) limited women's participation further. Synod delegates decided the Sisters
would no longer advise the Unity Elders Conference (as the General Directorate was now called), serving only as advisors to the Helpers Conference (subordinate to the Unity Elders Conference). Furthermore, no
standing female advisory committee would be recognized. It was "left up
to Helpers Conference as it saw fit" to gather together some Sisters for that
purpose.[13] After the next General Synod in 1775, leading women like Anna
Johanna Piesch could no longer ordain women as deaconesses. Leading
Sisters were not even allowed to assist a bishop at such an ordination.

The fact that Zinzendorf's successors dismantled women's offices so
speedily in the wake of his death suggests his policy on women had its
critics among the Church's male leaders during his lifetime. At the Synod
of 1747 Johannes von Watteville repeatedly criticized Zinzendorf's stance
on marriage, and worried about outsiders' reactions to it.[14] Anna Johanna
Piesch's description of her uneasiness after the deaths of Zinzendorf and
Nitschmann suggests her awareness of these critics:

> Now I was completely orphaned, and the grief and worry in my poor soul
> was great, not only because of these two dear people, but also primarily
> because the settlements and choirs had now lost their lead sheep and [because
> of] how things would go in the future. My anxious thoughts and premo-
> nitions did unfortunately come true in considerable measure, and to my
> inexpressible pain, I had to witness that these dear people were almost
> completely forgotten, especially the dear Mama [Anna Nitschmann].[15]

That Piesch harbored such anxious premonitions suggests that she had
heard undercurrents of criticism among leading Moravians about women's
roles during the Zinzendorf era and that she was aware of plans to undo
them. Because Zinzendorf's personal charisma and aristocratic power
were so great within the governing circles of the Church, his decisions
prevailed during his lifetime, but as soon as he was gone, the new leaders clearly lost no time in undoing them. Moreover, it seems they purposefully erased Nitschmann's pivotal role as a leader along with many of
Zinzendorf's innovations from the historical record in their effort to "improve" the image of the Moravian Church.

In less than four decades' time, the Moravian Church had experienced
two sweeping changes in women's position, the first when Zinzendorf

Figure 10.3 Portrait of Anna Johanna Peish (Seidel) (1726–1788). (Moravian Archives, Herrnhut, GS 171)

introduced new offices for women and the second when his successors took them away. Zinzendorf had not been motivated by a belief in the need for equal social rights when he created those offices.[16] Rather he believed that men and women should be separated to discourage extra-marital love relationships. As he especially wished to prevent contact between male ministers and female believers, because of its potential for inappropriate intimacy, he created spiritual offices for women, like Deaconess and Caretaker *(Pflegerin).* He also believed women would understand the spiritual problems of women better than men. And because only these new female spiritual leaders understood the condition of the Sisters' souls, they needed to participate on the governing boards in each Moravian settlement, in the central governing body of the Church, and in synods, to give reports about their work with the Sisters. We know from these written reports and Synod minutes that they took their responsibility seriously.

While Zinzendorf did not believe in women's equal social rights, leading Sisters may well have valued them. Many single women hesitated or even refused to enter into marriage. A number stated they did not want to give up their work in the Single Sisters Choir. Anna Johanna Piesch actually suggested she treasured her equal status as a leading Single Sister. On the proposal that she marry, she said:

> After these two dear people [Zinzendorf and Nitschmann] went home [in death], I thought from then on I would devote myself completely to my dear Single Sisters Choir and exert twice the steadfastness and diligence; I believed it to be more necessary now than ever, however, the Savior ordained otherwise and gave me a whole different field to till. I received my assignment in America and in addition, the dear Brother Nathanael Seidel was offered to me [in marriage]... To America I was very willing to go, but to enter into marriage, that cost me a great deal. There were many bitter pains, before I was able to submit my will to the Savior's. But He helped me get through [the ordeal] and stood strongly by my side.... As already mentioned, I went very unwillingly into this important state, but since it was the Savior's will, I prayed immediately upon my entry into [marriage] to grant me the favor, that he would help me bring him joy and honor and that he would give me the grace to be a loyal submissive [*untertänige*] wife from now on.[17]

Piesch's independence and status as a leading Single Sister was so important to her that she required the Savior's insistence before she would give them up. For Zinzendorf and the other Moravian men, however, the subjection of women was taken for granted. Yet how had Zinzendorf convinced other men to bring the Sisters into the leadership of the Church? How did he quiet the opposition?

One means was reliance on the Lot. Zinzendorf simply submitted proposed women for leading positions to the Lot. Moravians were supposed to lay their merely human proposals before the Savior, that is, write their suggestions as questions and draw lots to give the Savior the chance to answer yes or no. Meeting minutes from the 1730s and 1740s indicate many women were proposed to the Lot for office, and many came up positive, which meant the Savior had made his will known. Interestingly, Zinzendorf never drew a Lot on the general question of *whether* Sisters should hold leading offices in the central governing body of the Church, in the separate settlements, or in their choirs.

Zinzendorf's second way of circumventing criticism was to analyze the nature and abilities of the two genders and communicate his findings in countless sermons written for the different choirs. So, a sermon to the Single Brothers might say something about the Single Sisters, to emphasize contrasting character traits. He suggested that women could serve as good models for all Christians, because the ideal woman was completely submissive, intensely loving, and able to feel deeply—the very traits that defined the ideal relationship between every Christian and the Savior. Zinzendorf also claimed that a few women had the gift to govern well, although men were generally better at it.[18] These sermons were painstakingly copied in editions of the *Jüngerhaus Diarium* (Diary of the House of Disciples) and sent to Moravian settlements worldwide.

Zinzendorf also used ambiguity or even contradiction. In a single paragraph, he claimed one thing and then immediately modified or even denied it. On marriage, for instance, Zinzendorf said, "I greatly value equality in marriage and am marvelously happy when similar people marry each other," a statement contradicted by the next sentence, in which he preferred that "the saucy Sisters be a little weaker in knowledge than the Brothers, so that in their forwardness, they don't perceive things before their husbands do."[19] Whenever Zinzendorf introduced a new idea, this ambiguity could come in handy by suggesting he concurred with his critics on basic principles, thereby reassuring them innovation would be not so harmful after all.[20]

Scholars generally agree that the attack on female leadership after Zinzendorf's death was part of male leaders' program to make the Moravian Church more orthodox, but they are not quite sure why orthodoxy was so valued. Certainly orthodoxy was not pursued to attract new members. Moravians still agreed with Zinzendorf that they should avoid contributing to the proliferation of Protestant Churches. While the General Synod minutes show that the majority of male delegates favored limiting or even eliminating women's leading roles, the reasons for their stance are not obvious. The report of the ad hoc "Committee to Investigate the Participation and Influence of the Sisters in Choir, Congregation, and Church Affairs" (hereinafter the "men's Committee on Sisters") includes the following statements:

> One cannot deny, that the recent and still current practice of the Moravian Church concerning the service of the Sisters in the Church is certainly an important issue for the Synod, because it is evident that on the side of many a Brother, a fear remains [concerning that practice], which could easily lead to the other extreme.

> Consequences and reprimands [arise whenever] the Moravian Church deviates from tradition and authorizes the Sisters to assist in the celebration of Communion in gatherings of both sexes in the whole congregation.

> The wellbeing and misfortune of the Moravian Church depends in large part ... on this important ... matter.[21]

These quotes indicate that many Moravian men feared the consequences of the Church failing to modify untraditional service practiced by Moravian women. Indeed, they indicate they thought the future survival of the Moravian Church depended on it. It is known that the Church feared the impact of colossal debts incurred by borrowing from both members and nonmembers, and that it also feared disgrace in the eyes of the surrounding world because of its debt burden and the more extreme religious practices of the Sifting Time.

These burdens reflected tense relationships between the Moravian Church and the world, and delegates had good reason to be concerned. Under Zinzendorf's leadership, the Church had been subject to vehement attack from outsiders and apostates. The criticism centered on Zinzendorf's many innovations in theology, religious practice, and social structure, but especially on the unique social arrangements in Moravian communities.[22] While marriage and work in the patriarchal family had become the dominant structure for social and economic life in post-Reformation Germany, Moravian communities offered attractive alternatives.[23] Men and women could remain single and still lead meaningful, respected, and independent lives. If they married, they might well be asked to work with their spouses in ways that transcended their family interests and served the larger Moravian spiritual or economic enterprise. Having committed itself so solidly to marriage and the family as the basis for life and work since the sixteenth century, the outside world may well have perceived Moravian alternatives as threatening.

In addition, the class boundaries that still defined German society were blurred in Zinzendorf's Moravian communities. Men and women of humble backgrounds and people of the high nobility dressed alike, served with each other in governing councils and synods, worked with each other to plan community and choir festivals, and worshipped with each other while sitting on the same bench. An anonymous 1735 polemic complained the Moravian Church was a *Weiber-Religion* (feminine religion) and decried its mixing of classes: "A theologian in the neighborhood calls the Herrnhut revival a feminine religion, because it has been observed that this sex conforms itself especially to the Count [Zinzendorf], and that often a peasant maiden renounces her manners and habits when she enters the community of Sisters [Single Sisters Choir] and becomes overly refined and soft in her carriage. That the common people in Herrnhut immediately change their manners and become urbane beyond their station happens because they live with great lords and noble ladies in the most intimate association."[24] The insistent focus on women in this early critique of blurry class boundaries may hinge on the fact that lower-class Moravian women in positions of authority had crossed boundaries of both gender and class and were therefore perceived to be especially threatening to hierarchy. If Zinzendorf had pulled women leaders from his own class, the high nobility, would the public have reacted so strongly, given the long history of regency among noble women? Regardless, their success suggests that Moravian women may actually have been better than men at assuming upper-class bearing, as the observer suggested.[25]

The synod delegates believed they could counter persistent criticisms only if their practices matched those in other Protestant Churches.[26] Women's active participation must have been one of the most offensive differences in religious practice, an important example of the extremist tendencies of the Church under Zinzendorf. One Brother even connected the practices of the Sifting Time with the participation of the Sisters. In a letter that he directed to the men's Committee on Sisters, he wrote that he hoped "with all his heart" that the choirs could be preserved, but that he saw "a great difference between [on the one hand] that, which belongs to the heart of Jesus ... and to the choir concept and [on the other hand] the exaggerated principles and methods, which the teachings of Jesus do not include and [which] can cause only danger and unhappiness," and he wished, "that the latter might remain removed from the Moravian Church forever," whereupon the Sisters reminded the delegates "that this should be understood as applying only to the previous Period [that is, the Sifting Time]."[27] Although this Brother did not explicitly connect the service of the Sisters with the choir concept and the Sifting Time, the fact that he directed his remarks to the men's Committee on Sisters suggests this connection in his mind. The Sisters' response shows they understood his remarks as a criticism of their participation and their undue influence on the exaggerations of the Sifting Time. They tried to disconnect the two in their response by pointing out that the Sifting Time practices were no longer followed, though the Sisters still held their influential Church offices. If the Sisters had been more forthright, they could have pointed out that men had always set the tone, while the women followed their lead.

The goal of making the Moravian Church more orthodox was intended to ensure survival in a world grown wary of, or even vehemently opposed to the Moravian Church under Zinzendorf. This opposition in the face of an overwhelming debt burden convinced Moravian leaders they must improve their image to regain the trust of their creditors. In the Synods of 1764 and 1769, delegates expressed great concern about the perception of Moravians in the world, and especially what the world thought about women's participation in spiritual and administrative affairs.[28]

Male leaders then tackled the problem of how to limit women's office holding among the women themselves, who were committed to the Church and attended to their duties with evident energy and inspiration. How did the male leaders succeed in taking away these roles? Careful preparation for the Synod of 1764 on the part of several leading Brothers, including August Gottlieb Spangenberg, marked the first step. Prior to the synod Spangenberg collected countless quotes from Zinzendorf's writings that might apply to current issues. These quotations, many of them extensive, appear throughout the synod minutes and the ad hoc committee reports, including Zinzendorf's remarks about the position of the women in the Church, which suggests Spangenberg had intended to limit the roles of Moravian women long before the Synod began.

Prior to the meeting, Spangenberg and the twelve other Brothers present determined that all issues would have to be prepared by ad hoc committees before introduction at plenary sessions, that not all synod delegates should be present for all discussions, and that certain issues should be prioritized on the agenda, so that the "doubts [of the delegates about a difficult issue] could be satisfied ahead of time."[29] The four session chairs (who were to alternate in presiding over the various sessions) would be able to control the agenda and the direction of the discussions.

When the synod convened, the Sisters' participation was sharply limited. Only men were allowed to be present at the first in-depth discussion of women's leadership roles (implementing the stipulation that not all delegates would be present for all discussions). In this session, seven points were drawn up for the men's Committee on Sisters, which was actually not named until the next synod session. The cautious selection of committee members that followed was noteworthy. First the four session chairs and then the six congregation leaders in attendance were submitted to the Lot as two separate groups, and the Lot came up "yes" both times. Then eleven other Brothers were suggested but submitted to the Lot as individuals. Four were chosen, making fourteen members in all. A question on whether leading Sisters should be added to the committee was not approved by the Lot.[30] As a result of this unusual procedure, the most influential Brothers in the Church were committee members of this committee—a sign this issue was considered highly important. The female delegates had no part in suggesting members for this committee that would decide their future in the Church. They were, however, allowed to suggest names for a committee of their own that would meet separately, and after discussing the report of the men's Committee on Sisters, they would "be heard." The women suggested eleven candidates, but only five were approved by the Savior through the Lot.

Results of the Lot depended not only on the will of the Savior. Before the Lot could be consulted, people had to decide when to use it. Thus the delegates never asked whether Sisters should be members of the General Directorate or continue to hold "General Offices." The report of the men's Committee on Sisters simply stated that "such office holding was in no way suitable for Sisters, if they weren't supposed to have authority in all the settlements, as they have heretofore. The whole committee was unanimous on this."[31] The minutes for the plenary session concluded it was "deemed not good" for Sisters to hold general offices.[32] This decision was made by male leaders of the synod, not the Savior.

People also formulated questions to submit to the Lot. In the deliberations about who should have oversight for educating the girls in the settlements, only the following questions were presented to the Lot:

1. The oversight of the education of the children in the Girls House is to be taken care of by a School ["Anstalt"] Conference.
2. The oversight of the education of the children in the Girls House is to be given to a specific married couple alongside the Conference.[33]

These formulations allowed Single Sisters no opportunity to retain sole responsibility for the education of girls, as they had in the past. Still another method employed to diminish women's responsibilities turned on reminding all members of basic Moravian values. Delegates frequently heard some form of the admonishment "that the lust for power,…over choirs, settlements, or the whole Church, is not suitable for any human being, for maids of Jesus Christ least of all."[34] Sisters essentially had no defense available to them as the synod moved to limit their participation in Church administration.

Finally, Zinzendorf's successors supported their efforts to limit Moravian women's power by carefully reshaping the Church's relationship to its past. They attempted to show these changes as consistent with previous ones, simply stating that the Moravian Church had always done it this way or using a quotation from Zinzendorf to support a proposed change. The latter was especially effective because they used Zinzendorf's own words, with their studied ambiguity, to their advantage, as in this example: "The female sex must remain under the direction of the male Elders etc. [this was the Synod's inaccurate, partial quotation of Zinzendorf's remarks at the Synod in Gotha]; about that there is no question. It was stipulated this way at the Synod in Gotha and maintained since that time unchanged …. Therefore qualified Brothers must be put in charge of the Sisters Choirs by the Synod or in each settlement one Brother [must be put in charge of the Sisters Choirs].[35]"

This quote misrepresents the past in two ways. First, the delegates interpreted Zinzendorf's words incorrectly. As Paul Peucker has pointed, Zinzendorf said only that *one* Brother in the whole Church should direct the Sisters Choirs *through* their separate Eldresses and choir leaders. He did not intend that there be a Brother in each settlement to oversee the individual choirs at close hand. Zinzendorf actually had himself in mind as the one Brother, and was reconstituting authority to give female leaders *more* independence than usual.[36] Second, this actually marked a significant change from the past, as male curators would be assigned to the female choirs in every Moravian settlement for the first time.

Zinzendorf's successors also "manipulated" their history. In the 1764 Synod, it was decided that Spangenberg should write a biography of Zinzendorf, for which a number of different documents would be made available to him. Spangenberg's subsequent manuscript carefully formulated Zinzendorf's ideas and actions to be perceived as creative but not inoffensive, and many of the sources Spangenberg used were destroyed when he finished writing. Leaders and archivists also systematically destroyed many other documents from 1760 to 1810, especially those dealing with the Sifting Time or the activity of leading Sisters. The voluminous correspondence of Anna Nitschmann, Anna Johanna Piesch, and other leading Sisters, for example, was sought out and burned.[37]

The collective memory of the leading Sisters and their significant contributions to Moravian history were damaged too. Nitschmann, as the founder of the Single Sisters Choir and the originator of the Single Sisters' Covenant with the Savior, had been remembered on 4 May since at least as early as 1748 (when the single Sisters in Bethlehem began to keep their diary). In the descriptions of the festival for 1767 and 1770, she had to share the honor with Zinzendorf. After 1770, the entries reported only that 4 May was the anniversary of the covenant eighteen Single Sisters had made with Christ. Nitschmann had disappeared. From the mid 1780s on, the covenant was no longer mentioned. Instead 4 May simply marked a yearly blessing of the Single Sisters Choir and the admittance of the Older Girls into the single Sisters Choir. Even the hundredth anniversary in 1830 was celebrated only as an ordinary single Sisters Choir festival.

Given the importance of this day before Nitschmann's death in 1760, it is doubtful single Sisters had forgotten her contributions ten years later. This public "forgetfulness" must have been engineered as yet another way to distance Moravians from the roles Moravian women had held under Zinzendorf's leadership.

Women must have been shocked by the sudden limitation of their office holding in the Moravian Church. The 1764 Synod minutes state "when the [men's Committee on Sisters] was set up and the Sisters were not included, all kinds of emotional feelings surfaced, although the Sisters themselves realized that it should go that way."[38] During the rest of this Synod, the Sisters made cautious "reminders" *(Erinnerungen)* that reflected concern about the proposed changes. In one instance, the Lot had determined that Sisters would continue their membership in the Elders Conferences in Moravian congregations. The men's Committee on Sisters subsequently suggested this matter must come up in Elders Conferences, which "do not belong in [the Sisters'] jurisdiction." To avoid "taxing the patience of the Sisters" the local leader "must have the freedom … to look at such matters with the Brothers alone, without admitting the Sisters." The Sisters responded with the hope "that that [freedom] would just not be extended too far."[39]

Although such comments highlight the Sisters' underlying anxiety, no existing record indicates they suggested any changes in the basic principles being developed or (after their initial outburst) that they objected to the methods being used to reduce their influence and participation. One reason for their relative silence may have been that they still played important roles in this particular synod. In a large ad hoc committee formed to analyze the perilous financial situation of the Moravian Church, nine of the twenty-six members were women. When the Savior refused (through the Lot) to agree to any of their proposed solutions to their financial problems, the synod participants began to see his responses as an indictment of current Church shortcomings. The minutes show that the Sisters took part in these proceedings.[40] The committee then submitted these shortcomings to the Lot one by one, and the Savior indicated that twelve of them matched his concerns. After this heartfelt, soul-searching process, the delegates found the Savior ready to approve a number of their suggestions for dealing with the Church's problems. Because these Twelve Points were considered such a significant communication from the Savior, not only during the synod itself, but afterward as well, the Sisters involved must have felt included. And although the minutes do not identify the originator of each point, chances are some came from the Sisters. Such inclusion may have reassured the Sisters that they would continue to have influence under the new regime.

When the Synod of 1769 reduced women's responsibilities even further, the Sisters spoke with more candor. Delegates, having reintroduced the question of female participation in the central governing body, suggested perhaps they ought not allow women even the advisory role given them in 1764. The Sisters handed in a written request "that our dear Lord might be asked about that," putting the decision in the Savior's hands, not the Bothers'.[41] The women wrote again asking that a topic be submitted to the Lot, and even suggested some wording, in sharp contrast to the relative meekness of the female delegates at the synod five years earlier. Now they openly questioned the procedures by which decisions were being made and suggested alternatives. Interestingly, one of the Twelve Points from the 1764 Synod read: "Many Brothers settle their ideas without knowing the Savior's [wishes] concerning them." It is tempting to conclude that a Sister formulated that particular point.

The spiritual autobiography of Anna Johanna Piesch provides frank private reactions about the events of this transitional period in the Moravian Church. While different versions of her autobiography indicate certain parts have been "edited away," much has been preserved in the records of the congregation in Nazareth, Pennsylvania, where Piesch lived her last years. Her writings express her grief upon the deaths of Zinzendorf and Nitschmann—because she had lost people dear to her, but also because of her anxiety over what would happen to the Church and choirs. Recall also her comment that "[her] anxious thoughts and premonitions did unfortunately come true in considerable measure, and to [her] inexpressible pain, [she] had to witness that these dear people were almost completely forgotten, especially the dear Mama [Anna Nitschmann]." Surely these words reflect Piesch's unhappiness with women's limited roles following Zinzendorf's death. Although Piesch had not been present at the 1764 Synod, she attended the 1769 Synod. She wrote about the event: "I rejoiced to see many of my dear acquaintances from the past and to embrace them, and that was all, too, for otherwise I had no joy at all, only distress, and I cried many, many tears. As soon as the synod was over, we hurried back."[42] She never returned to Europe.

Anna Johanna Piesch knew Zinzendorf was the only Moravian man who consistently advocated for women's participation in the spiritual and administrative affairs of the Moravian Church. Without his support and that of Anna Nitschmann, Piesch must have felt heavily burdened. She probably took an active role in the 1769 Synod, a driving force behind the women's attempts to halt the attack on women's roles by calling for a change in procedures. Her personal reaction to these failed efforts is evident in her poignant observation: "otherwise I had no joy at all, only distress, and I cried many, many tears."

Notes

1. MAB, Autobiography of Anna Johanna Piesch Seidel.
2. Heide Wunder, *He Is the Sun, She Is the Moon: Women in Early Modern Germany* (Cambridge, 1998), 162.

3. *Zeremonienbüchlein: Kurze, zuverläßige Nachricht von der unter dem Namen der Böhmische-Mährischen Brüder bekanten Kirche Unitas Fratrum, Herkommen, Lehr-Begriff, äussern und innern Kirchen-Verfassung und Gebräuchen, aus richtigen Urkunden und Erzehlungen von einem ihrer christlich unpartheiischen Freunde herausgegeben und mit sechzehn Vorstellungen in Kupfer erläutert* (n.p., 1757), Plate N.IX, UA-Herrnhut.
4. There were probably at least two paintings originally. Beverly Smaby, "Female Piety Among Eighteenth-Century Moravians," *Pennsylvania History: A Journal of Mid-Atlantic Studies, Empire, Society and Labor: Essays in Honor of Richard S. Dunn*, vol. 64, Special Supplemental Issue (Summer 1997): 151–167.
5. See Carl Freiherrn von Schrautenbach, *Der Graf von Zinzendorf und die Brüdergemeine seiner Zeit* (1851) in Erich Beyreuther and Gerhard Meyer, eds., *Nikolaus Ludwig von Zinzendorf: Leben und Werk in Quellen und Darstellungen*, Series 2, vol. 9 (Hildesheim, 1972), 91–92; Erika Geiger, *Erdmuth Dorothea Gräfin von Zinzendorf: Die "Hausmutter" der Herrnhuter Brüdergemeine* (Ulm, 2000), 36–39, 48–93.
6. Wunder, *He is the Sun, She is the Moon*, 154–161.
7. Ibid., chapters 3, 4, 5, 7, and 11.
8. Paul Peucker, " 'In Staub und Asche': Bewertung und Kassation im Unitätsarchive 1760–1810," in *"Alles ist euer, ihr aber seid Christi": Festschrift für Dietrich Meyer*, ed. Rudolf Mohr, in *Schriftenreihe des Vereins für Rheinische Kirchengeschichte*, 147 (2000): 128.
9. UA-Herrnhut, R.2.B.44.1.c.2, 1764 General Synod Minutes, 1394.
10. UA-Herrnhut, R.2.B.44.1.c.2, 1764 General Synod Minutes, 1398.
11. UA-Herrnhut, R.2.B.44.1.c.2, 1764 General Synod Minutes, 1389–1391.
12. UA-Herrnhut, R.2.B.44.1.b, 1764 General Synod Minutes, 819–820.
13. UA-Herrnhut, R.2.B.45.1.e, 1769 General Synod Minutes, 1082–1083.
14. UA-Herrnhut, R.2.B.45.1, 1747 Synod Minutes, 625.
15. Autobiography of Anna Johanna Piesch Seidel.
16. *Verlass der vier Synoden der evangelishcen Brüde-Unität von den Jahren 1764, 1769, 1775, und 1782*, §§457–458, MAB; Beverly Smaby, "Gender in Eighteenth Century Bethlehem," forthcoming in *Backcountry Crucibles: From Settlement to Steel*, ed. by Jean Soderlund and Catherine S. Parzynski, Lehigh University Press.
17. Autobiography of Anna Johanna Piesch Seidel.
18. Smaby, "Gender in Eighteenth Century Bethlehem."
19. UA-Herrnhut, R.2.B.45.1, 1747 Synod Minutes, 625.
20. Smaby, "Gender in Eighteenth Century Bethlehem."
21. UA-Herrnhut, R.2.B.44.4.a.5, Report of the Ad Hoc Committee zur Untersuchung der Concurrenz und des Einflusses der Schwestern in Chor-, Gemein-, und Kirchensachen.
22. For a small selection of the anti-Moravian polemic literature, see Beyreuther and Meyer, eds., *Anti-Zinzendorfiana in Nikolaus Ludwig von Zinzendorf: Leben und Werk...*, Series 2, vols. 14–18 (Hildesheim, 1976)
23. See Wunder, *He is the Sun, She is the Moon*, especially chapters 3 and 4.
24. Anonymous, *Ausführliche Historische und Theologische Nachricht von der Herrenhuthischen Brüdershaft...* in Beyreuther and Meyer, eds., *Anti-Zinzendorfiana*, volume 14, 93–96.
25. Peter Trudgill, "Sex and Covert Prestige," in Jennifer Coates, ed., *Language and Gender: A Reader* (London, 1998); Robin Lakoff, *Language and Women's Place* (New York, 1976).
26. UA-Herrnhut, R.2.B.45.2.a, Unvorgreiffliche Anmerkungen und Desideria dem Ehrwürdigen General-Synodo zur Prüffung und Decision pflichtmässig dargelegt von dem verordneten Unitäts Syndicats Collegion nebst Beylagen Sub. Cit: A. bis Cit. H.
27. Report of the men's Committee on Sisters.
28. One example of concern about outsiders' views came up in a discussion about Moravian women's assistance in the celebration of Communion. 1764 Synod Minutes, August 9, 1764, 819.
29. UA-Herrnhut, R.2.B.44.4.a.1, Report of Preparatory Committee for the 1764 Synod.
30. UA-Herrnhut, R.2.B.44.1.c.2, 1764 General Synod Minutes, 11 August 1764, 1371.

31. Report of the men's Committee on Sisters.
32. UA-Herrnhut, R.2.B.44.1.c.2, 1764 General Synod Minutes, 14 August 1764, 1394.
33. UA-Herrnhut, R.2.B.44.1.c.2, 1764 General Synod Minutes, 1397–1398.
34. Report of the men's Committee on Sisters.
35. 1764 General Synod Minutes, UA-Herrnhut, R.2.B.44.1.c.2, 1387.
36. Paul Peucker, "'Gegen ein Regiment von Schwestern': Die Stellung der Frau in der Brüdergemeine nach Zinzendorfs Tod," *Unitas Fratrum*, 66.
37. Paul Peucker, "'In Staub und Asche," 127–158.
38. Report of the men's Committee on Sisters.
39. Report of the men's Committee on Sisters.
40. These proceedings are described in UA-Herrnhut, R.2.B.44.3.1, *Special-Conference Protocoll*, 27 July 1764, included in *Protocoll der vom Gen: Synodo verordneten Committee in der Diaconats-Materie.*
41. UA-Herrnhut, R.2.B.45.1.d, 1769 General Synod Minutes, 1064.
42. Autobiography of Anna Johanna Piesch Seidel.

Chapter 11

THE ROLE OF THE PASTOR'S WIFE IN THE PIONEERING GENERATION OF PROTESTANT GERMAN-SPEAKING CLERGY IN THE AMERICAN COLONIES

Marianne S. Wokeck

THE NUMBER OF UNIVERSITY-TRAINED professionals among more than 100,000 German-speaking immigrants in eighteenth-century North America was minute. Generally, professionals' training, interests and opportunities for making a living limited them to German lands.[1] Most pastors belonged to this group, and relatively few relocated to the American colonies.[2] Some ministers came leading immigrant groups, for instance John Martin Boltzius, who ministered to the Protestant refugees from Salzburg in Georgia, and Moritz Göttschi, who accompanied emigrants from Zurich bound for the Carolinas. The majority, however, were Churchmen who came to serve already established congregations. As the trickle of German migration across the Atlantic swelled to a substantial flow by the 1730s, the influx of sectarian voyagers was augmented by growing numbers of Reformed and Lutheran immigrants who settled in communities in desperate need of pastors.[3]

The immigrants' appeals to their homelands for ministers went mostly unheeded until Count Nicolaus Ludwig von Zinzendorf, Michael Schlatter, and Henry Melchior Mühlenberg arrived in the 1740s. These men and other pioneering pastors became trendsetters not only for their organization of German Protestant Churches in the American colonies but for the congregations they served. In those first formative decades of the German Reformed, Lutheran, and Moravian Churches in North America they played a crucial role in modeling ways to negotiate difficulties in unfamiliar territory. They maneuvered between competing and overlapping experiences and expectations based on Old World customs and traditions on one hand and, on the other, life in the new land. Since the pastorate was considered an exemplary office in its very nature, these pioneering pastors played a crucial role in establishing conduct, values, and activities for those who followed them.[4]

Defining pastors' role in local communities was a shared enterprise of the *"ganze Pfarrhaus,"* shouldered also by the *Pfarrfrauen* (parsons' wives) and other members of the pastors' households, especially children and servants. In Zinzendorf's household, the so-called House of Disciples *(Jüngerhaus),* included his close co-workers.[5] This essay focuses on the part of the parson's wife. As a group their character is difficult to describe because the sources that specify their activities and behavior, let alone thoughts and emotions, are scarce and scattered. As individuals they remain almost in the shadow, seen only through the lens of men, as a rule their husbands, who provide most of the observations and comments—the image of the woman is the image man has of the woman (Das Bild der Frau ist das Bild des Mannes von der Frau).[6] Despite the limitations of the sources, comparing the *Pfarrfrau* in the German homelands with the circumstances under which the parson's wife in German-speaking communities in the American colonies carried out her responsibilities allows us to speculate about how she influenced identities and framed choices for subsequent generations of pastors and their households in German-American congregations.

In Germany, Katharina von Bora, the former nun who married the Protestant reformer Martin Luther, began the process of defining the role of the *Pfarrfrau*.[7] In the "first parsonage" *(erste Pfarrhaus)* everything had to be improvised; nothing was regulated.[8] In subsequent generations, however, the transformation of the view of women from "obstacle to help," from the reality of dishonorable companions of clerics *(unehrenhaftes "papenwife")* before the Reformation to the virtuous parson's wife ideal, occurred in the territories where Protestantism prevailed.[9] Consequently the responsibilities of pastors' wives became integrated into the cities' and states' regulatory catalogs of privileges and obligations that determined the place Protestant clergy occupied in early modern Germany.

The Protestant territorial lords and the Church administrations succeeded in creating a new estate *(Stand)* for the clergy with a distinctive lifestyle, privileges, and social status, attainable only through ordination.[10] *Kirchenordnungen* (Church orders) controlled the lives of the ministers and spelled out their rights, most importantly freedom from taxes and levies in addition to direct responsibility to the consistory. Over time the clergy not only accepted the regulations but embraced them as the culture of their estate.[11] Since the pastorate had the monopoly on preaching the gospel truth, special training was required, which meant studying Protestant theology at a chosen university—a prerequisite for office that made pastors intellectually, socially, and culturally members of the cities' developing bourgeoisie, kept them remote from the courts of territorial lords and the mansions of the landed nobility, and left them outsiders in the parishes of the countryside.[12]

When the Protestant clergy achieved complete professionalization in the second half of the seventeenth century, certain characteristics of their social status had become typical. Pastors considered the parsonage and income from small tithes and interest on loans to rural parishioners status-specific property, which they not only defended but also sought to expand.[13] They expected sons to become their successors and daughters to marry the sons of other ministers.[14] The extent of political maneuvering necessary to arrange such desirable marriages and succession in office led to a clannish mindset among the orthodox clergy (*altprotestantische Pfarrstand*) that placed high value on the pastors' honor and ethos.[15]

If the Protestant clergy had developed a self-understanding about their place in society, their relationship to the territorial lords and to their parishioners was ambiguous.[16] Pastors were obligated to the territorial state that granted them privileges. Moreover, they had proven their usefulness as overseers of the poor and the nascent school system and as local guardians of moral order beholden to absolutist lords. Ministers had developed into the most important executive arm of the state and its Church on the local level.[17] Parishioners, on the other hand, had high expectations concerning their pastors' conduct in office, including demonstrating restraint in their use of material goods.[18] Such expectations, together with pastors' dependence on parishioners' payments for income, clashed with the increasing needs of the Protestant clergy to maintain their families.[19]

In the eighteenth century, the reform movement of Pietism brought radical changes well beyond the small circle of like-minded teachers and students of theology around Philipp Jacob Spener.[20] Pietism destroyed the unity among Lutheran clergy, in part by separating well-established and well-off pastors in the imperial cities and university towns, who had included writing devotional literature among their responsibilities, from the rest of their colleagues, in part by creating parties of pastors for or against reform.[21] Students, often the sons of pastors, sought out professors at certain universities for their stance on ideological issues and those of one mind kept in touch by meeting in conventicles, through correspondence, and partisan publishing activities. On the local level parishioners became separated into pious and not so pious Christians, the former with more equal access to their pastors and devout conversation, the latter definitely discouraged and excluded from such discourse.[22]

In this new constellation of orthodoxy and reform, certain pastors' households became nodes in the networks of Pietists and their far-flung organizational and publication activities that focused on solving social problems and affecting humankind. Their interests extended beyond local issues of Church and community and transcended political boundaries,

economic regions, and cultural spheres of influence.[23] Pietist social reform, intent on building the kingdom of God *(praxis pietatis)*, captured the
active involvement of other Protestant Church leaders worldwide as well
as prominent lay people, including influential women like Zinzendorf's
grandmother, Henriette von Gersdorf. Pietist reform developed in two
phases. The first, initiated by Spener, emphasized informal communication networks and *collegia pietatis;* the second phase directed efforts toward founding institutions, printing houses, and systems of supply
stations to support missionary efforts.[24]

Building on this reform impetus, some enlightened rulers used pastors' households to generate change in Church and society and as models
for the transformation of the family at large.[25] Especially in the early years,
even when congregations split over issues of reform, whole families joined
the Pietists. Women who rejected their traditional role in the patriarchal
structure were shunted into radical Pietism.[26] Their examples did not help
transform the role of women in the family.[27] Moravians, like Quakers,
fully acknowledged women's spiritual equality, granting them exceptional
roles in spiritual leadership, at least temporarily, in the organization and
government of their Church. The strength Moravian women gained from
their unconventional spiritual and administrative roles may have shaped
their own marriages without structurally redefining the proper place and
duties for Moravian wives generally.[28] As the Enlightenment and its supporters increasingly influenced absolutist rulers, Pietism lost ground among
the bourgeoisie, faltered in its commitment to reform efforts, and retreated
from the political arena and social opportunities for enterprising, increasingly secularized citizens—in defense of pious practice. In the second half
of the eighteenth century piousness became a more private affair. Pietism
remained strong in those more limited spheres because it offered a comprehensive theological system clear in its ethical conditions and reliant on
trusted persons for guidance in practicing piety.[29]

By the 1730s and 1740s, when the pioneering generation of pastors to
American congregations had been trained in German lands, Protestant
clergy—whether reform-minded or not—held established places in society, playing well-defined roles in the parishes they served. Their situation
depended on the university at which they trained and with whom, where
they secured ordination and what kind of parish they served, and who
they married. Well-off and well-connected young men based their decisions concerning university, professor, parish, and wife on the experience
and support derived from overlapping circles of family, friends, and
sponsors.[30] First-generation pastors, who were a minority, often lacked
this kind of support structure, instead depending heavily on some sort of
mentor, which usually came at the price of considerable, life-long obligation.[31] The situation was different, of course, for someone like Zinzendorf, whose ordination and leadership in the Moravian Church grew not
only out of his religious interests but more importantly, out of his status
as territorial lord.[32]

Upon installation into their first post, usually when they were thirty-one years old and had waited a considerable time in interim positions for a call, all pastors had had considerable exposure to the workings of *Pfarrhäuser*.[33] About half spent their childhood in one, observing father and mother in their respective duties as *Pfarrer* and *Hausvater*, *Pfarrfrau* and *Hausmutter*, also noting how siblings took on responsibilities according to their age and sex and how servants fit into the operations of the parsonage.[34] When the boy moved out of his father's house to pursue studies in preparation for higher education and then to attend university, he typically became a member of another pastor's household, a boarding young scholar under the tutelage of the *Hausvater*, obedient to both him and the *Hausmutter*.[35] Such boarding arrangements afforded the teenager another perspective on the organization of a *Pfarrhaus*.[36] Boys who attended Latin schools—usually boarding schools in cities or university towns—were often taught by students and candidates of theology.[37] At university it was common for exceptional students to board with their professors, whose households depended on the additional income—yet another *Pfarrhaus* experience for the pastor-in-training that modeled urban circumstances and the comportment of the privileged professoriate, both situations out of reach of most pastors.[38] Further exposure to the ways of parsonages occurred when the young man served several years as teacher or curate before receiving a call. In short, the experiences of the household in a succession of *Pfarrhäuser* helped shape a young pastor's ideas about what constituted good management of the parsonage and about the proper role of the *Pfarrfrau*.[39] Relatively few young men who became ministers of Moravian congregations, however, formed their ideas about these roles in the pastor's household this way. Their experience of living and learning grew out of the choir system, which grouped single members according to age and segregated them strictly by sex. It was also informed by the teachings of the Church about marriage, sex, and family and by observing the extended households of their leaders, foremost Zinzendorf's House of Disciples (*Jüngerhaus*).

For the *Pfarrfrau*, her world of experience and contacts centered on family and parish, excepting Moravian single Sisters, whose world was primarily defined by the choir system—a model of communal living and working different from that of the traditional family and local community.[40] The political, social, and cultural developments in the eighteenth century that affected the Pietist reform movement locally, regionally, and worldwide were of little consequence to the parson's wife, especially if she was far from cities and university towns.[41] Her role as helpmate to her husband and mother of his household (*Hausmutter*) was firmly embedded in a patriarchal system that remained fundamentally unchanged and even strongly reaffirmed in the structuring of Pietist philanthropic and educational enterprises.[42]

Together with her husband, the pastor's wife determined the regimen of the house, different from ordinary houses because it was the domicile of the pastor's household and also the house of the parish, making the *Pfarrhaus* both private and public.[43] In keeping with the dual role the pastor played as father of the house *(Hausvater* being a more common appellation than *Hausherr)* and as father to the parishioners, the parson's wife was mother of the house *(Hausmutter)* as well as mother to the parishioners *(Pfarrfrau).*[44] The *Pfarrfrau* was in a partnership, albeit an unequal one, where the roles of the pastor and his wife were complementary, like that of father *and* mother of the house—co-rulers, parents, united in their responsibility for the household and the upbringing of their children as well as preservation of community and Church. In effect, the parson's wife was defined by her relationship to her husband as well by her duty to the office of *Pfarrfrau*, underscoring the exemplary character of her conduct as well as her activities.[45] The partnership took on an additional dimension of teamwork among Moravians because in Zinzendorf's version of marriage—marriage militant or *Streiterehe*—the husband served the spiritual needs of the men in his pastoral care, the wife those of the women in the congregation.[46] As the pastor's companion *(Gefehrtin des Lebens)* and co-ruler of the house, the wife owed obedience to her husband so that she could serve as his "aide and support, not his footstool." In this the parson's wife was no different from all good Christian housewives of comparable status whose accomplishments were reflections to the public, but because of the *Pfarrfrau*'s responsibility she had to be an especially good housewife.[47]

The pastor's wife had to educate her children, manage the household, and lead a Christian life by caring for the poor and sick and by providing spiritual guidance to her family.[48] Fulfilling those high expectations under the difficult circumstances of eighteenth-century life was demanding for ordinary pastors' wives and especially those in the countryside because the standard of living in the *Pfarrhaus* depended in large part on their skillful household management.[49]

Vocation to the office of *Pfarrfrau* was an expectation only in that most Protestant women of bourgeois background became wives *(Ehefrauen)*; it became a strong likelihood for daughters whose fathers belonged to circles of university-trained functionaries where pursuing advantageous marriage strategies improved social status.[50] "Riches" and marriage into a "distinguished family" constituted "qualities of luck" *(Glücks=Qualitäten)* in addition to the other two important criteria for making a beneficial choice in wives, namely a good mind for pleasant conversation and competent housekeeping and also youth, health, and beauty to please her husband and bear healthy children.[51]

Becoming the wife of a pastor was like a career option, sometimes a true calling, because while marriage to a pastor usually resulted from negotiations between the woman's father and her prospective husband, it did not necessarily mean the woman had no say.[52] Not every father commanded, like Frederick William I of Prussia, that daughters abide by the paternal will and marry the husbands of his choice.[53] Since the life's work of Protestant women was marriage and the education of children, daughters of clerks, jurists, and other members of the urban bourgeoisie were expected to be able to read, write, and do arithmetic, know the basic tenets of Christianity, and have an aptitude for household management in addition to a command of other academic subjects, especially foreign languages.[54] Training in housewifery did not necessarily come through the mother, especially for daughters of the urban bourgeoisie who went to cloister-like public schools for girls or received instruction from live-in teachers.[55] In contrast, ordinary pastors' daughters often learned household management from their mothers and other female members of the household and relatives and studied most other subjects with their brothers, instructed by their fathers.[56]

At the age of twenty-three or so, when pastors' wives first married, young women were well trained and sufficiently experienced to take on the management of the *Pfarrhaus*, the epitome of the *"status oeconomicus."*[57] Pastors' households were complicated entities of six to eight persons that would include children, servants, kinsfolk, and young men and women under the tutelage of the pastor and his wife.[58] The central responsibility of the pastor's wife was to manage the household economically *(wirtschaftende Hausfrau)*, because income depended largely on her ability to turn the agricultural goods and services that she collected from parish members into food and clothing to sustain the pastor's household. Profits from products raised or manufactured as part of the parsonage's operations could supplement the pastor's salary, which came from the state and from payments of tithes and fees. Whether capitalizing on fruits of the garden, interest from loans to parishioners, paying boarders, tutoring and midwifery services, or beer brewing privileges, imaginative and prudent housekeeping was an essential strategy for hard times, when remunerations were late, fell off, or ceased, and when demands for care and charity increased.[59] In structuring the household regimen of the *Pfarrhaus* the pastor's wife not only had to manage material goods but was also responsible for the spiritual guidance of the children and servants and the poor and sick in the parish—activities that underscored the public role of her office.[60]

The wives of Moravian ministers faced challenges of household management and service to the parish that were comparable to those of Lutheran and Reformed *Pfarrfrauen*. The particulars and relative weight of their duties differed significantly, though, especially in the 1730s through the 1750s when the direct influence of Zinzendorf on women's role was strong.[61] Moravian women did not hone their skills for pleasing their husbands and managing an individual household; instead, when married, their commitment was to the wellbeing of the whole community, thereby expanding their responsibilities greatly and underscoring the religious nature of marriage. Consequently, for Moravian women the transition from Single Sister to Married Person was crucial, yet often difficult; some of them were also ordained as priests to mark the transformation.[62]

Among Lutherans and Reformed clergy, daily life was determined by the calendar of responsibilities set by the Church.[63] People in the *Pfarrhaus* rose early, the norm for most households, and began their day with morning prayers. They gathered to eat and began and ended each meal with prayer—common practice in many Protestant households. Formal business started at eight o'clock, allowing time for administrative duties in the morning. For this kind of business, and for the preparation of sermons and private consultation with parishioners, all *Pfarrhäuser* had a study *(Studierstube,* later, more officious, also *Amtszimmer)* designated solely for official purposes. Except for additional Church-related services and acts, ranging from prayer meetings to baptisms and funerals, afternoons and evenings were commonly spent tending to business necessary for the material support of the pastor's household. In rural parishes those chores were many and varied according to the seasons, presenting the housewife *(wirtschaftende Hausfrau)* with considerable challenges for labor organization and time management.[64]

Pioneering pastors who accepted calls to serve congregations in the American colonies, most commonly young men early in their careers, were familiar with pastors' households even if they lacked experience in heading one.[65] These forerunners could not draw on the professional and social support networks they were accustomed to in Germany. For immediate guidance they could rely on well-established laymen among their German-speaking congregations and on sympathetic colleagues from closely related Protestant denominations; for direction from their superiors in Europe they had to wait for letters that always arrived too late to address time-sensitive matters.[66] In other words, the founding Lutheran and Reformed clergymen, foremost among them Johann Martin Boltzius, Heinrich Melchior Mühlenberg, and Michael Schlatter, had to be self-reliant, devising new rules and organizational structures for their respective Churches in the colonies. The Moravians were better and more tightly organized in their missionary efforts in Pennsylvania and beyond, making effective use of the structural cohesion that was part of the choir system and maintaining frequent and vibrant transatlantic communication by letter and in person, including with Church leaders.

Pioneering German Lutheran and Reformed pastors envisioned establishing Churches in the image of the ones they had known in Europe. Yet they had to contend with a reality completely unlike anything they had experienced in the course of their preparation for the pastorate. While the founding pastors' struggle and success in building German-speaking Lutheran and Reformed Churches in North America is relatively well known, the emphasis has generally been on the organizational and structural elements of the challenge, for which European models presented powerful ideals despite the different realities in early America that forced accommodation and change.[67]

Although ample evidence attests to the achievements of the founding pastors under difficult circumstances, little attention has been paid to the local support structure that enabled those pioneers to concentrate on the daunting tasks they faced. Setting up an Old World-type *Pfarrhaus* was a critically important step. It demonstrated literally the place of the pastor in the community. It afforded the pastor visible independence from the master of the household where he was once a boarder and allowed him to take on the parallel role of *Hausvater* in the parsonage and parish. Forming a household, however, depended on finding a wife to become the *Hausmutter*.[68]

In the American wilderness, moving into a *Pfarrhaus* was neither ordinary nor automatically tied to the installation of the pastor in his post, as was typical in German parishes. Especially in congregations with many new settlers struggling to make a living, interim solutions for housing the parson were the norm, except among sectarians like the Mennonites, who migrated under the leadership of their preachers, and the Moravians, who carefully planned the settlement of missionary outposts in terms of building and staffing.[69] If the lack of parsonages was common in the early years and remained so in frontier settlements, choosing a wife presented the German Reformed or Lutheran pastor with a different kind of problem. The pioneering Churchmen were newcomers to their congregations as well as to the community at large. Unlike circumstances in German lands, where pastors were tied to an extensive network of familial and professional connections and where they often lived in densely populated towns and cities, the pioneering pastors in the American colonies had only begun the process of building professional relationships and making connections to local families. In short, while the marriage market for clerics in Europe was large, the American one was limited, especially if pastors sought to match customary ideas of the *Pfarrfrau* with eligible women. There were few German-speaking Reformed, or Lutheran, young women of bourgeois background and none who had grown up in a *Pfarrhaus* or had been instructed in the *Pfarrfrau*'s traditional ways. Moravians, who advocated marriage and were mindful of keeping marriages within the Church, recognized this difficulty for German-speaking Protestant ministers in the American colonies and solved it by arranging missionaries' weddings before they left Europe or set out from Bethlehem to missionary outposts in North Carolina, for example, a strategy that made sense in the spiritual development of men called to undertake pastoral duties and also ensured the proper operation of daily life in the overseas Church communities.[70]

If German Reformed and Lutheran pastors saw this situation as a disadvantage, having to choose an America-savvy woman as pastor's wife offered potential advantages, especially where Old World traditions were lacking or did not fit. American-born wives were spared the unhappiness and frustration of Esther Werndtlin-Göttschi, a middle-aged widowed *Pfarrfrau* and teacher who in 1737 complained bitterly to her sister in Zurich about the alien and confusing backwardness of Pennsylvania.[71] An astute pioneering pastor had a good chance of gaining the hand of a well-placed and well-off young woman in the German-speaking community—and with it the support and connections of her family, desirable *"Glücks=Qualitäten,"* which might well anchor the social status of the German churchman among the local and professional elites and help found a German-American dynasty of pastors.[72]

Satisfying the need for a wife with the right disposition was much easier in some regards than in others.[73] Women with a good mind for sensible conversation and ready communication with a variety of people, in German and English, had to rely on their natural abilities because opportunities for educating girls were mostly absent in the colonies. By contrast, they were well acquainted with examples of good housekeeping because they came from a German immigrant background where success often depended on the work of the *Hausfrau*.[74] Since all Protestant Christian wives were expected to be good household managers, becoming a pastor's wife did not present a fundamental change but instead raised the bar, in keeping with the exemplary role of the *Pfarrfrau*.[75] It is not surprising that, from a man's perspective, the *"Leibes=Qualitäten,"* or physical properties, of the ideal wife should include youth, beauty, and health. More remarkable were the reasons given for why she had to be young: her love was more tender because it was her first and, necessarily, a young woman would have sufficient respect for a husband ten years or more her senior; she also would think he was more intelligent than she and therefore submit more easily to his will. And, if the husband was clever, he could teach her as he saw fit and choose those subjects he thought proper for a woman.[76]

German-born and trained pastors took American-experienced women as wives to direct them in learning the *Pfarrfrau* role, and then developed it not only to fit the German Reformed and Lutheran diaspora churches in North America but to become part of the foundation on which distinctly American, or German-American, traditions could be built.[77] In turn, women in the American colonies who wed German Lutheran or Reformed pastors contributed to shaping the German-American *Pfarrfrau* in a critical way. Unlike their counterparts in Germany, they did not start their households and begin their offices in the congregation as outsiders. On the contrary, it was their familiarity with the local community that influenced their female networks. Wives of the pioneering Protestant pastors created a strong local base for the informal education of the second, native-born generation of German Reformed and Lutheran ministers who followed in the footsteps of their fathers and, even more importantly, for all of the education and training of the second-generation of *Pfarrfrauen*, who continued in the tradition their mothers had begun and married German Lutheran and Reformed pastors, contributing significantly to the development of the German-American pastorate during the American Revolution and the Early Republic. The situation of the Moravian ministers' wives was different in subsequent generations. If anything, the importance of the service of the minister's wife to the community grew—

in the tradition of spiritual commitment and consented to carefully by lot—to make her an effective helpmeet, though at the expense of limiting female leadership in all positions.[78] Excepting her responsibilities as mother and educator of her young children and teenaged daughters, from which she was usually relieved by the choir system, the nature of her tasks was becoming more like those of pastor's wives of the second and third generation of German Reformed and Lutheran clergy, narrowing the gap that had divided Moravian ministers' wives from Lutheran and Reformed *Pfarrfrauen.*

This preliminary reading of the literature makes it clear that the traditions that developed for German Reformed and Lutheran pastors' households in the American colonies were composite expressions of ideals and realities from both sides of the Atlantic, while for the Moravians the experimental, even daring, redefinition of the role of wife in the *Streiterehe* among the pioneering missionaries gave way to the more limited position of the minister's wife, which underscored her conventional function as his helpmeet in the community. Among Lutheran and Reformed Germans, the role of the pastor's wife blended women's New World experiences and circumstances with expectations and ideas that the pioneering pastors taught their wives deliberately or by happenstance. Out of this blending of traditional customs and local practices there emerged certain patterns of conduct, responsibilities, and activities that pastors' daughters learned from their mothers and fathers and used to manage their own households, whether they married pastors who belonged to the second generation of German Reformed and Lutheran clergy in the American colonies, or other men who were part of their families' networks among the local elites. The American model for the pastor's wife also influenced the minister's sons, for whom the experience in the *Pfarrhaus* set standards for choosing a wife to manage their households, irrespective of careers in the Church or outside of it. The exemplary nature of the pastor's household may very well have shaped the formation of local behavior and ritual—an assumption that begs to be explored more fully.

Notes

1. "German lands" refers here to the variety of countries, principalities, and territories in Central Europe in which German was the most commonly spoken language. Subsequent references to "Germans" stand for the more cumbersome "German-speaking people."
2. "Pastor" best describes men trained in Europe who became shepherds of German flocks of Protestants in North America, although "parson" and "minister" were used synonymously. In German, preferences for *"Pastor"* or *"Pfarrer"* tend to be regional. See the entries in Henry (Heinrich) Mühlenberg and Benedict J. Schipper, *Deutsch-Englisches und Englisch-Deutsches Woerterbuch (German-English and English-German Dictionary),* 2

vols. (Lancaster, PA, 1812). The preachers of radical Pietists and other sects that did not require formal or university training for ordination are omitted from consideration here.

3. Aaron Spencer Fogleman, *Hopeful Journeys: German Immigration, Settlement, and Political Culture in Colonial America, 1717–1775* (Philadelphia, 1996), chapter 3; Marianne S. Wokeck, *Trade in Strangers: The Beginnings of Mass Migration to North America* (University Park, PA, 1999), chapter 2.

4. German *traditionsbildend* (forming traditions) is an appropriately descriptive term.

5. Beverly P. Smaby, "'No one should lust for power...women least of all.': Dismantling Female Leadership among Eighteenth-Century Moravians," in this volume.

6. Jutta Jahn, "Hexe und Hausfrau: Feindbild und Leitbild negativ und positiv determinierter Verhaltensmuster für Frauen zur beginnenden Neuzeit," in *Leben und Gestalt. Studie zur Frauengeschichte in Halle*, ed. Halle Courage e. V, *Schriftenreihe zur Geistes- und Kulturgeschichte* (Halle, 1996), 11.

   I have only begun to analyze pertinent sources such as Kirchenordnungen; Visitationsberichte; Andachtenbücher (geistige Frauenzimmerspiegel); and also personal letters and accounts. Examples in the secondary literature include Rudolf Dellsperger, "Frauenemanzipation im Pietismus," in *Zwischen Macht und Dienst: Beiträge zur Geschichte und Gegenwart der Frauen im kirchlichen Leben der Schweiz*, ed. Sophia Bietenhard et al. (Bern, 1991); Brigitta Stoll, "Hausmutter und Himmelsbraut — Ein Andachtsbuch des 17./18. Jahrhunderts und sein Frauenbild," in Bietenhard et al., *Zwischen Macht und Dienst*, 142–43, 83, 94; Andrea van Dülmen, ed., *Frauenleben im 18. Jahrhundert* (Munich, 1992); Elke Kleinau and Christine Mayer, eds., *Erziehung und Bildung des weiblichen Geschlechts: Eine Kommentierte Quellensammlung zur Bildings- und Berufsbildungsgeschichte von Mädchen und Frauen*, vol. 1/1, Einführung in die pädagogische Frauenforschung (Weinheim, 1996).

7. Heide Wunder, *"Er ist die Sonn', sie ist der Mond": Frauen in der Frühen Neuzeit* (Munich, 1992), 71; Gerta Scharffenorth, "'Im Geiste Freunde werden': Mann und Frau im Glauben Luthers," in *Wandel der Geschlechterbeziehungen zu Beginn der Neuzeit*, ed. Heide Wunder and Christine Vanja (Frankfurt am Main, 1993).

8. Hartmut Lehmann, "'Das ewige Haus': Das lutherische Pfarrhaus im Wandel der Zeiten," in *Religion und Religiosität in der Neuzeit. Historische Beiträge*, ed. Manfred Jakubowski-Tiessen and Otto Ulbricht (Göttingen, 1996), 183.

9. Gottfried Maron, "Vom Hindernis zur Hilfe. Die Frau in der Sicht Martin Luthers," *Theologische Zeitschrift* 39 (1983); Luise Schorn-Schütte, "'Gefährtin' und 'Mitregentin': Zur Sozialgeschichte der evangelischen Pfarrfrau in der Frühen Neuzeit," in *Wandel der Geschlechterbeziehungen zu Beginn der Neuzeit*, Wunder and Vanja, 110.

10. Rudolf Vierhaus, *Germany in the Age of Absolutism*, trans. Jonathan B. Knudsen (Cambridge, 1988), 44; Luise Schorn-Schütte, *Evangelische Geistlichkeit in der frühen Neuzeit: Deren Anteil an der Entfaltung frühmoderner Staatlichkeit und Gesellschaft. Dargestellt am Beispiel des Fürstentums Braunschweig-Wolffenbüttel, der Landgrafschaft Hessen-Kassel und der Stadt Braunschweig*, ed. Gustav Adolf Benrath, vol. 62, Quellen und Forschungen zur Reformationsgeschichte (Gütersloh, 1996); Eberhard Winkler, *Zwischen Volkskirche und Diaspora: Eine Einführung in die praktisch-theologische Kybernetik* (Neunkirchen-Vluyn, 1998), 160–162.

11. Lehmann, "'Das ewige Haus,'" 187.

12. Mary Fulbrook, *Piety and Politics: Religion and the Rise of Absolutism in England, Württemberg, and Prussia* (Cambridge, 1983).

13. Schorn-Schütte, "Sozialgeschichte der evangelischen Pfarrfrau," 146–148.

14. Schorn-Schütte, *Evangelische Geistlichkeit*, 92–97.

15. Martin Hasselhorn, *Der altwürttembergische Pfarrstand im 18. Jahrhundert* (Stuttgart, 1958); Lehmann, "'Das ewige Haus,'" 187; Schorn-Schütte, *Evangelische Geistlichkeit*, 99–128, 139–140, 146–151.

16. Schorn-Schütte, *Evangelische Geistlichkeit*, 32

17. Lehmann, "'Das ewige Haus,'" 189.

18. Winkler, *Praktisch-theologische Kybernetik*, 128.
19. Schorn-Schütte, *Evangelische Geistlichkeit*, 285.
20. Spener's most influential publication was *Pia Desideria*. Hartmut Lehmann, *Protestantische Weltsichten: Transformationen seit dem 17. Jahrhundert* (Göttingen, 1998), 11.
21. Lehmann, "'Das ewige Haus,'" 189–190; Lehmann, *Protestantische Weltsichten*, 35–36.
22. Lehmann, *Protestantische Weltsichten*, 19; Lehmann, "'Das ewige Haus'," 190.
23. Lehmann, *Protestantische Weltsichten*, 16, 18.
24. Ibid., 22, 36; see also Winkler, *Praktisch-theologische Kybernetik*, 133.
25. Lehmann, *Protestantische Weltsichten*, 18–20; Klaus Deppermann, *Der hallesche Pietismus und der preussische Staat unter Friedrich III. (I.)* (Göttingen, 1961); Carl Hinrichs, *Preußentum und Pietismus: Der Pietismus in Brandenburg-Preußen als religiös-soziale Reformbewegung* (Göttingen, 1971); Renate Wilson, *Pious Traders in Medicine: A German Pharmaceutical Network in Eighteenth-Century North America* (University Park, PA, 2000); Ulrike Witt, *Bekehrung, Bildung und Biographie. Frauen im Umkreis des Halleschen Pietismus*, ed. Hartmut Lehmann et al., vol. 2 (Tübingen, 1996).

    On the household (usually *Haus* or *"ganzes Haus"*), see Otto Brunner, "Das 'ganze Haus' und die alteuropäische 'Ökonomik,'" in idem, *Neue Wege der Verfassungs- und Sozialgeschichte* (Göttingen, 1968); Richard van Dülmen, *Kultur und Alltag in der Frühen Neuzeit: Das Haus und seine Menschen*, 3 vols. (Munich, 1990), 1:12–23; W. Freitag, "Haushalt und Familie in traditionellen Gesellschaften," *Geschichte und Gesellschaft* 14 (1988): 5–37; for a characterization of the *"ganze Pfarrhaus,"* see Schorn-Schütte, *Evangelische Geistlichkeit*, 288–309.
26. Marilyn J. Westerkamp, *Women and Religion in Early America, 1600–1850*, ed. Hugh McLeod, Christianity and Society in the Modern World (London, 1999); Sara Mendelson and Patricia Crawford, *Women in Early Modern England, 1550–1720* (Oxford, 1998).
27. Lehmann, *Protestantische Weltsichten*, 22–23.
28. Smaby, "Dismantling Female Leadership."
29. Ibid., 25, 38.
30. Horst Schmidt-Grave, *Leichenreden und Leichenpredigten Tübinger Professoren (1550–1750)* (Tübingen, 1974), 65.
31. Schorn-Schütte, *Evangelische Geistlichkeit*, 198.
32. Dietrich Meyer, *Bibliographisches Handbuch zur Zinzendorf-Forschung* (Düsseldorf, 1987); Erich Beyreuther, *Studien zur Theologie Zinzendorfs* (Neukirchen, 1962).
33. Ibid., 314, 329.
34. In the parlance of the *"ganze Pfarrhaus"* girls other than daughters in the household, including maids, became *"Haustöchter."*
35. Schorn-Schütte, *Evangelische Geistlichkeit*, 191, 197–211, 226; *Schulen machen Geschichte: 300 Jahre Erziehung in den Franckeschen Stiftungen zu Halle* (Halle, 1997), especially Gertrud Zaeparnick, "Kurzer Bericht vom Pädagogikum Regium, 1695–1784," 67–82; Schorn-Schütte, *Evangelische Geistlichkeit*, 293; and Schorn-Schütte, "Sozialgeschichte der evangelischen Pfarrfrau," 110, 112–113.
36. The letter of Gotthilf August Francke, a student in Jena, to his mother provides good evidence. Thomas Müller and Carola Wessel, eds., *Hertzliebe Mama: Briefe aus Jenaer Studientagen, 1719–1720* (Halle, 1997).
37. Most of the Lutheran pastors whose regular calls to service in German-speaking congregations in the American colonies were channeled through the Franckesche Stiftungen had served as teachers in the schools of the foundation.
38. Gotthilf August Francke did not paint a favorable picture of his *Hausmutter* in Jena. See, for example, letters 2–5, 8 in Müller and Wessel, *Hertzliebe Mama*.
39. Francke's 1694 letter; reproduced in exhibit catalog, *Vier Thaler und sechzehn Groschen. August Hermann Francke. Der Stifter und sein Werk* (Halle, 1998), 86–87.
40. Beverly Prior Smaby, *The Transformation of Moravian Bethlehem: From Communal Mission to Family Economy* (Philadelphia, 1988), 10.
41. Warren Sabean, *Power in the Blood*, 17.
42. See especially Wilson, *Pious Traders*; Witt, *Bekehrung*.

43. Robert Beachy, "Business Was a Family Affair: Women of Commerce in Central Europe, 1650–1880," *Histoire Sociale—Social History*, vol. 34, no. 68 (2002): 307–330; and "Women Merchants and the Erosion of Gender Tutelage in Germany, 1680–1830," in *Family Welfare: Gender, Property and Inheritance since the Seventeenth Century*, ed. David R. Green and Alastair Owens (Westport, CT, 2004).

44. van Dülmen, ed., *Frauenleben*, 21.

45. Schorn-Schütte, "Sozialgeschichte der evangelischen Pfarrfrau," 110, 112–113, 117, 119 (*"Vorbildlichkeit des Amts der Pfarrfrau,"* 113); *Evangelische Geistlichkeit*, 290–291, 312; van Dülmen, *Frauenleben*, 29, 30, 31.

46. Smaby, *Moravian Bethlehem*, 159.

47. Schorn-Schütte, "Sozialgeschichte der evangelischen Pfarrfrau," 119 (*"Gehülffe und Tragstab und nicht Fusschemel"*), 120, 132–33, 153; Bernd Moeller, "Die Brautwerbung Martin Bucers für Wolfgang Capito: Zur Sozialgeschichte des evangelischen Pfarrstandes," in *Philologie als Kulturwissenschaft: Studien zur Literatur und Geschichte des Mittelalters. Festschrift für K. Stackmann zum 65. Geburtstag*, ed. L. Grenzman (Göttingen, 1987), 319; also Schorn-Schütte, *Evangelische Geistlichkeit*, 293.

48. In an early visitation report this was recognized and expressed simply: "Seine Ehefrau is uffrichtig, ziehet die Kinder wol, können auch ziemlich beten" (his wife is sincere, educates the children well, and can pray properly), cited in Schorn-Schütte, *Evangelische Geistlichkeit*, 305.

49. Schorn-Schütte, "Sozialgeschichte der evangelischen Pfarrfrau," 133.

50. Schorn-Schütte, *Evangelische Geistlichkeit*, 133–134, 221, 222.

51. Christoph August Heumann, *Der politische Philosophus: Das ist, Vernunftmäßige Anweisungen zur Klugeheit Im gemeinen Leben*, 3d ed. (Frankfurt, 1724), 87–94.

52. See, for example, Nicolaus Ludwig von Zinzendorf's letter proposing marriage to Dorothea Erdmuthe von Reuß. Wilhelm Jannasch, *Erdmuthe Dorothea, Gräfin von Zinzendorf, geb. Gräfin Reuss zu Plauen: Ihr Leben als Beitrag zur Geschichte des Pietismus und der Brüdergemeine* (Herrnhut, 1915), 71–72.

53. Gustav Bertold Volz, ed., *Friedrich der Große und Wilhelmine von Baireuth.*, vol. 1: *Jugendbriefe, 1728–1740* (Leipzig, 1924), 459–460; Ingeborg Weber-Kellerman, ed., *Wilhelmine von Bayreuth. Eine preußische Königstochter. Glanz und Elend am Hofe des Soldatenkönigs in den Memoiren der Markgräfin Wilhelmine von Bayreuth* (Frankfurt am Main, 1990).

54. Ulrike Witt, "Das hallesche Gynäceum," in Daniel Cyranka, ed., *Schulen machen Geschichte: 300 Jahre Erziehung in den Franckeschen Stiftungen zu Halle* (Halle, 1997), 85–103; Witt, *Bekehrung*, 87–146; van Dülmen, *Kultur und Alltag*, 1:101–121.

55. See, for example, the advertisement in Frankfurt's newspaper for such a private institution. Marie Belli-Contard, ed., *Leben in Frankfurt am Main: Auszüge aus der Frag= und Anzeigungs=Nachrichten von ihrer Entstehung 1722 bis 1821*, 10 vols. (Frankfurt am Main, 1850–1851), 1:51–52 (reprinted in van Dülmen, *Frauenleben*, 189–190). See also Rita Bake and Birgit Kiupel, eds., *Margarete Elizabeth Milow: Ich will nicht murren* (Hamburg, 1987), 10–11; Robert Beachy, "Business Was a Family Affair," 6; August Hermann Francke's "Ordnung für Waisenmädchen," in van Dülmen, *Frauenleben*, 187–189.

56. Schorn-Schütte, "Sozialgeschichte der evangelischen Pfarrfrau," 133–136; also *Evangelische Geistlichkeit*, 306, 312.; van Dülmen, *Frauenleben*, 208.

57. Schorn-Schütte, "Sozialgeschichte der evangelischen Pfarrfrau," 146–147; Schorn-Schütte, *Evangelische Geistlichkeit*, 317; van Dülmen, *Das Haus und seine Menschen*, 133–197.

58. Schorn-Schütte, *Evangelische Geistlichkeit*, 303–305; and "Sozialgeschichte der evangelischen Pfarrfrau," 141–143; van Dülmen, *Das Haus und seine Menschen*, 11–78.

59. Schorn-Schütte, "Sozialgeschichte der evangelischen Pfarrfrau," 147–148, 151.

60. Schorn-Schütte, "Sozialgeschichte der evangelischen Pfarrfrau," 148–151.

61. Smaby, "Dismantling Female Leadership"; on Zinzendorf and women see Otto Uttendörffer, *Zinzendorf und die Frauen* (Herrnhut, 1919).

62. Smaby, *Moravian Bethlehem*, 159–164; Katherine M. Faull, ed. and transl., *Moravian Women's Memoirs: Their Lives, 1750–1820* (Syracuse, 1997), xxix.

63. Schorn-Schütte, *Evangelische Geistlichkeit*, 320–322.

64. Georg Heinrich Zincke, *Teutsches Real=Manufactur= und Handwercks=Lexicon* (Leipzig, 1745), 773, excerpted in van Dülmen, *Frauenleben*, 53–54.

65. For establishing my database of the pioneering generation, Charles H. Glatfelter, *Pastors and People: German Lutheran and Reformed Churches in the Pennsylvania Field, 1717–1793*, 2 vols., vol. 1: *Pastors and Congregations, Publications of The Pennsylvania German Society* (Breinigsville, PA, 1980), has been most helpful. For statistical characteristics, see Wilson, *Pious Traders*, 124–126 (Tables 4.2 and 4.3); for some preliminary results, see Marianne S. Wokeck, "The *Pfarrhaus* as Model in Defining German-American Identities," in *Halle Pietism in Colonial British North America and the Young United States*, ed. Hans-Jürgen Grabbe (Stuttgart, 2003).

66. Ironically, extant correspondence between pastors in the American colonies and their superiors in Germany, especially Halle, contains important details about the beginnings of the German Reformed and Lutheran Churches in the American diaspora.

67. A. G. Roeber, *Palatines, Liberty, and Property: German Lutherans in Colonial British America* (Baltimore, 1993); Thomas Müller, *Kirche zwischen zwei Welten: Die evangelische Obrigkeitsproblematik bei Heinrich Melchior Mühlenberg* (Stuttgart, 1994); and Wilson, *Pious Traders*.

68. Among the pioneering generation of Lutheran pastors, Peter Brunnholz remained unmarried.

69. Daniel B. Thorp, *The Moravian Community in Colonial North Carolina: Pluralism on the Southern Frontier* (Knoxville, TN, 1989), 42–49.

70. Ibid., 60.

71. Leo Schelbert and Hedwig Rappolt, eds., *Alles ist ganz anders hier. Auswandererschicksale in Briefen aus zwei Jahrhunderten* (Olten, 1977), 113–118.

72. Heumann, *Philosophus*, 94.

73. Ibid., 87.

74. Zincke, *Handwercks=Lexicon*.

75. Mühlenberg, in letters to his superiors in Halle, praises his wife's household management.

76. Heumann, *Philosophus*, 88.

77. In my forthcoming book, *Charting New Courses for Social Identities of German Speakers in the American Colonies*, I analyze the background, training, and life courses of pastors' wives. Kurt Aland, ed., *Die Korrespondenz Heinrich Melchior Mühlenbergs: Aus der Anfangzeit des deutschen Luthertums in Nordamerika*, 5 vols. (Berlin, 1986–1993), 1:395, 400–401, 437, 494.

78. Smaby, "Dismantling Female Leadership"; Smaby, Moravian Bethlehem, 107–116; Faull, *Moravian Women's Memoirs*, xxx–xxxi; Thorp, *Moravian Community*, 82–83.

– Chapter 12 –

UNLIKELY SISTERS: CHEROKEE AND MORAVIAN WOMEN IN THE EARLY NINETEENTH CENTURY

Anna Smith

WHILE TRAVELING BACK AND FORTH to Washington in the 1830s, Chero-kee delegations often stopped at the Moravian town of Salem, North Carolina, founded by the pietistic United Brethren in 1766. The arrival of one group prompted Jane Ross, a Cherokee student at the Moravians' academy for young women, "to go down and greet them in-dividually, giving her father's name and her own name."[1] The delegation immediately asked "Would not the Chief's daughter give us some bread?" Ross ran inside to request that the principal provide food, and the Chero-kees were offered a "substantial and comfortable meal."[2] Up and down the Atlantic seaboard Moravians built and sustained their relationships with native people in such relatively mundane ways. The simple act of sharing food with travelers, however, also represents the intersection of two cultural traditions, Cherokee and Moravian.[3] On many issues, Chero-kee and Moravian views diverged, but on some, from hospitality to the value of community, enough common ground allowed them to build strong relationships that lasted decades and linked generations. In particu-lar, relationships between Cherokee and Moravian women transcended ethnicity and bound them in a community of women. In both societies women worked together gardening, gathering, cooking, housekeeping, and sewing, as well as caring for the sick and raising children.

Most scholars have focused on the cultural differences of missionar-ies and native people in the early nineteenth century.[4] The differences are undeniable. Yet, this focus obscures the similarities that existed between these two groups of women who found comfortable familiarity in the pattern of their lives. When several Cherokee women joined the United Brethren, they formed a sisterhood with Moravian women rooted in shared faith, as well as work, that enabled them to entrust their children to the care of the Moravian Sisters. Within this sisterhood Cherokee women had some authority in spiritual matters and held leadership roles.[5]

The Moravians, a small German-speaking pacifistic religious group from Bohemia, Moravia, and Poland, came from Europe to Savannah, Georgia, in 1735. The Moravians began a mission and school for the Indians nearby, but in less than five years, war broke out between the English and Spanish, and the Moravians, refusing to bear arms, abandoned their settlement.[6] They moved to Bethlehem, Pennsylvania, where they began widespread mission work to the Native Americans in Pennsylvania and the Ohio Valley. In later years the Moravians ventured from Bethlehem to Wachovia in North Carolina, where the community of Salem developed into a key commercial town.[7] They did not hold land individually; the Church owned the land and leased it to members.[8] Many Moravians cared little for wealth, political power, or expansionism, but they did care about education.[9] Because they believed the Scriptures contained truths that an individual must read to understand, education was central to their congregational life. Although most Moravians were artisans and not highly educated, their leaders, who had attended European universities, created a higher standard for education.[10] The reputation of Moravian schools extended beyond their community, and non-Moravians in the area surrounding Salem sought their daughters' admission to the Girls' School that opened in 1772. The Moravians agreed to accept the daughters of outsiders, constructing a building to house them that became known as the Girls' Boarding School.[11] The tuition it generated became a significant source of income for the Salem community.[12]

Motivated by spiritual experience and the desire to spread God's word, Moravians wanted to live among the Indians and teach their converts through example as well as in their churches and schools. Abraham Steiner and Frederic de Schweinitz attended the Cherokee Council in October 1800, and with the support of two influential Cherokees, James Vann and Charles Hicks, obtained permission to establish a mission among them.[13] Neither Vann, Hicks, nor other Cherokees exhibited interest in Christianity, but they valued the Moravians' willingness to educate their children. In 1801 the Moravians began a mission at Springplace, adjacent to James Vann's plantation in what is today North Georgia.[14]

In subsequent years other denominations opened missions and schools in the Cherokee Nation. The Presbyterian minister Gideon Blackburn followed the Moravians, settled in Tennessee, and employed lay schoolmasters. In 1817 the American Board of Commissioners for Foreign Missions, consisting of Congregationalists and Presbyterians, began Brainerd, the first of eight American Board mission schools.[15] The American Board and the Moravians worked in similar areas, often with the same groups of

Figure 12.1 Mission sites among the Cherokee, c. 1825. (Reprinted from *The Brainerd Journal: A Mission to the Cherokees, 1817–1833,* ed. by Joyce B. Phillips and Paul Gary Phillips by permission of the University of Nebraska Press)

people. The Baptists labored among the poorest Cherokees in the mountains, and the Methodists were the last denomination to enter the Nation when they began their circuit in 1823.[16]

Unlike the other missionaries to the Cherokees, however, the Moravians believed in strict gender division. Women served as spiritual advisors and taught the girls and women, and men advised and taught the boys and men. Women shared the work of running the school and mission and participated in decision-making. Husband and wife teams typically served in the Moravian missions. When a qualified single brother accepted the role of missionary, the Moravians chose a single or widowed woman, whose attributes suited the project, for him to marry.[17] Marriage, however, did not insinuate husbands into wives' economic or spiritual lives. Consequently, married Moravian women enjoyed considerable autonomy. Similarly, married Cherokee women enjoyed comparable autonomy. Cherokee couples lived in the extended household of the wife's kin, and title to houses and fields was vested in the women of the lineage. Husbands and wives held personal property separately, and they engaged independently in commercial transactions.

Moravian missionary women and the women of the Cherokee Nation encountered each other for the first time at the Springplace Mission. Adhering to a hospitality ethic, the women in the Vann household welcomed their new neighbors. James Vann had married a number of times, and at least three of his wives were sisters.[18] His wives and their mothers, grandmothers, aunts, and children visited the mission often. Vann's sister Nancy and his mother, whom the missionaries called Old Mother Vann, also lived on the plantation. At first Mother Vann did not hold the missionaries in high esteem because, she once complained, they only knew how to talk about the Savior.[19] As time passed, however, her views softened. Other members of the Vann family embraced the mission with more enthusiasm. James Vann's youngest daughter Sally was the first student at the mission; she received instruction one hour a day.[20] After Vann's death, his widow, Peggy Scott Vann, became the mission's first convert.[21]

The Vann family was wealthy, and although they adhered to many traditional Cherokee practices such as polygamy, they had considerable familiarity with Euro-American ways. Some of the family spoke English, making communication without a translator possible since the Moravians spoke English as well as their native German.[22] Like other elite Cherokees, James Vann had acquired his fortune through commerce and agriculture, and cultivated his extensive acreage with African-American slaves. In 1805 he built an elegant red brick mansion with white columns and furnished it in Euro-American style. The Vanns, no doubt, seemed reassuringly familiar to the Moravians in many ways. Their shared ideas about appropriate housing, furnishings, and dress expanded to include broader cultural values that linked Cherokee and Moravian women.

In both Cherokee and Moravian societies men and women lived in separate worlds. In Cherokee society, men hunted, went to war, and engaged in diplomacy while women farmed, gathered, and maintained their households. Traditionally the Cherokees lived close together in towns with communal fields, where women shared the responsibilities of the household, the care of children, and the production and preservation of crops and other foodstuffs on which their economic and political power partially rested. Men hunted in territory that often lay at a considerable distance.[23] Towns also served as social, political, and religious centers. Typically several households from each clan lived in each town, and the clan-based matrilineal kinship system connected the towns. Eighteenth-century warfare helped break up the Cherokees' town system, as enemy armies and small raiding parties repeatedly attacked towns during the French and Indian War and the Revolutionary War.[24] In their aftermath, headmen and warriors ceded large tracts of land. Consequently, war destroyed many Cherokee towns and treaty negotiations took the land where towns had once existed. Fearful that towns created easy targets for their enemies, many Cherokee moved to individual farms.[25] Meanwhile, the rapidly expanding market economy of the late eighteenth century prompted many Cherokee men to turn from hunting to running stores and taverns, operating toll roads and ferries, herding livestock, and participating in commercial agriculture with the use of slave labor. The loss of the Cherokee town network diminished the clan system and the power of Cherokee women, though women continued to engage in subsistence agriculture, gather wild foodstuffs, prepare food, care for children, and make most household goods.

In Moravian communities, similarly, the division of labor between men and women began almost at birth. The female choirs in Salem, which organized women's social and economic lives, cultivated large gardens and fields that provided food for the community. In 1786, one third of the Single Sisters and Older Girls in Salem were "trained for house and field."[26] Women cared for and taught children, prepared food, and sewed. Men conducted trade, ran the brewery and the dye shop, and practiced artisanal trades in the community.[27] Both Cherokee and Moravian men and women had clearly defined work specific to their gender, and each enjoyed a distinct arena of power grounded in the sexual division of labor.

Because of this similarity in labor systems, Cherokee men appreciated the enormous effort required of missionary women, which helped resolve a dispute with the Moravians. Missionaries were unable to teach and provide board for seven young scholars to attend the mission school, as they originally had agreed, and ultimately wanted to accept only four. At first, the Cherokee Council insisted that the Moravians fulfill their agreement. Chief Chuleoa stated "the food can't amount to much, our children only need corn; that's what they're used to, and it does after all, grow." Abraham Steiner, a Moravian missionary, replied that the problem was not just growing the corn, but the "labor" of grinding it and making bread.[28] This explanation appeased Chuleoa, who understood that the pounding of corn with mortar and pestle, as Cherokee women did, was intensive work, although Moravians actually used millstones to grind grain, a chore assigned to men. Chuleoa concluded that the children's board was within the domain of women, where men had little power.

Like Cherokee women, Moravian women traditionally worked in the fields and gardens.[29] Cherokee women soon discovered that at least one Moravian woman understood their special connection to the plant world. Missionary Anna Rosina Gambold's avid gardening and gathering became apparent soon after she arrived at the Springplace Mission, when she enlarged the existing garden and added another one.[30] Elias Cornelius, a visitor to Springplace in 1817, described her botanical garden plotted along Linnaen lines. "For some distance around, the land was cleared, and … in the highest state of cultivation … Mrs. G. is quite a botanist, and has a very good garden of plants, both ornamental and medicinal."[31] The sheer volume of Anna Rosina's samples suggests a collaborative enterprise. In 1818 she sent Rev. Henry Steinhauer between 12,000 and 14,000 specimens of dried plants, almost 100 packets of seeds, and several minerals from the Cherokee Nation. Steinhauer estimated that, under the most favorable conditions, the gathering took six months of "undivided attention," which Anna Rosina could hardly have afforded.[32] Almost certainly, she had help.[33]

Gathering remained important to the Cherokee women in the nineteenth century. Native and Moravian women and children probably searched the woods and riverbanks together for wild plants, seeds, leaves, roots, and nuts. Rosina published an article on plants found in the Cherokee Nation near the Connasarga River in the *American Journal of Science and Arts*. Daniel McKinley, her biographer, has concluded that "these were plants that she was told by the Cherokees that they used as sources of medicines, foods, dyes, and fibers."[34] Her descriptions of their uses imply considerable collaboration with her Cherokee neighbors: "*Alliums.–* The Indians are fond of, for culinary purposes. *Angelica.–* The same. *Cercis canadensis.–* Children are fond of eating the blossom. *Ilex.–* Of the wood, spoons are made. The berries of service in colics. *Sanguinaria canadensis.–* The root is used for the red die [*sic*] in basket making."[35]

Anna Rosina used many of these as medicines to treat the Cherokee and African-American population for everything from rashes to consumption.[36] As her reputation as a healer grew, Cherokee people sought medical advice and medicine from Springplace. She nursed children at the mission and sent medicine to those who were ill in distant places. While she acquired some knowledge of the medicinal uses of plants academically, she almost certainly enhanced that knowledge through contact with Cherokee women

The information in Anna Rosina's published list points to the connection between acquired botanical knowledge and shared experiences. One notation in particular reflects a specific event that appears in the historical record. The entry read, "*Calycanthus floridus.–* The roots are used as (though very strong) emetics. The seeds to poison wolves."[37] In 1824 the smoke from controlled burns in the forest drove wolves into the "neighborhood of the mission and one Indian woman was torn up by them."[38] Cherokee women used fire to clear fields or burn underbrush so they could collect nuts in the fall, but the fire sometimes forced wild animals into populated areas. They killed fleeing wolves by poisoning them with seeds. Cherokee women had shared this technique with Anna Rosina before the tragedy of 1824, when the practice apparently failed, but the notation and the event firmly connect Anna Rosina's academic exercise to Cherokee experience.

In addition to teaching the missionaries, the Cherokee women learned from them. Although women traditionally had constructed clothing from skins using needles made of bone and thread of sinew, they no longer wore skins by the time the Moravians had arrived, and they were eager to adapt their traditional role as seamstresses to the textiles that traders had introduced early in the eighteenth century.[39] Peggy Vann and her sister asked the missionaries' wives to teach them to sew in 1801, and in exchange for the sewing lessons, the Indian women stayed with Sister Dorothea Byhan while her husband was away.

Reciprocity, valued in both societies, made it easy for the women to exchange favors. In the fall of 1819, when missionaries and Peggy Vann gave refuge to Keren-Happuch Sandford Turner Haskins, an abused Indian woman, the woman repaid their kindness by sewing, spinning, and weaving.[40] As Cherokees joined the mission in subsequent years, the members offered their help and that of their African American slaves to reciprocate for the hospitality offered by the missionaries after services and on holidays.[41] In 1818 Mother Vann lent her African American slaves to cut lumber for the meetinghouse. Interestingly, her name is listed in a group of prosperous Cherokee men, Joseph Crutchfield, Charles Hicks, and Joseph Vann, who also sent their African American slaves to help with the construction of the meetinghouse.[42] After the death of Anna Gambold, Mother Vann again came to the aid of the mission when she sent her African American slave Betsy to help Sister Gertraud Schmidt with washing and scrubbing for a week.[43] The mission was short of help, and Vann wanted to assist the missionaries during this time of loss. Furthermore, as head of a large family she understood the amount of work involved in boarding and teaching the children at the mission school. The community of women at the Springplace Mission offered help to one another as their resources allowed; the Cherokee women's ability to lend slaves underscored the wealth and autonomy they enjoyed.

Numerous Cherokee women less prominent than the Vann women were part of the extended community of Springplace. They visited the mission and worshiped and worked with the women there for varying lengths of time. Parents often visited children who lived at the mission or in nearby homes while attending school. Some parents remained for several days, attending services and getting to know the Moravian women with whom their children studied and lived, while Moravians learned from them about Cherokee cultural pratices. Missionaries understood that the Cherokee mother and her family determined the children's care and education. In the Cherokees' matrilineal kinship system, descent was traced through the women; children were the kin of their mother and her sisters, mother, grandmother, and brothers. The father and his family belonged to another clan and were not considered blood kin to the children.[44] Even though fathers often brought children to the mission to school or took them home, the child's presence at school was dictated by the mother.[45]

The missions served as gathering places for women, especially after 1818. Scholars have suggested that as people left traditional towns to live on individual farms, the mission communities provided a place where women and children could gather and participate in social and religious activities as they had in their towns.[46] Indeed this appears to have been the case at Springplace, even though only four to eleven students attended the mission yearly. Parents of former students, however, continued to be part of the community. When five former students of the Springplace Mission gained admission to the Cornwall Institute in Connecticut for advanced education, the Gambolds and missionaries from the Brainerd mission assembled items and money the boys would need at school and, with Peggy Crutchfield translating, the missionaries explained the opportunities at Cornwall to their parents.[47] Anna Gambold wrote her friends in Salem and Bethlehem requesting a place for the boys to stay on their journey north, tours of the towns they passed through, and entertainment during their visits.[48] At Gambold's behest, the Moravians in Salem provided accommodations, a musical performance, and community tours, including one at the Girls' Boarding School.[49] Children fostered prolonged bonds between Cherokee and Moravian women even when they traveled great distances from their parents. Cherokee parents dictated letters to Anna Gambold for their children, and she read the boys' letters to their parents, translated by students or Peggy Crutchfield. The mothers of three of the five attending Cornwall had become communicant members of the Moravian congregations by 1822.

Moravian missionaries at Springplace respected Cherokee women and permitted them to participate in the activities of the mission, take leadership roles, and, once they became communicant members, have a voice in the congregation. Sister Crutchfield instructed possible converts and served as an interpreter for the missionaries.[50] She also taught Sunday school for African American slave girls and women while her husband taught the men and boys.[51] Sister Crutchfield, like the leaders in the Sisters' choirs in Bethlehem and Salem, instructed and advised slave women about spirituality. Another example of Moravians' acceptance of Cherokee women occurred at a Christmas Service in 1818 attended by "brown, black, and white people," as well as two highly respected Cherokee chiefs, Charles Hicks and Major Ridge. John Gambold gave Susanna Ridge his seat, a public expression of the esteem in which she and other Cherokees were held.[52]

One did not need to convert to Christianity to win acceptance into the community of women at Springplace. A number of the Vann women, for example, never converted. To participate fully in the spiritual family of the Moravians, however, one had to become a communicant member. To gain membership, a man or woman had to have a religious experience. Missionaries then provided copious instruction and finally submitted the name of the candidate for baptism to the Lot.[53] If the lot was positive, the person received instruction and baptism. After still further instruction and close observation, the religious community finally admitted the candidate to communion.[54] Moravians believed literally that through Christ's blood, taken during communion as the sacrament, a person joined in a spiritual kinship.

Becoming a communicant member of the Moravian congregation at Springplace made a woman the "Sister" of the missionaries, a concept that resonated deeply with Cherokee women. Missionaries used the kinship terms "Sister" and "Brother" when addressing someone with whom they shared a spiritual kinship. Cherokees also used kin terms to describe relationships.[55] In their matrilineal system, Cherokees recognized as "brothers" and "sisters" individuals who did not share their biological parents but who belonged to their clan and generation.[56] The mother of a Cherokee child named Nicky, who had come to the mission when she heard that her son was deathly ill, "was completely astonished and beside herself with joy when he ran to meet her when he saw her coming. He was completely healthy and fit. Upon this occasion she assured Sister Gertraud Schmidt that she loved her like her own daughter and that she always felt well when she was here."[57] That she "felt well" when she was at the mission demonstrates that she perhaps felt the same comfort with this community of women as she did with members of her own lineage or clan. When Nicky's mother told Sister Gertraud Schmidt that she "loved her like her own daughter," she likened the relationship to the strongest possible Cherokee tie, that of mother and daughter. This kin tie implied the responsibility of caring for the children as though they were her own. The use of kin terms confirmed that Sister Gertraud Schmidt was fulfilling her obligation.[58]

Cherokees marked adoptions and other special events with ceremonies, so the Moravians' baptizing ritual must have seemed appropriate to them.[59] Cherokee mission members, students, and friends questioned and instructed the prospective candidates. The missionaries did not speak the Cherokee language; consequently, Mother Vann, who spoke no English, was prepared for her baptism by Peggy Crutchfield, her Cherokee daughter-in-law, who taught her when to kneel and respond as the liturgy was read.[60] The baptism ceremony took place in the barn at Springplace since the church would not hold the sixty people in attendance. While the children sang, Mother Vann entered the barn dressed in white, the color Cherokees associated with peace and prosperity. Her "spiritual sisters," Peggy Vann Crutchfield and Anna Rosina Gambold, walked by her side, ushering her into their spiritual family.[61] Since Cherokee women made adoption decisions, the ceremony was reminiscent of familiar rituals.[62]

Mother Vann's baptism affected many of those present. Prior to Vann's baptism in 1819 the Moravians had accepted only three Cherokees into communicant membership. Following Vann's baptism, the Moravians accepted thirteen as members, eleven of them women, the two men being husbands of members.[63] Eight of the thirteen converts lived in Oochgelogy, about thirty miles from Springplace. A number of Cherokees wanted the Moravians to begin a second mission and school here. Sarah "Sally" Hicks, who had joined the mission at Springplace, and her husband William Hicks lived at Oochgelogy.[64] When John Gambold sprinkled her with baptismal water, Sally immediately presented her baby to share in the experience.[65] Since she had joined the Moravians, she believed her children had become part of her new spiritual family.[66] Sally may have hoped her baptism would prompt the Moravians to care for and educate her children by beginning a second mission and school in Oochgelogy.

Cherokee women likely interpreted their baptism and acceptance by the Moravians through their own worldview. They certainly perceived Peggy Crutchfield to be a spiritual leader. She counseled Sally Hicks, Mother Vann, and Susanna Ridge, who joined the Church shortly after Sally, in their homes as well as the mission. She translated the missionaries' instruction and sermons and added her own comments.[67] Often the missionaries' ability to communicate with and influence the Cherokee women depended on Peggy, who was "fluent and literate in English" and became an "intermediary" between the missionaries and many Cherokees who neither wrote nor spoke English.[68] Crutchfield's importance to the mission during these years cannot be overstated.

Although Cherokee women joined the mission church at Spring-place, they continued to observe many Cherokee practices. After her con-version, Crutchfield hired a conjuror to treat one of her sick slaves and predict the outcome of the slave's illness by dropping beads into a con-tainer of water.[69] She also maintained an intense interest in Cherokee af-fairs and was one of the most respected women in the Cherokee Nation. She participated in a women's council that petitioned the National Coun-cil through Charles Hicks in 1818 to continue the practice of holding land in common and to halt further cessions of Cherokee land. On the way home from the council she stopped by Springplace, where she described the trials of her people and told Anna Rosina Gambold and other mis-sionaries about the petition.[70] The Moravian women must have em-pathized, for they knew well the importance of commonly owned land.

Gambold and Crutchfield shared their lives with each other for more than a decade. During the final days of Crutchfield's life, Gambold took her dear friend into the mission to care for her.[71] The Moravians held communion several times beside her bed before her deathbed and more than a hundred people attended her funeral at Springplace. Sister Gam-bold died shortly thereafter, and the Moravians buried her beside Sister Crutchfield. Edmund Schwarze, author of the classic work on Moravian missions to the Cherokees, described the fictive kin relationship of these women when he wrote of Gambold's burial. "Beside her Cherokee sister, whom she loved as her own flesh and blood, was she tenderly bedded in the Springplace graveyard."[72] Cherokees probably would have under-stood the relationship in the same way.

The death of these two stalwarts of the Springplace Mission did not mark the end of a Cherokee-Moravian community of women. Instead, their passing signaled a strengthening bond that linked generations of Moravians and Cherokees. Shortly after the deaths of Peggy and Anna Rosina, three prominent men in the Nation, William Hicks, Major Ridge, and Ridge's brother David Watie asked Salem to open a second mission and school at Oochgelogy, which occurred shortly after Crutchfield and Gambold's death.[73] Men conducted political negotiations and business outside the Nation, so it was fitting that the formal request would come from men.[74] Moravians Abraham Steiner and John Gambold supported the idea, telling Salem leaders that William and Sally Hicks and Susanna Ridge were now members. They and others in the area "earnestly desire [d] to have a teacher live among them, particularly Moravian, the sooner the better."[75]

Although men made the request, the Cherokee women proved the force behind the new mission.[76] They not only sought to educate their children in the language and the ways of the dominant culture, but also wanted to create a place where women could gather. In this highly accul-turated Oochgelogy area, Cherokees farmed, raised livestock, and worked an ever increasing number of slaves on large acreages, which prevented them from living in towns.[77] The Moravian leadership in North Carolina had difficulty understanding why it was impossible for the Oochgelogy area to follow the mission compound model that had been successful among the Delaware and other tribes in the North.[78] Abraham Steiner and John Gambold attempted to explain the difficulties in their lengthy account, "Minutes of the Mission Conference Held in Springplace." Slave-holding among the elite Cherokees was central to their argument.[79] Most of their members owned four to ten African American slaves. If the Moravians established a mission community, "considerable space would be needed for the dwellings and the maintenance of the Negroes and fur-ther that it would be more of a Negro town than an Indian." Many of the men and women adopted the changes, encouraged by the US govern-ment's "civilization program," long before they asked the Moravians to come to the area.[80] In this transformation of Cherokee society, women were often isolated in nuclear families on farms. The Moravians' school and the mission community with its sisterhood of Cherokee and Mora-vian women provided a place where women could share daily activities and spiritual life. Susanna Ridge confirmed this hope when she pleaded with the missionaries in 1820: "Will you not move to our place at Ooch-gelogy? Oh, what a joy that would be to see you climb out of the wagon in front of our house! Oh, if you lived at our place, no grass would grow on the road to our house! We neighbors would meet together very often in your house although we now see each other seldom."[81]

Mission communities in Oochgelogy and Springplace recreated towns, like those of the past, where networks of kinship linked the Mora-vian converts to larger and stronger communities of women that existed in Bethlehem and Salem. Within the sisters' choirs, the women mission-aries attended school, labored together, held leadership positions, han-dled their own finances, and shared their spiritual life. Moravian women who served in the Cherokee missions were part of those choirs, and the educational practices used in the mission schools attempted to duplicate education in Bethlehem and Salem. Cherokee women witnessed these ed-ucated and independent Moravian sisters' abilities, and confidence in them encouraged Cherokee women to send their daughters to study with them. Moravian women participated in religious activities and made de-cisions about life in the towns and missions. Perhaps Moravian women offered the Cherokees a way for their daughters to acquire the education and skills needed to survive in the society of the day, yet maintain some of the independent ways of Cherokee women.

In 1823 the Girls' Boarding School in Salem, North Carolina, admit-ted Mary and Martha McNair, the daughters of Delilah Vann McNair and granddaughters of James Vann.[82] The Salem diary explained that Delilah "is a member of the little Cherokee congregation at Springplace."[83] In years to come Delilah's granddaughter attended the Girls' Boarding School, as did other girls from the extended family of Delilah's daughters.[84]

The women missionaries at Springplace knew the teachers and admin-istrators of the boarding school in Salem, and their influence in securing

Figure 12.2 Sally Ridge, c. 1854. (Courtesy of Paul and Dorothy Ridenour from the McNair Family Collection)

admission to the school for their Cherokee sisters' children was significant.[85] In 1824 Major Ridge, a prominent Cherokee headman, applied for his daughter's admission to the Girls' Boarding School, only to have it rejected. Prosperous families paid handsomely for their children to attend the boarding school, a significant source of income for the Single Sisters and the Moravian community as a whole. Correspondence between the missionaries at Oochgelogy, Springplace, and educators at the Salem school concerning Sally Ridge's admittance revealed not only that Brother Schmidt opposed "dragging the Indians out of the Country," but also that he and Brother Schmidt, missionaries in the Cherokee Nation, doubted Major Ridge's ability to pay.[86] Two years later, however, the boarding school in Salem accepted Sally Ridge.[87] Frances Griffin has speculated that because this time it was Susanna Ridge, a communicant, who had applied for her daughter's admission, the Brethren relented, feeling they could not turn down a member of their own faith.[88] Here was a Cherokee "sister" asking that her daughter be accepted into the community of women that extended from the Cherokee Nation to North Carolina.[89] Furthermore, Susanna Ridge had property of her own and may have been able to pay the tuition herself, a circumstance that would have eased the decision.[90]

Delilah McNair and Susanna Ridge visited Salem while their daughters were enrolled in school.[91] Ridge watched her daughter Sally perform at her examinations. "She wore a man's fur hat without ornament and dressed very plainly although neatly, but it was observed that the white ladies in their silks and satins left the seat of honor beside the principal on the front row for her."[92] The author of this account, a teacher, pointed out that while Susanna's clothes lacked the quality and ornamentation of the other women's dresses, they were certainly acceptable by Moravian standards. Describing Susanna as possessing "intelligence in her own right," the teacher's comments suggest she perceived Susanna as an equal. Ridge demonstrated her pride in Sally's education by her very attendance at the examinations. Like the Moravian sisters, she valued women's education. The "white ladies" visiting the Moravian community to attend their children's examinations probably did not know how to interact with a plainly dressed Cherokee woman who did not speak English, a situation Moravians were at ease with, although they also spoke no Cherokee. The connection of the Cherokee women to the Moravians ran deeper than superficial appearances.

Together these women had found a common ground. They cared for one another in sickness, death, and distress, and they united in educating their children. Communicant membership strengthened the cross-cultural bond, and Native women found familiarity in this sisterhood. In 1915, a photograph of Jane Ross Nave, the girl who had greeted the Cherokee delegation in 1830, appeared in *The Academy*, a publication of the Girls' Boarding School, along with an article by Sara Vogler, the daughter of Miles and Sophia Vogler, missionaries to the Cherokee, and a teacher at the Girls' Boarding School. She stated about the experience of Springplace: "Here was laid the foundation of a friendship which, for many a year has existed between the Moravians and the Cherokee Indians. It was this acquaintance that brought a number of Indian girls to Salem Academy."[93] A common ground does not deny differences. Indeed, Cherokees and Moravians must have found many aspects of each other's culture unfathomable. The tendency of their contemporaries as well as modern scholars to focus on difference, however, has obscured the remarkable relationship that developed between a group of Cherokee women and German-American Moravians in early nineteenth-century America.

Notes

1. Jane Ross attended the Girls' Boarding School from 12 June 1835 until 6 July 1838. Student card in Salem College Library vault, Winston-Salem, NC; Gary E. Moulton, *John Ross, Cherokee Chief* (Athens, GA, 1978), 73.
2. J. B. Lienbach, "Some Recollections of the School Before and Since the Civil War," *The Academy* 28 (March 1905): 4141, 4142.
3. Jane Merritt, "Cultural Encounters along a Gender Frontier: Mahican, Delaware, and German Women in Eighteenth-Century Pennsylvania," *Pennsylvania History* 67 (2000): 515; MA-SP, Springplace Diary, 25 October 1821.
4. William G. McLoughlin, "Native American Reaction to Christian Missions," in *The Cherokees and Christianity 1794–1870: Essays on Acculturation and Cultural Persistence*, ed. Walter H. Cosner, Jr. (Athens, 1994).
5. Merritt, "Cultural Encounters," 508, 509, 515–517.
6. Kenneth G. Hamilton and J. Taylor Hamilton, *History of the Moravian Church: The Renewed Unitas Fratrum, 1722–1957*, (Bethlehem, PA, 1967), 84.
7. Gillian Gollin, *Moravians in Two Worlds: A Study of Changing Communities* (New York, 1967); Beverly Prior Smaby, *The Transformation of Moravian Bethlehem: From Communal Mission to Family Economy* (Philadelphia, 1988); Daniel B. Thorp, *The Moravian Community in Colonial North Carolina: Pluralism on the Southern Frontier* (Knoxville, TN, 1989).

8. Daniel Crews, *Faith and Tears: The Moravian Mission among the Cherokee* (Winston-Salem, NC, 2000), 42, n.1; Jerry Surratt, "From Theocracy to Voluntary Church and Secularized Community: A Study of the Moravians in Salem, North Carolina, 1772–1860" (PhD diss., University of North Carolina, 1968), 5.

9. William G. McLoughlin, *Cherokees and Missionaries, 1789–1839* (New Haven, CT, 1984), 36.

10. Frances Griffin, *Less Time for Meddling: A History of Salem Academy and College, 1772–1866* (Winston-Salem, 1979), 6.

11. Ibid., 4.

12. Ibid., 144.

13. Edmund Schwarze, *History of the Moravian Missions Among Southern Indian Tribes of the United States* (Bethlehem, PA, 1923).

14. Crews, *Faith and Tears*, 1–5; McLoughlin, *Cherokees and Missionaries*, 35–53; Schwarze, *History of Moravian Missions*, 32–82.

15. McLoughlin, *Cherokees and Missionaries*, 128.

16. William G. McLoughlin, *Cherokees and Missionaries: Champion of the Cherokees, Evan and John B. Jones* (Princeton, NJ, 1980); Rowena McClinton Ruff, "To Ascertain the Mind and Circumstance of the Cherokee Nation, Springplace, Georgia, 1805–1821"(MA thesis, Western Carolina University, 1992); Rowena McClinton, "The Moravian Mission Among the Cherokees at Springplace Georgia" (PhD diss., University of Kentucky, 1996); Joyce B. Phillips and Paul Gary Phillips, eds., *The Brainerd Journal: A Mission to the Cherokees, 1817–1823* (Lincoln, NE, 1998); Wade Alton Horton, "Protestant Missionary Women As Agents of Cultural Change: Transition Among Cherokee Women, 1801–1839" (PhD diss., Southern Baptist Theological Seminary, 1991); Schwarze, *History of Missions.*

17. Crews, *Faith and Tears*, 14, 15, 56, 57; Merritt, "Cultural Encounters," 508; Katherine M. Faull, "Relating Sisters' Lives: Moravian Women's Writings from 18th Century America," *TMHS* 31 (2000): 17.

18. Charles Hudson, *The Southeastern Indians* (Knoxville, TN, 1976, repr. 1994), 199.

19. MA-SP, Springplace Diary, 4 March 1809.

20. Ibid., 25 March 1802.

21. Ibid., 16 June 1810 and 16 April 1813. Charles Hicks, her uncle, was the second convert; Peggy's second husband, Joseph Crutchfield, joined after their marriage. These were only Cherokee members of the Moravian mission until 1819.

22. Schwarze, *History of Missions*, 145.

23. Louis-Philippe, *Diary of My Travels in American: Louis-Philippe, King of France, 1830–1848*, trans. Stephen Becker (New York, 1977), 73; Henry Timberlake, *Lieut. Henry Timberlake's Memoirs 1756–1765*, ed. Samuel Cole Williams (Johnson City, TN, 1927), 68.

24. Laura F. Klein and Lillian A. Ackerman, eds., *Women and Power in Native North America* (Norman, OK, 1995); Theda Perdue, *Cherokee Women: Gender and Culture Change, 1700–1835* (Lincoln, NE, 1998), 13–15.

25. Perdue, *Women*, 104–108.

26. *RMNC*, 5: 2394, 2395.

27. Surratt, "Theocracy to Church," 99, 100.

28. MA-SP, Springplace Diary, 27 August 1803.

29. *RMNC*: 2, 671, 672; 5, 2394, 2395.

30. Daniel McKinley, "Anna Rosina (Kliest) Gambold (1765–1821), Moravian Missionary to the Cherokees, With Special Reference to Her Botanical Interest," *TMHS* 28 (1994): 59–99; John Witthoft, "An Early Cherokee Ethnobotanical Note," *Journal of Washington Academy of Sciences* 39 (1947): 73–75; Kenneth G. Hamilton, ed. and trans. "Minutes of the Mission Conference Held in Springplace," *Atlanta Historical Bulletin* 15 (1970): 39.

31. McKinley, "Anna Rosina," 59, 87 n. 4; Thurman Wilkins, *Cherokee Tragedy: The Ridge Family and the Decimation of a People* (Norman, OK, 1986), 111, 112.

32. McKinley, "Anna Rosina," 90, n. 21.

33. Perdue, *Women*, 20.

34. McKinley, "Anna Rosina," 60.

35. Anna Rosina Gambold, "Plants of Cherokee Country," *American Journal of Science and Arts* 1 (1819): 245–251.
36. MA-SP, Springplace Diary, 8 February 1819, 6 March 1819; McKinley, "Anna Rosina," 82, 83.
37. Gambold, "Plants," 250, 251.
38. Schwarze, *History of Missions*, 174.
39. Perdue, *Women*, 22.
40. Schwarze, *History of Missions*, 128.
41. Hamilton, "Minutes Mission Conference," 41.
42. Springplace Diary, 12 September 1818; Theda Perdue, *Slavery and the Evolution of Cherokee Society 1540–1866* (Knoxville, TN, 1979).
43. MA-SP, Springplace Diary, 25 April 1821, 28 January 1819.
44. Perdue, *Women*, 41–44, 46–50.
45. Wilkins, *Tragedy*, 114; Springplace Diary, 23 March 1804.
46. Theda Perdue, "Catharine Brown," in *Sifters: Native American Women's Lives* (New York, 2002), 83.
47. Wilkins, *Tragedy*, 112–153; Schwarze, *History of Missions*, 109–113.
48. Gambold to Jacob Van Vleck, 26 September 1818.
49. Wilkins, *Tragedy*, 119, 121; Schwarze, *History of Missions*, 109, 110; Crews, *Faith and Tears*, 11; MA-SP: Gambold to Jacob Van Vleck, 26 September 1818; John Ridge to Gambold, 24 October 1818; Darcheechee to Gambold, 24 October 1818.
50. Hamilton, "Minutes Mission Conference," 44.
51. MA-SP, Springplace Diary, 5 April 1818; Horton, "Protestant Missionary Women," 141.
52. MA-SP, Springplace Diary, 25 December 1818 and 23–25 September 1818.
53. To determine the Lord's guidance, slips of paper bearing three choices—yes, no, or wait—were drawn. Daniel Crews, *Moravian Meanings: A Glossary of Historical Terms of the Church, Southern Province* (Winston-Salem, NC, 1992), 18.
54. Hamilton, "Minutes Mission Conference," 42, 44, 45; Schwarze, *History of Missions*, 103.
55. Perdue, *Women*, 46.
56. Perdue *Women*, 41–59; MA-SP, Gambold to Rev. John Herbst, 10 November 1810.
57. MA-SP, Springplace Diary, 13 April 1821 and 30 May 1821.
58. MA-SP, Springplace Diary, 14 May 1820.
59. Perdue, *Women*, 54, 69.
60. MA-SP: Gambold to Jacob Van Vleck, 8 March 1819; Springplace Diary, 14 March 1819.
61. MA-SP, Springplace Diary, 14 March 1819.
62. Jane T. Merritt, "Dreaming of the Savior's Blood: Moravians and the Indian Great Awakening in Pennsylvania," *William and Mary Quarterly* 54 (1997): 723–746.
63. McLoughlin, *Cherokees and Missionaries*, 147.
64. Gambold to Jacob Van Vleck 11 January 1819, MA-SP; Hamilton, "Minutes Mission Conference," 55.
65. MA-SP, Gambold to Van Vleck, 16 September 1819.
66. Ibid., 29 December 1819.
67. Schwarze, *History of Missions*, 127.
68. Sara H. Hill, "Weaving History: Cherokee Baskets from the Springplace Mission," *William and Mary Quarterly* 53 (1996): 134.
69. Schwarze, *History of Missions*, 121, 122.
70. MA-SP: John and Anna Rosina Gambold to Jacob Van Vleck, 17 July 1818; Springplace Diary, 1 July 1818 and 15 November 1818.
71. MA-SP, Springplace Diary, September 1820 and 18 March 1820.
72. Schwarze, *History of the Missions*, 142, 143.
73. MA-SP, Springplace Diary, 19 February 1821.
74. Crews, *Faith and Tears*, 56.
75. Hamilton, "Minutes Mission Conference," 54.
76. The Springplace Diary of 1819 demonstrates that the pressure for the mission came from the women in the Oochgelogy area.

77. Wilkins, *Tragedy*, 33

78. Crews, *Faith and Tears*, 12–14; McLoughlin, *Cherokees and Missionaries*, 144, 145; Hamilton, "Minutes Mission Conference," 54–57.

79. Hamilton, "Minutes Mission Conference," 31–59; Crews, *Faith and Tears*, 12; Jon F. Sensbach, *A Separate Canaan: The Making of an Afro-Moravian World in North Carolina, 1763–1840* (Chapel Hill, NC, 1998).

80. Hamilton, "Minutes Mission Conference," 37; Theda Perdue and Michael D. Green, *The Columbian Guide to American Indians of the Southeast* (New York, 2001), 72–100.

81. MA-SP, Springplace Diary, 12 April 1820.

82. MA-SP, Abraham Steiner to brother Jacob and all dear brothers and sisters, 11 October 1819. Four years later Mary and Martha McNair attended the Girls' Boarding School from 13 February 1823 until 23 May 1825. Student card in Salem College Library vault, Winston-Salem, NC.

83. *MRNC*, 8:3621.

84. Delilah McNair's great granddaughter, Albina Rogers, attended the Girls' Boarding School from 9 November 1839 until 30 October 1843. Student cards in Salem College Library vault, Winston-Salem, NC.

85. MA-SP, Springplace Diary, 14 March 1819; Gambold to Van Vleck, 11 January 1819.

86. MA-SP, J. R. Schmidt to Andrew Benade, 16 February 1824; Schwarze, *History of Missions*, 138, 139.

87. Sarah "Sally" Ridge came to the boarding school on 26 December 1826 and left 23 May 1829. Student card in Salem College Library vault, Winston-Salem, NC.

88. Griffin, *Less Time*, 165, 166.

89. *MRNC*, 8: 3771.

90. Perdue, *Women*, 152.

91. *MNRC*, 8: 3738.

92. Eliza Vierling Kremer, "Bits of Old Salem Gossip." Handwritten account in the Salem College Archives, Winston-Salem, NC.

93. Sara A. Vogler, *The Academy* 39 (1915): 6525.

Chapter 13

MORAVIAN MISSIONS IN TIMES OF EMANCIPATION: CONVERSION OF SLAVES IN SURINAME DURING THE NINETEENTH CENTURY

Ellen Klinkers

IT WAS ALMOST DARK WHEN the Moravian brother Th. C. Calker and his wife went ashore at the mission post Worsteling Jacobs. Nobody heard them arrive and nobody was there to welcome them at the pier. Once this had been a flourishing community where the Moravian couple Bleichen had lived happily. Now the almost deserted post made a sad impression. As they walked to the dilapidated and unoccupied house, a few slaves finally arrived to open the door for them. They climbed the shaky steps carefully and walked cautiously across the rotten veranda to the door. The rowers carried their luggage inside and hung their hammocks. Calker put the iron suitcase with the books in the wooden partitions to protect them from the many rats. They drank the tea and ate the bread, ham, and cake they had brought from home. They tried to make it as cozy as possible, but missed the enthusiastic welcome of a congregation of "Brothers" and "Sisters." Calker held a service the next morning with the twelve slaves still present.[1]

This experience of the missionary couple Calker at the almost deserted mission post Worsteling Jacobs illustrates the course of the Moravian mission among the slaves of Suriname, where success and disappointment alternated with one another. It was 1860 when the Calkers visited the mission post, and slavery was still an everyday reality. It would take three more years before its abolition was finally realized on 1 July 1863, years after the British, the French, and the Danish had freed their slaves in the Caribbean.

The slaves in Suriname were only introduced to Christianity during the last decades before Emancipation, when German Moravians visited their plantations to preach the Gospel. This period of transformation was not an easy mission for the Brethren. The future was anticipated eagerly by the slaves and feared by their owners. In addition, the Brethren had to deal with an Afro-Caribbean religion and culture, deeply rooted after almost two centuries of social isolation from white Christian culture. Nevertheless, the Brethren gained confidence among the slaves, many of whom converted to Christianity. But was the new religion firmly enough entrenched to survive the radical changes following Emancipation?

Conversion to Christianity: A Twofold Mission

The first attempt to convert the slaves in Suriname was made by the Dutch minister J.G. Kals in 1731. Kals ran up against strong opposition, however, when he presented his plans to the slave owners. They stated: "So vicar, let us convert those who have our skin and have our color, and leave those damned children of Cham with the devil. They are made to plant coffee and sugar for us."[2] Their refusal was intended to emphasize the inferiority of the slaves and keep a safe social distance between their own world and that of the slaves.

The first Moravians arrived in Suriname in 1735. They started their missionary work under the most difficult circumstances in the interior of Suriname among the Maroon and Indian communities. On the whole, their attempts to convert the Maroons and the Indians were unsuccessful, and eventually they decided to close the mission posts.[3] The Moravians carefully started their missionary work among the slaves in the town of Paramaribo in the second half of the eighteenth century. Cupido, a 45-year-old servant of a tailor, was the first slave to be baptized by the Moravians, in 1776.[4]

It was not until the 1830s that the plantation administrators changed their mind about converting the slaves. The abolition of the slave trade in 1814—a prohibition that was only observed in 1826 when the illegal trade was finally gotten under control—and later on the inevitable abolition of slavery gave Christian conversion a different meaning. In effect, the declining slave population amounted to the threat of a labor shortage, since the number of newborns could never make up for the deaths. Planters and colonial government agreed something had to be done to stop the dramatic decline of the slave population, which could no longer be supplied by new slave imports. One implication was that the slaves should receive better care. The colonial authorities forced the planters to improve the conditions of the slaves with laws.[5] Planters and the colonial government also hoped conversion would encourage family life among slaves, according to Christian traditions, which would presumably increase birth rates. A second aim of the conversion of slaves was to improve the industriousness of the slaves and, more importantly, help to retain them as plantation laborers after Emancipation.[6]

In 1828 the Society for the Advancement of Religious Education among the Heathens of Suriname (*Maatschappij ter bevordering van het godsdienstig onderwijs onder de heidense bevolking in Suriname*) was founded. This Protestant society entrusted the conversion of the slaves exclusively to the Moravians and supported them financially. The planters trusted the Moravians because they made it clear that they were not opposed to the enslavement of blacks and would therefore not harm their business interests.[7] In addition, the Moravians had proven their spiritual dedication in the interior of Suriname, even though their efforts to convert the Indians and the Maroons had remained almost fruitless.

The declaration of the plantation managers Gulcker and Le Chavalier in 1841 illustrates the attitude of the planters. They decided to invite Moravian missionaries to their coffee plantations because "the education of the Moravians in the colony of Suriname is in every respect suitable to impress religiousness and moral sense on the Negroes. This education will teach them respect for their masters and inspire them with zest for work."[8] Thus did the Moravians' wish come true when the slave owners finally welcomed them to their plantations in the 1830s. From this moment on the Moravian mission in Suriname grew rapidly. The working area was expanded from eleven plantations in 1830 to 190 in 1863. In that year, when the Surinamese slaves gained their freedom, the Moravian community counted 27,500 members, mostly slaves—served by 70 Brethren.[9]

Catholic missionaries also came to Suriname to convert slaves. However, the Catholic mission suffered from a lack of money and a shortage of missionaries. Moreover, the managers favored the Moravians and often refused the Catholic missionaries access to their plantations. The Catholic missionaries worked in Paramaribo, on plantations in the district of Coronie and in the leper colony Batavia. Petrus Donders became the well-known missionary of the lepers. By 1862, only 8,249 slaves had been converted to Catholicism.[10]

At the Managers' Mercy

In December 1862, S. Limes, manager of the Schoonoord plantation, put his slave Sancousie in irons because of "excessive impudence." Limes even called soldiers from Sommelsdijk, who planned to take Sancousie in their boat (to be taken to court in Paramaribo). But they never got the chance. Several slaves released Sancousie and gave him refuge in a cabin, while shouting victory. When more soldiers arrived, the slaves only became more agitated, continued shouting, and began pelting the military with stones. At last Lieutenant Bechtold gave orders to shoot, and several slaves were killed or wounded; Martha died, as did Eduard Barend after he was taken to the city, and in January, Gerrit was still under the care of a doctor for his injuries. Seven men and three women were finally taken to court in Paramaribo. Many slaves repented to the missionaries for the rebellion, and some even declared that the devil had brought them to do this. One Moravian brother blamed the managers of Schoonoord, since feelings had run high already before the incident, but he also lectured the slaves for their behavior.[11]

Planters and managers expected that conversion would discipline the slaves and turn them into loyal and subservient workers. When slaves rose in resistance, the Brethren arbitrated the dispute, usually in favor of the managers. They succeeded in preventing some rebellions and managed to calm rebellious slaves.[12] Still, it would be wrong to consider missionaries and slaveholders to have been of one mind. Often the Brethren were at the mercy of the managers, who could deny them entrance to the plantations and send them back empty-handed. This happened often at the height of the season, when crops had to be planted or harvested. At the Schoonoord sugar plantation, the relations between missionaries and managers turned out to be tense for a long time, as the following report indicates.

> 3 Sept 1859: H. Colli cannot just hide his anger and hatred against us with gestures (that would be the least) but also not with words…. Yesterday, when I arrived, he gave me permission to preach, while the other day on the 5th, the 8th and the 9th he sent us away without any course or reason.[13]

More and more owners gave permission to the Moravian missionaries to convert their slaves, but since many lived in Europe they could not assure that their managers would carry out their orders and welcome the missionaries at their estates. Some managers required slaves who attended Church to make up for lost time on their free Sunday.[14] The missionaries had to accomplish their work within the limits set by the managers, but they did not neglect the interests of the slaves. They treated the slaves with respect, learned to speak their language, *Sranan Tongo*, and were the first to document this language by translating the Bible in *Sranan*.[15]

Despite their good intentions, the Brethren did not oppose slavery. Sometimes they condemned the harsh managers in their private notes, but they had learned not to interfere in the existing social relations and advocated only for the spiritual freedom of the slaves. However, this passive attitude was condemned when abolitionist thought gained ground in Europe. Not the powerless Dutch antislavery movement but the British and Foreign Anti-Slavery Society criticized the Moravians for being slave owners themselves. Around 1845, the British abolitionists leveled their criticism directly at the Moravian missionaries in Suriname, who continued buying slaves. Under pressure from the abolitionist movement, the Brethren, beginning in 1846, allowed their 61 slaves to purchase their freedom. This implied they had to work for the Brethren until they had compensated their purchase price.[16]

In response to the accusations of the British abolitionists, Brother Otto Tank stated in 1846 that it was far too early for the Brethren to liberate their slaves.[17] In 1847 there were still 38,369 slaves in Suriname.[18] But in several letters and a circular in 1848, he also condemned the cruelty of slavery in Suriname and protested the working conditions imposed by his fellow Brethren.

> To the slaves we have to preach respect and obedience towards their masters, while these masters themselves trample on the first duties of humanity and on the respect for the rights of other people. And this while these masters refuse further obedience to most of the Commandments of God by virtue of their legal right to own slaves.

Tired of being used to discipline the slaves, Tank even suggested that "it was better to give up Christian education, than to make it subservient to purposes which it can never promote."[19] Tank's circular did not go unnoticed. Furious, the slave owners called the Moravian missionaries to account for Tank's statements. Under the direction of Praeses Calker, the Moravian missionaries in Suriname distanced themselves from Tank's writings. Tank never returned to Suriname and ultimately resigned from the Moravian Church.[20] Suriname was not yet ready for Tank's progressive point of view. For the time being, the Brethren compromised between the opposing interests of the slaves and their managers, and their own ideals.

Christianity in a Creole World

By the nineteenth century, when the Word of God was spread across the plantations of Suriname, slaves had already been shaping their own religious and cultural world for a long time. The Moravians faced a tremendous challenge in bridging the substantial gap between the world of the slaves and that of the white minority, separated consciously for almost two centuries. But from several mission posts scattered across the plantation areas, the Brethren traveled in their boats from one plantation to another. In notebooks or *specialiën* kept about each plantation, they recorded conversations with community members, names of newcomers, and promotions in the Church hierarchy, as well as the exclusion of community members and other daily experiences.

Due to the large distances and difficult transportation, the missionaries visited most plantations only once every five or six weeks. During their absence, their most loyal converts, men as well as women, looked after their affairs. These helpers or *Nationalhelpers* watched over the members, and kept the missionaries informed about the slaves' conduct. They also assisted in various tasks when the Brethren were present.[21] These helpers had prestige in the slave community, and it was honorable to be appointed. But at the same time, their position was difficult and contentious. As brother F. J. G. F. Jansa explained:

> In every respect it is not an easy post, because the helpers have to tolerate all kinds of hostilities from their fellow slaves when they practice their job with loyalty. They are hated by many and often called slanderers when they inform their teacher against somebody's sinful life. It needs a lot of self-denial and most of our helpers have too much fear and are short of faith in God, although they lead a good life themselves.[22]

At the Schoonoord plantation, for instance, the helper was often in trouble:

> There is a lot of disagreement here, in particular among the women. Many of them turned against the *dienerschwester* [servant sisters], who urged me to dismiss her from the job. Because of all the uproar, this afternoon I declared at Church that to our regrets there was hardly any good spirit—with the exception of a few—after such a long period of teaching Christianity. Moreover, I declared I would not remove the *dienerschwester*. The fact that so many were opposed to her was precisely the evidence that she performed her job with loyalty.[23]

Slaves also ran the risk of being expelled from the Moravian community when they attended Afro-Caribbean religious practices or committed adultery. The stability of family life and lasting monogamous relations between men and women was of major concern for the Brethren. No other subject received more attention in their *specialiën* than adultery and domestic quarrels. In 1850, the Brethren established the *Verbond* (alliance), a religious commitment that had no legal status. With this alliance the Brethren gave recognition to the relationships between men and women who were not allowed to contract a civil marriage. However, slaves were very reluctant to marry, so the alliance never became popular.[24]

But this should not imply that family life and communal loyalty were unimportant to the slaves. A steady flow of recent research has emphasized the importance of family life, in spite of all the obstructions of slavery. The African background and the particular circumstances of enslavement, however, gave family life a specific character.[25] Often women were the focus in the household, but also nuclear families and, to a lesser extent, polygynous arrangements existed. Households were embedded in extended families and community networks, often crossing the plantation boundaries. These extended families took care, so to speak, of the instability of some nuclear households. When a mother died, her family took care of her children. Hardly any orphans were entered in the registers kept shortly before the abolition of slavery. Fathers, aunts, grandmothers, and other kin took care of motherless children.[26]

Old slaves, neglected by their masters, were dependent on the care of their children and grandchildren. Without family, these people lived in terrible circumstances, as Brother Räthling vividly described:

It was very touching to see two old women at plantation John. They were living together in a cabin with a broken roof and the beautiful blue sky was visible through a hole. The remaining rafter could tumble down any moment. It's true, nobody is freezing in Suriname, but one needs shelter against rain and sunshine. This is how things are when slaves are old and not capable of working anymore. They are a burden for their masters, who don't care for them anymore. When they have no family, they lack any care and suffer bitter need.[27]

Räthling writes in the same report:

When I visited the sick at the Burnside plantation, I met the old Cristina Lucretia every week.... As long as she could, she didn't miss one single meeting, although she had to walk to Church for more than thirty minutes. Now she doesn't have the strength anymore and she can't stand it that she is not capable of doing as much as she could do before. She feels abandoned and thinks she suffers a lot. That is not the case, because she lives quite well, compared to many others. She has many children, adult grandchildren and several great-grandchildren.[28]

In spite of the intensity of family life in the slave communities, it seemed almost impossible for the Brethren to accept forms of domestic organization other than the ideal of the Western nuclear family. True enough, Moravian doctrine allowed the Brethren to accept polygynous associations prior to conversion. Those associations were not a reason to withhold baptism from partners.[29] However, the Brethren did not tolerate slaves becoming involved with a second partner after they became engaged with the Moravian community. In that case, polygyny was considered adultery and the slaves involved were punished with expulsion. This rule was less straightforward for slaves who united Christianity with Afro-Caribbean traditions.[30]

Besides promoting the nuclear family, managers hoped Christianity would discipline slaves. As shown above, the Brethren advocated humility and servitude, and sometimes managed to mollify rebellious slaves. But when tensions between slaves and masters increased, slaves might withdraw from the Church and find consolation in the Afro-Caribbean *Winti*-religion. *Basya's,* slaves who worked as overseers, were often the leaders of this religion, and their religious authority confirmed their secular power in the communities. It is no surprise then that some *basya's* resisted the arrival of the Moravians, while others asserted their influence in the Moravian community by becoming helpers.[31]

Essential in the *Winti*-religion is the belief in supernatural beings who can take possession of humans or eliminate their consciousness. At the top of a pantheon of gods is the supreme God, *Gran Gado,* who leaves control of the world to the many gods on earth, the *Winti's.*[32] There is no indication that the *Winti*-religion by itself made slaves rebellious. However, as Eugene Genovese has argued, it was more difficult to persuade slaves to rebel "when master and slave appealed to the same God, the same book, the same teachings," and "the difference came not with the abstract character of the Christian tradition but with the reduction of revolutionary potential inherent in the deeper separation of religion from class and especially ethnicity."[33]

The *watramama* dance, where dancers entered a trance, had been forbidden in Suriname since 1776. The white overseers and managers feared that the arousing music and the hypnotized dancers would make the participants rebellious.[34] But the dance never disappeared, which was usually no secret to the whites, who could hear the roll of drums from afar. Moreover, whites' anxiety about these dances seems to have diminished in the nineteenth century, and they were mentioned less often in contemporary literature than in earlier writings. Ironically some managers even encouraged Afro-Caribbean religious and secular dances, to the great grief of the Brethren.[35] Brother Tank wrote of "conjuration dances," by which dancers jumped around a fire, fell under the devil's spell, and performed supernatural feats while committing dreadful atrocities.[36] Some managers deliberately obstructed the Brethren by instigating Afro-Caribbean celebrations. For others, the celebrations were entertaining spectacles in the boring life at the estates.

More and more slaves converted to Christianity through time, but the persistence of Afro-Caribbean culture and customs demonstrates that slaves maintained control of their own lives. As Gert Oostindie has argued, the Brethren swung between hope and despair.[37] Slaves welcomed the Brethren into their communities some ten to thirty years before the abolition of slavery. In this short twenty-year period many accepted Christianity, though it often was merged with their Afro-Caribbean religion.

The Abolition of Slavery

On 1 July 1863, slavery was finally abolished in Suriname. Following the British example, the abolition of slavery was succeeded by a period of apprenticeship. Ex-slaves had to work for ten more years on the plantations, although they were free to choose their own employer and they received pay for their work. Compared to the four years of apprenticeship in the British Caribbean, this arrangement lasted exceptionally long in Suriname, supposedly to prevent social and economic upheaval.[38]

The Emancipation Act received royal approval almost a year before it was enacted, and this news spread rapidly among the slaves of Suriname. Some managers announced the news to the slaves themselves, while others entrusted this to the Brethren. After Brother Räthling received the declaration in *Sranan* on 12 October 1862, he and his wife arranged a Church meeting to announce it to all. The Church was packed with slaves who listened happily and carefully to Räthling as he read the declaration. The missionary explained every line and asked the slaves if they had understood his words. Everyone was full of joy, wrote Räthling, who was himself elated that the slaves of Suriname would finally be free. Many claimed they would never have believed the news if it had not been their *leriman* [teacher/instructor] who told them. At the end of the evening they asked Räthling to thank the king and the governor for the great gift of freedom.[39]

True, the slaves were happy about their impending freedom, but they also had mixed feelings about what was about to happen. The obligatory contract concerned them, particularly, and they feared it might enslave them once again. The missionaries had their own worries. Although many were pleased about the abolition of slavery, the Brethren realized this meant drastic changes in their missionary work.[40]

On 1 July 1863 the Moravians mounted festivities all over the country to celebrate Emancipation. At the Church of the Catharina Sophia estate the ex-slaves of surrounding plantations gathered early in the morning to celebrate their freedom. Thirty-two persons from the plantation Kent had traveled all night to attend the ceremony. The Church was too small for the crowd and some had to sit in front of the door. White folks also came to listen to the sermons of the Moravians, and Brethren Bau and Calker wrote a song for the occasion, *"gi koning Willem bigi nem"* (King Willem is respected). It was not until seven o'clock in the evening that the celebration came to an end in the Church decorated with flowers and garlands. Elsewhere at the plantation, wrote Calker, a "worldly" party was going on with much dancing and drinking. To Calker's great annoyance many baptized youth attended this feast, and he blamed the managers since they had paid for the party and frustrated the Moravian community, consciously or unconsciously.[41]

In whatever manner the first day of freedom was celebrated, for the former slaves it was a joyful day. A new era had begun; slavery was left behind forever. In the following weeks, the rivers brimmed with boats carrying goods and people, mostly ex-slaves who had left their old estates to sign their contract elsewhere. Some managers lost many workers, and labor shortages loomed. Contract laborers were recruited from the Caribbean and Asia to save Suriname's plantation economy.[42] Although the migration among plantations slowed down in the course of time, after the ending of the apprenticeship in 1873 it started all over again. Many ex-slaves wanted to rebuild their lives outside the plantation regime as peasants, craftsmen, or gold diggers. Others continued as contract workers on the plantations, often renting themselves out for specific jobs for a limited period of time only. The changes of residence during apprenticeship and the withdrawal from the plantations were above all acts of resistance against former masters who hoped to coerce the ex-slaves back into plantation labor, but this itinerancy was likewise a search for independence.[43] Brother Kühn explained that the ex-slaves liked to move on to another plantation, even if there was actually no reason to leave: "Often, by leaving he makes clear to his master, that this master is dependent on him since Emancipation. At best, he gives his permission to make a new contract after hesitating for a while."[44] The changing of residences was remarkable in the face of staunch plantation communities and family ties, as well as the trauma of forced removals following slave sales before 1863.[45] Still, there were communities that resisted the changes brought on by Emancipation and remained together, forming a stable basis for peasant communities after the end of the apprenticeship.[46]

The abolition of slavery also introduced a period of uncertainty for the Moravians. Although the Brethren were generally delighted with Emancipation, they had to face a loss of control over the Church communities. For the first time in centuries their flock of followers declined. The Moravians remained the largest Christian community among the Creole population, but they still lost 3,924 members during this apprenticeship period.

The plantation slave communities had laid the foundation for a black Christian Church with an organization and administration. But the migration between and then withdrawal from plantations disturbed the unity of the Church communities, and it became difficult to monitor the conduct of the members. The missionaries did their best to keep the Christian communities together, but they often failed. In 1863 Brother Menze talked with the community members till deep into the night, trying and tried to convince them to stay at the plantation and improve their way of life. Some gave in, but many others did not.[47] After 1873 some plantations were increasingly deserted. For example, the plantation around the mission post Leliëndaal had the largest Moravian community in Suriname with 2,273 members in 1872, just before the end of the apprenticeship. By 1880 only 938 members were left. Two estates were almost deserted, and the managers were delighted when they finally caught sight of a steamer with contract laborers from India approaching up the river Commewijne in July 1873.[48] In this sense the Brethren were not treated differently from any other employer, as they also lost laborers after 1873; Brother Meissel, for example, complained that since workers were not committed to a contract, they left when they did not like the job.[49] On the Schoonoord estate, brother Voigt held the last meeting on 4 June 1878: "Held Church in the morning. Ten adults were present. Almost all residents of the plantation have left ... It is not worth anymore to keep service here."[50]

Alongside the breakup of communities, the Brethren encountered a strong spirit of liberty among the ex-slaves. In particular the young ex-slaves rebelled against authority, including the Brethren. It became even more difficult to find loyal helpers after Emancipation. The job had lost prestige, and the helpers had to endure even more criticism and mockery than before. No wonder then that helpers were reluctant to report on the conduct of community members. Their warnings were neglected and Church attendance was limited. The spirit of liberty also became apparent with the overt profession of the Creole *Winti*-religion.[51]

The advancement of Christianity was part of the politics of assimilation for the colonial government, which was continued and even reinforced after Emancipation. It seemed contradictory, but cultural freedom was more limited after Emancipation than ever before.[52] Creoles had to be part of one national language and cultural community. Despite the politics of assimilation, the ex-slaves preserved the Creole language *Sranan Tongo*, traditional medical treatment, and religion. Compulsory education in Dutch was introduced in 1876, but could not replace *Sranan*.[53] Participation in "heathen practices" was criminalized but with little success, since the Afro-Caribbean religion was practiced openly. Most charges against practicing the Afro-Caribbean religion were made in 1872, when twenty-two persons were accused of heathen practices. Although Moravian missionaries were the principal plaintiffs, most of them seemed to realize the law was not the best way to keep their flock together.[54]

At the mission post of Bersaba, Brother and Sister Braukmann heard the roll of the drums more and more on Saturday evenings. In the beginning, they thought of young people making music and dancing, but later they realized that Afro-Caribbean religious meetings were being held. Their helper told them on 1 October 1868 that his "heathen" family members were organizing a feast of the dead the following Saturday. As the helper explained to Brother Braukmann, his family members had to keep a promise made to their deceased father or mother but would then put those "heathen things behind them" and join the Church. When Braukmann recorded his memories three years later, they still had not become members. The feast was well prepared: the participants made cakes, slaughtered pigs, and invited all their friends from other plantations. At nine o'clock in the evening they started singing and playing the drums. In the beginning it was soft, like a solo. Later, the others joined in. This alternation was repeated several times during the night. At midnight, the singing became weaker and weaker. For several minutes Braukmann and his wife could hear only one voice. They were startled when suddenly the crowd joined in, and made a "demoniacal roaring," as Braukmann wrote. The feast went on till six in the morning. When the missionary couple woke up, it was silent at last. Only a few attended Sunday mass that morning. In the afternoon the roll of the drums started again, but Braukmann was not to be put off and rang the bells for the evening mass. Their helper asked them to postpone the service until after the ceremony. Braukmann did not give in and rang the bells again. The drumming stopped, and a few loyal members of the community came to Church. Braukmann realized it was no use fighting the Afro-Caribbean religion with force. He did not want to demolish places of gods because he realized they would be rebuilt quickly, which had happened before.[55]

The Brethren had hoped that Emancipation would change attitudes about family life. Now that the ex-slaves were taking full charge of their own lives and were able to contract civil and religious marriages, the Brethren hoped the ex-slaves would adopt European customs with respect to marriage and family. The government, which offered benefits to married couples during apprenticeship, supported the aspirations of the Brethren.[56] But even with the reduction or elimination of women's work obligations, the majority of the couples could not be persuaded to marry.

The Brethren held celebrations with the married community members, but were frustrated by the many people who although married lived as if they were single. The references to the reluctance of ex-slaves to marry are many in the writings of the Moravians.[57] The stereotype of the fragile Afro-Caribbean family life did not change after Emancipation. Some stated that relationships between men and women became even weaker because of the many changes of residence.[58]

There are no indications, however, that Emancipation had a structurally debilitating impact on family life. In those areas where ex-slaves did not move out, both the extended families and the old plantation communities formed the basis for the rising peasant economies. The socioeconomic meaning of the household became stronger, but this does not mean that marriage and the nuclear family became the standard. Only a few marriages were conducted in the peasant regions Para and Coronie. Brother Braukmann even stated that in no other district were there so few married couples as in Para. Moreover, it was the only region in Suriname where polygyny was still practiced. In 1871, the Moravians accepted thirteen men, each living with two wives; one was even allowed to keep his three wives. Among the new members, fifteen men had two wives. Thirteen others were expelled from the community because they entered into polygynous relations after being baptized.[59]

The Moravians tried hard to persuade ex-slaves to lead their life according to Western norms at the expense of Creole culture. In those years divorced people were not allowed to marry again, and community members who wanted to marry "heathens" were excluded from the community. Couples who promised to marry were allowed to live together, but it was decided in 1870 that this arrangement could not last for more than one year, and even more exclusions from Church were the result. This situation lasted into the 1880s, when Church discipline was relaxed.[60]

Suddenly, during this period of transformation, the Catholic missionaries revealed themselves as real competitors in the struggle for converts. The Catholic missionaries had been less successful than their Protestant colleagues during slavery because they lacked financial means, missionaries, and the support of owners and the colonial government. In 1865, Suriname became an apostolic vicariate, and the possibilities for Catholicism grew rapidly. Although the Catholic missionaries and the Moravian Brethren shared the same ideals about family life, the Catholics were more liberal in practice. Unlike the Moravians, they baptized children of unbaptized parents, and they accepted marriages between Catholics and partners of a different religious persuasion as long as the couple promised to raise their children as Catholics. Undoubtedly, this attitude contributed to their success.[61] The Brethren looked with suspicion at the growing competition. The Catholic missionaries, on the other hand, expressed their dislike for the Moravians in sharp criticism and complained about the "moravianized" population. This clash between the two religions lasted until the 1890s. In the twentieth century, Catholics and Moravians gradually became closer and ultimately began to cooperate.[62]

Conclusion

The timing, the double standards of the managers, and the strong Creole culture of the slaves made the conversion of slaves a difficult mission. Christianity, it was hoped, would prepare the slaves for Emancipation by promoting monogamy and the nuclear family, improving labor ethics, and abolishing "heathen practices." As of 1830, the state and the plantation owners encouraged the conversion of slaves by the Moravians. The Moravian Brethren did not share the goals of the planters and the state, which nonetheless allowed them to realize their own ambition: the conversion of slaves. The Moravians did their work with inspiration and converted many slaves. However, the Creole *Winti*-religion never disappeared, but persisted alongside of or in the place of Christianity, even among the converted.

After the abolition of slavery, the ex-slaves wanted to experience their freedom. In their longing for independence they opposed not only their former masters but also the Brethren. The Brethren preached humility and servitude, but the ex-slaves wanted freedom without restraint. More than before, the ex-slaves showed their resentment of the interference by the Brethren. The situation in Suriname was in this respect very similar to the one described by Nigel Bolland for the British Caribbean: "The widespread persistence of Afro-Caribbean beliefs and customs, as well as the continuing resentment of and resistance to the authority systems of the colonial plantation society, are eloquent testimony to the ultimate failure of the indoctrination process among the ex-slaves in the British Caribbean."[63] But by the end of the nineteenth century, the Moravians had regained the confidence of the Creole population. This time, together with the Creole population, the Moravian Church could build a firm and lasting Christian community in Suriname.

Notes

I wish to thank Tony Robben for his editorial suggestions and correction of my English.

1. UA-Herrnhut, 15 La 8 (14), 23-02-1860.
2. Johannes Kals, *Neerlands Hooft- en Wortel-sonde, het verzuym van de bekeringe der Heydenen, aangewesen en ten toon gespreit door Drie Leer-Redens gedaan en gemeen gemaakt door drie der voornaamste kerk-voogden in Engeland* (Leewarden, 1756), 44.
3. Jan Van der Linde, *Het visioen van Herrnhut en apostolaat der Moravische Broeders in Suriname, 1735–1863* (Paramaribo, 1956); Maria Lenders, *Strijders voor het lam: leven en werk van Herrnhutter-broeder en –zusters in Suriname, 1735–1900* (Leiden, 1996), 53–152.

4. Lenders, *Strijders voor het Lam*, 124.
5. Ernst Van den Boogaart and Pieter C. Emmer, "Plantation Slavery in the Last Decade before Emancipation: The Case of Catharina Sophia," in *Comparative Perspectives on Slavery in New World Plantation Societies*, ed. Vera Rubin and Arthur Tuden (New York, 1977), 205–225.
6. Ellen Klinkers, *Op hoop van vrijheid: Van slavensamenleving naar Creoolse gemenschap in Suriname, 1830–1880* (Utrecht, 1997), 23; Lenders, *Strijders voor het Lam;* Gert Oostindie, *Roosenburg en Mon Bijou: Twee Surinaamse plantages, 1720–1870* (Dordrecht, 1989), 192–195; Gert Oostindie, *Het Paradijs overzee: De 'Nederlandse'Caraïben en Nederland* (Amsterdam, 1997), 34, 50–53.
7. Karel Zeefuik, *Herrnhutter zending en Haagsche Maatschappij, 1828–1867: Een hoofdstuk uit de geschiedenis van de zending en emancipatie in Suriname* (Utrecht, 1973), 27; See also J. C. S. Mason, *The Moravian Church and the Missionary Awakening in England, 1760–1800* (Woodbridge, 2001), 90–113.
8. UA-Herrnhut, 15 La 10, dokumente 1768–1857.
9. *Koloniale Verslagen* 1851–1863; Klinkers, *Op hoop van vrijheid*, 56–57.
10. Joop Vernooij, *De Rooms-Katholieke gemeente van Suriname vanaf 1866* (Paramaribo, 1974), 25, 33; A. Bossers, *Beknopte geschiedenis der katholieke missie in Suriname door een pater Redemptorist* (Gulpen, 1884), 25.
11. RU, Evangelische Broedergemeente Suriname (EBGS), 373, 25 February 1863; J. F. Zeegelaar, *Suriname en de opheffing der slavernij in 1863* (Amsterdam, 1871), 54–56.
12. Ellen Klinkers, "De zending onder de plantageslaven in Coronie," *OSO: Tijdschrift voor Surinaamse Taalkunde, letterkunde, cultuur en geschiedenis* 1 (1994): 36–37.
13. RU, EBGS, 372.
14. Lenders, *Strijders voor het Lam*, 222.
15. Johan Jones, *Tussen Kwakoe en Christus* (Brussels, 1980).
16. The Moravians had already taken action to liberate their slaves in the Danish West Indies. The Danish Governor gave permission to the Brethren to free their slaves in 1843. Lenders, *Strijders voor het Lam*, 217–232; Jon F. Sensbach, *Rebecca's Revival: Creating Black Christianity in the Atlantic World* (Cambridge, MA, 2005), 242–245.
17. Lenders, *Strijders voor het Lam*, 219.
18. Cornelis van Sijpesteijn, *Beschrijving van Suriname: Historisch-, geografisch- en statistisch overzigt* (Gravenhage, 1854), 152.
19. RU, Het Archief van het Zeister Zendingsgenootschap (ZZG), 823.
20. Lenders, *Strijders voor het Lam*, 224–225; Zeefuik, *Herrnhutter zending en Haagsche Maatschappij*, 120–137.
21. Mason, *Moravian Church and the Missionary Awakening*, 98–99; Sensbach, *Rebecca's Revival*, 94–100.
22. *Nachrichten aus der Brüdergemeine* (1859): 385.
23. RU, EBGS, 373, 4-6-1861.
24. Klinkers, *Op hoop van vrijheid*, 78–79; Lenders, *Strijders voor het Lam*, 245–250.
25. The extensive recent work on slave families includes Michael J. Craton, "Changing Patterns of Slave Families in The British West Indies," *Journal of Interdisciplinary History* 10 (1979): 1–35; Wilma A. Dunaway, *The Afro-Caribbean Family in Slavery and Emancipation* (Cambridge, 2003); Karen Fog Olwig, "Finding a Place for the Slave Family: Historical Anthropological Perspectives," *Folk* 23 (1981): 345–358; Jacqueline Jones, *Labor of Love, Labor of Sorrow; Black Women, Work and the Family from Slavery to the Present* (New York, 1995); Barry W. Highman, *Slave Populations of the British Caribbean, 1807–1834* (Baltimore and London, 1884). See for Suriname: Huub Everaert, *Een zoektocht naar de aard van man-vrouw relaties onder Surinaamse slaven* (Amsterdam, 1999); Klinkers, *Op hoop van vrijheid*, 69–105; Humphrey Lamur, *De kerstening van de slaven van de Surinaamse plantage Vossenburg, 1847–1878* (Amsterdam, 1985); Oostindie, *Roosenburg en Mon Bijou*, 157–163, 264–267; Alex van Stipriaan, *Surinaams contrast: Roofbouw en overleven in een Caraïbische plantagekolonie, 1750–1863* (Leiden, 1993), 340–346.

26. Landsarchief Suriname: Archief van de Gouverneur, brievenboeken 1863; Centraal Bureau Bevolkingsregister Suriname: emancipatieregisters.
27. RU, EBGS, 560.
28. Ibid.
29. Mason, *Moravian Church and the Missionary Awakening*, 97.
30. Klinkers, *Op hoop van Vrijheid*, 91–94; *Nachrichten aus der Brüdergemeine* 1847: 501 and 1851: 472.
31. Lamur, *De kerstening van de slaven*, 27–33.
32. Charles Wooding, *Winti: Een Afroamerikaanse godsdienst in Suriname: Een cultureel-historische analyse van de religieuze verschijnselen in de Para* (Meppel, 1972).
33. Eugene D. Genovese, *From Rebellion to Revolution: Afro-Caribbean Slave Revolts in the Making of the Modern World* (Baton Rouge, LA, 1979), 32.
34. Anthony Blom, *Verhandelingen van den landbouw in de colonie Suriname, volgens eene negentien-jaarige ondervinding zamengesteld, door Athony Blom: En met de noodige opheldering en bewysredenen voorzien, door Floris Visscher Heshuysen* (Amsterdam, 1786), 391–392, 398; Eensgezindheid, *Verzameling van uitgezochte verhandelingen, betreffende den Landbouw in de kolonie Suriname; Opgesteld door het Landbouwkundig Genootschap: De eensgezndheid, gevestigd in de devisie Matappica, binnen dezelve Kolonie* (Amsterdam, 1804), 17; Jan Jacob Hartsinck, *Beschryving van Guiana, of de Wilde Kust, in Zuid-America* (Amsterdam, 1770), 909; Jacob Schiltkamp and Jacobus. Th. de Smidt, eds., *West Indisch Plakaatboek II* (Amsterdam, 1973), 896; for discussion of trance and resistance see Ioan Lewis, *Estatic Religion: A Study of Shamanism and Spirit Possesion* (London, 1991); James Scott, *Domination and the Arts of Resistance: Hidden Transcripts* (New York, 1990), 140–142; Brian Morris, *Anthropological Studies of Religion: An Introductory Text* (Cambridge, 1993), 231–232.
35. At plantation Osembo, for example, the managers encouraged *Winti*-assemblies. RU, EBGS, 539, 10 October 1858, 22 July 1860.
36. UA-Herrnhut, 15 La 8 (12).
37. Oostindie, *Roosenburg en Mon Bijou*, 193–194.
38. Pieter Emmer, "Between Slavery and Freedom: The Period of Apprenticeship in Suriname (Dutch Guyana), 1863–1873," *Slavery and Abolition* 14 (1993): 87–113.
39. UA-Herrnhut, 15 Lb Salem.
40. UA-Herrnhut, 15Lb 11b Catharina Sophia; See also UA-Herrnhut, 15 Lb 15 Salem; RU, EBGS, 376, Hooiland Plantation.
41. Ibid.
42. Hoefte, *In Place of Slavery: A Social History of British Indian and Javanese Laborers in Suriname* (Gainesville, FL, 1998).
43. O. Nigel Bolland, "The Politics of Freedom," in Frank McGlynn and Seymour Drescher, eds., *The Meaning of Freedom: Economics, Politics, and Culture after Slavery* (Pittsburgh, PA, 1992), 139; Sidney W. Mintz, *Caribbean Transformations* (Baltimore, 1989), 154–156.
44. UA-Herrnhut, 15 La 9c (2) Kühn: Visitationsbericht u. beilagen 1-XXXIII 1870–1871, *Einige bemerkungen über die zukunft die neger*.
45. Van Stipriaan, *Surinaams Contrast*, 389–392.
46. Mintz, *Caribbean Transformations* and "Slavery and the Rise of Peasantries," *Historical Reflections* 6 (1979).
47. RU, EBGS, 831. *Ein Missions-bild aus Suriname*, 16–17.
48. UA-Herrnhut, 15 La 8 (15), 15 lb Leliëndaal.
49. UA-Herrnhut, 15 Lb Leliëndaal.
50. RU, EBGS 374, 4 June 1878.
51. UA-Herrnhut, 15 La 9c (2) Kühn, Visitationsbericht u. Beilagen I-XXXIII 1870–1871; 15 Lb 14 Leliëndaal; RU, 377, 28 April 1878; *Nachrichten aus der Brüdergemeine* (1969), 849; Klinkers, *Op hoop van vrijheid*, 179.
52. Klinkers, 69–105. See also Diane J. Austin-Broos, "Redefining the Moral Order: Interpretations of Christianity in Postemancipation Jamaica," in McGlynn and Drescher, *The Meaning of Freedom*, 221–244.

53. *West Indiër* 3 June 1874, 15 December 1880.
54. Emmer, *Between Slavery and Freedom*, 109; Klinkers, *Op hoop van vrijheid*, 130–133.
55. UH-Herrnhut, 15 Lb 11a Bersaba; *Nachrichten aus der Brüdergemeine* (1872), 854, 855. During slavery, the Brethren often demolished Afro-Caribbean religious objects and the places of their gods. Lenders, *Strijders voor het Lam*, 233.
56. Emmer, *Between Slavery and Freedom*, 112.
57. UA-Herrnhut, 15 La 9c (2) Kühn, Visitationsbericht and 15 Lb 11a Bersaba; RU, EBGS, 671; Nachrichten (1871): 763 and (1873), 1057.
58. *Koloniaal Verslag* 1878. Brother Illy noticed partners breaking up because one of them did not want to leave their estate, UA-Herrnhut, 15 Lb 11b Catharina Sophia. See also the *Specialiën*, RU, EBGS, 373, 374, 376, 377.
59. UA-Herrnhut, 15 La 9c (2) Kühn, 1871; 15 Lb Salem.
60. Lenders, *Strijders voor het Lam*, 357, 358.
61. Lenders, *Strijders voor het Lam*, 343; KDC: Bestuursarchief van de Nederlandse provincie van de Congregatie van de Redemptoristen—vice-provincie Suriname, 3140, 3578.
62. Vernooij, *De Rooms-Katholieke gemeente van Suriname*, 12, 27–45; KDC: Bestuursarchief van de Nederlandse provincie van de Congregatie van de Redemptoristen—vice-provincie Suriname, 3140, 3578.
63. Bolland, *The Politics of Freedom*, 136, 137.

– Chapter 14 –

SLAVERY, RACE, AND
THE GLOBAL FELLOWSHIP:
RELIGIOUS RADICALS CONFRONT
THE MODERN AGE

Jon Sensbach

IN 1738 MORAVIAN MISSIONARIES in the Danish West Indian colony of St.
Thomas faced a quandary. The mission they had begun among enslaved
Africans in 1733 converted several hundred people, making their house
too small for meetings. Local planters suspicious of Moravian motives believed the meetings were a breeding ground for slave insurrection, so
they harassed converts and mission workers, often violently. The missionaries were poor. Recipients of sparse funds from the central Church in
Germany, they were expected to support themselves by whatever handi-
work they could pick up, usually not enough. They devised a solution to
these problems, convincing a friendly planter to buy them a plantation
and slaves of their own. On this site they would build a Church where
they could worship freely, and the slaves would work the sugar cane fields
to support them. They named it Posaunenberg–Trumpet Mountain.[1]

Reminiscent of Spanish mission sites among Indians in the New World,
Posaunenberg became an odd hybrid of working plantation and spiritual
refuge, whose captive labor force doubled as a congregation. A Moravian
etching from the 1760s depicts the plantation's African slave village with
rows of huts lining a hillside near the fields. A Church, a tannery, and sta-
bles form an adjacent compound, and at the top of the hill, surveying
everything, is the sugar boiling house where workers rendered the cane
to molasses and poured it into barrels for shipment to world markets.
Slavery ended in the Danish islands in 1848, but the Church built on the

plantation by Africans in the early 1740s stands today. Its congregation, still active as the New Herrnhut Moravian Church, is both the oldest Moravian and the oldest African-American Protestant congregation in the Western hemisphere.[2]

Posaunenberg symbolized the melding of religious and social impulses that shaped the Renewed Unity of Brethren in the eighteenth century. In an age of reason, their worldview was militantly antirationalist. In their home communities, their diaspora settlements, and their missions around the world, they wanted only to live by their understanding of God's word, shunning worldliness and the things they associated with it—acquisitiveness, politics, militarism, the intellect, immodesty. Yet with no sense of irony and no moral qualms, they participated in the quintessential invention of the modern world, the American plantation system and all it entailed: the African slave trade, international capital, management of an enslaved agricultural and industrial labor force. All this they grafted onto their vision of a New Testament community of believers who worked in the Lord's cane fields.

The Moravian Church had a deeply ambivalent relationship to some of the key indexes by which many Europeans measured their ideas of progress, and their national identities, in the eighteenth century. Though they saw themselves as reacting against modernity, they also embraced and promoted it. In their quest to spread God's kingdom across the earth, they exemplified important aspects of European outreach in the first centuries of globalization. In the spaces between their disdain for the modern world and their need to act within it, they forged their longest-lasting legacy.

This essay explores this duality by examining some aspects of their mission work, Moravians' most visible projection of themselves into a public arena. The Brethren were not the earliest Protestant missionaries—Puritans, Anglicans, Dutch Reformed, Hallensian Pietists, and even Quakers long preceded them. But they were the first to realize the implications of the worldwide spread of European imperialism for disseminating Christianity. They established more outposts and preached to more people than any other Protestant Church in the eighteenth century. Historians have not adequately explained the source of the dynamic impulse that, just five years after the consecration of the Renewed Unity in 1727, compelled hundreds of missionaries around the globe to take the Gospel to so many people. These squadrons of disciples considered themselves martyrs in God's service, unfazed by their enormous mortality in climates both tropical and frozen.

What made this small sect ubiquitous on the frontlines of the encounter between Europeans and non-Christians in Suriname, Jamaica, St. Thomas, Nicaragua, Ohio, Pennsylvania, Greenland, Labrador, South Africa, Russia, and Ceylon? Why was the largest massacre of civilians during the American Revolution the Whig slaughter of Moravian Delawares at Gnadenhuetten, Ohio? Why, at the end of the eighteenth century, was the great majority of the world's black Protestants Moravian? What does it mean for the history of that endeavor when the huge preponderance of Church membership today, as in many Churches, is found not in Europe or the United States but in the Caribbean and southern Africa? Until we better understand these dimensions of the Brethren's appeal, we cannot appreciate how they anticipated and helped define the global outreach of evangelical Protestantism between the early modern period and our own time. To study the eighteenth-century Moravian Church is to enter a vast laboratory where Christianity mixed with European ideas about race, civilization, and slavery at the same time that evangelicalism furnished thousands of colonized people a new belief system to reckon with their subjugation.[3]

Several generations of scholars have emphasized the social, intellectual, and cultural volatility around the Atlantic rim set in motion by European colonization of the Americas. We are coming to understand how the flow of capital and human energy linked such distant ports as Bristol, Gambia, and Charleston. The European diffusion to the western hemisphere brought many consequences, but several of the most prominent include: a prolonged cycle of confrontation and, often, a melding of peoples from America, Europe, and Africa; a series of cultural frontiers with permeable boundaries between colonizers, colonized, and enslaved; constant attempts by Europeans to classify those they encountered in emerging racial and ethnic categories; the creation of new systems of knowledge and language blending assumptions from the Old World with lessons from the New; and a multidirectional, transatlantic, and often reciprocal flow of people, ideas, and information between metropolitan and imperial centers. These aspects figured prominently in the Brethren's view of themselves and how they projected that image into the world. We should understand them not as self-contained communities of religious mystics insulated from the world but as global sojourners engaged with the complexity of these new realities, often involving difficult choices for themselves and for those with whom they came into contact.[4]

The Moravians' ambiguous relationship to the question of European empires illustrates their attempts to navigate those complexities. The eighteenth-century Brethren thought of themselves as latter-day apostles, free to go where God directed them to spread the word. As members of a spiritual fellowship and German-speaking natives of territories fractured by religion and politics, the Brethren did not link their mission to German national or imperial identity. In that regard they were unlike the missionary wing of the Church of England, the Society for the Propagation of the Gospel in Foreign Parts, which regarded evangelism among the enslaved Africans in the American colonies as a valuable service not only to Christianity but also to English civilization and empire. Although the Brethren considered themselves attached to no one's expansionist agenda, free from the ideological requirements of nationalism and colonialism, in fact the Church was tied to a number of imperial Protestant apron strings.

Count Zinzendorf used his friendship with the royal court of Denmark to secure patronage for the first mission in 1732 to St. Thomas, and, in quick succession, to the other colonies of the Danish Atlantic, St. Croix, St. John, and Greenland. Permission from the Dutch and British likewise enabled the Brethren to take their mission worldwide, following Dutch colonization to South Africa, Suriname, and Ceylon and British conquests in the West Indies and North America.

Whatever their own intentions, the Brethren came to be seen by colonial administrators as bulwarks of imperialism, whose teachings helped pacify captive or potentially resistant populations. Ironically, at the outset of their mission work they had the opposite reputation as social incendiaries, fomenters of slave rebellion. How they came to be seen as social conservatives is an instructive case study of their relationship to imperial power. On St. Thomas, where the enslaved African population outnumbered the Danish and Dutch colonists 3,741 to 650 in the mid 1730s, the missionaries gained a foothold by befriending sympathetic planters who allowed them to preach on their plantations, believing that Christianity would help "civilize" their slaves. The preachers, including young Bishop August Spangenberg, who visited the island in September and October 1736, sympathized deeply with the slaves and were privately aghast at the atrocities they saw committed against them by the *Blancken,* as white colonists were called. "They treat the Negroes so cruelly it would make a stone wail," wrote the bishop. To convince the slaves that Christianity was an empathetic religion, missionaries gained their confidence by becoming their friends and allies. They visited the quarters to shake hands and hold searching conversations, addressing listeners as "Brother" and "Sister." They held nightly meetings in which they taught Afro-Caribbean students to read the Bible and to write, a risky tactic in that slave society. They preached a Christianity that exalted the slaves while emphasizing their fellowship in the community of the spirit. One pupil named Mingo "asserted on the authority of his teacher that black men were no less creatures of God than were the Whites."[5]

A key to this approach lay in an explicit biblical critique of the slaveholders themselves. As Spangenberg explained, "When they learn to read the testimony of the Scriptures, the Negroes can see for themselves how to avoid the false teachings and wicked life of the so-called Christians under whom they live." He believed the planters promoted promiscuity among their bondspeople to expand their workforce, and condemned them for denying baptism to slaves. "Damned are the authorities who want to take that honor from the Lord and rule over the conscience of the people." The Moravian preachers did not advertise their criticism to the planters, nor were they urging pupils to develop a biblical attack on slavery or to resist the social order. Their strategy was to encourage the enslaved to set themselves apart from, and spiritually above, the "so-called Christians" who purported to rule them.[6]

The times were dangerous for such doctrines. The planters of St. Thomas were acutely aware of the slave revolts that had peppered the Caribbean during the 1730s, including a major rebellion in 1733 that convulsed the Danish colony of St. John, where Africans slew several dozen whites and captured the island before being suppressed. The St. Thomas planters, terrified of a revolt on their own soil, grew alarmed as they became aware that slaves were absorbing potentially inflammatory messages from the Moravians. "If one wants to have a Rebellion in St. Thomas in which all the *Blanken* would lose their lives, the surest way is to continue tolerating" the Brethren, according to one colonial official. The *Blanken* responded violently, beating up the missionaries and whipping black congregants for attending meetings. One master made a practice of setting fire to the Bible and beating out the flames on his slaves' faces. Another chained slaves to the ground to keep them from devotions. In 1738 the authorities arrested several missionaries, including the married couple Matthäus Freundlich and his wife Rebecca, a free woman of color from St. Thomas who had become an important leader in the mission. Authorities feared the interracial marriage would threaten the ordered slave society. After four months in jail, the missionaries were released through the fortuitous intervention of the Moravian leader, Count Nicolaus Ludwig von Zinzendorf, who happened to visit the island and lobbied the governor to set them free. Many planters nonetheless remained determined to suppress the spread of black Christianity and stepped up their attacks.[7]

To placate them, Zinzendorf assembled three hundred Afro-Christian worshipers for a pep talk in January 1739. Speaking in Dutch, which a black assistant translated into Dutch Creole, the slaves' lingua franca, the count told the audience he was glad so many had found their way to Christ, but urged them to remember who they were. "[R]emain faithful to your masters and mistresses," he said. "Perform all your work with as much love and diligence as if you were working for yourselves." God, he said, "has made everything himself—kings, masters, servants, and slaves. And as long as we live in this world, everyone must gladly endure the state into which God has placed him and be content with God's wise counsel." Because God had "punished the first Negroes with slavery," conversion did not liberate their bodies, but "it does remove all evil thoughts, deceit, laziness, faithlessness, and everything that makes your condition of slavery burdensome." The count, identifying sin as the ultimate slavery, made no mention of oppressive work regimes, a lack of physical freedom, and violent punishments as factors contributing to the burden of slavery.[8]

These positions were consistent with the count's own conservative worldview, so he made no ideological compromise by telling slaves to obey their masters. To save the mission, he articulated positions that would become the Brethren's party line on African slavery in the Americas, their trump to the planters' hostility. The Moravians, courageous advocates of the slaves in so many ways, now enslaved themselves to biblical and racialist defenses of bondage. The radical impulses that had driven them just a few years earlier—celebrating the slaves as God's chosen people, criticizing the planters as cruel and ungodly—began to drift away. Now they would become the planters' best friends. The strategy worked; planters remained skeptical of the Brethren for several more years, but with their much more explicitly Pauline emphasis on submission in their preaching the Moravians made the masters aware, according to missionary and historian Christian Oldendorp, that "exposure to Christian teachings tended to convert formerly rebellious, disobedient, and wild slaves into benevolent, faithful, and genuinely devoted people." By the 1750s, planters welcomed the Brethren. Masters, according to Oldendorp, were completely justified in their brutal control over the slaves. Because of "the sinful nature of the heathen Negroes, these uncivilized people can be restrained in the exercise of their vicious inclinations by nothing other than fear of punishment that is as inexorable as it is severe." All talk of the planters' cruelty and moral failure ended. Meanwhile, the Brethren bought plantations and slaves themselves.[9]

The Moravian Church's new, militantly proslavery principles were spelled out by August Spangenberg, the very man who had been so critical of the planters in 1736, when he chastised them as immoral and violent while praising the slaves as Christ's beloved elect. In 1788, then in his eighties, he wrote a treatise describing the Brethren's mission work, which by then they carried out in dozens of posts around the world. It was a kind of advertisement for their services, aimed at West Indian and North American planters. The Brethren, he wrote, "will faithfully inculcate to the heathen that they must avoid all fraud and deceit, which are so peculiar to the heathen. We will never omit diligently to set before the negroe slaves the doctrines which the apostles preached to servants. We will put them in mind that it is not by chance, but it is of God, that one man is a master and another a slave. We will frequently remind the heathen of what Paul said: 'Let every soul be subject to the higher power; for there is no power but of God.'" That message earned them favor with the planters and invitations to preach in other colonies. As late as 1848, missionaries in Suriname insisted to planters that when "the poor slaves patiently accept the roads whence God leads them, and when they do not complain about this and are complacent, then God will bless them for it and look upon the services that they perform obediently for you gentlemen as if they therewith served Him." In following their calling as Christian apostles, white Moravian Brethren allowed themselves to be manipulated in the service of imperialist and economic ends.[10]

The question of Moravian cooperation with power becomes more complicated when we consider the attitudes of the Brethren toward the cultures of the Mandinkas, Saramakas, Delawares, and Inuits they so indefatigably sought to convert. Did the Moravians further lend themselves to a colonial agenda by linking their teachings to a belief in the conjoined superiority of European values and fair-skinned, or "white," physiognomy? Historians and theorists have shown that Europeans and Euro-Americans, through their encounters with indigenous peoples in the early modern period, refined a related cluster of ideas about science, knowledge, nature, and physical beauty that reified Western civilization. An evolving concept of "race," measurable and grounded in the emerging social science of anthropology, classified people—and assigned them a corresponding social value—by phenotype, presumed intelligence, national or ethnic character, and cultural attainment. Philosophers disagreed whether differences among people occurred naturally or were the product of breeding and environment. Still, the idea of quantifiable—and probably permanent—human difference was fundamental to the Enlightenment, to progress, to Europeans' self-assessment of themselves in comparison with others, to modernity itself.[11]

As an extension of the eighteenth-century Pietist movement, Moravians had little interest in attempts to classify race or categorize peoples scientifically. They were concerned only with bringing them to salvation through an awareness of Christ. In their world, there were only the saved and the unsaved, a condition upon which skin color, cranial size, or physique had no bearing. They were interested in finding the spiritual essence underneath the outer shell. Thus, the Brethren expounded a philosophy opposed to the Enlightenment's efforts to distinguish between people and, by implication, to separate them accordingly. By the Lord's yardstick, all people were essentially equal in spirit, or had a chance to be.

The "First Fruits" paintings by Moravian artist Valentin Haidt from the 1740s and 1750s celebrate this spiritual multiculturalism with their many-hued gallery of redeemed figures from mission fields in the Americas, Asia, and Africa, all delighting in God's bounty. Though much of the emotional impact of the "First Fruits" is allegorical, the Brothers and Sisters of this international fellowship, no mere abstract collection of exotic species, are individuals with names and specific conversion narratives: "The Mingrel, Thomas Mammucha," "Guly from Persia," "David the Armenian," "Sam, the Savage from Boston," "Thomas of the Hurons," "The Carolina Negro Johannes," "Francesco from Florida," "The Hottentot Kibbodo," and others. The implications of the alternative vision contained in the paintings were potentially large, for it might have challenged the presumed right of Europeans to rule the world's people by virtue of their own superior civilization. Certainly, the evangelical search for underlying similarities between people, and the belief in a bond of emotion, not intellect, hinted at a proto-Romanticist celebration of the noble savage.[12]

On the other hand, the Brethren positioned themselves in the mainstream of a set of unquestioned European assumptions, drawn from a pastiche of premodern, modern, and religious sources, about the depravity of non-Westerners. Zinzendorf encouraged missionaries in their work among the "savages, slaves, and other heathen" to "pay attention to the culture of their hearers and express spiritual truths in terms and expressions which could be readily understood by the people." But if that culture was to be paid attention to, it was the better to change it. "A heathen," the count told the assembly of enslaved African converts at Posaunen-berg on St. Thomas in 1739, "cannot be naturally inclined to do as much good as a man who has been taught to do good and to avoid evil since childhood. For a heathen is accustomed to evil since his youth and has not learned anything better." Practices like polygamy, sex out of wedlock, the worship of non-Christian gods, the use of amulets and fetishes, and the singing of traditional music were to be stamped out.

In the case of enslaved Africans, the Brethren followed the lead of many other theorists by making an explicit connection between "heathen" culture and physiognomy as a rationale for slavery. "There is not much good to say about a people for whom Paul's expression in Ephesians 5:8, *For ye were sometimes darkness* has to be applied in the literal sense," wrote the missionary Oldendorp. Zinzendorf was even more explicit in identi-fying slavery as a positive precondition for African or African American Christianity: "The Lord wishes to make slaves of the Moors first before they are blessed, because they are so proud." Taking the standard religious justification for African slavery—it was an institution ordained by God, and Christianity would not emancipate the bodies of the enslaved—Zinzendorf gave it a radical new twist. Because of a permanent character flaw, black people *must* be enslaved before they can be saved. White Breth-ren simply accepted uncritically, and even gave new weight to, the spiri-tual foundation of the American plantation system, in which they now participated fully.[13]

Missionary Oldendorp expounded on the question of Africans' "na-ture." He believed their character was corrupt, wicked, and obstinate, and he asked rhetorically "how could one expect it to be otherwise, since from their childhood on, they have been accustomed to follow only the impulses generated by their passions?" Any virtues they might possess stemmed from "instinct and have no relation to religion or reason." In at-tributing Africans' "ignorance" to their native land, Oldendorp came close to a kind of racial or cultural determinism. "It would be pointless to view this deficiency as a necessary consequence of their slave status, because there is no doubt that true virtue can manifest itself in this as in other circumstances. ... The cause of the gross ignorance of Negroes in things both natural and made by man is to be found exclusively in the lack of exercise of their reasoning abilities. This is particularly the case with those from the interior of Africa. Since their needs there are reduced to the barest minimum, the arts of civilization which were discovered by other nations in order to meet their own various needs, are unknown to them." Converted Africans might not necessarily become more intelligent, but they would shed their corruption and become virtuous by accepting their "lowly fate from the hand of God's wise goodness," becoming patient and faithful in their bondage.[14]

Here the Brethren, like many early modern Europeans, both religious and secular, were poised on the cusp of a complex problem. Was a person's "nature" permanent, or could it be changed? And if so, might Africans be able to change the things that caused them to be enslaved? The Moravian answer was that Africans' cultures and beliefs, though initially assigned by God, and of grossly inferior quality, were indeed changeable. Their souls were as worthy of salvation as anyone's. God saw them as spiritually equal to white people, and by converting, they could become culturally white. Pushed to its most radical edge, this doctrine might have challenged slaveholders' belief in the inferior and unchanging nature of Africans that was said to justify their enslavement. But the Brethren made no such intellectual leap. The reason for Africans' dark skin (punishment for the "first Negroes"), and hence their enslavement, was not changeable, even though baptism washed away the sins that brought about that divinely assigned mark of shame. White Moravians endorsed a racial basis for enslaved Africans' "lowly fate" at God's merciful hand. Perceiving no conundrum in how some parts of a person's nature might be changeable but others not, the Brethren's answer was that real slavery was spiritual, not physical, so that the question of bodily freedom was irrelevant. Christianity served as a conservative social force; African bodies were required to remain in bondage while they searched for ways to free their souls at Posaunenberg. This logic led missionaries like Oldendorp to endorse severe treatment of slaves as necessary to suppress their inclination to laziness, obstinacy, and corruption.[15]

In similar fashion, Moravians saw their mission to the Cherokees in the early nineteenth-century United States as an attempt to "civilize" a people that some white Americans wished to drive away or exterminate. Emerging "scientific" ideas of race were even invoked to argue that Cherokees and other Indians were biologically and culturally different from Euro-Americans and could never be assimilated into American society. By contrast, the Brethren (as well as the Baptists and Methodists) hoped that, by bringing the Cherokees up to the stature of white America, the Indians would demonstrate themselves worthy of respect, thereby preserving their nation. The Brethren stood well apart from modern racialist ideas. But, with a combination of respect and condescension, in their attempt to change native and enslaved people culturally and spiritually, they embraced another idea fundamental to modernity: that Christianity and Western civilization would save the world.[16]

In their quest to bring this vision about, the Moravians employed the most modern of methods, many of them grounded in literacy and the production of texts. A highly developed mission bureaucracy helped spread and maintain the Unity's worldwide reach. Mission boards and officials proliferated in Germany and in other provinces outside Europe. Missionaries in the field kept thorough records of all their instructional activities among converts and students, requiring them to spend a major part of each day simply writing. Hundreds upon hundreds of reports, diaries, and letters poured in to Herrnhut each year from evangelists in dozens of posts to be collected, read and filed. Extracts from each were gathered and published in the Unity's newsletter, the "Gemein Nachrichten," which was sent back out into the field to keep missionaries abreast of their fellows' progress on the global frontlines of heathenism.[17]

Literacy for their catechumens was a crucial element of the missionaries' strategy, one indicative of their belief that the egalitarian embrace of the Gospel should be open to all. Teaching enslaved Africans to read and write was a revolutionary concept that got the Brethren in trouble with slaveholders in the West Indies, but as a strategy that incorporated missionaries and converts alike into an Enlightenment emphasis on education, it was brilliant. Not only could hundreds of slaves, as well as indigenous people in other mission sites, now go to the Bible and seek learning for themselves, but they had the ability to write their own letters baring their souls to each other and God. Many also followed Moravian tradition by writing their own autobiographies, or memoirs, a literary form that Katharine Faull contends was "definitely part of the Western Enlightenment 'discovery' of the self." Not only did literacy enable students to receive and transmit knowledge, it also prepared the way for the production of new kinds of knowledge. Missionaries busily worked to translate the Bible and other texts, including hymns, into many native and creole languages, making them available to people with new reading skills. In the Danish West Indies during the early 1760s, missionary Johann Boehner translated excerpts from the Bible into Dutch Creole, along with hymns, and a history of the life of Jesus drawn from the four gospels. David Zeisberger produced a similar outpouring in the Delaware language, while others did the same on mission frontiers elsewhere. Fully in keeping with the cultural interflow and mingling brought on by European expansion, translations, literacy, and multilingualism created entirely new groups of Moravian missionaries and converts who moved back and forth between languages and ethnic groups.[18]

To understand better the cultures they were trying to change, missionaries refined their skills as observers and recorders of the practices they encountered. Writers like Zeisberger and Oldendorp produced sophisticated ethnographic reports based on extensive interaction with informants. Zeisberger spent years living among the Delawares in Ohio, while Oldendorp interviewed hundreds of enslaved Africans during his year-long stay in the Danish West Indies in 1767, differentiating skillfully in his writing among dozens of ethnic groups. These careful observations, besides containing a catalogue of "savage" customs, were practical guides as well, for missionaries could use descriptions of particular practices to explain similar or parallel concepts from Christianity to students. Such writings often balance disdain with a tone of respect for their subjects. It was not enough to lump all Africans, or all Indians, together as alike. Rather, it was essential to understand them as human beings who, though laboring in the grip of false beliefs and customs, were no less worthy of divine grace than anyone else. Thus, a missionary had to grasp the difference between Mandingo and Mondongo people because they were God's creations as well. Though they had their own religious motivations for conducting such studies, the Brethren were well within the emerging Enlightenment social science of anthropology, with its attempts to observe and categorize the world's "exotic" people, and its ambiguous relationship to imperialism and notions of race.[19]

Perhaps most importantly of all, the Moravian Church, for better or worse, became the vehicle through which increasing numbers of indigenous and enslaved people negotiated the bewildering challenges of the modern world. Whatever white Brethren thought of them, the crucial point was what *they* thought of the missionaries and their teachings and what purpose they believed Christianity served, if any, in shielding them from slavery, the fracturing of families, the loss of land, or other consequences of their encounters with Europeans. As they weighed the Christian alternative presented by Moravian preachers, they considered not only a sacred system of beliefs, symbols, and rituals, but a social system, bound together by Jesus' blood, that ordered its adherents' lives. The Brethren had their major successes when they were perceived as allies and their teachings seemed to provide protection against abuse. Non-Christians converted almost in proportion to the amount of worldly power they wielded, influencing the degree to which they believed the Christian message and congregational order articulated opposition to the violence and oppression they endured. Here again, the Danish West Indian example is instructive, for missionaries noticed that "those slaves who enjoyed the greatest freedom and had to face the fewest obstacles were also the least likely to become converts." In the early years of that mission, when congregants endured beatings and arrest by the authorities, the missionaries boosted their credibility by retreating to the bush with their students to hold secret meetings. When the three missionaries were arrested, tried, and held in jail for four months between 1738 and 1739, the sense of shared persecution caused Church membership to increase by more than two hundred, or half again as many.[20]

Because the mission was so popular with the slaves, many plantation owners wanted to stamp it out. Hundreds of people would regularly walk miles over the rugged mountains to attend meetings. The missionaries depended on a core of black exhorters to spread the word in the slave quarters. Congregants divided themselves by gender into small groups of six to ten for prayer and discussion led by black "helpers" who were "loved and respected by their fellow slaves." Thus, the spread of Protestant Christianity across St. Thomas became a movement promoted and managed by Afro-Caribbean worshipers themselves.[21]

Literacy, in this regard, became both a means of self-expression for enslaved Moravian converts and a tool they could use to defend themselves, sometimes aggressively, by tapping into a deep wellspring of spiritual power. One woman in 1737 ended her abuse from a hostile overseer by reading Scriptures to him, causing him to relent and become more "indulgent" with plantation workers. Another slave used her knowledge of the Bible to intimidate whites into silence. "She speaks to some [whites] with such authority about what she has read in the Bible that they cannot open their mouths against her." And, the slaves pointed out, the book of Revelation, which many of them could read for themselves, proved the slaveholders' wickedness for all the world but themselves to see. One woman told a missionary that "the Christians do not serve their God," and that, though she was a slave, she could see the world would come to an end and the masters had no idea of the punishment they would face.[22]

Potential converts weighed a complex set of spiritual and utilitarian factors when deciding whether to join the faith. They were expected to renounce their previous beliefs as heathenish (though many Africans and Indians continued to practice traditional devotions furtively), and enslaved Brethren had to reconcile their own fellowship in a religious order that sanctioned their captivity as God's will. Against these deterrents were possible benefits of conversion. Africans whose families and communities were destroyed by the transatlantic slave trade could forge new connections in the Congregation with an extended web of spiritual mentors, godparents, "Brothers" and "Sisters," and other fictive kin. They could also attain positions of leadership and responsibility as class leaders, teachers, and lay preachers. Women especially profited from this status, since the Brethren interpreted the Scriptures liberally and encouraged women to testify and lead in Church.[23]

These factors help explain why, even with the emphasis on obedience, black Christians continued streaming into a Church that sanctioned their enslavement. The mission spread rapidly from St. Thomas to the other Danish Caribbean islands of St. Croix and St. John during the 1740s. By the missionaries' count, about ten thousand African and Afro-Creole converts were baptized in the Danish West Indies by the 1780s, joined by another five thousand in Antigua, where a mission began in 1757. They comprised the most thriving Afro-Protestant congregations in the Americas in the eighteenth century. For those worshipers and the growing number of African-American converts in English-speaking North America, Christianity would have had no appeal at all if it had simply represented another command to submit. There had to be some large purpose to it, and that purpose was to salvage a spiritual reckoning with enslavement.[24]

In some cases, Christian fellowship even provided social and geographic mobility, including an avenue out of slavery. The Church sent small cohorts of converts from its worldwide missions to Germany for immersion in congregational life and training in mission work. Thus, Moravian towns like Herrnhut, Herrnhaag, and Marienborn became anachronistic experiments in racial and religious identity, where European Brethren lived and worshiped alongside Africans from the West Indies, Indians from Ohio and Pennsylvania, Inuits from Greenland, and Tartars from Russia. The Pennsylvania towns of Bethlehem, Lititz, and Nazareth contained African and Delaware congregants; in North Carolina, white and enslaved black Brethren worshiped together until the early years of the nineteenth century, when the increase of slavery as a labor system in Moravian communities fed a rise of antiblack sentiment and the eventual segregation of black congregants into a separate church building.[25] The transcultural, multiracial Moravian fellowship derived from, and expressed, many of the contradictions of the eighteenth century. It signified movement and collision of ideas and people in a worldwide arena. It represented a crossing of ethnic, racial, and religious borders, a shifting of identities among Brothers and Sisters in the Church. The Unity provided a new set of options to besieged people responding to European encroachment and colonialism along an immense set of geographic and cultural frontiers, but those options often involved a complex calculus of gains and losses by those electing to join the Brethren. Moravian teachings sought to shield non-Europeans from some depredations, but they also defended and even participated in a conservative social order that witnessed some of the most horrific abuses of the age, most notably the African slave trade. Did the Christianity offered by the Brethren offer a way out for people caught in these traps? Only the casualties of modernity in the first age of globalization could answer.

Notes

1. Christian Georg Andreas Oldendorp, *History of the Mission of the Evangelical Brethren on the Caribbean Islands of St. Thomas, St. Croix, and St. John*, ed. Johann Jakob Bossard (1777), English trans. and ed. Arnold R. Highfield and Vladimir Barac (Ann Arbor, MI, 1987), 340. Oldendorp's original manuscript, severely edited for its original publication, has been published as Christian Georg Andreas Oldendorp, *Historie der caribischen Inseln Sanct Thomas, Sanct Crux und Sanct Jan: Kommentierte Edition des Originalmanuskriptes*, ed. Gudrun Meier, Stephan Palmie, Peter Stein, and Horst Ulbricht (Berlin, 2000, 2002).
2. The etching by C. G. A. Oldendorp, titled "Aussicht von Neu-Herrnhut auf St. Thomas von der Ostseit," is included in Oldendorp, *History of the Mission*, 571.
3. Joseph E. Hutton, *A History of Moravian Missions* (London, 1922); J. Taylor Hamilton, *A History of the Missions of the Moravian Church during the Eighteenth and Nineteenth Centuries* (Bethlehem, PA, 1901); Jane Merritt, *At the Crossroads: Indians and Empires on a Mid-Atlantic Frontier, 170–1763* (Chapel Hill, NC, 2003); Britta Rupp-Eisenreich, "Les freres moraves, ethnologues de la condition esclave? (Iles Vierges, Petites Antilles, 1731–1768)," in *Naissance de l'ethnologie? Anthropologie et missions en Amerique, XVI–XVIIIe siecles*, ed. Claude Blanckaert (Paris, 1985), 125–172; Jon Sensbach, *Rebecca's Revival: Creating Black Christianity in the Atlantic World* (Cambridge, 2005).
4. Nicholas Canny, "Writing Atlantic History: or, Reconfiguring the History of Colonial British America," *Journal of American History* (1999): 1093–1114; Karen Kupperman, *America in European Consciousness, 1493–1750* (Chapel Hill, NC, 1995); C. Schnurmann, *Europa trifft Amerika: Atlantische Wirtschaft in der Frühen Neuzeit, 1492–1783* (Frankfurt am Main, 1998).
5. August Spangenberg, "Kurze Nachricht von einigen in St. Thomas erweckten Negern und von dem Segen des Herrn unter Ihnen," manuscript diary from August through October 1736, quote from 11 October, UA-Herrnhut; Oldendorp, *Caribbean Mission*, 322; N.A.T. Hall, *Slave Society in the Danish West Indies: St. Thomas, St. John, and St. Croix*

(Mona, 1992); Waldemar Westergaard, *The Danish West Indies under Company Rule, 1671–1754* (New York, 1917).

6. Spangenberg, "Kurze Nachricht," 10 and 17 September 1736.
7. Oldendorp, *Caribbean Mission*, 328, 345–360; Albin Feder to Leonhard Dober, 4 August 1739, R15.Ba.11, UA-Herrnhut; Sensbach, *Rebecca's Revival*.
8. Oldendorp, *Caribbean Mission*, 362–363.
9. Ibid., 230, 335.
10. August Gottlieb Spangenberg, *An Account of the Manner in Which the Protestant Church of the Unitas Fratrum, or United Brethren, Preach the Gospel* (London, 1788); Gert Oostindie, "The Enlightenment, Christianity and the Suriname Slave," *Journal of Caribbean History* 26 (1992): 159.
11. Ivan Hannaford, *Race: The History of an Idea in the West* (Baltimore, 1996); Anthony Pagden, *European Encounters with the New World: From Renaissance to Romanticism* (New Haven, CT, 1993).
12. Hugh Honour, *The Image of the Black in Western Art, Part IV: From the American Revolution to World War I, vol. 1: Slaves and Liberators* (Cambridge, 1989), 58–59, 313–14; Gordon M. Sayre, *Les Sauvages Americains: Representations of Native Americans in French and English Colonial Literature* (Chapel Hill, NC, 1997).
13. Oldendorp, *Caribbean Mission*, 362–363; Zinzendorf, *Texte zur Mission* (original edition 1748, repub. Hamburg, 1979), 56; Peter Sebald, "Christian Jacob Protten Africanus (1715–1769) - Erster Missionar Einer Deutschen Missionsgesellschaft in Schwarzafrika," in *Kolonien und Missionen: Referate des 3 Internationalen Kolonialgeschichtlichen Symposiums 1993 in Bremen*, ed. Wilfried Wagner, (Hamburg, 1994), 117–18. See also Katharine Faull, "Self-Encounters: Two Eighteenth-Century Memoirs from Moravian Bethlehem," in *Crosscurrents: African Americans, Africa, and Germany in the Modern World*, ed. David McBride, Leroy Hopkins, and C. Aisha Blackshire-Belay (Columbia, SC, 1998), 41, n. 42.
14. Oldendorp, *Caribbean Mission*, 243, 247–248.
15. Ibid., 228.
16. William G. McLoughlin, *Cherokees and Missionaries, 1789–1839* (New Haven, CT, 1984); Reginald Horsman, *Race and Manifest Destiny: The Origins of American Racial Anglo-Saxonism* (Cambridge, 1981).
17. J. Taylor Hamilton and Kenneth G. Hamilton, *History of the Moravian Church: The Renewed Unitas Fratrum, 1722–1957* (Bethlehem, PA, 1967), 113.
18. Faull, "Self-Encounters," 31; Daniel B. Thorp, "Chattel with a Soul: The Autobiography of a Moravian Slave," *Pennsylvania Magazine of History and Biography* 112 (1988): 433–51.
19. Hermann Wellenreuther and Carola Wessel, eds., *Herrnhuter Indianermission in der Amerikanischen Revolution: Die Tagebücher von David Zeisberger, 1772 bis 1781* (Berlin, 1995); Oldendorp, *Historie*; Anthony Pagden, *The Fall of Natural Man: The American Indian and the Origins of Comparative Ethnology* (New York, 1982).
20. Oldendorp, *Caribbean Mission*, 361, 369.
21. Ibid., 333.
22. Oldendorp, *Caribbean Mission*, 328; UA-Herrnhut, R15. Ba.10, St. Thomas diary, 30 March and 28 May 1737.
23. Oldendorp, *Caribbean Mission*, 332–335; Arnold R. Highfield, "Patterns of Accommodation and Resistance: The Moravian Witness to Slavery in the Danish West Indies," *Journal of Caribbean History* 28 (1994): 138–164; Peter Vogt, "A Voice for Themselves: Women as Participants in Congregational Discourse in the Eighteenth-Century Moravian Movement," in *Women Preachers and Prophets Through Two Millennia of Christianity*, ed. Beverly Mayne Kienzle and Pamela Walker (Berkeley, CA, 1998), 227–247.
24. "A Short Account of the Endeavours of the Episcopal Church Known by the name of Unitas Fratrum," 1787 manuscript in MA-SP; Sylvia R. Frey and Betty Wood, *Come Shouting to Zion: African American Protestantism in the American South and British Caribbean to 1830* (Chapel Hill, NC, 1998).
25. Jon Sensbach, *A Separate Canaan: The Making of an Afro-Moravian World in North Carolina, 1763–1840* (Chapel Hill, NC, 1998).

CONCLUSION

MORAVIANS AND THE CHALLENGE
OF WRITING A GLOBAL HISTORY
OF DIASPORIC CHRISTIANITY

A. G. Roeber

THIS VOLUME CHALLENGES US to see German-speaking Moravians in a non-European context. In the eighteenth century such a context primarily meant the Atlantic World, but given the global vision both Moravians and their Lutheran contemporaries at the Francke Foundations shared, even that Atlantic World assumes its proper contours only within a global framework. The essays in *Pious Pursuits* invite us to understand issues ranging from print culture to gender roles and piety in comparative contexts and press us to consider a more global perspective for understanding early modern Moravians.[1]

By examining the application of Moravian pietism among enslaved Africans in a plantation world, Jon Sensbach's essay explores implicitly an old theme in the history of the Reformation—namely, whether this religious movement should be thought of as an atavistic attempt at repristination of a supposedly golden Apostolic Age, or whether radical departures from past pieties, beliefs, and practices were the intended, or perhaps unintended, significance of the Reformation. Sensbach, along with Robert Beachy, Emily Conrad Beaver, and Michael Shirley, argue that whereas Moravians saw themselves in strong reaction against modernity, they somewhat paradoxically still embraced and promoted it. Each author explores this central dilemma, and on the whole, profitably instructs us to recall that the Moravians were "the first Protestant church to realize the implications of the worldwide spread of European imperialism for disseminating Christianity." One might quibble about whether the Moravians initially saw themselves as a separate "church" before Nicolaus Graf von Zinzendorf's vision of a pan-Protestant cooperative world mission came to grief in the early 1740s. One could plausibly argue that by the first decade of the eighteenth century, Halle's August Hermann Francke had already understood the significance of the cultivated contacts to the courts in Denmark and Great Britain very well, and was under no illusions about the role state power would play in the dissemination of the Gospel—he lived in Prussia, after all.[2]

Sensbach in particular is interested in the relationship between Moravian religious ideology and practice as it applies to the modern system of plantation slavery. He makes a good case for the Moravian lack of interest in the "attempts to classify race or categorize peoples scientifically." This position begs an explicit comparison with the Halle missionaries, since part of their instructions included keeping elaborate records of flora, fauna, and people, all of which went back to Halle and in some ways became part of the early Enlightenment's fascination with systems of classification. By the late eighteenth century, Halle's neologist theologians had distanced themselves from the more confident convictions of Christianity's absolute truth claims that had characterized Halle Pietism at the century's beginning. Thus Moravians may very well have been atavistic and more determined, as Roman Catholic missionaries seemed to be, to acknowledge culture and context, but to insist absolutely on the transhistorical and transcultural universal validity of the Christian message. That conviction goes some distance in explaining the hierarchy of races and practices the Moravians shared with other Europeans of their age. But the supposition of European superiority in issues defined as "civilization" did not necessarily mean that others—especially Native Americans—could not share in that process. Scholars might be a bit bolder, then, and ask whether, for example, the famous environmentalist arguments that underlay so much of the later philanthropic experiments in "civilizing" Native Americans were ones the Moravians shared?[3]

Perhaps it may not be so helpful to expect that the Moravians should have debated whether a person's "nature" was permanent. Nearly all early modern Christians—Roman Catholic, Orthodox, or Protestant, save for a few liberal speculators—believed that the basic "nature" of humans was set and determined because of the sin of Adam and Eve that had nonetheless not canceled out an established set of "orders" in the created, natural world. Moravians, as a predominantly German-language Pietist movement, shared those convictions.[4] But that belief did not necessarily preclude those who had formerly been outside the realm of Christian civilization from improving their lot in this life. This is a very ancient debate within Christianity, and the Byzantine Rite even incorporated the debate into its liturgy, singing its praises to Christ, who made known the Gospel "to the civilized world" but whose clear command was to preach among the heathen, with the presumption that they too, would become civilized, and saved.[5] This assumption raises another question. Did the Moravians believe that the Gospel was the agency of civilization, or did one have to civilize first, and then patiently see the Gospel spread among the former barbarians? Rather than simply concluding that Moravians embraced the idea that Christianity and Western civilization would save the world, we might be wiser to probe more precisely the sequence of which came first for Moravians—and it might well prove to be the case that they, like the English, changed their minds over time.

From confident agents of the Gospel among Elizabethans, Joseph Lucas has discovered, English and Scottish theorists by the eighteenth century had turned into pessimists, concluding that only after long epochs of civilizing programs would the Gospel finally be implanted among the heathen. While Sensbach concludes that the Africans and Native Americans who became Moravians apparently found the message of the Gospel far more convincing than they did the behavior of Europeans, once again affirming the ancient pattern that had witnessed Christianity flourish in times of persecution and martyrdom, Anna Smith suggests the reverse, in that it was Cherokee women's comfort with Moravian women and their work that brought them to the Gospel.

The most significant part of this volume is its general insistence on tracing the gradual decay of the universal confidence in the Gospel and the decline of the Moravians into more conventional nineteenth-century provincial Protestants. Asking that they should have successfully resisted what was part of the general collapse of the more global vision of eighteenth-century Pietism may be somewhat impertinent, though their own initial breadth of vision certainly seems to have become especially impoverished as they entered the age of nationalism and racialist thinking.[6]

Pious Pursuits asks us to think about the shared perspective held at various levels by a wide variety of people in the eighteenth-century world. Thus Renate Wilson, in her essay, hints that in other, more subtle ways, what we might call "national" or ethnic differentiation in medical practices seems to have been emerging by the end of the eighteenth century. Specifically where the Moravians are concerned, she argues that the practitioners more resembled the French Catholic diaspora medical practitioners than the individual German practitioners—not surprising, given the communal ideology of the Moravians and their close ties to the medical institutions of the Francke Foundations. Did the new self-help manuals that characterized English-language publishing in the later eighteenth century play a key role in this change? Or did the transformation reflect what she later describes as the "pragmatic approach" to colonial medical practice in the absence of an academic medical hierarchy? Wilson suggests that English speakers in the lower Southern colonies came to express "distaste" for the Halle preparations, which may have reflected ethnic preferences for specific *materia medica*. This observation, in turn, points us toward a close examination of what specific botanical ingredients varied, for example, from Barbados to Georgia among Moravian practitioners.[7]

242 I A. G. Roeber

We lack sufficient evidence to understand where the Moravian practitioners fit in this larger development. That they also were committed to
ease of access to medical knowledge seems clear. Whether their own preferences for *material medica* simply replicated the Halle preparations, or
whether they adjusted to the new conditions and regional indigenous
sources of plants, for example, remains unknown. If Moravians in their
overall Christian ideology became provincial and less globally oriented,
as some essays suggest, did their medical knowledge and practice mirror
this development as well? In short, did they become quickly indistin-
guishable from their Anglophone neighbors by the early nineteenth century? What was the fate of Moravian medical knowledge in the changing
landscape of Western Christianity by this time?[8]

Pious Pursuits invites us to take the "long view" of Moravian contact
with peoples, flora, and fauna in the Atlantic diaspora from the middle of
the eighteenth century onward. As the globally confident conviction of
Christianity's universality and superiority began to waver toward that
century's end, Pietism as an international movement faltered, only briefly
inspiring a more secular, "enlightened" view of European superiority and
inevitable triumph. But the Moravian experience, whether with non-
European peoples or as part of the gradual eclipse of European medicine
in the more provincial climate of the early nineteenth-century republics
and colonies, effectively hid from view Moravians' earlier patterns of
confident engagement. In that story, we shall surely have to reexamine,
more carefully than has been the case heretofore, just what to make of the
entire topic of Christian "missions." At all costs, students must be trained
to transcend the convenient indictments of the agents of this global faith
as mere colonialist agents or gullible pawns of imperialism.[9] Protestant
Europeans did not wholly lose their interest in global missions as they
entered the nineteenth-century world of Congress Europe. As Hartmut
Lehmann has persuasively argued, the renewed emphasis on the "inner
mission" to marginalized and impoverished Europeans in urban centers
between 1814 and 1848 did not unfold in isolation from continued zeal to
spread the Gospel in Africa, Asia, and the Americas.[10]

Finding the proper voice to articulate Moravian roles in these transformations will take us beyond the sphere of Moravians in the Atlantic
World. To assess accurately to what extent Moravian vision became my-
opic in the Early Republic, one has to bear in mind the somewhat breathtaking global sight they enjoyed in the previous century. But first-hand
accounts of Moravians among Native Americans, for example, or Halle
Pietists in India, were filtered through European publishers and contributed
to a more "uniform" conviction of European superiority, perhaps in in-
verse proportion to the discovery of how pluriform and difficult to comprehend were the cultures Pietists struggled to convert. In ways the Pietists
themselves did not always seem to comprehend, their laudable attempts to
translate the Christian Gospel into new languages unwittingly pulled "the
trigger of a loaded gun: the translator cannot recall the hurtling bullet."[11]

Whether "Western" Christians were peculiarly susceptible to the illusion of their own cultural superiority is a question that can only be assessed comparatively, for example, by contrasting Russian Orthodox missions, whether in Alaska or the southern Eurasian territories, to Catholic and Protestant struggles with the problem of civilization and Christianity. Although promising work has begun, we know next to nothing of the Byzantine history of missions, even as background, and work on eighteenth- and nineteenth-century Orthodox missions cannot rightly be assessed without this "long view" of the numerically large but poorly understood Orthodox Christian interactions with non-Christian peoples and cultures. The identical lack of familiarity hampers our understanding of the spread of scientific and medical knowledge in these communities.[12]

Finally, it might be worth reflecting upon the Moravians as another of the "diasporic communities" whose interactions with indigenous peoples and botanicals could never be negotiated apart from the dominant English-speaking world in which they settled. *Pious Pursuits* affirms the wisdom of Richard Ross's observation: "cultural exchange among diasporic communities emphasized contexts both broader and narrower: the transnational sources of ideas and values as well as the local terrains of their negotiations."[13] As the global shift of Christianity's own history continues, our assessments of Moravian identities will not only incorporate Tom Brady's wise advice to keep medieval Catholic inheritances in mind. We will also be compelled to ask for as much imaginative research in the many diasporic Moravian communities scattered across the globe as intrepid scholars can muster. Only then will the promise of this volume find appropriate fulfillment.

Notes

1. Ronnie Po-Chia Hsia, *The World of Catholic Renewal, 1540–1770* (Cambridge, 1998); Robert Bireley, *The Refashioning of Catholicism, 1450–1700* (Washington, D.C., 1999); A. G. Roeber, "The Migration of the Pious: Methodists, Pietists, and the Antinomian Character of North American Religious History," in *Visions of the Future in Germany and America*, ed. Norbert Finzsch and Hermann Wellenreuther (Oxford, 2001), 25–47.

2. Carl Hinrichs, *Preussentum und Pietismus: Der Pietismus in Brandenberg-Preussen als religiös-soziale Reformbewegung* (Göttingen, 1971); Daniel L. Brunner, *Halle Pietists in England: Anthony William Boehm and the Society for Promoting Christian Knowledge* (Göttingen, 1993).

3. Bernard W. Sheehan, *Seeds of Extinction: Jeffersonian Philanthropy and the American Indian* (Chapel Hill, NC, 1973); Mark Haeberlein, "Contesting the 'Middle Ground': Indian-White Relations in the Early American Republic," in *The Construction and Contestation of American Cultures and Identities in the Early National Period*, ed. Udo J. Hebel (Heidelberg, 1999), 1–23; Joseph R. Lucas, "Conquering the Passions: Indians, Europeans, and Early American Social Thought, 1580–1840" (PhD dissertation, Pennsylvania State University, 1999).

4. A. G. Roeber, "What the Law Requires Is Written on Their Hearts: Noachic and Natural Law among German-Speakers in Early Modern North America," *William and Mary*

Quarterly 58 (2001): 883–912; Roeber, "The Orders of Creation in Halle Pietism," in Udo Straeter et al., eds., *Proceedings of the First International Pietism Congress* (Halle, 2003).

5. Dale T. Irvin and Scott W. Sunquist, *History of the World Christian Movement: Volume I: Earliest Christianity to 1453* (Maryknoll, NY, 2001); Elizabeth DePalma Digeser, *The Making of a Christian Empire: Lactantius and Rome* (Ithaca, NY, 2000), in *First Things* 92 (2001): 36–40.

6. George M. Frederickson, *Racism: A Short History* (Princeton, NJ, 2002); Richard Carwardine, "Evangelicals, Politics, and the Coming of the American Civil War: A Transatlantic Perspective," in *Evangelicalism: Comparative Studies of Popular Protestantism in North America, The British Isles, and Beyond, 1700–1990*, ed. Mark A. Noll, David W. Bebbington and George A. Rawlyk (New York, 1994), 198–218.

7. Henry Lowood, "The New World and the European Catalog of Nature," in *America in European Consciousness, 1493–1750*, ed. Karen Ordahl Kupperman (Chapel Hill, NC, 1995), 295–323.

8. Unfortunately, besides Renate Wilson's own brilliant work *Pious Traders in Medicine: A German Pharmaceutical Network in Eighteenth-Century North America* (University Park, PA, 2000), little has been done on the transmission of medical knowledge outside Europe. For an insightful work on the European networks, see for example Bruce T. Moran, "Patronage and Institutions: Courts, Universities, and Academies in Germany; an Overview 1550–1750," in *Patronage and Institutions: Science, Technology, and Medicine at the European Courts, 1500–1700*, ed. Bruce T. Moran (Rochester, NY, 1991), and for the English context, Andrew Wear, *Health and Healing in Early Modern England: Studies in Social and Intellectual History* (Aldershot, 1998).

9. Dana L. Robert, "From Missions to Mission to Beyond Missions: The Historiography of American Protestant Foreign Missions Since World War II," in *New Directions in American Religious History*, ed. Harry S. Stout and D.G. Hart (New York, 1997), 362–393; Karl Mueller and Werner Ustorf, eds., *Einleitung in die Missionsgeschichte: Tradition, Situation und Dynamik des Christentums* (Stuttgart, Berlin, and Cologne, 1995); the most promising approach to the history of Christianity in a global context is Irvin and Sunquist, *History of the World Christian Movement: Volume I: Earliest Christianity to 1453*. For the present-day shift of the centers of Christianity toward the southern hemisphere and its implication for reconceptualizing the history of Christianity, see Philip Jenkins, *The Next Christendom: The Coming of Global Christianity* (New York, 2002).

10. Hartmut Lehmann, *Protestantische Weltsichten: Transformationen seit dem 17. Jahrhundert* (Göttingen, 1998), 69–90.

11. Lamin Sanneh, *Translating the Message* (Maryknoll, NY, 1989), 53; see also, for example, Hermann Wellenreuther and Carola Wessel, eds., *Herrnhuter Indianermission in der Amerikanischen Revolution: Die Tagebücher von David Zeisberger 1772 bis 1781* (Berlin, 1995), 82–88; Axel Utz, "Cultural Exchange and the Promotion of Uniformity: Pietists in Europe, North America, and South Asia, 1733–1765" (PhD diss., Pennsylvania State University, 2006).

12. Alexander A. Krivonosov, "Where the East Meets the West: A Landscape of Familiar Strangers: Missionary Alaska, 1794–1898" (PhD dissertation in progress, Penn State University); Matthew P. Romaniello, "Monastic Colonization on the Russian Frontier: Urban Networks in the Volga-Ural Region, 1552–1682," unpublished paper delivered at the Third Biennial Meeting of the Forum on European Expansion and Global Interaction, St. Augustine, Florida, 17–19 February 2000. On scientific knowledge, see for example Dimitris Dialetis, Kostas Gavroglu, and Manolis Patiniotis, "The Sciences in the Greek Speaking Regions during the 17th and 18th Centuries: The Process of Appropriation and the Dynamics of Reception and Resistance," in *The Sciences in the European Periphery During the Enlightenment*, ed. Kostas Gavroglu (Volume 2 in Jed Z. Buchwald, ed., *Archimedes: New Studies in the History and Philosophy of Science and Technology*) (Dordrecht, Boston, and London, 1999), 41–71.

13. Richard J. Ross, "Forum: Jews and Pietists in Early America Introduction: Intersecting Diasporas," *William and Mary Quarterly* 58 (2001): 849–854, quotation at 853–854.

CONTRIBUTORS

Craig D. Atwood is John Comenius Visiting Professor of Moravian Studies at the Divinity School at Wake Forest University and Theologian-in-Residence at the Home Moravian Church in Winston-Salem, North Carolina. He also teaches at the Moravian Theological Seminary. He received his PhD in religion and the history of Christianity at Princeton Theological Seminary and his Master of Divinity from Moravian Theological Seminary. His many publications include his latest book, *Community of the Cross: Moravian Piety in Colonial Bethlehem* (2004).

Robert Beachy is Associate Professor of History at Goucher College and was recently a Fellow at the National Humanities Center. He completed his PhD in history at the University of Chicago and is the author of *The Soul of Commerce: Credit, Property, and Politics in Leipzig, 1750–1840* (2005). He is coauthoring *German Civil Wars: Nation-Building and Historical Memory, 1756–1914*, and his latest book project is *Berlin: Gay Metropolis, 1860–1933*.

Emily Conrad Beaver, who earned her BA at Wake Forest University in 2003, completed an internship at the Museum of Early Southern Decorative Arts, and received her MA in history at the University of North Carolina-Greensboro in 2005.

Katherine Carté Engel is Assistant Professor of History at Texas A & M University. She received her doctorate in American History at the University of Wisconsin-Madison, and has been a Dissertation Fellow of the Institute for the Advanced Study of Religion at Yale. Her current book project is titled *Of Heaven and Earth: Religion and Economic Activity Among Bethlehem's Moravians*.

Michele Gillespie is Kahle Family Associate Professor of History at Wake Forest University. She received her PhD from Princeton University. Her publications include *Free Labor in an Unfree World: White Artisans in Slaveholding Georgia, 1789–1860* (2000).

Ellen Klinkers studied cultural anthropology at *Utrecht University* and graduated in 1997 with a PhD in history at *Leiden University*. Her dissertation is entitled "Op Hoop van Vrijheid: Van Slavensamenleving naar Creoolse Gemeenschap in Suriname, 1830–1880" (In Hope of Liberty: From Slave Society to Creole Community in Suriname, 1830–1880), and she worked from 1998 to 2004 as a researcher at the *Institute of Dutch History*, the Hague.

A. G. Roeber is Professor of Early Modern History and Religious Studies and the Co-Director of the Max Kade German-American Research Institute at Pennsylvania State University. He received his PhD from Brown University. He has published widely in American and European history, and his works include *Palatines, Liberty, and Property: German Lutherans and Colonial British North America* (1993) and *Faithful Magistrates and Republican Lawyers: Creators of Virginia Legal Culture, 1680–1810* (1981). His current project is *Renewing the Ordered Body: German Pietists and Marriage in the Early Modern Atlantic World*.

S. Scott Rohrer is an independent scholar and journalist who received his PhD from the University of Virginia. His publications include *Hope's Promise: Religion and Acculturation in the Southern Backcountry* (2005).

Jon Sensbach is Professor of History at the University of Florida. He has been an NEH Fellow at the National Humanities Center. He received his PhD from Duke University. He is the author of *A Separate Canaan: The Making of an Afro-Moravian World in North Carolina, 1763–1840* (1998) and *Rebecca's Revival: Creating Black Christianity in the Atlantic World* (2005).

Michael Shirley directs public programs for the National Endowment of the Humanities. He received his PhD from Emory University and his publications include *From Congregational Town to Industrial City: Culture and Social Change in a Southern Community* (1994).

Beverly P. Smaby recently retired as Professor of History at Clarion University of Pennsylvania. She completed her PhD in American civilization at the University of Pennsylvania. Her scholarship focuses on gender history in colonial America and includes *The Transformation of Moravian Bethlehem: From Communal Mission to Family Economy* (1988).

Anna Smith is an independent scholar who graduated from Salem College in Winston-Salem. Her research centers on a group of young Cherokee women educated by the Moravians at Salem. She is the founder of the Cherokee-Moravian Historical Association.

Elisabeth Sommer completed her PhD in history at the University of Virginia and has held both teaching and research positions at a range of universities and museums. Her publications have focused on the German Moravians in North Carolina and include *Serving Two Masters: The Moravian Brethren in Germany and North Carolina 1727–1801* (2000).

Mack Walker is Emeritus Professor of History of Johns Hopkins University. After receiving his PhD from Harvard University, he taught at Cornell University. He has held numerous fellowships and professional offices, and his scholarship has included extensive research and publications on early modern and nineteenth-century German and European history. His works include *Germany and the Emigration 1816–1885* (1964), *German Home Towns: Community, State, and General Estate 1648–1871* (1971, 2d ed. 1998), *Johann Jakob Moser and the Holy Roman Empire of the German Nation* (1981), and *The Salzburg Transaction: Expulsion and Redemption in Eighteenth Century Germany* (1992). He is currently conducting research in Halle on German Pietism.

Renate Wilson is Senior Research Associate and Adjunct Associate Professor in the Department of Health Policy and Management, in the School of Hygiene and Public Health, and in the Institute for the History of Science, Technology, and Medicine at the School of Medicine at Johns Hopkins University. She received her PhD from the University of Maryland-College Park in German area studies. She is the author of numerous articles and book chapters, as well as *Pious Traders in Medicine: A German Pharmaceutical Network in Eighteenth-Century North America* (2000). She has received several awards and fellowships, including, for her last book, the Kremers Award from the Institute for the History of Pharmacy.

Marianne S. Wokeck is Professor of History and Director of American Studies at Indiana University-Purdue University Indianapolis. She received her M.A. from Hamburg University and her Ph.D. from Temple University. She has numerous publications on German immigrants in colonial America, including *Trade in Strangers: The Beginnings of Mass Migration to North America* (1999).

SELECTED BIBLIOGRAPHY

Altman, Ida, and James Horn, eds. *"To Make America": European Emigration in the Early Modern Period*. Berkeley, 1991.

Anderson, Benedict. *Imagined Communities: Reflections on the Origin and Spread of Nationalism*. Rev. ed. London, 1991.

Anderson, Fred. *Crucible of War: The Seven Years' War and the Fate of Empire in British North America, 1754–1766*. New York, 2000.

Atwood, Craig. *Community of the Cross: Moravian Piety in Colonial Bethlehem*. University Park, PA, 2004.

———. "The Mother of God's People: The Adoration of the Holy Spirit in the Eighteenth-Century Brüdergemeine." *Church History* 68 (1999): 886–909.

———. "Sleeping in the Arms of Christ: Sanctifying Sexuality in the Eighteenth-Century Moravian Church." *Journal of the History of Sexuality* 8, no. 1 (1997): 25–51.

———. "The Joyfulness of Death in Eighteenth-Century Moravian Communities." *Communal Societies* 17 (1997): 39–58.

Bailyn, Bernard. *Atlantic History: Concept and Contours*. Cambridge, MA, 2005.

———. *The Peopling of British America*. New York, 1986.

———. *Voyagers to the West: A Passage in the Peopling of America on the Eve of the Revolution*. New York, 1986.

———. *The New England Merchants in the Seventeenth Century*. Cambridge, 1955.

Bailyn, Bernard, and Philip D. Morgan, eds. *Strangers within the Realm: Cultural Margins of the First British Empire*. Chapel Hill, NC, 1991.

Balmer, Randall. *A Perfect Babel of Confusion: Dutch Religion and English Culture in the Middle Colonies*. New York, 1989.

Barthold, Friedrich W. "Die erweckten im protestantischen Deutschland während des Ausgangs des 17. und der ersten Hälfte des 18. Jahrhunderts, besonders der frommen Grafenhöfe." In *Historisches Taschenbuch*, 3d series. Leipzig, 1853. Pp. 129–390.

Becker, Bernhard. *Zinzendorf im Verhältnis zu Philosophie und Kirchentum seiner Zeit*. Leipzig, 1866.

Becker, Laura. "Diversity and Its Significance in an Eighteenth-Century Pennsylvania Town." In *Friends and Neighbors: Group Life in America's First Plural Society*, ed. Michael Zuckerman. Philadelphia, 1982.

Berlin, Ira. *Many Thousands Gone: The First Two Centuries of Slavery in North America*. Cambridge, 1998.

———. "From Creole to African: Atlantic Creoles and the Origins of African-American Society in Mainland North America." *William and Mary Quarterly* 53 (1996): 251–288.

Bettermann, Wilhelm. *Theologie und Sprache bei Zinzendorf.* Gotha, 1935.

Beyreuther, Erich. *Die Grosse Zinzendorf-Biographie.* Marburg an der Lahn, 1957–1961.

———. *Nikolaus Ludwig von Zinzendorf in Selbstzeugnisse und Bilddokumente.* Hamburg, 1965.

Beyreuther, Gottfried. *Sexualtheorie im Pietismus.* Munich, 1963.

Blackburn, Robin. *The Making of New World Slavery: From the Baroque to the Modern 1492–1800.* London, 1997.

Blickle, Peter. *Kommunalismus: Skizzen einer gesellschaftlichen Organisationsform.* 2 vols. Munich, 2000.

Boles, John B. *The Great Revival: Beginnings of the Bible Belt.* Lexington, KY, 1996.

Bosher, J. F. "Huguenot Merchants and the Protestant International in the Seventeenth Century." *William and Mary Quarterly* 52 (1995): 77–101.

Brady, Thomas J. *Communities, Politics and Reformation in Early Modern Europe.* Leiden, 1998.

Brecht, Martin, et al, eds. *Geschichte des Pietismus.* 3 vols. Göttingen, 1993–2000.

Breen, T. H. "'Baubles of Britain': The American and Consumer Revolutions of the Eighteenth Century." *Past and Present* 119 (1988): 73–104.

Breward, Christopher. *The Culture of Fashion.* Manchester, 1995.

Brooke, John L. *The Refiner's Fire: The Making of Mormon Cosmology, 1644–1844.* Cambridge, 1994.

Brown, Dale W. *Understanding Pietism.* Grand Rapids, MI, 1978.

Brown, Kathleen. *Good Wives, Nasty Wenches and Anxious Patriarchs: Gender, Race and Power in Colonial Virginia.* Chapel Hill, NC, 1996.

Bruford, Walter H. *Germany in the Eighteenth Century: The Social Background of the Literary Revival.* Cambridge, 1935.

Brunner, Otto. "Das 'ganze Haus' und die alteuropäische 'Ökonomik'." In idem, *Neue Wege der Verfassungs- und Sozialgeschichte.* Göttingen, 1968.

Burke, Peter, and Asa Briggs. *A Social History of Media: From Gutenberg to the Internet.* Cambridge, 2002.

Bushman, Richard. *From Puritan to Yankee: Character and Social Order in Connecticut, 1690–1765.* Cambridge, 1967.

Bynum, Caroline Walker. "Violent Images in Late Medieval Piety." *German Historical Institute Bulletin* 30 (Spring 2002).

———. "Jesus as Mother and Abbot as Mother: Some Themes in Twelfth-Century Cistercian Writing." In Bynum, *Jesus as Mother: Studies in the Spirituality of the High Middle Ages.* Berkeley, CA, 1984. Pp. 110–169.

Canny, Nicholas, ed. *Europeans on the Move.* Oxford, 1994.

Chartier, Roger. *The Cultural Uses of Print in Early Modern France.* Princeton, NJ, 1987.

Crane, Elaine Forman, ed. *The Diary of Elizabeth Drinker.* Boston, 1991.

Crawford, Michael J. *Seasons of Grace: Colonial New England's Revival Tradition in Its British Context.* New York, 1991.

Dallimore, Arnold. *George Whitefield: The Life and Times of the Great Evangelist of the Eighteenth-Century Revival.* 2 vols. Edinburgh, 1980.

Davis, Fred. *Fashion, Culture, and Identity.* Chicago, 1992.

Ditz, Toby. "Shipwrecked; or, Masculinity Imperiled: Mercantile Representations of Failure and the Gendered Self in Eighteenth-Century Philadelphia." *Journal of American History* 81 (1994): 51–80.

Douglass, Mary. *Purity and Danger: An Analysis of the Concepts of Pollution and Taboo.* New York, 1989.

———. *Natural Symbols: Explorations in Cosmology.* New York, 1973.

Doerflinger, Thomas M. *A Vigorous Spirit of Enterprise: Merchants and Economic Development in Revolutionary Philadelphia.* New York, 1986.

Durnbaugh, Donald F. "Communitarian Societies in Colonial America." In *America's Communal Utopias,* ed. Donald E. Pitzer. Chapel Hill, NC, 1997.

Elliott, J. H. *Britain and Spain in America: Colonists and Colonized.* Reading, PA, 1994.

Eltis, David. *The Rise of African Slavery in the Americas.* Cambridge, 2000.

Engelsing, Rolf. "Die Perioden der Lesergeschichte in der Neuzeit." *Archiv für Geschichte des Buchwesens* 10 (1969): 944–1002.

Erbe, Hans-Walter. *Zinzendorf und der fromme hohe Adel seiner Zeit.* Leipzig, 1928.

Erbe, Hellmuth. *Bethlehem, Pa.: Eine kommunistische Herrnhuter Kolonie des 18. Jahrhunderts.* Stuttgart, 1929.

Eybl, F. M. "Leichenpredigt." In *Historisches Wörterbuch der Rhetorik,* ed. Gert Ueding. 5+ vols. Tübingen, 1992–. 5:124–151.

Egnal, Marc. *New World Economies: The Growth of the Thirteen Colonies and Early Canada.* New York, 1998.

Fauchier-Magnon, Adrien. *The Small German Courts in the Eighteenth Century.* London, 1958.

Faull, Katharine M. *Moravian Women's Memoirs: Their Related Lives, 1750–1820.* Syracuse, 1997.

Fogleman, Aaron. "Jesus is Female: The Moravian Challenge in the German Communities of British North America." *William and Mary Quarterly* 60 (2003): 295–332.

———. "From Slaves, Convicts, and Servants to Free Passengers: The Transformation of Immigration in the Era of the American Revolution." *Journal of American History* 85 (1998): 43–76.

———. *Hopeful Journeys: German Immigration, Settlement, and Political Culture in Colonial America, 1717–1775.* Philadelphia, 1996.

Francke, August Hermann. *Werke in Auswahl.* Ed. Erhard Peschke. Berlin, 1969.

Frantz, John B. "The Awakening of Religion among the German Settlers in the Middle Colonies." *William and Mary Quarterly* 33 (1976): 266–288.

Freeman, Arthur. *An Ecumenical Theology of the Heart: The Theology of Nicholas Ludwig von Zinzendorf.* Bethlehem, PA, 1998.

Fries, Adelaide, ed. *Records of the Moravians in North Carolina.* 7 vols. Raleigh, NC, 1922–1943.

Fries, Adelaide, Stuart Thurman Wright, and J. Edwin Hendricks. *Forsyth: A County on the March.* Rev. ed. Chapel Hill, NC, 1976.

Gäbler, Ulrich, ed. *Der Pietismus im neunzehnten und zwanzigsten Jahrhundert.* Göttingen, 2000.

Galenson, David W. "The Settlement and Growth of the Colonies: Population, Labor, and Economic Development." In *The Cambridge Economic History of the United States, Vol. I,* ed. Stanley L. Engerman and Robert E. Gallman. Cambridge, 1996. Pp. 135–207.

Girard, Renè. *Violence and the Sacred.* Trans. Patrick Gregory. Baltimore, 1972.

Glatfelter, Charles H. *Pastors and People: German Lutheran and Reformed Churches in the Pennsylvania Field, 1717–1793.* 2 vols. Breinigsville, PA, 1980.

Gollin, Gillian. *Moravians in Two Worlds: A Study of Changing Communities.* New York, 1967.

Greene, Jack P. "Beyond Power: Paradigm Subversion and Reformulation and the Re-Creation of the Early Modern Atlantic World." In Greene, *Interpreting Early America: Historiographical Essays.* Charlottesville, NC, 1996.

———. *Pursuits of Happiness: The Social Development of Early Modern British Colonies and the Formation of American Culture.* Chapel Hill, NC, 1988.

Grubb, Farley. "The Market for Indentured Immigrants: Evidence of Forward-Labor Contracting in Philadelphia, 1745–1773." *Journal of Economic History* 45 (1985): 855–868.

Guram, Phillipp. "Wirtschaftsethik und Wirtschaftspraxis in der Geschichte der Herrnhuter Brüdergemeine." In *Unitas Fratrum: Herrnhuter Studien/Moravian Studies,* ed. Mari P. Buijtenen, Cornelis Dekker, and Huib Leeuwenberg. Utrecht, 1975.

Hahn, Hans-Christoph, and Hellmut Reichel, eds. *Zinzendorf und die Herrnhuter Brüder: Quellen zur Geschichte der Brüder-Unität von 1722 bis 1760.* Hamburg, 1977.

Hall, Timothy. *Contested Boundaries: Itinerancy and the Reshaping of the Colonial American Religious World.* Durham, NC, 1994.

Hamilton, Kenneth G., trans. *The Bethlehem Diary: Volume 1, 1742–1744.* Bethlehem, PA, 1971.

Hamilton, Kenneth G., and J. Taylor Hamilton. *History of the Moravian Church: The Renewed Unitas Fratrum, 1722–1957.* Bethlehem, PA, 1967.

Harrington, Virginia D. *The New York Merchant on the Eve of the Revolution.* New York, 1935.

Hardtwig, Wolfgang. *Genossenschaft, Sekte, Verein in Deutschland: Vom spätmittelalter bis zur Französischen Revolution.* Munich, 1997.

Hatch, Nathan O. *The Democratization of American Christianity.* New Haven, CT, 1989.

Heyrman, Christine Leigh. *Southern Cross: The Beginnings of the Bible Belt.* New York, 1997.

———. *Commerce and Culture: The Maritime Communities of Colonial Massachusetts, 1690–1750.* New York, 1984.

Hutton, J. E. *A History of the Moravian Church.* 2d ed. London, 1909.

Innes, Stephen. *Creating the Commonwealth: The Economic Culture of Puritan New England.* New York, 1995.

Isaac, Rhys. *The Transformation of Virginia, 1740–1790.* Chapel Hill, 1982.

Jordan, John W. "Moravian Immigration to Pennsylvania, 1734–1767, with Some Account of the Transport Vessels." *TMHS* 5 (1899):40–90.

Katz, Stanley N., John Murrin, and Douglas Greenberg, eds. *Colonial America: Essays in Politics and Social Development.* 4th ed. New York, 1993.

Kennedy, Ruby Jo Reeves. "Single or Triple Melting Pot? Intermarriage Trends in New Haven, 1870–1940." *American Journal of Sociology* 49 (January, 1944): 331–339.

Kinkel, Gary S. *Our Dear Mother the Spirit: An Investigation of Zinzendorf's Theology and Praxis.* Lanham, MD, 1990.

Knox, R. A. *Enthusiasm.* Oxford, 1950.

Koslofsky, Craig. *The Reformation of the Dead: Death and Ritual in Early Modern Germany, 1450–1700.* London, 2000.

Kulikoff, Allan. *Tobacco and Slaves: The Development of Southern Cultures in the Chesapeake, 1680–1800.* Chapel Hill, NC, 1986.

Kupperman, Karen Ordahl. *America in European Consciousness, 1743–1750.* Chapel Hill, NC, 1995.

———. "Errand to the Indies: Puritan Colonization from Providence Island through the Western Design." *William and Mary Quarterly* 45 (1988): 70–99.

Lambert, Frank. *"Pedlar in Divinity": George Whitefield and the Transatlantic Revivals, 1737–1770.* Princeton, NJ, 1994.

Lehmann, Hartmut. *Protestantische Weltsichten: Transformationen seit dem 17. Jahrhundert.* Göttingen, 1998.

Lehmann, Hartmut, Hermann Wellenreuther, and Renate Wilson, eds. *In Search of Peace and Prosperity: New German Settlements in Eighteenth-Century Europe and America.* University Park, PA, 2000.

Lenz, Rudolf, ed. *Leichenpredigten als Quelle historischer Wissenschaften.* 3 vols. Marburg, 1975–1984.

Levy, Barry. *Quakers and the American Family: British Settlement in the Delaware Valley.* New York, 1988.

———. "The Birth of the 'Modern Family' in Early America: Quaker and Anglican Families in the Delaware Valley, Pennsylvania, 1681–1750." In *Friends and Neighbors: Group Life in America's First Plural Society,* ed. Michael Zuckerman. Philadelphia, 1982. Pp. 26–63.

Levering, Joseph Mortimer. *A History of Bethlehem, 1741–1892.* Bethlehem, PA, 1903.

Lewis, A. J. *Zinzendorf the Ecumenical Pioneer.* Philadelphia, 1962.

Linebaugh, Peter, and Marcus Rediker. *The Many-Headed Hydra: Sailors, Slaves and the Atlantic Working Class in the Eighteenth Century.* Boston, 2000.

Mason, J. C. S. *The Moravian Church and the Missionary Awakening in England, 1760–1800.* Woodbridge, UK, 2001.

Matson, Cathy. *Merchants and Empire: Trading in Colonial New York.* Baltimore, 1998.

McCusker, John J., and Russell R. Menard. *The Economy of British America, 1607–1789.* Chapel Hill, NC, 1991.

McCusker, John J., and Kenneth Morgan, eds. *The Early Modern Atlantic Economy.* Cambridge, 2000.

McFarlane, Anthony. *The British in the Americas 1480–1815.* London, 1994.

McKendrick, Neil. *The Birth of a Consumer Society: The Commercialization of Eighteenth Century England.* Bloomington, IN, 1982.

Mcpherson, M. P., ed. and trans. *The Works of Aelred of Rievaulx 1: Treatises and Pastoral Prayer.* Spencer, MA, 1971.

Merritt, Jane. *At the Crossroads: Indians and Empires on a Mid-Atlantic Frontier, 1700–1763.* Chapel Hill, NC, 2003.

———. "Cultural Encounters along a Gender Frontier: Mahican, Delaware, and German Women in Eighteenth-Century Pennsylvania." *Pennsylvania History* 67 (2000): 515.

———. "Dreaming of the Savior's Blood: Moravians and the Indian Great Awakening in Pennsylvania, *William and Mary Quarterly* 54 (1997): 723–746.

Mezezers, Valdis. *The Herrnuterian Pietism in the Baltic and its Outreach into America and Elsewhere in the World.* North Quincy, MA, 1975.

Miller, Perry. *The New England Mind: From Colony to Province.* Cambridge, 1953.

Morgan, Philip D. *Slave Counterpoint: Black Culture in the Eighteenth-Century Chesapeake and Low Country.* Chapel Hill, NC, 1998.

Mueller, Joseph. *Zinzendorf als Erneuer der alten Brüderkirche.* Leipzig, 1900.

Noll, Mark, ed. *God and Mammon: Protestants, Money, and the Market, 1790–1860.* New York, 2002.

Norton, Mary Beth. *Founding Mothers and Fathers: Gendered Power and the Forming of American Society.* New York, 1996.

O'Brien, Susan. "A Transatlantic Community of Saints: The Great Awakening and the First Evangelical Network, 1735–1755." *American Historical Review* 91 (1986): 811–832.

Oldendorp, Christian Georg Andreas. *History of the Mission of the Evangelical Brethren on the Caribbean Islands of St. Thomas, St. Croix, and St. John.* Ed. Johann Jakob Bossard (1777). English trans. and ed. Arnold R. Highfield and Vladimir Barac. Ann Arbor, MI, 1987.

Peterson, Mark. *The Price of Redemption: The Spiritual Economy of Puritan New England.* Palo Alto, CA, 1997.

Peucker, Paul. "'Blut auf unsre grünen Bändchen:' Die Sichtungszeit in der Herrnhuter Brüdergemeine." *Unitas Fratrum: Zeitschrift fur Geschichte und Gegenwartsfragen der Brudergemeine,* nos. 49–50 (2002): 41–94.

Pfister, Oskar. *Die Frömmigkeit des Grafen Ludwig von Zinzendorf: Ein psychoanalytischer Beitrag zur Kenntnis der religiösen Sublimierungsprozesse und zur Erklärung des Pietismus.* Leipzig, 1910.

Plitt, Hermann. *Zinzendorfs Theologie.* Vol. 1: *Die ursprüngliche gesunde Lehre Zinzendorfs (1723–1742).* Vol. 2: *Die Zeit krankhafter Verbildungen in Zinzendorfs Lehrweise (1743–1750).* Vol. 3: *Die wiederhergestellte und abschließende Lehrweise Zinzendorfs (1750–1760).* Gotha, 1869–1874.

Podmore, Colin. *The Moravian Church in England, 1728–1760.* Oxford, 1998.

Reichel, Gerhard. *Zinzendorfs Frömmigkeit im Licht der Psychoanalyse.* Tübingen, 1911.

Ribeiro, Aileen. *Dress in Eighteenth-Century Europe.* New York, 1984.

Richter, Daniel K. *Facing East From Indian Country: A Native History of Early America.* Cambridge, 2001.

Ritschl, Albrecht. *Geschichte des Pietismus.* 3 vols. Bonn, 1880–1886.

Roeber, A. G. *Palatines, Liberty, and Property: German Lutherans in Colonial British America.* Baltimore, 1993.

Rohrer, S. Scott. *Hope's Promise: Religion and Acculturation in the Southern Backcountry.* Tuscaloosa, AL, 2005.

———. "Searching for Land and God: The Pietist Migration to North Carolina in the Late Colonial Period." *NCHR* 79 (October, 2002): 409–439.

Sawyer, Edwin. "The Religious Experience of the Colonial American Moravians." *TMHS,* 18:1–227.

Schwartz, Sally. *"A Mixed Multitude": The Struggle for Toleration in Colonial Pennsylvania.* New York, 1987.

de Schweinitz, Edmund. *The Financial History of the American Province of the Unitas Fratrum and of Its Sustentation Fund.* Bethlehem, PA, 1877.

Scoville, James A. *Old Merchants of New York.* 3d eries. New York, 1865.

Sellers, Charles. *The Market Revolution: Jacksonian America, 1815–1846.* New York, 1991.

Sensbach, Jon S. *A Separate Canaan: The Making of an Afro-Moravian World in North Carolina, 1763–1840.* Chapel Hill, NC, 1998.

———. *Rebecca's Revival: Creating Black Christianity in the Atlantic World.* Cambridge, MA, 2005.

Sessler, John Jacob. *Communal Pietism Among Early American Moravians.* New York, 1933.

Shammas, Carole. *The Pre-Industrial Consumer in England and America.* New York, 1990.

Shirley, Michael. *From Congregational Town to Industrial City: Culture and Social Change in a Southern Community.* New York, 1994.

Smaby, Beverly Prior. *The Transformation of Moravian Bethlehem: From Communal Mission to Family Economy.* Philadelphia, 1988.

Snydacker, Daniel. "Kinship and Community in Rural Pennsylvania, 1749–1820." *The Journal of Interdisciplinary History* (summer 1982): 41–61.

Sommer, Elisabeth W. *Serving Two Masters: Moravian Brethren in Germany and North Carolina, 1727–1801.* Lexington, KY, 2000.

Spangenberg, August Gottlieb. *An Account of the Manner in Which the Protestant Church of the Unitas Fratrum, or United Brethren, Preach the Gospel.* London, 1788.

Stocker, Harry Emilius. *A History of the Moravian Church in New York City.* New York, 1922.

Stoeffler, Ernst. *German Pietism During the Eighteenth Century.* Leiden, 1973.

———. *The Rise of Evangelical Pietism.* Leiden, 1965.

Stoeffler, Ernst, ed. *Continental Pietism and Early American Christianity.* Grand Rapids, MI, 1976.

Surratt, Jerry Lee. *Gottlieb Schober of Salem: Discipleship and Ecumenical Vision in an Early Moravian Town,* Macon, GA, 1983.

———. "The Role of Dissent in Community Evolution among Moravians in Salem, 1772–1860," *NCHR* 52, no. 3 (1975).

———. "From Theocracy to Voluntary Church and Secularized Community: A Study of the Moravians in Salem, North Carolina, 1772–1860." PhD diss., University of North Carolina, 1968.

Thorp, Daniel B. *The Moravian Community in Colonial North Carolina: Pluralism on the Southern Frontier.* Knoxville, TN, 1989.

———. "Chattel with a Soul: The Autobiography of a Moravian Slave," *Pennsylvania Magazine of History and Biography* 112 (1988): 433–51.

———. "Assimilation in North Carolina's Moravian Community." *Journal of Southern History* 52, no. 1 (1986): 19–42.

Thyssen, Anders Pontoppidan. "Christiansfeld: Die Herrnhuter im Spannungs-feld zwischen Pietismus und Aufklärung." In *Aufklärung und Pietismus im dänischen Gesamtstaat 1770–1820,* ed. Hartmut Lehmann. Neumünster, 1983.

Tise, Larry E. *The Yadkin Melting Pot: Methodism and Moravians in the Yadkin Valley, 1750–1850.* Winston-Salem, NC, 1967.

Tönnies, Ilse. "Die Arbeitswelt von Pietismus: Erweckungsbewegung und Brüdergemeine; Ideen und Institutionen: Zur religiös-sozialen Vorgeschichte des Industriealisierungszeitalters in Berlin und Mitteldeutschland." *Jahrbuch für die Geschichte Mittel und Ostdeutschland* 20 (1971): 89–133; 21 (1972): 140–183.

Tolles, Frederick B. *Meeting House and Counting House: The Quaker Merchants of Colonial Philadelphia, 1682–1763.* Chapel Hill, NC, 1948.

Trommler, Frank, and Elliott Shore, eds. *The German-American Encounter: Conflict and Cooperation Between Two Cultures, 1800–2000.* New York, 2001.

Uttendörfer, Otto. *Zinzendorf und die Mystik.* Berlin, 1952.

———. *Wirtschaftsgeist und Wirtschaftsorganisation Herrnhuts und der Brüder-gemeine von 1743 bis zum Ende des Jahrhunderts.* Herrnhut, 1926.

———. *Alt-Herrnhut: Wirtschaftsgeschichte une Religionssoziologie Herrnhuts während seiner ersten Zwanzig Jahre (1722–1742).* Herrnhut, 1925.

Valeri, Mark. "Religious Discipline and the Market: Puritans and the Issue of Usury." *William and Mary Quarterly* 54 (1997): 747–768.

van Dülmen, Richard. *Kultur und Alltag in der Frühen Neuzeit: Das Haus und seine Menschen.* 3 vols. Munich, 1990.

Vogt, Peter, and Craig D. Atwood, eds. *The Distinctiveness of Moravian Culture: Essays and Translations in Honor of Vernon Nelson.* Nazareth, PA, 2003.

Ward, W. R. *The Protestant Evangelical Revival.* Cambridge, 1992.

Weigelt, Horst. *Geschichte des Pietismus in Bayern: Anfänge – Entwicklung – Bedeutung.* Göttingen, 2001.

Weinlick, John. *The Moravian Diaspora: A Study of the Societies of the Moravian Church within the Protestant State Churches of Europe.* Nazareth, PA, 1959.

Wellenreuther, Hermann, and Carola Wessel, eds. *Herrnhuter Indianermission in der Amerikanischen Revolution: Die Tagebücher von David Zeisberger, 1772 bis 1781* (Berlin, 1995).

Westerkamp, Marilyn J. *Triumph of the Laity: Scots-Irish Piety and the Great Awakening, 1625–1760.* New York, 1986.

Williams, Eric. *Capitalism and Slavery.* London, 1944.

Wilson, Renate. *Pious Traders in Medicine: A German Pharmaceutical Network in Eighteenth-Century North America.* University Park, PA, 2000.

Ward, W. W. "Zinzendorf and Money." In *The Church and Wealth,* ed. W. J. Sheils and Diana Wood. Oxford, 1987.

Wagner, Hans. *Abraham Dürninger & Co., 1747–1939.* Herrnhut, 1940.

Walker, Mack. *The Salzburg Transaction: Expulsion and Redemption in Eighteenth-Century Germany.* Ithaca, NY, 1992.

———. *Johann Jakob Moser and the Holy Roman Empire of the German Nation.* Chapel Hill, NC, 1981.

———. *German Home Towns: Community, State, and General Estate, 1648–1871.* Ithaca, NY, 1971.

———. *Germany and the Emigration, 1816–1885.* Cambridge, 1964.

Weber, Max. *The Protestant Ethic and the Spirit of Capitalism.* Trans. Talcott Parsons. London, 1992; orig. pub. 1930.

Webster, Jonathan Howes. "The Merchants of Bordeaux in Trade to the French West Indies, 1664–1717." PhD diss. University of Minnesota, 1972.

Weinlick, John R. "The Moravians and the American Revolution: An Overview." *TMHS* 23 (1977).

Wilkenfeld, Bruce M. "The New York City Shipowning Community, 1715–1764." *American Neptune* 37 (1977). 50–65.

Wokeck, Marianne S. *Trade in Strangers: The Beginnings of Mass Migration to North America.* University Park, PA, 1999.

Wolf, Stephanie Grauman. *Urban Village: Population, Community, and Family Structure in Germantown, Pennsylvania, 1683–1800.* Princeton, NJ, 1976.

Zimmerling, Peter. *Gott in Gemeinschaft: Zinzendorfs Trinitatslehre.* Giessen, 1991.

Zinzendorf, Nicolaus Ludwig Graf von. *Nine Public Lectures on Important Subjects in Religion Preached in Fetter Lane Chapel in London in the Year 1746.* Trans. and ed. George W. Forell. Iowa City, 1973.

———. *Hauptschriften in sechs Bänden,* ed. Erich Beyreuther and Gerhard Meyer. 6 vols. Hildesheim, 1962–1963.

INDEX

.